Sexual INJUSTICE

Sexual INJUSTICE

Supreme Court Decisions from *Griswold* to *Roe*

Marc Stein

The University of North Carolina Press Chapel Hill

This book was published with the assistance of the
Thornton H. Brooks Fund of the University of North Carolina Press.

Library of Congress Cataloging-in-Publication Data
Stein, Marc.
Sexual injustice : Supreme Court decisions from Griswold to Roe / Marc Stein.
p. cm.
Includes bibliographical references and index.
ISBN 978-0-8078-3412-1 (cloth : alk. paper)
1. Constitutional law—United States—Cases. 2. Sex and law—United States—Cases. 3. Gays—Legal status, laws, etc.—United States—Cases. 4. United States. Supreme Court. I. Title.
KF4550.S74 2010
342.73—dc22

2010010140

Portions of this book were drawn from previous publications: "The U.S. Supreme Court's Sexual Counter-Revolution," *Organization of American Historians Magazine of History* 20, no. 2 (Mar. 2006): 21–25; "Crossing the Border to Memory: In Search of Clive Michael Boutilier (1933–2003)," *torquere* 6 (2004): 91–115 [published Nov. 2005]; and "*Boutilier* and the U.S. Supreme Court's Sexual Revolution," *Law and History Review* 23, no. 3 (Fall 2005): 491–536. Used by permission.

14 13 12 11 10   5 4 3 2 1

Contents

In the early 1970s, when I was about nine years old and living with my family in suburban New York, my parents decided to purchase new furniture, carpets, and wallpaper for my sister's bedroom and the room my younger brother and I shared. My brother and I selected a colonial-style desk and dresser, a navy blue shag carpet, and wallpaper that featured red, white, and blue stripes, stars, soldiers, guns, and drums. The celebration of the U.S. bicentennial was approaching, and I suspect that our selections reflected a combination of popular design trends, conventional masculine aspirations, immigrant family identifications, and my own peculiarly strong patriotic fervor, which later found expression in my passionate devotion to the Broadway musical *1776* and the photographic images of the White House, Capitol, and Supreme Court that I taped to the back of our bedroom door. My parents tried to make us understand that we would have to live with our design choices for many years. We persisted, however, and sure enough that furniture, carpeting, and wallpaper remained in my childhood bedroom until 1999, when my parents sold their house. When I traveled from Canada, where I had moved recently, to visit my parents for the last time before their departure, my partner used my brother's bed, I claimed my old one, and we slept surrounded by the colors and symbols of a country that was no longer my home.

I begin with this story to measure the distance I have traveled in the last few decades and to give my readers a sense of the personal and political journeys that led me to and through this book. All historians bring to their work a set of motivations, interests, and concerns that influence their interpretations. Those who claim to approach the past with disinterested and dispassionate objectivity not only suffer from a lack of honest interest and genuine passion, but also mislead readers into wanting forms of historical analysis that are as unrealistic as they are undesirable.[1] I bring to this project the profound disappointments of a U.S. citizen who once believed deeply in the guiding visions of my country but who has lived for much of the last twelve years as an expatriate ex-patriot in Canada.

As is the case with many U.S. Americans, my childhood patriotism was attached in particularly strong ways to the U.S. Constitution and Supreme Court.² This reverential loyalty was based on two principal beliefs: that the Constitution protects liberty, freedom, equality, and democracy and that the Court defends the Constitution by striking down laws and practices that violate the country's fundamental principles. Nurtured by the mystique that has been cultivated by the Court and consumed by the country, these beliefs are widely shared across the nation's political spectrum, and they may well have taken hold in particularly strong ways for those of us who grew up after World War II, when the United States was encouraging and compelling other countries to adopt constitutions and courts modeled on the U.S. system. My generation came of age in the aftermath of the Court's ruling against racial segregation in *Brown* (1954) and in the midst of the constitutional crises of the Watergate era, when the Court played a key role in prompting President Nixon to resign. When I first visited the Court with my family in the 1970s, I still had patriotic faith in the Constitution and the Court.³

Had I known then what I was taught later about the Court's controversial rulings on sex, marriage, and reproduction in the late 1960s and early 1970s, my faith in the Constitution and Court might well have been even stronger. I was almost two years old when the Court struck down some of Connecticut's restrictions on access to contraceptives for married people. At the time, my family lived about twenty miles from the Connecticut border; had we resided in that state before the Court's ruling, my married parents could not have used contraception legally. In turn, that ruling set in motion a series of developments that enabled my sexual partners and me to obtain birth control legally when I was a university student in Connecticut. I was two years old when the Court ruled in a Massachusetts obscenity case that sexual materials with redeeming social value were constitutionally protected. Two decades later, when I was working in Boston as the coordinating editor of *Gay Community News*, some of the newspapers I helped produce might have been censored had it not been for the Court's earlier ruling. I was three years old when the Court struck down state laws against interracial marriage. About fifteen years later, I began the first of several interracial relationships that, even if they had been heterosexual, could not have been legitimized by marriage in parts of the United States before the Court's ruling. I was seven years old when the Court struck down a Massachusetts law restricting unmarried people's access to birth control. A decade later, this helped my partners and me avoid unwanted pregnancies and sexually transmitted diseases at a time when the former was subject to intensified public scrutiny and the latter included HIV/AIDS. I was nine years old when the Court struck down restrictive state laws against abortion. This was too late for one of my grandmothers, who had an illegal abortion when my grandfather was overseas in the military during World War II, but the ruling, by improving access to safe abortions, may have saved the lives of several of my friends a decade later. I remember none of these decisions from the late 1960s and early 1970s, but when I first began to learn more about the Court during the post-Watergate era, my faith in the Constitution and the Court deepened.[4]

By the time I visited the Court for the second time, that faith had been shaken to its core, first by lessons learned in the 1980s about the Constitution's and Court's historical roles in institutionalizing class, race, and sex oppression and then by the news that the justices had upheld state sodomy laws in *Bowers* (1986).[5] It is difficult to capture the despair I remember feeling as I read the ruling in the *New York Times*. Up to that point, I had retained some hope that the Court would uphold the principles I had been taught were enshrined in the Constitution. Now those hopes felt desperately innocent and naive. And so in 1987 I had my second direct encounter with the Court, this time during the March on Washington for Lesbian and Gay Rights, which brought hundreds of thousands of people to the nation's capital, in part to protest *Bowers*. Two days after the main demonstration, I joined hundreds of activists who marched on the Court and were arrested for committing nonviolent civil disobedience. My small affinity group, sporting yellow rubber gloves with purple nail polish to mock the police who claimed they were wearing gloves to protect themselves from catching AIDS, managed to maneuver around the police barricades. As we ran toward the Court and then sat down, arms linked and voices raised, I remember thinking about the boy who had spent endless hours looking at the picture of that building on the back of his bedroom door.

I had my third significant encounter with the Court in the early 1990s, when I was a graduate student at the University of Pennsylvania and was taking a legal history seminar taught by Mary Frances Berry, then a member and later the chair of the U.S. Civil Rights Commission. While doing preliminary work on the research that would form the basis of my book on Philadelphia's lesbian and gay history, I came across documents mentioning the long-forgotten Homosexual Law Reform Society (HLRS), which had been active in the United States in the 1960s. The HLRS had supported the litigation in *Boutilier* (1967), one of the Court's first major gay rights cases. In this case, the justices upheld the deportation of a Canadian man who had been living in the United States for more than a decade on the grounds that, under the Immigration and Nationality Act of 1952, "homosexual" aliens were excludable and deportable as "afflicted with psychopathic personality."[6] While working on

Boutilier for my seminar paper, I learned that *Bowers* was not the gay and lesbian movement's first major defeat at the Court and that the loss in *Boutilier* had occurred in the midst of a set of "liberalizing" rulings on birth control, obscenity, interracial marriage, and abortion. I wondered how *Boutilier* could be reconciled with these other rulings. *Bowers*, I began to understand, could not be blamed exclusively on the Court's shift in direction in the late 1970s and 1980s and the politics of conservative backlash. The roots of the Court's denial of gay and lesbian rights lay further back, in the so-called "sexual revolution" of the 1960s.

When I began work on this project, I did not know that in 1998 I would cross the same border Boutilier had crossed when he was deported from the United States thirty years earlier. The grandchild of European Jews who had moved to the United States in 1929, I was thirty-four years old, one year younger than Boutilier had been when he was forced to leave the United States.[7] I had visited Canada only once before, ironically during the U.S. bicentennial celebrations in 1976, when my family vacationed for the first time outside the United States. Now I had a job interview at York University in Toronto for a position as a U.S. political historian. Having decided to present my work on *Boutilier* during the interview, I was curious about how much my audience would know about the U.S. Constitution and Supreme Court. Canada is a parliamentary democracy (not a presidential republic) and did not have its own comprehensive and constitutionally entrenched statement of fundamental rights until the 1980s, when the Canadian Charter of Rights and Freedoms was adopted. I quickly learned that Canadians know much more about the United States than U.S. Americans know about Canada. When York offered me its position, I marveled at the relationship between the story of Boutilier, a "homosexual" man forced by the U.S. government to return to Canada, and my story, that of a "gay" man whose migration across the same border was made possible by my work on *Boutilier*.

About six months later, I crossed the border again to begin my new job in my new country. Soon I began thinking more actively about a question that had haunted me for many years: what happened to Boutilier after he was deported? Telephone calls to Boutiliers listed in the Toronto telephone directory did not yield any clues, but in 2001 I received an e-mail message from one of Boutilier's nieces, who was responding to an inquiry I had posted on a genealogical website. Over the next several months, Boutilier's niece told me that he had been in a terrible car accident in New York while awaiting deportation after the Supreme Court ruling and that he had been in a coma for thirty days, suffering brain damage as a result. She believed that her uncle's injuries were the result of a suicide attempt, and she wrote that her siblings shared this view. With Boutilier requiring long-term medical assistance, his stepfather and mother, who had emigrated from Canada to the United States with several of her grown children, moved to southern Ontario to take care of him. One e-mail message from the niece stated that Boutilier, who had moved to a group home for the disabled after his mother was no longer able to care for him, could dress and feed himself but "walks as if in a drunken stupor." Boutilier's niece believed that he remembered his former "lifestyle" because one of her nephews was gay and Boutilier had once said, "He has the problem, too, doesn't he?" I wondered if the justices knew what happened to Boutilier and his family.

Unfortunately, my efforts to meet Boutilier were not successful. His niece wrote that under no circumstances would her mother or grandmother allow me to meet him; they did not want to "open old wounds," and the niece was certain that her "grandmother drummed it into his head that what happened was to never be brought into the light of day ever again." I began to wonder if Boutilier had been living under the control of antigay family guardians for more than thirty years or if he had come to believe that homosexuality, rather than antihomosexual attitudes, had caused his troubles. I also began to think of him as a person with disabilities, not only in his post-accident life but also in the period when the U.S. government labeled him psychopathic.[8] Though I made many efforts to contact Boutilier, offering to speak with his mother or sister before contacting him or to send questions his niece could ask, his niece would not reveal the contact information I needed to write to him directly. Because Boutilier's niece was the only family member who was communicating with me, I did not want to alienate her. One day in 2002, my e-mail message to her bounced back undelivered; I feared the trail had gone cold. I did not hear from her again until 2003, when she informed me that on 12 April Boutilier had died of complications related to a heart condition. As far as I know, no newspaper, magazine, or other news source reported on his death until I wrote an article for the electronic History News Network nearly seven months later.[9]

Meanwhile, I had experienced my own border troubles.[10] In 1998, I applied to become a permanent resident of Canada, which required that I contact the Federal Bureau of Investigation (FBI) so that Canadian officials could determine whether I had ever been arrested or convicted of a crime. Fortunately, the FBI report contained no mention of my civil disobedience at the Supreme Court. Nor did it indicate that I had broken state laws against adultery, cohabitation, fornication, and sodomy. But there was another potential problem. In early 1999, Citizenship and Immigration Canada informed me that I would have to be tested for HIV/AIDS as part of the permanent residency application process. This derived from a complicated set of developments in the United States and Canada. Under U.S. law, "homosexual" aliens had been excludable and deportable as "psychopathic personalities" or "sexual deviates" until 1990, when the United States removed these restrictions around the same time that it adopted policies to exclude and deport aliens with HIV/AIDS. These policies remained in effect until 2010. Canada had passed an explicit restriction on "homosexual" immigration in 1952, which remained in effect until 1977. In the 1980s, Canada officially regarded people with HIV/AIDS as a danger to public health and rejected most applications for permanent residency by those known to have HIV/AIDS. Some defenders of this policy argued that since the Canadian public health care system was far more generous than its U.S. counterpart, U.S. citizens with HIV/AIDS would immigrate in large numbers to Canada if these restrictions did not exist. In 1991, Canada adopted a new policy that excluded most categories of immigrants with HIV if they were expected to place an "excessive demand" on public health or social services. From 1991 to 2000, HIV testing of permanent residency applicants was selective and could be ordered if the test seemed to be clinically indicated, which it apparently was in my case. I suspect that what prompted my HIV test requirement was the section of the application in which I had to list my previous organizational memberships, which included multiple groups with "gay" or "AIDS" in their names. In 2000, Canada announced a new policy under which HIV testing for permanent residency applicants fifteen years of age or older became mandatory. Canada retained the "excessive demand" exclusion, which applied if the estimated cost of the individual's health care was greater than that of the average Canadian.[11] In short, had I tested positive for HIV my application for permanent residency could have been denied, and had I applied before 1977 as an openly gay man my application also would have been denied.

For these and many other reasons, I was profoundly moved by Boutilier's story and the related stories of thousands of people excluded unjustly from the United States, and I was horrified by the Supreme Court decisions that permitted this to occur. As I worked on this book, I continued to be disappointed in the Court's rulings, even as I developed a more complicated understanding of the many constraints on the Court's powers. After deciding *Boutilier* in 1967, the Court refused to hear oral arguments on gay and lesbian rights cases until 1984. Over the subsequent fifteen years, the Court upheld not only state sodomy laws but also the refusal of the U.S. Olympic Committee to allow the "Gay Olympics" to use the word "olympics" and the exclusion of "homosexuals" from the military, the Boy Scouts, and Boston's St. Patrick's Day parade. To be sure, there were rulings such as *Lawrence* (2003) that were interpreted as sexual freedom decisions, but these fell short of affirming comprehensive sexual equality.

These are some of the concerns that motivated my work on this project, but the fact that I began this project with a commitment to sexual equality does not mean I was not surprised or influenced by the evidence I uncovered. Nor do my convictions mean that my arguments were predetermined by a political agenda. Acknowledging that my life has influenced my interpretations is not meant to suggest the existence of a linear, cause-and-effect relationship between the two; I would no sooner argue that the opinions of the justices were the inevitable results of their familial, marital, reproductive, and sexual histories. These reflections are offered instead as a strategy to resist the pretenses of historical objectivity, a way of thinking about the effects of the past and present on one another, and a means of encouraging readers to consider how their histories will inform their readings of this book.[12]

Sexual INJUSTICE

Introduction

In its controversial 2003 decision in *Lawrence v. Texas*, the U.S. Supreme Court struck down state sodomy laws for violating constitutional rights.[1] These laws, which existed in thirteen states at the time of *Lawrence*, were enforced infrequently but were often used to legitimate sexual discrimination. In this sense, they functioned like state laws against adultery, cohabitation, and fornication. Rarely utilized and widely flouted, these prohibitions were available for use in conflicts and debates about sexual rights and social citizenship.[2]

As was evident in *Lawrence*, such laws were not just vestiges of older systems of sexual regulation. In March 2000, for example, the *New York Times* reported that Kimberly Henry and Richard Pitcher, an unmarried couple, had been charged with violating New Mexico's cohabitation statute. Pitcher's ex-wife, who had cohabited with Mr. Pitcher before becoming a born-again Christian after her fourth marriage, filed a complaint because of her concerns about the lessons the unmarried couple was teaching their child about "moral values." In covering this case, the *Times* mentioned that earlier in 2000 Arizona's legislature had "rebuffed efforts . . . to repeal its own 80-year-old cohabitation law after a committee chairman described it as a bulwark against the 'decaying fabric of society.'" In January 2001, the Eleventh Circuit Court upheld an Alabama obscenity law banning the sale of "any device designed or marketed as useful primarily for the stimulation of human genital organs." According to the court, the law served the state's interests in promoting "public morality" and "discouraging prurient interests in autonomous sex." In April 2001 the *Charlotte Observer* reported that federal judge Carl Horn was regularly invoking a North Carolina law banning fornication and adultery in cases involving cohabiting defendants. Declaring that he would not release a criminal defendant "knowing that he or she will break the law," Horn had been saying that "they won't be freed on bond until they agree to get married, move out of the house or have their partner leave." Just before *Lawrence* was announced in 2003, the North Dakota Senate voted against repealing a law that made it a crime for an unmarried heterosexual couple to live together "openly and notoriously." As one state senator declared, the law "stands as a reminder that there is right and there is wrong."[3]

After *Lawrence*, many of these laws continued to be enforced. In January 2004, the *New York Times* reported that a sales representative of Passion Parties, a sex toy company that uses "Tupperware-style marketing," had been arrested for violating a Texas law that prohibited the sale of obscene devices. In July of that year, the Eleventh Circuit again upheld the Alabama law against selling sex toys, arguing that ruling otherwise might jeopardize laws against incest, prostitution, and obscenity. Four years later, the Fifth Circuit struck down the Texas law, but the Eleventh Circuit in 2007 and the Alabama Supreme Court in 2009 upheld Alabama's ban. Courts also continued to uphold the use of sodomy laws in specific types of cases. In 2004, the Kansas Court of Appeals upheld a seventeen-year prison sentence for a man who, when eighteen years old, had consensual sex with a fourteen-year-old boy, even though the maximum sentence would have been fifteen months if the boy had been a girl. The differential penalty was struck down by the Kansas Supreme Court in 2005, but according to Lambda Legal Defense lawyers several states were continuing to enforce their sodomy laws in public solicitation and prison sex cases. In 2004, the U.S. Court of Appeals for the Armed Services upheld the military's ban on sodomy. Laws against cohabitation also continued to be enforced. In 2005, the *New York Times* reported that a North Carolina woman had been forced to resign from her job as a sheriff's dispatcher after her boss claimed she was violating a state law prohibiting unmarried couples from "lewdly and lasciviously" cohabiting. A state court later overturned this law, but the *Christian Science Monitor* reported in 2006 that seven states continued to ban nonmarital cohabitation. Shortly thereafter, a national gay and lesbian magazine reported that thousands of municipal ordinances prohibited households containing more than three individuals not related by "blood, marriage, or adoption"; one such law in Missouri had been used recently against an unmarried heterosexual couple and their children. Meanwhile, in 2005 a Georgia jury convicted a man of aggravated child molestation for having consensual oral sex with a fifteen-year-old girl when he was seventeen. Sentenced to ten years in prison, the man was released in 2007 after the Georgia Supreme Court ruled that this constituted "cruel and unusual punishment." In short, consensual sexual expression continues to be criminalized in 2010.[4]

In the aftermath of *Lawrence*, critics on the right warned that laws against adultery, bestiality, incest, pedophilia, polygamy, prostitution, and same-sex marriage were now vulnerable to challenge, while critics on the left attacked the ruling for not addressing sexual discrimination in the public sphere and not protecting consensual sex more generally. Anticipating the decision just before it was announced, Senator Rick Santorum warned, "If the Supreme Court says that you have the right to consensual sex within your home, then you have the right to bigamy. Then you have the right to polygamy, you have the right to incest, you have the right to adultery." On the other side of the political spectrum, a *History News Network* column declared, "The *Lawrence* decision does not give gays all of the same rights as straight Americans, and it theoretically leaves the door open to certain types of discrimination. This is actually a step backward."[5] At stake in these discussions were sharply conflicting views about the proper role of the state in society, an issue that divides both the right and the left. Yet despite these disagreements, the vast majority of commentators agreed with the claim made in Justice Anthony Kennedy's majority opinion that *Lawrence* was consistent with Supreme Court precedents from the 1960s and 1970s.[6]

Sexual Injustice challenges this view, arguing that it is based on a fundamental misunderstanding or a revisionist interpretation of what the Court did several decades ago in cases concerning birth control, obscenity, homosexuality, interracial marriage, and abortion. The evidence more convincingly suggests that *Lawrence* transformed the conservative vision of sexual freedom, equality, and citizenship that had guided the Court since the 1960s. This book does not address the question of what the Court should have done in these cases. Nor does it offer an interpretation of the U.S. Constitution. My work concentrates on what the Court said, what roles liberal and leftist advocates played in the development of the Court's doctrine, and how the Court's decisions were subsequently interpreted and remembered.

After providing an overview of the history of the sexual revolution and the role of the Court, this book advances three main claims. First, in the period from 1965 to 1973 the justices developed a sexual rights doctrine that was not broadly libertarian or egalitarian; instead, the doctrine affirmed the supremacy of adult, heterosexual, marital, monogamous, private, and procreative forms of sexual expression. The doctrine was heteronormative in two senses: it favored heterosexuality and it favored particular forms of heterosexuality. While allowing for some flexibility in what counted as normative, the doctrine was based on the notion that normative heterosexuality had been, was, and always should be privileged.[7] Second, liberal and leftist advocates contributed to the development of the doctrine as they worked within the constraints of the legal system. In other contexts, these advocates may have adopted more libertarian and egalitarian positions, but the arguments they presented to the Court condoned sexual discrimination. Third, the mass media, lower courts, and scholarly experts depicted the Court's decisions as more sexually libertarian and egalitarian than the texts of the rulings indicated or implied. These depictions suggested to various types of sexual criminals, including those who engaged in nonmarital heterosexual sex, that their rights to engage in previously illegal behaviors had been recognized by the Court. This had the effect of securing their allegiance to the dominant sexual order. Without understanding this history, the U.S. public in the post-*Lawrence* era is again more likely to interpret the nature of the rights recognized by the Court in ways that diverge from the justices' interpretations. At the same time, this history suggests that, over the long term, what the public thinks the Court has decided can be as important or more important than what the Court thinks it has decided, eventually convincing even the justices to adopt revisionist interpretations of the Court's precedents.

The Sexual Revolution?

When historians discuss the post–World War II sexual revolution, they generally highlight a set of developments. Many focus on behavioral indices, such as the percentage of the population engaging in nonmarital and nonreproductive sex, the popularity of nonmarital cohabitation, and the incidence of nonmarital reproduction, all of which appear to have increased. For many scholars, the main issue is not changing behaviors but changing norms, which they argue came into greater alignment with behavioral patterns, thereby reducing social disapproval of certain forms of nonmarital sex, reproduction, and cohabitation. To account for these changes, researchers focus on competing and complementary developments. Movements committed to racial equality, student power, countercultural rebellion, sexual liberation, women's liberation, gay liberation, and lesbian feminism challenged sexual repression and oppression, often in different or opposing ways. Transformations in gender roles influenced sexual discourses and practices. The dynamics of advanced capitalism contributed to the commodification of sex and encouraged sexual entrepreneurs to seek greater profits in an increasingly sexualized public sphere. And various technological innovators and technocratic elites came to see products such as the diaphragm, the birth control pill, and the condom and procedures such as abortion and sterilization as the keys to solving social problems such as unwanted pregnancies, sexually transmitted diseases, poverty, hunger, and overpopulation.[8]

Although many in the midst of the sexual revolution believed themselves to be living through a period of significant changes, the timing, character, and extent of the changes remain unclear. Did the revolution begin in the Roaring

Twenties, which some see as the era of the "first sexual revolution," or in the Great Depression and World War II, when major social transformations occurred? What about the late 1940s and 1950s, which witnessed the emergence of *Playboy*, the release of the Kinsey sex reports, the rise of hipsters and Beats, and the founding of the homophile movement? The origins of the sexual revolution are more commonly traced to the early 1960s, when the birth control pill was approved by the Food and Drug Administration, *Sex and the Single Girl* was published, and commentators began referring to "the sexual revolution." Or the revolution is said to have begun in the late 1960s and early 1970s, when sexual radicals, radical feminists, and gay liberationists achieved greater influence.[9]

As for the revolution's character, here, too, the picture remains unclear. For instance, many women's liberationists from multiple racial and religious communities promoted the legalization of birth control and abortion, but did not necessarily see themselves as aligned with African American, Native American, Puerto Rican, and disability activists concerned about forced sterilization; nor did they typically align themselves with technocrats trying to control population growth. Students who cohabited did not necessarily see themselves as having much in common with promiscuous sex radicals, free lovers, swinging singles, or married couples who swapped spouses. Countercultural youth interested in "natural" and "authentic" sex did not necessarily support the publishers of *Playboy* and *Hustler*. What many pornographers celebrated as the liberation of desire was denounced by many women's liberationists as quintessential forms of objectification. What many women's liberationists wanted in reconstructed heterosexual partnerships was criticized by many lesbian feminists as "sleeping with the enemy." The men many lesbian feminists saw as the enemy were seen by many gay liberationists as objects of desire. In assessing the sexual revolution, most scholars have stressed its liberating dimensions, but some have emphasized its limitations.

We can say with greater certainty that in a vortex of complicated forces there were revolutionary sexual possibilities. As is generally the case in potentially revolutionary contexts, key elements of the dominant order appeared to be vulnerable, and a variety of competing groups hoped to participate in the construction of a new social order. Some elements of the old order changed while others did not. Answers to the question of whether the sexual revolution was revolutionary depend on how the key elements of the old order are defined, what conclusions are reached about the extent and rapidity of the changes that occurred, and whose perspectives are considered when answering these questions. While this book does not make a general argument about the sexual revolution, it concludes that insofar as the old order was based on the dominance of heteronormative forms of sexual expression, the Court's role was counterrevolutionary.

The Supreme Court

The Supreme Court is a unique institution in the U.S. system of checks and balances, and its role in the sexual revolution was also unique.[10] Appointed for life terms by the president with the advice and consent of the Senate, the nine members (one chief justice and eight associate justices) decide cases involving conflicts between states, hear appeals concerning federal law, and pass judgment on whether federal, state, and local laws and practices violate the Constitution. In theory, the system is designed so that the Court will not be accountable to electoral majorities or political authorities and will stand up to them when they violate the law. Like the U.S. system as a whole, the court system is federal: the states have their own constitutions and courts, and cases that deal exclusively with state matters will not be accepted by the Supreme Court unless they concern conflicts between states. The Court's decisions have special significance, though not because they are the only way to effect legal change. Executive and legislative actions at local, state, and federal levels, and judicial decisions at levels below the Court were responsible for significant reforms in the legal regulation of sex, marriage, and reproduction. Many states, for example, revised their abortion, birth control, and interracial marriage statutes before the Court ruled on the constitutionality of the remaining laws. Decisions by the Court have special significance in part because they have the power to nationalize legal reforms that might otherwise vary by state. They also set the basic parameters within which governments operate in the United States, and on a cultural level they are very influential, cited frequently by those who believe authority and legitimacy can be gained by invoking Court decisions.

The Court is often described as a reactive institution with limited powers, responding to cases brought to it rather than initiating action. In each annual term in the post–World War II era, the justices and their clerks reviewed a large number of written petitions (*writs of certiorari*) asking the Court to hear appeals of lower court rulings. If four justices supported the request, the case was accepted for consideration and the Court either issued a summary judgment or scheduled oral arguments. Only a small percentage of cases was accepted for argument; in other cases the Court generally let stand the lower court ruling or issued a summary judgment. After reviewing briefs submitted by the opposing sides and by *amici curiae* (friends of the court) and after listening to oral arguments, the justices met in private to discuss the case. By custom, the chief justice spoke first, followed by the other justices in order of seniority. Voting then proceeded in the opposite direction. If the chief voted with the majority, he determined who would draft the majority opinion. Otherwise, the senior justice in the majority decided who would do so. The process of producing, circulating, and revising the drafts might take days, weeks, or months. In some cases, justices switched sides during this process and in doing so could change the results. Justices also sometimes produced concurring opinions, which might agree with the majority judgment but not its reasoning or agree with the judgment and reasoning but make additional points not contained in the majority opinion. After all revisions were complete, the Court announced the results.

Along the way, the justices acted in strategic ways. In theory, for example, the justices accepted cases for argument if there were major unresolved constitutional questions involved, if two appellate courts issued conflicting rulings, or if the justices disagreed with lower court rulings. But some justices voted for other reasons: to avoid having the Court endorse lower court rulings they opposed, to encourage the Court to take positions that might support particular outcomes in future cases, to wait for cases whose features might be more favorable to the outcome desired, or to delay in the hopes that resignations or deaths on the Court might lead to different results. The justices also behaved strategically in oral arguments, interrupting, intimidating, and challenging lawyers whose arguments they opposed and asking helpful questions and providing answers to lawyers whose arguments they supported. In some instances, the chief justice and the more senior justices cast their votes to ensure that they would select the drafter of the majority opinions. In many cases, the justices who were selected to write the opinions were chosen for strategic reasons. A certain justice could be asked to write the majority opinion because he might best be able to hold together a fractious majority or because his support for the winning side appeared to be weak. In the revision process, the justices praised and criticized, suggested additions and deletions, granted and withheld endorsements, prepared concurrences, and changed their votes. Some justices disliked narrow majorities and switched their votes to increase the authority of the decisions; others relished their roles as dissenters.

Like their predecessors, the justices who served from 1965 to 1973 were drawn from very narrow demographic elements of the U.S. population. Fifteen men, ranging in age from late forties to mid-eighties, served on the Court in this period. Hugo L. Black (1937–71) and William O. Douglas (1939–75) were appointed by Franklin Roosevelt; Tom C. Clark (1949–67) by Harry Truman; Earl Warren (1953–69), John M. Harlan (1955–71), William J. Brennan Jr. (1956–90), and Potter Stewart (1958–81) by Dwight Eisenhower; Byron R. White (1962–93) and Arthur J. Goldberg (1962–65) by John Kennedy; Abe Fortas (1965–69) and Thurgood Marshall (1967–91) by Lyndon Johnson; and Warren E. Burger (1969–86), Harry A. Blackmun (1970–94), Lewis F. Powell Jr. (1972–87), and William H. Rehnquist (1972–2005) by Richard Nixon. Eight of these men were appointed by Republican presidents, seven by Democrats. The Republican appointees were not necessarily more conservative than the Democratic ones; Warren, Brennan, and Blackmun, appointed by Republicans, were generally more liberal on sexual issues than Clark and White, both appointed by Democrats. All of the justices were at least middle class when serving on the Court, but several grew up in working-class families. Fourteen were Euro-American; one (Marshall) was African American; thirteen were Christian; two (Fortas and Goldberg) were Jewish. Warren served as chief justice from 1953 until 1969; Burger replaced him and served until 1986.

According to the biographical literature on the members of the Court, the justices were fully immersed in the problems, pleasures, and possibilities of heterosexuality, marriage, and procreation. Several were the children of unhappy and contentious marriages (Black, Brennan, Douglas, Harlan, and Warren); at least one had parents who conceived a child before marriage (Marshall); and one discovered that his father had syphilis (Blackmun). In their youths, at least one was warned about the dangers of masturbation (Douglas); at least one read pornography (Black); there are hints that one had sexual experiences with prostitutes (Warren); and most dated, courted, and had intimate relationships with women other than their eventual spouses. Marshall later claimed that he was engaged to be married at least nine times, that he lost a testicle while trying to jump into a truck during a college escapade, and that he failed a class after challenging a professor's assertion that the only reason to have sex was to reproduce. One justice was a Christian whose marriage to a Jew was blocked by her parents (Black); another justice married while he was a student, despite promises to parents to wait until after graduation (Marshall); one kept his marriage secret from his and his wife's parents while he was a student (Brennan); and another kept his marriage secret so he could live in unmarried student housing (Douglas). Three married significantly younger women (Black, Douglas, and Marshall); several married widows or divorcees (Black, Douglas, Fortas, Harlan, and Warren); two married across religious and/or racial boundaries (Fortas and Marshall); at least three had extramarital relationships (Douglas, Fortas, and Marshall); and one married four times (Douglas). Collectively these fifteen justices married twenty-one times.[11]

As for their reproductive histories, one justice tried but failed to have children with his first wife and conceived a child premaritally with his second (Marshall); another justice and his wife reportedly had difficulty having children (White); one wife volunteered for Planned Parenthood (Stewart); and one justice once advised a young law firm colleague after his girlfriend died of complications from an illegal abortion (Powell). As far as we know, these fifteen justices had thirty-eight biological children, but their parents had more than seventy, suggesting that the justices limited their reproductive sex to a far greater extent than their parents had. Biographers have not, for the most part, discussed the justices' children in their coverage of sexual matters, but the justices watched their children and grandchildren live through the "sexual revolution" and some had difficult relationships with their children during this tumultuous time. Several of the children married across religious and/or racial boundaries; several divorced; and one justice (Warren) asked the F B I to investigate his daughters' boyfriends. One justice's daughter became pregnant as a teenager, contemplated abortion, married her boyfriend, and then miscarried (Blackmun). The biographical literature also reveals that one justice took testosterone shots to increase his virility (Black); the same justice's wife counseled a future first lady (Mamie Eisenhower) about her husband's sexual affairs; this justice's wife later committed suicide; and two had their personal papers destroyed to protect their privacy (Black and White).

The work of the Court during these years intersected with these and other aspects of the justices' lives. The justices heard cases referencing abortion, birth control, cohabitation, homosexuality, interracial marriage, nonmarital sex, nonmarital reproduction, obscenity, and rape. Douglas's four marriages, three divorces, and multiple extramarital affairs generated substantial public discussion and contributed to calls for his impeachment, as did the appearance of his work in periodicals considered pornographic. Court staff were kept busy ensuring that Douglas's wives did not encounter his lovers; staffers also tried to make sure that the Court was not sullied by allegations about Douglas's unwanted sexual advances to associates, secretaries, and visitors. Before, during, and after this period the Court was the site of workplace romance: Black married his secretary in the 1950s, Brennan did so in the 1980s, and an interracial relationship between two Court employees was a source of controversy beginning in 1972. According to a member of Douglas's staff, "Other justices . . . had mistresses . . . , but they would employ them as secretaries or keep them away from the Court building." During oral arguments, chairs with brass nameplates were reserved for Mrs. Warren and the other wives, but the justices also noticed other women in the room. In 1971, one justice wrote to another during oral arguments, "Note 'blond' in second row center. She is here almost daily—at least since you came!" In 1973, one justice referred to a female lawyer in a note passed to another justice: "How would you like to try to change the lady's position on any matter—where to have dinner for example?"[12]

Meanwhile, many of the justices and clerks regularly gathered in the Court basement to review movies, magazines, and books that were at issue in obscenity cases. According to one biography, Marshall "always took a front-row seat and wisecracked loudly" and "if the action on-screen got especially heated, he would commend the performance and even ask for a copy of the film so he could have it to show his kids when they reached college age." Journalists Joyce Murdoch and Deb Price write that Harlan, "nearly blind with cataracts," held "graphic pictures two inches from his face—a fact that continually amused him," purposely sat beside "prudish colleagues" during the movies, and demanded "a blow-by-blow description." Some justices refused to attend. As Brennan later recalled, "Warren was a terrible prude.... I'd read the book or see the movie and he'd go along with my views." In the midst of these rulings, *Playboy* founder Hugh Hefner (or someone pretending to be Hefner) sent Brennan a pornographic card "with love and kisses." During the oral arguments in *Fanny Hill*, Black announced to his neighbor on the bench, "I'm the court's expert on sex." Fortas joked in a 1966 memorandum to Brennan that he was "glad to join you and *Fanny Hill*." In 1967, as the Court heard arguments in *Loving*, Fortas wrote sexually suggestive poems that he shared with Douglas. Rehnquist later passed similar missives to Blackmun. Douglas once joked that the reason the Court seemed to be moving in a liberal direction in obscenity cases was that the legal test was "whether the material arouses a prurient response in the beholder." As he explained, "The older we get the freer the speech." In 1972, one clerk wrote embarrassed memoranda to the other clerks and the chief justice about "exhibits in obscenity cases" that had gone missing. On occasion, the justices themselves were featured in sexually risqué representations: in February 1974, *National Lampoon* featured a centerfold illustration depicting the justices engaging in various transgressive sexual acts.[13]

The justices also had significant encounters with homosexuality. Douglas and Black served on the Court in the 1940s with Frank Murphy, who was rumored to be gay. G. Harold Carswell, a Nixon nominee for the Court who was rejected by the Senate in 1970, was arrested in 1976 for allegedly making a sexual advance to an undercover policeman in a Florida bathroom. Murdoch and Price have identified twenty-two gay and lesbian Supreme Court clerks, the earliest of whom served in the 1950s. They also note that Clark had a gay nephew, whom he knew to be gay and treated "like a beloved son." One clerk recalls that Harlan once said he would "have no difficulty whatever having a clerk who was homosexual," and the clerk was "sure" that Harlan "had friends who were homosexual." All of the justices knew about the 1964 resignation of presidential aide Walter Jenkins, a married man with six children who was twice caught having sex with a man in a YMCA restroom. Douglas's widow Cathy Douglas Stone told Murdoch and Price that Douglas mentioned the Jenkins incident many times: "He kept saying to me, 'Can you imagine somebody on the police force actually hanging out in public toilets. . . . What do they say to their children when they say, "Daddy, what did you do today?"' It was so ludicrous to him. It was pathetic and sad to him the way people were treated." According to Stone, Douglas had many gay friends and viewed homosexuality as part of the "tapestry of life." Douglas wrote in his autobiography about a college friend who "expressed his sexual interest" in the future justice "in an unmistakable way." He referred to a senator and an undersecretary of state "reputed" to be gay and mentioned the use of Lafayette Park in Washington, D.C., as a "meeting place for homosexuals." Douglas was also friendly with his lesbian neighbors in Goose Prairie, Washington. Other justices were less friendly. Black told his son that when he worked as a judge in Alabama, he handled a case in which a man charged with assault claimed that his victim had "made advances." Black "threw out the charges and found the pervert guilty of disorderly conduct and gave him the maximum sentence." "That kind of thing will destroy a society, Son," Black reportedly said. One recent study claims that "the person who spearheaded the greatest antihomosexual Kulturkampf in American history was California's governor, Earl Warren."[14]

One justice had a particularly significant encounter with homosexuality in the 1960s. Fortas's biographies suggest that the justice participated in various "extramarital activities," had at least two serious affairs with women during his marriage, and "did not regard anyone, not even his wife's friends, as off limits." Closely aligned with President Johnson, Fortas was the first person Walter Jenkins called when news of his second arrest became public; Fortas quickly sent Jenkins to a hospital and pleaded unsuccessfully with journalists to delay their stories. In 1967, J. Edgar Hoover sent a trusted lieutenant from the FBI to visit Fortas at his home to inform him about an "allegation" that implicated Fortas in "homosexual activities." According to an FBI memorandum shown to Fortas, an "active and aggressive homosexual" who was a "reliable" informant claimed that he had "balled" with Fortas several times before he joined the Court. The informant defined "to ball" as "to have a homosexual relationship." The FBI assured Fortas that it was handling the matter "discreetly and informally" but wanted to inform him for his own "protection and knowledge." Fortas responded that the charges were "ridiculous" and "absolutely false" and that "while he might be properly accused of normal sexual relations while a young man and during his married life, he most certainly had never committed homosexual acts." The FBI may have been trying to blackmail Fortas, influence his votes, encourage his resignation, or prevent his appointment as chief justice. Two years later, Johnson nominated Fortas to replace Warren as chief justice. But in the wake of ethics accusations concerning financial improprieties, political questions about his role as a presidential adviser, sensational attacks linking him with liberal rulings in rape and obscenity cases, and anti-Semitic concerns about his Jewish background, Fortas withdrew from consideration. He resigned from the Court shortly thereafter.[15]

Because most of the justices supported or accepted the notion that the Court's mystique, majesty, and authority could be maximized by keeping their private and sexual lives hidden from public view, they tended (with the exception of Douglas) to eschew many of the forms of personal publicity favored by U.S. presidents, senators, and representatives. Their families were on public display at key moments in the life of the Court, but not nearly to the extent that was the case for their executive and legislative branch counterparts. Meanwhile, the black robes worn by the justices when performing their official functions conveyed the impression that the justice dispensed was depersonalized and disembodied.[16] On the one hand, the politics of judicial respectability required that the justices maintain the appearance of conventional family, reproductive, and sexual lives (or pay a price). On the other hand, the politics of legal objectivity demanded that the justices not allow their personal prejudices, which theoretically included biases in favor of conventional family values, to affect their judgments. When the Court considered cases dealing with sexual matters, the tensions between these two demands were often eased by the presumption that heteronormative respectability was a universal aspiration.

The point of referencing these biographies is not to suggest that there were direct and causal relationships between the justices' personal experiences of sex, marriage, and reproduction and their legal opinions. Relationships there were, but these were complex. Personal experiences may have predisposed the justices to uphold heteronormative values, but the members of the Court were capable of making decisions that seem at odds with what is known about their personal histories. Eva Rubin has argued that "the most likely source of the image of family life depicted in the [Court's] opinions," which she describes as "idealized" and "mythological," was "the personal family experience of the Justices." If it is true that the justices romanticized the heteronormative "haven in the heartless world," they may have done so precisely because their own havens sometimes proved rather heartless.[17]

It is tempting to search for moments in the work of the Court that seem related to the personal histories of the justices. Douglas waxed rhapsodic about the sacred character of marriage in *Griswold*; at that time he was on his third marriage and soon there would be a fourth. In *Boutilier*, Fortas pressed a government lawyer on the question of whether homosexuality was psychopathological; a few months later the FBI called his attention to allegations about his homosexuality. In the oral arguments in *Loving*, Warren asked whether states could prohibit marriages between people of different religions; one of Warren's sons-in-law was Jewish. Blackmun defended abortion rights in *Roe* several years after his daughter revealed an unwanted pregnancy to her parents. It would be naive to assume that the justices were disembodied rational arbiters on these subjects or that the "wise old men" had no personal sexual interests. Having benefited from the special rights and privileges associated with heterosexuality, marriage, and reproduction, the justices were rendering legal opinions on these practices and institutions. They were doing so in the early years of a post–baby boom era in which marriage and fertility rates were declining, divorce rates were increasing, and the sexual revolution was underway. This book will not have much more to say about the relationship between the justices' experiences and their opinions, but the former certainly influenced, without fully determining, the latter.

New Perspectives

Because of its decisions in civil rights and other types of cases, the Supreme Court has been identified as a leading agent of change, including sexual change, in the 1960s and 1970s. Scholars working on the subject generally concur that in a series of major rulings the Court redefined relationships between law and sexuality in the United States. Five of the most significant decisions, *Griswold v. Connecticut* (1965), *Fanny Hill v. Massachusetts* (1966), *Loving v. Virginia* (1967), *Eisenstadt v. Baird* (1972), and *Roe v. Wade* (1973), recognized new constitutional rights in cases concerning birth control, obscenity, interracial marriage, and abortion. In *Griswold*, the Court ruled five to two (with two additional judgment concurrences) that a state law forbidding the use of contraceptives by married couples infringed on rights of marital privacy. In *Fanny Hill* (whose official name was *A Book Named "John Cleland's Memoirs of a Woman of Pleasure" v. Attorney General of the Commonwealth of Massachusetts*), six of nine justices restricted the reach of obscenity laws, with a controlling plurality of three declaring that only materials that were "utterly without redeeming social value" could be suppressed. In *Loving*, the Court ruled unanimously that laws prohibiting marriages between people of different races violated the Constitution. In *Eisenstadt*, the Court issued a four to one ruling (with two additional judgment concurrences and two vacancies) that struck down a state law banning the distribution of contraceptives to unmarried people. And in *Roe*, seven of nine justices found that restrictive anti-abortion laws interfered with rights of reproductive privacy. In apparent contrast, in *Boutilier v. the Immigration and Naturalization Service* (1967) six of nine justices ruled that "homosexual" aliens could be excluded and deported from the country under the "psychopathic personality" provisions of the 1952 Immigration and Nationality Act.[18]

Historians of the sexual revolution have produced groundbreaking studies exploring various dimensions of change and continuity, but have not paid much attention to the Court. When mentioning the Court, they usually highlight the liberalizing aspects of rulings in the late 1960s and early 1970s and situate conservative decisions in the context of rightwing backlash in the late 1970s, 1980s, and 1990s. Discussing *Griswold*, they do not typically point out that most of the justices made comments suggesting that laws against adultery, fornication, and homosexuality were constitutional. Historians do not usually emphasize that the obscenity rules adopted in *Fanny Hill* relied on the discriminatory concept of "community standards" and that the Court, on the same day it ruled in favor of *Fanny Hill*, upheld obscenity convictions in two other cases. When exploring *Loving*, they do not generally mention the passage that based the ruling on a narrowly reproductive conception of marriage and a narrowly marital conception of reproduction. Nor do they acknowledge that *Eisenstadt* and *Roe* embraced reproductive rather than sexual privacy. To take just one example, David Allyn's book on the sexual revolution describes *Griswold* as a "solid victory for . . . the forces of sexual freedom," claims that "American censorship law finally collapsed in 1966," and asserts that *Roe* was "the crowning achievement of the sexual revolution." The problem is not that these historians are wrong in emphasizing that the Court was moving in a liberal direction, but their work has obscured the rulings' conservative elements.

They have made reformers appear like revolutionaries.[19] None of the most notable books on the history of the sexual revolution mention *Boutilier*.[20]

Leading historians of the sexual revolution appear unfamiliar with the arguments of legal studies scholars and political scientists, some of whom have emphasized the limitations of the Court's rulings on sex, marriage, and reproduction.[21] In turn, most legal studies scholars and political scientists who have worked on this subject have not favored the archival research methods and interpretive strategies commonly used by historians. With important exceptions, much of their work focuses on the decisions themselves, paying less attention to the activists and advocates who took these cases to the Court.[22] There is also an unfortunate tendency to dismiss or ignore gay and lesbian rights litigation before the 1970s. No scholar has examined the homophile movement's adoption of a Supreme Court strategy in the 1960s, the work of the Philadelphia-based Homosexual Law Reform Society (H L R S), or the extraordinary coalition of activists and advocates who came together to defend *Boutilier*.[23]

Legal studies scholars and political scientists have explored the relationship between the Court and public opinion, which is another major concern of this book, and some of this research examines cases about sex, marriage, and reproduction. In general, however, this work concentrates on policy support and opposition rather than legal reasoning. Work on *Roe*, for instance, typically asks whether the Court's decision led to increased or decreased support for abortion rights, not whether the public's understanding of the justices' reasoning was consistent with the justices' understanding of their own reasoning.[24] There is a related literature on "popular constitutionalism," emphasizing that the Court is not the only influential interpreter of the Constitution. This work has shaped the analysis offered in this book, but no scholar has carefully examined the language of the decisions considered here and compared this to the language used by readers of the Court's opinions. The story of how the Court's language about marital and reproductive rights came to be understood as implicating sexual rights has remained untold.[25]

Another limitation of the existing scholarship is that it downplays relationships between different types of cases that addressed sex. Many legal scholars would argue, for example, that what the Court does in a sexual privacy case might have no relationship to what it does in sex-related immigration and obscenity cases. This helps explain why the literature on *Boutilier* has tended to remain separate from the literature on the other cases examined in this book. One result is that we have many works on birth control and abortion *or* obscenity *or* interracial marriage *or* homosexuality, but few that adopt a broader perspective. These tendencies have made it difficult to consider the hetero-normative reasoning that influenced decisions across different types of cases. Also, they have made it difficult to examine the relationships of these cases to one another. As this book demonstrates, however, when abortion, birth control, homosexuality, and interracial sex are labeled obscene, when obscenity rulings are invoked in cases about reproductive and gay and lesbian rights, when obscenity is viewed as a violation of privacy rights, and when decisions about any of these subjects refer to laws against adultery, cohabitation, fornication, and prostitution, it becomes useful to adopt a broad sexuality studies framework. *Boutilier* is usually regarded as an immigration case, not a free-speech or privacy case, but Boutilier's speech-acts about private conduct led to his deportation. Moreover, while privacy was not discussed in *Boutilier*, the related concept of secrecy was invoked when the government expressed concern about homosexual aliens who might sneak into the country.[26] *Boutilier* also had implications for privacy rights because if Congress could classify certain types of consensual sexual conduct as psychopathological and if there was no right to be psychopathological in private, there was no right to engage in these forms of sexual conduct in private. In other words, there is much to be learned about privacy and free speech by examining a case that does not apparently focus on either. Another reason to consider these subjects together is that doing so encourages attention to relationships between sexual rights and national citizenship. As this book emphasizes, important birth control, interracial marriage, and gay rights cases involved aliens, not citizens. Examining cases involving citizens and aliens alongside one another can help cast light on the policing of sexual, legal, and national borders, while contributing to our understanding of the meanings of sexual, legal, and national citizenship.

Before outlining what the book's chapters do, it may be helpful to emphasize what they do not do. This is not a comprehensive study of the sexual revolution or a broad survey of sex and the law. The book does not focus on the legislative, executive, state, or local branches of government. It is not an expansive social history of sexual practices, a general cultural history of sexual discourses, or a multifaceted political history of sexual reform. It does not place the United States in transnational context or search for the roots of the Court's decisions in the distinctive American character or the exceptional history of the country. There is much that could be said about how, why, and whether the history recounted here diverges from the histories of other countries; scholars doing this type of comparative analysis typically emphasize structural factors (including the Constitution, the federal system, and the checks and balances of the executive, legislative, and judicial branches), cultural factors (including religion, race, and regionalism), or both. The goals of this monograph are more modest and the methods more microhistorical. Challenging the received wisdom about the Court's sexual revolution has been sufficiently ambitious, and doing so has required careful attention to rhetoric and reasoning.

It may also be helpful to emphasize that my training as a social, cultural, political, and legal historian has informed my approach. I have read broadly and deeply in legal studies and political science literature, but this does not mean I have adopted their methods. To take one example, many constitutional law scholars distinguish between the "holdings" of Supreme Court decisions and the "dicta," which are passages in the opinions that do not relate directly to the issue at hand and are not necessary for the legal judgment. For these scholars, dicta do not have the precedential weight of holdings and should not be regarded as the Court's considered judgment. For instance, if the justices overturn a birth control law but comment in passing that laws against fornication are constitutional, these scholars would say that the Court has not necessarily determined the constitutional status of fornication laws. Others disagree, pointing out that the justices do not formally distinguish between holdings and dicta in their opinions, they frequently cite dicta in their rulings, and the distinction between holding and dicta is not always clear. My approach acknowledges the distinction, but uses dicta when this helps reveal the meanings of the holdings. In *Griswold*, for example, the meanings of the Court's conclusions about marital privacy are clarified when dicta referring to laws against adultery, fornication, and homosexuality are considered. Along similar lines, while some constitutional law scholars believe that the Court's refusal to consider a particular appeal should not be taken as evidence of the justices' conclusions about the merits of the case, this book acknowledges the distinction between cases accepted and rejected for argument but regards as meaningful the Court's actions in both types of cases. They are differently meaningful, but meaningful nonetheless.[27]

The book's first two chapters develop the argument about the Court's heteronormative doctrine. Instead of taking up the question of whether the justices interpreted the Constitution correctly or asserting that the anti-gay majority in *Boutilier* contradicted the liberalizing decisions on abortion, birth control, interracial marriage, and obscenity, these chapters explore the Court's consistent logic. Examining *Griswold*, *Fanny Hill*, *Loving*, *Eisenstadt*, and *Roe* (chapter 1) in relation to *Boutilier* (chapter 2) and exploring more broadly the Court's various rulings on sexual matters helps reveal the scope and limits of the Court's sexual revolution. This allows us to see how the law constructed normative heterosexuality, non-normative heterosexuality, and deviant homosexuality in dynamic and hierarchical relationships to one another. Doing so demonstrates that the Court, during its most liberal period in the post-1945 era, was sexually conservative. Exploring these cases together shows that the Court offered a vision of sexual citizenship that was not broadly libertarian and egalitarian; it did not endorse the libertarian principle that consenting adults may do as they please in private or the egalitarian notion that marital and nonmarital sex should be treated equally. Instead, the Court authorized special rights and privileges for adult, heterosexual, marital, monogamous, private, and procreative forms of sexual expression. The heteronormative doctrine simultaneously contributed to the ongoing formation of class, gender, and race hierarchies in the United States. From this perspective, post-*Roe* decisions, which are typically seen as reversing or limiting the reach of pre-*Roe* precedents, now appear more consistent with the earlier rulings. In short, the broadly libertarian and egalitarian rights of sexual freedom that many U.S. Americans assume are enshrined in the Constitution were not recognized by the highest court in the land. The Court helped institutionalize classed, gendered, and racialized principles of heteronormative supremacy.

Was this inevitable given the backgrounds of the justices and the state of sexual politics in this period? Is it ahistorical to imagine the Court ruling in different ways? Would it be better to see the Court as taking steps, in a progressive, evolutionary way, toward a broader doctrine of sexual freedom? Chapters 1 and 2 show that the rulings were not inevitable. The justices were quite capable of voting in ways that seem at odds with the details of their personal lives and the country's dominant values. In the pre-1965 era, the Court extended free-speech protection to several gay publications and used a legal technicality to rule against the deportation of a gay alien.[28] As far as *Boutilier* is concerned, three justices dissented, a fourth initially sided with Boutilier, and a fifth declared that he would switch his vote if the majority supported Boutilier. Beyond *Boutilier*, the abortion, birth control, interracial marriage, and obscenity cases could have been decided without the conservative language used by the justices. And if the United States is placed in a comparative framework alongside two of its closest allies, Canada and Great Britain, it becomes evident that the rulings were not inevitable.[29] The same points are relevant in considering whether it is ahistorical to imagine the Court ruling differently. If the goal is to understand the past on its own terms, what is ahistorical about suggesting that the Court's doctrine was heteronormative? Moreover, if ahistoricism means that the historian is projecting values from the present onto the past, then all works of history are ahistorical. As for the alternative view, that the Court was taking small steps in the direction of sexual freedom, it is difficult to sustain this position when the Court's conservative language is taken seriously. The justices did not limit themselves to the particular types of laws involved in these cases and leave other types for future consideration; they affirmatively signaled that laws against nonmarital sex were constitutional. To the extent that the Court used rhetoric and reasoning that could be cited in later cases, these decisions had profoundly conservative features.

Having established in the first two chapters the parameters of the heteronormative doctrine, this book then takes another look at the same rulings, examining the strategies used by legal advocates and movement activists, first in the cases that yielded liberalizing rulings (chapter 3) and then in *Boutilier* (chapters 4 and 5). Cases do not generally reach the Court simply because an individual decides to file an appeal; usually it is necessary to have the support of a movement or an organization. Among the groups discussed in these chapters are the American Civil Liberties Union (ACLU), the American Committee for the Protection of the Foreign Born (ACPFB), the Homosexual Law Reform Society (HLRS), the Japanese American Citizens League, the National Association for the Advancement of Colored People (NAACP), the National Organization for Women (NOW), and the Planned Parenthood Federation of America (PPFA). While scholars have examined the strategies used by some of these groups, they have not analyzed the strategies comparatively, and no one has studied Boutilier's defenders. These chapters show that the justices and their clerks were not the only authors of the final decisions; the Court relied on conservative concepts endorsed by liberals and leftists, who helped the justices set limits on what many perceived as a dangerous and disorderly sexual revolution.

The narrow conception of sexual freedom, equality, and citizenship was the product of a complex dynamic in which the Court's prior rulings shaped the arguments that legal advocates made, and, in turn, their arguments shaped new rulings. Historical agency rested not only with the Court but also with advocates, clients, and the movements that made litigation possible. To maximize their chances of winning, the lawyers tailored their arguments to fit prior rulings. If they succeeded, their arguments created new precedents. To more fully understand these decisions, then, it is necessary to go beyond the texts of the rulings. The strategies used by activists and advocates in selecting cases, choosing jurisdictions, mobilizing resources, securing allies, developing arguments, generating publicity, and responding to decisions are also important to explore. These strategies were shaped not only by the content of prior rulings but also by various legal structures and conventions, including the incrementalist tradition whereby the Court claims that it avoids making rulings that are broader than necessary, the precedential tradition whereby the Court claims that it prefers to rely on the language of prior rulings rather than innovate with new formulations, and the advocacy tradition whereby lawyers are supposed to act in the best interests of their clients and not necessarily larger causes.

Influenced by these traditions, many advocates relied on strategies that minimized potential challenges to the dominant order. In explicit and implicit ways, they argued that their reasoning did not imply that laws against nonmarital sex were unconstitutional. In several instances the advocates discussed among themselves the possibility of making more sexually radical claims, but over and over again they rejected these arguments in favor of those that emphasized marital and reproductive rights. Many birth control and abortion rights supporters invoked population control and eugenic arguments that reinforced class and race inequalities. These advocates relied on privacy claims that were compatible with conservative antigovernment politics and opposition to state intervention in cases of family violence.[30] They deferred to scientific experts whose authority was rooted in hierarchical social structures, and they frequently deployed strategies of respectability.[31] *Griswold*'s lawyers deliberately set up a test case that concerned married couples given birth control by a doctor. *Fanny Hill*'s advocates defended a work of recognized literary merit with a conclusion that celebrates the redemption of a prostitute who finds happiness in monogamous marriage. *Boutilier* concerned an English-speaking white Canadian who had come to the United States with his family, whose parents and siblings included U.S. citizens and U.S. military servicemen, and who could be described as a discreet, honest, churchgoing, hardworking, and masculine man. The lawyers who pursued *Loving* looked for and found an interracial couple featuring a white man and a nonwhite woman rather than a more transgressive pairing. *Eisenstadt* concerned a speaker who gave out contraceptives after a university lecture. *Roe* is the exception that proves the rule, as Norma McCorvey's lawyers hindered discussion of her lesbian past, her alcohol and drug use, and her prior pregnancies by assigning her a pseudonym. Sometimes the strategies were part of a long-term litigation plan; at other times they emerged in the crucible of legal circumstances; in some instances they are best thought of as strategic in effect rather than intention. But in each of these examples, liberal and leftist advocates attempted to secure victories by appealing to conservative values. When these values were highlighted in the Court's rulings, the results were victories for marital and reproductive rights, but defeats for sexual freedom, equality, and citizenship.

Given all of this, how did significant segments of the public come to believe that the Court had developed an expansive vision of sexual rights? Why was there public surprise when local officials enforced laws against nonmarital sex in the post-*Roe* era? Understanding this requires exploration of a dynamic discussed in chapters 6 and 7. While the Court had the power to render judgments in the cases it chose to hear, it could not control public interpretations of those rulings. Nor could it control later judicial interpretations. The justices devoted substantial attention to their finely detailed and carefully reasoned arguments, but much of the public developed an understanding of what the Court had done that was at odds with what the justices wrote in their opinions. Playing crucial mediating roles were the mass media, lower courts, and research scholars. To the extent that their accounts presented the Court as affirming an expansive vision of sexual freedom, equality, and citizenship, the public was led to believe that it had rights that would be upheld. When this did not happen, the public thought that the Court had reversed direction, which then prompted new political and legal responses. Public perceptions of the law played critical roles in the dynamic historical process.

In effect, popular interpretations of the Court's rulings as libertarian and egalitarian obfuscated and mystified the ongoing construction of a legal regime of heteronormative supremacy. In so doing, accounts of these rulings by journalists, judges, and scholars worked against the emergence of forms of public consciousness that might have been quicker to demand sexual justice. Regardless of their intentions, these interpretations secured the allegiance of various types of sexual criminals (including those who broke laws against nonmarital sex) to the dominant order on the false belief that they had constitutionally protected and legally recognized sexual rights. This curtailed the building of a broad-based majority coalition of sexual criminals who might otherwise have used democratic institutions to pursue sexual freedom and equality.

Responding to sexual revolutions from below, the Court tried to limit their effects from above. At an American Bar Association prayer breakfast in 1972, Justice Lewis Powell expressed concern about "excessively tolerant views" of "sexual morality." He was specifically troubled by a recent media story that asked, "'What happens when the liberated young return (home)for the weekend with a friend of the opposite sex and expect to share the same bedroom.'" Bemoaning the loss of the world depicted in the film *Fiddler on the Roof*, where "the feeling of individual serenity in the common bond of family life was com-

plete," Powell declared that "the relationships clustered around the home, between husband and wife and parents and children, are the most sacred of all
human relationships." Neglecting to point out that the serenity of the Jewish
family in *Fiddler* was shattered first by the relationships the daughters formed
with a poor man, a communist, and a non-Jew and then by anti-Semitic violence, Powell instead issued a jeremiad about sexual immorality. Chief Justice
Warren Burger also addressed changing sexual mores. In a 1973 obscenity case,
Burger declared, "One can concede that the 'sexual revolution' of recent years
may have had useful byproducts in striking layers of prudery from a subject
long irrationally kept from needed ventilation. But it does not follow that
no regulation of patently offensive 'hard core' materials is needed or permissible; civilized people do not allow unregulated access to heroin because it is
a derivative of medicinal morphine."[32]

In the end, however, while the Court sought to limit and contain the sexual
revolution, it could not fully control the roles its decisions would play in long-
term developments. This becomes clear in the book's epilogue, which reviews
key episodes in later years. While a set of post-1973 cases introduced minor
modifications to the doctrine developed from *Griswold* to *Roe*, in general the
heteronormative doctrine continued to hold sway through the end of the
twentieth century. Social movements, anxious to maintain the Court's liberal doctrine in an increasingly conservative era, continued to participate in
the construction of a heteronormative regime. At the same time, journalists,
judges, and scholars continued to depict the decisions as far more sexually
libertarian and egalitarian than the texts of the opinions stated or implied.
Eventually, in a striking demonstration of the power of the public to generate
new legal meanings, the Supreme Court itself accepted the revisionist interpretation of its precedents.

In its 2003 decision in *Lawrence*, the Court reinterpreted *Griswold*, *Eisenstadt*, and *Roe* in ways that rejected, without acknowledging, the earlier
Court's view that there is no constitutional right to have sex outside of marriage. In this respect, the Court not only overturned *Bowers* but also abandoned the logic of decisions from *Griswold* to *Roe*, developing a new constitutional doctrine with parameters that will only emerge with time. On the
one hand, Kennedy's majority opinion endorsed a broadly framed "spatial"
and "transcendent" conception of liberty that includes intimate sexual conduct. On the other hand, Kennedy's opinion narrowly emphasized the rights
of adult homosexuals in coupled relationships to have consensual sex with
their partners in their private homes, "absent injury to a person or abuse of

an institution the law protects," and the opinion distinguished this right from the rights of formal relationship recognition. Only future developments will make evident the Court's and country's new systems of sexual regulation, but we will be better prepared for the struggles ahead if we understand more about the struggles of the past.[33]

PART 1 : *Decisions and Doctrines*

1 : Liberalization's Limits from *Griswold* to *Roe*

Before 1965, U.S. federal, state, and local laws policed and produced sex in countless ways. Bans on oral and anal sex prohibited particular uses of specific body parts, promoting others in the process. Restrictions on adultery, bestiality, cohabitation, fornication, homosexuality, and incest distinguished between unacceptable and acceptable partners, as did statutes dealing with those deemed incapable of consent. Laws that regulated interracial marriage, marriage involving minors, marriage between members of the same family, plural marriage, and same-sex marriage identified some liaisons as less legitimate than others. Statutes criminalizing rape and assault constructed boundaries between involuntary and voluntary sex. Laws related to prostitution and other forms of sex work constituted some purposes of sex as less valid than others. Restrictions on sex in the military, prisons, and public space created institutional and geographic parameters for illegal and legal intimacies. Abortion, birth control, and sterilization statutes influenced the potentially reproductive consequences of sex, as did laws concerning illegitimacy, inheritance, and parenting. Sex was also policed and produced through laws on disorderly conduct, indecency, nudity, obscenity, sexual psychopathy, and sexually transmitted diseases. Meanwhile, in policy areas such as education, employment, health, housing, immigration, taxation, and welfare, legislation that seemingly had nothing to do with sex encouraged and discouraged specific forms of sexual expression.[1]

The overwhelming majority of these laws remained constitutional in 1973 after the Supreme Court's rulings in *Griswold*, *Fanny Hill*, *Loving*, *Eisenstadt*, and *Roe*. The Court had struck down state laws forbidding the use of contraceptives by married couples, prohibiting interracial couples from marrying, criminalizing the distribution of birth control materials to the unmarried, and imposing strict restrictions on abortions. The Court had also limited the application of obscenity laws by protecting materials with "redeeming social value." These were major achievements, but the Court had not overturned a vast array of laws related to sex, leaving them presumptively constitutional.

Most of the justices had suggested in cases concerning other matters that laws against nonmarital sex were constitutional.

This chapter examines the rulings in *Griswold*, *Fanny Hill*, *Loving*, *Eisenstadt*, *Roe*, and related cases, arguing that the Court in this period developed a doctrine of heteronormative supremacy. Recognizing special rights and privileges for adult, heterosexual, marital, monogamous, private, and procreative forms of sexual expression, the Court permitted denials of equal rights and privileges for other forms. Some have accused the Court of inconsistency in these rulings, asking, for instance, how the justices could recognize a right of sexual privacy while affirming the constitutionality of laws against nonmarital sex. Others have argued that no matter what the Court said, the decisions are best understood as affirming sexual freedom and equality. This chapter, in contrast, argues that the Court in the late 1960s and early 1970s never recognized rights of sexual privacy, freedom, or equality. More generally, chapter 1 identifies the consistent heteronormative principles articulated in these rulings and the ways in which these decisions were implicated in the ongoing formation of gender, class, and race hierarchies.

Searching for doctrinal consistency across these five rulings is difficult. To begin with, the Court's makeup changed: of the nine justices who decided *Griswold* in 1965, only four were on the Court when *Roe* was decided in 1973. Moreover, the justices changed their minds and their reasoning over time, and some treated previous rulings in which they had dissented as legitimate precedents for later rulings. In addition, the lead opinions in these five cases were credited to four different authors and in all five at least one justice agreed with the decision but not the reasoning of the lead opinion.

Nevertheless, the justices attempted, except in unusual circumstances, to make their decisions appear consistent, and this was their intention in the cases considered here. For example, although the rulings in *Griswold*, *Eisenstadt*, and *Roe* differed in important respects, the Court depicted them as consistent. Moreover, if we focus on the votes in these five cases, eight of the fifteen justices who served in this period—Blackmun, Brennan, Douglas, Fortas, Goldberg, Marshall, Powell, and Warren—consistently supported the Court's judgments in the cases in which they participated. After dissenting in *Griswold*, Stewart joined the liberalizing justices in the remaining cases. Rehnquist dissented in *Roe*, but he and Powell joined the Court too late to participate in the earlier decisions. The remaining five justices voted with the majorities in some but not all of the cases, primarily because of differing definitions of obscenity and conflicting views on whether privacy was protected by the Constitution. In short, it is possible to find elements of a collectively authored doctrine supported by a majority of the justices in these decisions. Key passages in the rulings from *Griswold* to *Roe* make it clear that the Court rejected sexual libertarianism and egalitarianism. Different passages may have suggested otherwise, but the presence of conservative and limiting language, available for use in later contexts, meant that sexual freedom and equality had not been secured.

Griswold (1965)

Griswold is often regarded as the foundational decision recognizing a constitutional right of sexual privacy, but the Court's ruling did not mention *sexual* privacy. What the Court affirmed was a right of *marital* privacy, and a majority of the justices made comments suggesting that laws against nonmarital sex were constitutional. In other words, *Griswold* was a pro-marriage ruling, and given the nature of marriage and sex law in 1965, the decision strengthened the supremacy of heteronormative sexual expression. As for procreation, although it may seem counterintuitive to argue that a ruling that increased legal access to contraception favored reproductive forms of sex, *Griswold* did just that by extending special protection to one type of sex, the type that was potentially reproductive.[2]

Writing for a majority of five (two other justices concurred with the decision but not the reasoning), Douglas offered a narrative of conflict between Estelle Griswold and C. Lee Buxton on the one hand and the state of Connecticut on the other. Griswold was described as the executive director of the state's Planned Parenthood League. Buxton was presented as a licensed physician, a Yale professor, and the medical director of the League's center in New Haven. According to Douglas, Griswold and Buxton were arrested for giving "information, instruction, and medical advice to *married persons* as to the means of preventing conception." The statutes cited criminalized "any person who uses any drug, medicinal article or instrument for the purpose of preventing conception" and "any person who assists, abets, counsels, causes, hires or commands another to commit any offense." Griswold and Buxton were found guilty of the latter, but the Court concluded that they also had "standing to raise the constitutional rights of the married people with whom they had a professional relationship."[3]

The Court's conclusion was that the statute violated the constitutional privacy rights of married couples.[4] Acknowledging that the Constitution nowhere explicitly mentions privacy, Douglas argued that "penumbras" and "emanations" originating in various constitutional provisions effectively established privacy rights. These provisions included the First Amendment's references to rights of speech and assembly; the Third Amendment's prohibition on the peacetime quartering of soldiers without homeowner consent; the Fourth Amendment's invocation of the rights of the people to be "secure in their persons, houses, papers, and effects, against unreasonable searches and seizures"; the Fifth Amendment's restriction on forced self-incrimination; and the Ninth Amendment's declaration that rights not mentioned in the Constitution are "retained by the people." According to Douglas, the Court had recognized a "right to privacy" in previous rulings, including an 1886 decision that rejected "all governmental invasions 'of the sanctity of a man's home and the privacies of life.'"[5]

How far did the right of privacy extend? In *Griswold*, Douglas made it clear that he was writing specifically about privacy within marriage. Having referred to the "married persons" and "married couples" served by Griswold and Buxton, the rights of "married people," and the operation of the law on the "intimate relation of husband and wife," Douglas concluded with dramatic rhetorical flourish: "Would we allow the police to search the sacred precincts of marital bedrooms for telltale signs of the use of contraceptives? The very idea is repulsive to the notions of privacy surrounding the marriage relationship." He continued, "We deal with a right of privacy older than the Bill of Rights—older than our political parties, older than our school system. Marriage is a coming together for better or for worse, hopefully enduring, and intimate to the degree of being sacred. It is an association that promotes a way of life, not causes; a harmony in living, not political faiths; a bilateral loyalty, not commercial or social projects. Yet it is an association for as noble a purpose as any involved in our prior decisions." In this formulation, marriage was a pre-constitutional institution and the bedroom was the married couple's privileged space. Protecting that space was the concept of privacy, which Douglas located at the boundaries of marriage, "surrounding" it. Outside of these boundaries were politics, commerce, and society. Inside was a sacred, intimate, and harmonious relationship.[6]

Goldberg's concurring opinion, joined by Warren and Brennan, also endorsed "the right of privacy in marriage," but emphasized the Ninth Amendment and the Fourteenth Amendment, according to which states may not "deprive any person of life, liberty, or property, without due process of law." After citing one precedent that affirmed the right "'to marry, establish a home and bring up children,'" another that recognized "'the liberty of parents and guardians to direct the upbringing and education of children,'" and a third that referred to "'the private realm of family life which the state cannot enter,'" Goldberg endorsed Harlan's dissent in an earlier case, *Poe* (1961), which had declared, "Of this whole 'private realm of family life' it is difficult to imagine what is more private or more intimate than a husband and wife's marital relations." Goldberg concluded, "Although the Constitution does not speak in so many words of the right of privacy in marriage, I cannot believe that it offers these fundamental rights no protection. The fact that no particular provision of the Constitution explicitly forbids the State from disrupting the traditional relation of the family—a relation as old and as fundamental as our entire civilization—surely does not show that the Government was meant to have the power to do so."[7]

Deciding that the Constitution protected marital privacy did not fully determine the outcome of *Griswold*, as the Court generally argued that federal and state laws could violate fundamental rights if there were legitimate, compelling, and substantial state interests at stake and if the laws were narrowly tailored and necessary to serve those interests. This was the Court's "strict scrutiny" test, which it also used if a law relied on suspect classifications such as race. Douglas did not mention the interests claimed by the state, but cited the Court's general rule that "a 'governmental purpose to control or prevent activities constitutionally subject to state regulation may not be achieved by means which sweep unnecessarily broadly and thereby invade the area of protected freedoms.'" The implication was that the law was not narrowly tailored to serve legitimate state interests, presumably because it affected the married and unmarried alike.[8]

Goldberg's concurrence addressed the asserted state interests more directly and in so doing took a significant step beyond the majority opinion. Douglas emphasized the right of privacy in marriage but did not discuss specific types of laws, other than the type exemplified by Connecticut's anticontraception law, that would or would not violate this right. Goldberg did, identifying two hypothetical laws that would not be constitutional and several existing laws that were. The hypothetical laws declared that "all husbands and wives must be sterilized after two children have been born to them" or, more generally, a law mandating "compulsory birth control." Goldberg was challenging the dissenters for suggesting that states could do anything not specifically prohibited by the Constitution, a position he described as permitting "totalitarian limitation of family size." Even in these imaginary scenarios, Goldberg indicated that such laws might be constitutional if there was a "compelling subordinating state interest." Goldberg also named specific types of existing sex laws that were constitutional. In the course of emphasizing that Connecticut's statute interfered with marital rights, Goldberg noted that "the discouraging of extra-marital relations" was "a legitimate subject of state concern," that state "regulation of sexual promiscuity or misconduct" was "proper," and that the constitutionality of laws prohibiting "adultery and fornication" was "beyond doubt." Making his position clear, Goldberg included another excerpt from Harlan's dissent in *Poe*, which declared, "Adultery, homosexuality and the like are sexual intimacies which the State forbids . . . but the intimacy of husband and wife is necessarily an essential and accepted feature of the institution of marriage, an institution which the State not only must allow, but which always and in every age it has fostered and protected. It is one thing when the State exerts its power either to forbid extra-marital sexuality . . . or to say who may marry, but it is quite another when, having acknowledged a marriage and the intimacies inherent in it, it undertakes to regulate by means of the criminal law the details of that intimacy." Endorsing Harlan's historically inaccurate claim about the universal state promotion of marriage and his tacit acceptance of laws against interracial marriage, Goldberg's formulation implied that marriage was a fragile institution in need of state support and offered constitutional means by which the state could protect and promote marriage by prohibiting nonmarital sex.[9]

Harlan and White, both of whom concurred with the *Griswold* decision but not the reasoning used by Douglas, also made it clear that the relevant rights were marital and highlighted the constitutionality of laws banning sex outside of marriage. Harlan filed a concurring opinion that reaffirmed his dissent in *Poe*. White criticized the law "as applied to married couples." Noting that "the statute is said to serve the State's policy against all forms of promiscuous or illicit sexual relationships, be they premarital or extramarital, concededly a permissible and legitimate legislative goal," White wrote that he failed to see "how the ban on the use of contraceptives by married couples in any way reinforces the State's ban on illicit sexual relationships." White did not invoke "privacy," preferring to emphasize the related concept of "liberty," but he too argued that Connecticut's law violated the rights of married people, and he too suggested that other types of sex laws were constitutional.[10]

Griswold did not recognize a broadly libertarian right to sexual privacy but a narrower right held by married couples only. It may be tempting to dismiss as "dicta" the Court's comments about laws against nonmarital sex, but these passages help clarify what the Court meant when it referred to marital privacy. According to the ruling, rights of privacy do not establish a literal sphere (i.e., the bedroom, home, or private property) in which consenting adults may do as they please. Instead, these rights create a quasi-literal and quasi-figurative sphere in which married people have certain privileges that unmarried people do not have. Although seven justices voted to strike down Connecticut's law, an equal number suggested that laws against nonmarital sex were constitutional, and neither of the other two (Douglas and Clark) disagreed.[11]

Theoretically, *Griswold* affirmed that all married U.S. citizens had special privacy rights, but in various ways the decision reflected and contributed to the country's ongoing formation of class, race, and gender hierarchies. One of the first issues addressed in the majority opinion was whether Griswold and Buxton had standing to address the rights of the married women served by the clinic. To establish their standing, Douglas invoked several precedents, including *Barrows* (1953), which held that "a white defendant, party to a racially restrictive covenant . . . , was allowed to raise the issue that enforcement of the covenant violated the rights of prospective Negro purchasers." Just as a white property owner had standing to raise questions about the rights of prospective black buyers, health care professionals had standing to raise questions about the rights of their clients. In this sense, just as prospective black buyers did not speak for themselves in *Barrows*, married women served by Planned Parenthood did not speak for themselves in *Griswold*. This takes on added significance when it is recognized (as is discussed in chapter 3) that Griswold and Buxton were white citizens while the three women who acknowledged receiving birth control at the clinic were a white citizen, a black citizen, and a white alien.[12]

Beyond the biographies of the case's protagonists, *Griswold* was a classed, gendered, and racialized decision in other ways. To begin with, the Court's romanticized and idealized conception of marriage had links to the rise of the bourgeois, male-dominated, white nuclear family in the eighteenth and nineteenth centuries. The Court did not acknowledge, for example, that in some contexts marriage was viewed as an economic relationship, romantic love was associated with nonmarital relationships, and married couples shared their bedrooms with others. Moreover, while the model of a two-parent, child-centered family that practices birth control had cross-class and cross-racial appeal, middle-class whites had long used this model to differentiate themselves from others. In addition, insofar as rates of formal marriage were higher among middle-class whites than among others, *Griswold* disproportionately benefited the country's dominant class and race. At the same time, White's observation that Connecticut denied birth control to "disadvantaged citizens" suggested that the law interfered with their adoption of white, middle-class family limitation strategies. To the extent that privacy rights could be invoked by men to restrict state interference in abusive marital relationships, the decision also provided a new tool for male supremacy. None of this means that the *Griswold* decision was opposed by nondominant groups, but it shows that the Court's reasoning was classed, gendered, and racialized.[13]

This is also evident in the Court's references to "civilized" values. As suggested above, traditional family relations were, for Goldberg, as old and fundamental as "our entire civilization." Goldberg also cited a well-known dissent by Justice Louis Brandeis that had described "the right to be let alone" as "'the right most valued by civilized men.'" Using the same key term, Brennan wrote privately to Douglas as the latter worked on *Griswold*: "In our civilization, the marital relationship above all else is endowed with privacy." As Gail Bederman has pointed out, discourses of "civilization" have been linked with class oppression, male dominance, and white supremacy.[14] In addition, in repeatedly referring to "our" civilization, "our" society, "our" people, and "our" institutions, the justices were relying on classed, gendered, and racialized beliefs about other civilizations, societies, peoples, and institutions. In a related formulation, Goldberg's hypothetical "totalitarian" law requiring "compulsory birth control" referenced Cold War beliefs about countries thought to have such laws.[15]

Finally, the justices decided *Griswold* in the midst of a classed, gendered, and racialized public discussion about nonmarital sex and reproduction that focused on delinquency, welfare, and poverty in the early 1960s. This discussion intensified after the release of Daniel Patrick Moynihan's controversial report, *The Negro Family*. Moynihan, an assistant secretary of labor in the Johnson administration, argued that the fundamental problem facing the black community was the "tangle of pathology" produced by low rates of long-term, cohabitational marriages and high rates of promiscuity, illegitimacy, and matriarchal households. Moynihan submitted his report in March 1965 and on 4 June some of the report's findings were incorporated into a speech that Johnson delivered at Howard University. After listening to the oral arguments in *Griswold* on 29 March and working on their opinions in the following months, the justices did not reference the "Negro" family explicitly in their June *Griswold* decision. Nonetheless, in the context of heightened white middle-class anxieties about the marital, reproductive, and sexual practices of nonwhites and the poor, the Court's celebration of marriage and its comments about nonmarital sex can be interpreted as having classed, gendered, and racialized meanings. As the justices recognized special rights and privileges for heteronormative sexual expression, they contributed to the reconstitution of class, gender, and race hierarchies.[16]

Fanny Hill (1966)

Griswold was the Court's key birth control ruling, but it is more difficult to identify one obscenity ruling as most important. In the 1950s, 1960s, and 1970s, the Court considered dozens of obscenity cases, and in none were the justices able to resolve, in an enduring way, the basic constitutional questions. In most instances in the period from 1965 to 1973, the Court divided into three factions. One (composed of Black and Douglas) argued that obscenity was protected by the First Amendment. A second (including Brennan, Fortas, Goldberg, Marshall, and Stewart, with the support of Harlan, Warren, and White in some cases) believed that obscenity was not protected but defined obscenity in ways that limited the scope of permissible government action. A third (consisting of Blackmun, Burger, Clark, Powell, and Rehnquist, with the support of Harlan, Warren, and White in some cases) agreed that obscenity was not protected but defined obscenity more broadly, which allowed for more substantial government action. The second and third groups agreed that obscenity was not protected, but the first and second groups restricted the reach of obscenity laws. The Court's *Fanny Hill* ruling exemplifies this dynamic, and of the many obscenity cases considered in this period, it produced the most influential framework. That framework afforded some protection to transgressive sexual expression, but used heteronormative standards for judging sexual materials. The inequality embedded in these standards is especially apparent when *Fanny Hill* is considered alongside *Ginzburg* and *Mishkin*, which were announced on the same day as *Fanny Hill*.[17]

According to the plurality opinion authored by Brennan and joined by Warren and Fortas, *Fanny Hill* involved a conflict between Massachusetts, where state laws permitted officials to have a book declared obscene by a court, and an eighteenth-century English novel by John Cleland titled *Memoirs of a Woman of Pleasure*, commonly known as *Fanny Hill* and published in the United States by Putnam. Under state law, obscene books could not be published, bought, sold, or distributed. After the Massachusetts Supreme Judicial Court judged the book obscene, the publisher appealed to the U.S. Supreme Court, which reversed the lower court in a 6–3 vote.[18]

Brennan's opinion reaffirmed the obscenity test developed in the 1957 *Roth* decision, which asked "whether to the average person, applying contemporary community standards, the dominant theme of the material taken as a whole appeals to prurient interest." He then asserted in *Fanny Hill*, "Under this definition, as elaborated in subsequent cases, three elements must coalesce: it must be established that (a) the dominant theme of the material taken as a whole appeals to a prurient interest in sex; (b) the material is patently offensive because it affronts contemporary community standards relating to the description or representation of sexual matters; and (c) the material is utterly without redeeming social value." According to Brennan, the Supreme Judicial Court had misapplied the third criterion when it held that "a book need not be 'unqualifiedly worthless before it can be deemed obscene.'" Because the Massachusetts court had concluded that *Fanny Hill* had "a modicum of literary and historical value," the Supreme Court ruled that the book was not obscene.[19]

With only two other justices supporting Brennan's reasoning, his judgment would not have carried the day were it not for concurrences by Stewart, Black, and Douglas. Stewart, whose position was closest to Brennan's, reaffirmed the position he had taken in *Jacobellis* (1964): only "hardcore pornography," which Stewart left undefined, could be governmentally suppressed.[20] Douglas and Black, in contrast, affirmed their longstanding position that obscenity was protected by the First Amendment. Douglas declared in *Fanny Hill*, "Publications and utterance were made immune from majoritarian control by the First Amendment. . . . No exceptions were made, not even for obscenity."[21]

Six justices thus extended protection to *Fanny Hill*, but seven rejected Douglas and Black's libertarian position, which would protect all sexual speech. What types of sexual speech could be restricted? A narrow majority of five (Brennan, Fortas, Warren, Clark, and White) endorsed the central holding in *Roth*. A narrow plurality of three (Brennan, Fortas, and Warren) accepted the three-part formula of *Fanny Hill*. This trio could determine the outcome of obscenity cases by aligning with their more or their less censorious brethren.

On abstract levels, *Roth* and *Fanny Hill* privileged normative sexual expression. As noted above, the *Roth* test was "whether to the average person, applying contemporary community standards, the dominant theme of the material taken as a whole appeals to prurient interest." This established hierarchies of sexual representations based on the imagined perspectives of "average" people applying imagined "community" standards. By the law of averages, "deviant" representations were vulnerable to unequal treatment. Brennan's "elaboration" in *Fanny Hill* mentioned both "community standards" and "social value." Douglas warned that this imposed majority rule "where minorities were thought to be supreme." Black pointed out that evaluations of "prurient interest" would "depend to a large extent upon the judge's or juror's personality, habits, inclinations, attitudes and other individual characteristics." He also raised questions about whether the "community standards" were local,

national, or global. As for the meaning of the phrase "utterly without redeeming social value," Black remarked that this was "as uncertain, if not even more
uncertain, than is the unknown substance of the Milky Way." He concluded
that the rulings would "make it exceedingly dangerous for people to discuss
either orally or in writing anything about sex." Douglas also criticized the "redeeming social value" test, asking, "Does it mean a 'value' to the majority?
Why is not a minority 'value' cognizable? . . . 'Redeeming' to whom? . . . If a
publication caters to the idiosyncrasies of a minority, why does it not have
some 'social importance'?"[22]

Fanny Hill also carved out a major exception to its basic holding. According to Brennan's Fanny Hill opinion, "The circumstances of production, sale,
and publicity are relevant in determining whether or not the publication or
distribution of the book is constitutionally protected. Evidence that the book
was commercially exploited for the sake of prurient appeal, to the exclusion of
all other values, might justify the conclusion that the book was utterly without redeeming social importance." Brennan's majority opinion in Ginzburg,
joined by Fortas, Warren, Clark, and White, used this exception to uphold a
conviction under a federal law prohibiting the mailing of obscene materials.
Referring to the "commercial exploitation of erotica solely for the sake of their
prurient appeal" and condemning "the sordid business of pandering—'the
business of purveying textual or graphic matter openly advertised to appeal to
the erotic interest of their customers,'" the Ginzburg majority concluded that
these were "sales of illicit merchandise, not sales of constitutionally protected
matter."[23]

Another exception to the basic holding in Fanny Hill was revealed in
Mishkin, which upheld a conviction based on a New York law against publishing and possessing obscene books with intent to sell. Mishkin concerned
materials aimed at people whom Brennan, joined by the same four justices
who endorsed his Ginzburg opinion, referred to as "deviants." Responding to
the appellant's argument that the materials were protected under the Roth
test because they "do not appeal to a prurient interest of the 'average person,'" Brennan argued that this was "an unrealistic interpretation" of the precedents: "Where the material is designed for and primarily disseminated to
a clearly defined deviant sexual group . . . , the prurient-appeal requirement
of the Roth test is satisfied if the dominant theme of the material taken as a
whole appeals to the prurient interest in sex of the members of that group."[24]

If Fanny Hill, Ginzburg, and Mishkin privileged normative sexual expression
in theory, how did they function in practice? What signals did the Court send
about how the Roth and Fanny Hill tests should be used? Brennan's Fanny Hill

opinion referred to experts who emphasized the book's "moral, namely, that sex with love is superior to sex in a brothel." Douglas's concurrence characterized *Fanny Hill* as "an erotic novel" that tells the story of a "young girl who becomes a prostitute" and then "abandons that life and marries her first lover" when she discovers the "'charms of virtue.'" Clark's dissent provided a more complete inventory of the novel's sexual "scenes," which included "lesbianism, female masturbation, homosexuality between young boys, the destruction of a maidenhead with consequent gory descriptions, the seduction of a young virgin boy, the flagellation of male by female, and vice versa, followed by fervid sexual engagement, and other abhorrent acts." Brennan and Douglas did not dispute this, but reached contrary conclusions about the novel's "moral." The Court seemingly overturned the obscenity determination because *Fanny Hill* championed heteronormative sex.[25]

In *Ginzburg*, the Court upheld an obscenity conviction. According to Brennan's majority opinion, the materials consisted of "EROS, a hard-cover magazine of expensive format; Liaison, a bi-weekly newsletter; and *The Housewife's Handbook on Selective Promiscuity*." In support of the Court's finding that Ginzburg had engaged in pandering, Brennan emphasized that the publisher tried to obtain mailing privileges for *EROS* from "Intercourse and Blue Ball, Pennsylvania" and succeeded in mailing the magazine from "Middlesex, New Jersey." The majority also determined that Ginzburg advertised with the "'leer of the sensualist'" and "deliberately emphasized the sexually provocative aspects." Douglas's dissent suggested that the Court's decision was motivated by normative values. One of the items in *EROS*, he observed, was "a photo essay entitled 'Black and White in Color,' which dealt with interracial love: a subject undoubtedly offensive to some." He also wrote, "Some of the tracts for which these publishers go to prison concern normal sex, some homosexuality, some the masochistic yearning." Discussing masochists, Douglas asked, "Why is it unlawful to cater to the needs of this group?" He continued, "Another group also represented here translates mundane articles into sexual symbols. . . . Why is freedom of the press and expression denied them?" Meanwhile, Stewart's *Ginzburg* dissent borrowed language from the Solicitor General to describe materials classifiable as "hardcore": "'photographs . . . with no pretense of artistic value, graphically depicting acts of sexual intercourse, including various acts of sodomy and sadism, and sometimes involving several participants in scenes of orgy-like character.'" When the Court applied its tests in *Ginzburg*, five justices ruled against sexual materials portraying adultery, promiscuity, homosexuality, interracial sex, masochism, or fetishism, and

Stewart indicated that he would join the majority in cases involving graphic depictions of sodomy, sadism, and group sex.[26]

In *Mishkin*, Brennan, again writing for a majority of five (Harlan filed an additional concurrence), applied the Court's tests and upheld another conviction. Mishkin had been charged under a New York law that prohibited the publication for sale of materials "designed, composed or illustrated as a whole to appeal to and commercially exploit prurient interest" through "the description, portrayal, or deliberate suggestion of illicit sex, including adultery, prostitution, fornication, sexual crime and sexual perversion." According to Brennan, "Some [of the fifty books] depict relatively normal heterosexual relations, but more depict such deviations as sado-masochism, fetishism, and homosexuality," which he elsewhere described as "flagellation, fetishism, and lesbianism." As noted above, Brennan's ruling revised the *Roth* test for materials "designed for and primarily disseminated to a clearly defined deviant sexual group." This had significant implications. First, insofar as *Mishkin* revised *Roth*'s "average person" test, it suggested that the test could be modified when it did not yield the desired results. Second, the Court signaled its acceptance of a law that discriminated against sexual representations of adultery, fetishism, fornication, prostitution, sadomasochism, and same-sex sex. Third, *Mishkin* suggested that materials could be declared obscene if the average person, applying contemporary community standards, thought the materials appealed to the prurient interests of deviants.[27]

To be sure, in other cases the Court reached seemingly different conclusions. In 1958, the Court simply cited *Roth* when, by a 5–4 vote in *ONE*, it struck down an obscenity ruling against a homophile movement magazine. In the absence of a full opinion, however, the Court left ambiguous the basis of the ruling, and *ONE* was among the country's most respectable gay publications. The limits of this ruling became apparent in 1961, when the Court voted 8–1 in *Womack* to let stand an obscenity conviction based on the mailing of advertisements for nude male photographs. In *Manual* (1962), the Court overturned the Post Office's determination that three male physique magazines were obscene, but three of the six justices who ruled this way did so on procedural grounds—that Congress had not authorized the Postmaster General to take this action. One year later, the Court denied *cert* in *Darnell*, which upheld the conviction of a man who had mailed a "filthy" letter to another man's wife that described her husband's preference for sex with him. In *Jacobellis* (1964), six justices overturned an obscenity conviction based on a film adaptation of D. H. Lawrence's *Lady Chatterley's Lover*, but Brennan's opinion emphasized that the film depicted "a woman bored with her life and marriage who abandons her husband and family for a young archaeologist with whom she has suddenly fallen in love." The majority and concurring opinions depicted the woman's actions in a sympathetic light and highlighted the representation of "love" rather than "sex." Before 1966, the Court applied *Roth* in ways that privileged representations that were more respectable, more heterosexual, and more loving.[28]

After 1966, the Court applied the *Roth* and *Fanny Hill* tests in ways that also tended to accept and promote sexual discrimination. *Landau* (1967) affirmed a ruling against a film by Jean Genet that was said to "promote homosexuality, perversion, and morbid sex practices." *G.I. Distributors* (1967) let stand an obscenity conviction based on homoerotic and sadomasochistic magazine photographs. And *Ginsberg* (1968) upheld a conviction in a case concerning the sale of "girlie" magazines to a sixteen-year-old "boy." In contrast, *Redrup* (1967) and other rulings favored materials seemingly aimed at heterosexual adult men. Perhaps the most significant obscenity ruling after *Fanny Hill* was *Stanley* (1969), which unanimously overturned an obscenity conviction based on the viewing of films in a private home. Writing for six justices, Marshall declared that "the mere private possession of obscene matter cannot constitutionally be made a crime" and "a state has no business telling a man, sitting alone in his own house, what books he may read or what films he may watch." After 1966, the Court reinforced the discriminatory standards it adopted in *Roth* and *Fanny Hill*.[29]

By 1973, the politics of the Court had shifted to the right thanks to Nixon's four appointments. In *Miller*, *Paris*, and three other cases decided in 1973, Burger achieved his longstanding goal of uniting a majority around more conservative obscenity tests. In these cases, the four new justices voted with White to reaffirm *Roth* and modify *Fanny Hill*. According to Burger's majority opinion in *Miller*, the constitutional test of obscenity was "(a) whether 'the average person, applying contemporary community standards' would find that the work, taken as a whole, appeals to the prurient interest . . . ; (b) whether the work depicts or describes, in a patently offensive way, sexual conduct specifically defined by the applicable state law; and (c) whether the work, taken as a whole, lacks serious literary, artistic, political, or scientific value." *Miller* revised *Fanny Hill*'s reference to "social" value, announced that "community standards" need not mean "national standards," and confirmed that materials "aimed at a deviant group" could be evaluated on the basis of their impact on "a particularly susceptible or sensitive person" rather than "the average person."[30]

Burger's success in the 1973 cases prompted Brennan, Marshall, and Stewart to move closer to the libertarian position supported by Black and Douglas, though by this time Black was no longer on the Court. In dissents joined by Marshall and Stewart, Brennan now abandoned his earlier stance, declaring that the *Roth* and *Fanny Hill* tests had failed to work. Obscene speech, they now concluded, could not be restricted, with exceptions for materials distributed to minors or nonconsenting adults. In a twist that demonstrated the compatibility of sexual conservatism and privacy discourse, Brennan based the exception for nonconsenting adults on the privacy rights of people who did not want to encounter obscenity.

Although *Miller* and *Paris* signaled a conservative shift in obscenity jurisprudence, their discriminatory standards were based on the Court's liberalizing decisions. In *Paris*, Burger wrote, "It is unavailing to compare a theater open to the public for a fee, with the private home of *Stanley* . . . and the marital bedroom of *Griswold*." Citing *Griswold*, *Loving*, *Stanley*, *Eisenstadt*, and *Roe*, Burger affirmed that the right of privacy "protects the personal intimacies of the home, the family, marriage, motherhood, procreation, and child rearing," but not the right "to watch obscene movies in places of public accommodation." Burger also wrote, "For us to say that our Constitution incorporates the proposition that conduct involving consenting adults only is always beyond state regulation is a step we are unable to take." In a footnote, he listed "constitutionally unchallenged" types of laws involving consenting adults, including laws against adultery, bigamy, fornication, and prostitution.[31]

As the Court's obscenity rulings privileged heteronormative sexual expression, they reinforced class, gender, and racial hierarchies. Obscenity tests that granted special rights to average citizens and public majorities, which were presumed to have unique appreciation for community standards and social values, had discriminatory implications. More specifically, the Court's obscenity decisions relied on classed language and logic. Brennan's *Fanny Hill* opinion emphasized the testimony of "experts" who addressed the novel's "literary merit" and labeled it a "work of art." This rejected the populist conclusions of the state court, which had noted that "the opinions of English professors, authors and critics . . . , no matter how distinguished they may be, cannot be substituted for those of average persons." Instead, Brennan sided with the publisher's lawyer, who had argued, "Appreciation of art and literature can often be gained only through an expenditure of effort; a certain level of cultivation or a certain amount of background may be required. . . . There is no snobbishness in this principle." Notwithstanding this denial, the Court's decision privileged elite over popular perspectives.[32]

While the *Fanny Hill* decision protected "literature," *Ginzburg* and *Mishkin* rejected a different class of materials. The "pandering" test adopted in *Ginzburg* emphasized the "commercial exploitation of erotica," which reproduced historically bourgeois divisions between the public exchanges of the marketplace and the private intimacies of the home. Writing in the *Atlantic* shortly after the ruling, Jason Epstein detected "class bias" in Brennan's "choice of such prejudicial epithets as 'pandering' and 'the leer of the sensualist,'" which suggested that Ginzburg was "a vulgarian" who "had no right to trade in a market whose delicate and dangerous products must be limited only to gentlemen and scholars." In *Mishkin*, Brennan depicted the books as "cheaply prepared paperbound 'pulps' with imprinted sales prices that are several thousand percent above costs." These rulings were based on class-based distinctions between literature and smut, art and commerce, elite and popular culture, and private consumption and public display.[33]

The rulings also relied on racialized reasoning and rhetoric. In *Ginzburg*, Brennan approvingly quoted the words of Judge Learned Hand, who in a different case had upheld a conviction based on the indiscriminate dissemination of materials that "might . . . have been lawfully sold to laymen who wished seriously to study the sexual practices of savage or barbarous peoples." Brennan used this to emphasize the context of sale and distribution, but the example was meaningfully racialized. Several of the obscenity rulings used racialized language in referring to the rights of "civilized man," the history of "civilized societies," and the laws of "Western civilization." As for the interracial photographs in *Ginzburg*, Edward de Grazia, who argued several obscenity cases before the Court in this period, has linked Attorney General Robert Kennedy's political calculations about white voters and officials in the U.S. South to his decision to prosecute Ginzburg on the basis of the interracial photographs. Before the case was decided, one of Harlan's clerks noted in a memorandum, "It was probably the picture study of the interracial couple that caused all the excitement; I doubt that there would be any fuss if the pictured couple was of the same color." One of Clark's clerks wrote, "I am a genuine southerner, I think, and I realize the implications of encouraging intermarriage, etc. But that is far from calling these things obscene. I really suggest that you take a look at these, for they are beautifully done." Douglas's dissent in *Ginzburg* stopped just short of accusing the majority of racism. Discussing *EROS*, he quoted critic Dwight Macdonald, who had stated, "If you object to the idea of a Negro and a white person having sex together, then, of course, you would be horrified by it."[34]

Just as Jason Epstein called attention to the class bias in the obscenity decisions, various commentators suggested that the decision had racialized elements. A letter sent to Harlan by the managing editor of the *Chicago Defender* stated, "I gather that color pictures of a Negro man embracing a white woman in 'Eros' produced the demand that Ginzburg be severely punished. Certainly, these pictures served to merge the hunt for obscenity with the distaste for desegregation." Ginzburg was later quoted in a *New York Times* interview as saying, "I suppose if it had been a white man and a black woman, nobody would have given it a second thought." In a 1966 *Playboy* interview, Ginzburg was asked "to what extent do you think . . . 'Black and White in Color' . . . was a factor in rousing the authorities against you?" Ginzburg responded, "To a tremendous extent. About three or four days after that issue was deposited in the mails, two members of Congress from the South cried out for my head." *Playboy* also asked if anti-Semitism played a role; Ginzburg, who was Jewish, replied, "I think so, although it's impossible to document on official levels. Some have suggested—and I personally don't believe this to be the case—that Fortas' vote against me might have been a manifestation of reverse anti-Semitism. As the sole Jew on the Court, he didn't want to be associated with me."[35]

The Court's rulings also relied on gendered perspectives and positions. Brennan's *Fanny Hill* opinion emphasized the female protagonist's gendered path from sin to virtue. In *Mishkin*, Brennan observed that many of the books had "covers with drawings of scantily clad women being whipped, beaten, tortured, or abused." As for *Ginzburg*, Brennan's majority opinion noted that *The Housewife's Handbook* offered the female author's views on "the equality of women in sexual relationships." Douglas's *Ginzburg* dissent argued that *The Housewife's Handbook* would be "especially" suitable for "teen age young women" who could be "disabused of some of the unrealistic notions about marriage and sexual experiences." He also emphasized that the book would help "the average man . . . gain a better appreciation of female sexuality." According to Douglas, one *EROS* article was "a discussion . . . of erotic writing by women," which critic Dwight Macdonald had described as containing "remarkable quotations from the woman who had put down her sense of lovemaking, of sexual intercourse . . . in an extremely eloquent way." Macdonald continued, "I have never seen this from the woman's point of view. I thought the point they made, the difference between the man's and the woman's approach to sexual intercourse was very well made and very important." Later, when Marshall in *Stanley* ruled that "a state has no business telling a man, sitting alone in his own house, what books he may read or what films he may watch," the Court used gender-specific language. The use of "man" is not easily dismissed given *Roth*'s reference to "average *person*" and Brennan's correction of a lawyer who repeatedly referred to the "average *man*" test during the oral arguments in *Ginzburg*.[36]

Gendered perspectives can also be seen in the "private" rules developed by the justices for defining hardcore obscenity. According to Bob Woodward and Scott Armstrong's *The Brethren*, which relies heavily on interviews with Court clerks, White had a "personal definition of hard-core pornography," which was "no erect penises, no intercourse, no oral or anal sodomy." Brennan's "private definition of obscenity" was "no erections." To the extent that the justices applied a "no erections" rule, representations of aroused women would be less likely than their male counterparts to be found obscene. These rules privileged sexual representations of women aimed at heterosexual men, while preserving and protecting the mystique of the erect penis.[37]

Loving (1967)

Two years after announcing its decision in *Griswold*, the Court considered another major case concerning marriage. In *Loving*, a unanimous Court struck down state laws banning interracial marriage. Once again affirming the privileged status of marriage and the special rights associated with adult, monogamous, and heterosexual relationships, the justices declared that these privileges and rights could not be denied on the basis of race. In basing their ruling on the notion that marriage was necessary for reproduction, the justices also affirmed the privileged status of reproductive marriage and marital reproduction.[38]

Warren's majority opinion positioned Mildred Jeter, described as "a Negro woman," and Richard Loving, described as "a white man," against the state of Virginia. According to Warren's account, in 1958 Jeter and Loving, both Virginia residents, had married in Washington, D.C. Shortly thereafter they returned to Virginia, where several months later they were charged with violating the state's ban on interracial marriage. Virginia law contained penalties "if any white person intermarry with a colored person"; voided all such marriages; and made it a crime if "any white person and colored person shall go out of this State, for the purpose of being married, and with the intention of returning, and be married out of it, and afterwards return to and reside in it, cohabiting as man and wife." In 1959, the Lovings pleaded guilty and were sentenced to a year in jail, but the judge suspended the sentence for twenty-five years, provided that the couple leave Virginia and not return for twenty-five years. The Lovings moved to Washington, but in 1963 they went back to court, charging that Virginia's law violated the Fourteenth Amendment.[39]

Warren's opinion, endorsed by all of the justices except Stewart, declared that Virginia's interracial marriage law and similar laws in fifteen other states violated the Fourteenth Amendment's equal protection and due process clauses. Challenging the lower court's finding that "the regulation of marriage should be left to exclusive state control," the Court indicated that state marriage laws were subject to the terms of the Fourteenth Amendment. As far as equal protection was concerned, the Court rejected the argument that Virginia's law applied equally to "whites and Negroes" and concluded that the statute constituted "invidious racial discrimination." According to the Court, "the fact that Virginia prohibits only interracial marriages involving white persons" (and not other types of interracial marriage) demonstrates that the laws were "designed to maintain White Supremacy," which was not a permissible state interest. Most of Warren's opinion focused on equal protection, but the final two paragraphs dealt with due process, declaring that insofar as "marriage is one of the 'basic civil rights of man,'" Virginia's laws deprived the Lovings of "liberty without due process." This meant there were two reasons to apply "strict scrutiny": the law interfered with a fundamental constitutional right (the right to marry) and it relied on a suspect classification (race). Stewart's concurring opinion emphasized equal protection, but did not address due process.[40]

Did *Loving* have implications for other types of laws that regulated marriage and sex? The Court said nothing about marriage restrictions based on age, bans on plural marriage, rules about marriage between family members, and customary prohibitions on same-sex marriage, but the focus on race as a suspect classification suggested that they were constitutional. Significantly, the majority opinion did not mention *Griswold*, which is best explained by Warren's desire to win the votes of Black, Stewart, and White, who had not accepted *Griswold*'s privacy arguments. Instead, the opinion repeatedly cited *McLaughlin* (1964), which unanimously overturned a Florida cohabitation law that criminalized "any negro man and white woman, or any white man and negro woman, who are not married to each other, who shall habitually live in and occupy in the nighttime the same room." Writing for seven justices in *McLaughlin* (Stewart and Douglas concurred for different reasons), White had made it clear that the Court was not overturning Florida's "general" and "neutral" laws against nonmarital sex and cohabitation but was rejecting the differential treatment of intraracial and interracial cohabitation. *McLaughlin* and *Loving* thus struck down cohabitation and marriage laws that included race distinctions, but left in place laws that privileged marriage and marital sex. According to the logic of *McLaughlin* and *Loving*, Jeter and Loving, if they had had sex or lived together outside of marriage, would have been vulnerable to prosecution under race-neutral fornication and cohabitation laws.[41]

Warren's use of another precedent makes it evident that *Loving* also privileged procreative forms of sexual expression. According to the majority opinion, "The freedom to marry has long been recognized as one of the vital personal rights essential to the orderly pursuit of happiness by free men. Marriage is one of the 'basic civil rights of man,' fundamental to our very existence and survival." For the quotation within this quotation, Warren cited the Court's 1942 ruling in *Skinner*, a sterilization decision authored by Douglas, but the remainder of Warren's sentence paraphrased *Skinner*, which had declared, "Marriage *and procreation* are fundamental to the very existence and survival *of the race* [my emphases]."[42] Setting aside for a moment the final three words, Warren's identification of marriage as fundamental to "existence" and "survival" offered a narrowly procreative conception of marriage and a narrowly marital conception of procreation. After all, while procreation might be necessary for human existence, marriage is not. *Skinner* linked marriage and procreation more explicitly than *Loving* did, but in deleting the explicit reference to procreation *Loving* strengthened the presumptions that marriage was necessary for reproduction and that reproductive marriage was necessary for human existence.[43]

As for class, gender, and race, it may seem counterintuitive to argue that a ruling striking down bans on interracial marriage contributed to a classed, gendered, and racialized doctrine of heteronormative supremacy, but this is what *Loving* did. To begin with, *Loving* did not question Virginia's classification of Richard as "white" and Mildred as "Negro," though later accounts would emphasize the long history of racial mixing in their community and Mildred would be described as having European, African, and Native American ancestry. *Loving* also expanded access to an institution (marriage) that, as discussed above, had played an important role in the ongoing formation of class, gender, and racial hierarchies. Moreover, when Warren argued that "this Court has consistently repudiated '[d]istinctions between citizens solely because of their ancestry' as being 'odious to a free people whose institutions are founded upon the doctrine of equality,'" he erased the history of the Court's acceptance and endorsement of racial distinctions. Significantly, this passage contained an excerpt of *Hirabayashi*, a ruling that had *upheld* the harsh treatment of Japanese Americans during World War II. One of the key words here was "solely." While *Loving* rejected laws based "solely" on ancestry, racial laws justified on other grounds (such as national security) remained constitutional.[44] And notwithstanding Warren's deletion of *Skinner*'s reference to the existence and survival "of *the* race," he was citing a decision that in another passage had affirmed "a right which is basic to the perpetuation of *a* race—the right to have offspring [my emphases]." This formulation does not seem to refer to the perpetuation of the *human* race; it seems to refer to the perpetuation of each particular race. Elsewhere *Skinner* expressed concern about "the power to sterilize" because "in evil or reckless hands it can cause races or types which are inimical to the dominant group to wither and disappear," which again means that *Loving* relied on a decision that invoked the reproductive rights of distinct "races" and not the singular human race.[45] Paradoxically, *Loving* struck down laws against interracial marriage on the basis of a racialist precedent that affirmed the right of each race to reproduce itself.

Eisenstadt (1972)

In striking down Connecticut's birth control law, *Griswold* granted special privacy rights and privileges to married couples who engaged in potentially reproductive sex. Seven years later, *Eisenstadt* partially decoupled marriage and reproduction, striking down laws banning the distribution of contraceptives to single people. Some commentators who acknowledge that *Griswold* did not recognize a right of sexual privacy argue that *Eisenstadt* did, but *Eisenstadt* never mentioned sexual privacy. Insofar as *Eisenstadt* suggested that laws against nonmarital sex remained constitutional, it made clear the distinction between sexual and reproductive privacy.[46]

Only seven justices voted in *Eisenstadt*, since Black and Harlan had resigned and Powell and Rehnquist were not confirmed in time to decide the case. Writing for a majority of four that included Douglas, Marshall, and Stewart, Brennan presented the case as a conflict between Thomas Eisenstadt, a Massachusetts county sheriff, and William Baird, who had been convicted for (1) "exhibiting contraceptive articles" and (2) "giving a young woman a package of Emko vaginal foam" after a lecture at Boston University. The state law targeted "whoever sells, lends, gives away, exhibits or offers to sell, lend or give away . . . any drug, medicine, instrument or article whatever for the prevention of conception." Exceptions were made for health care professionals, but only in relation to married persons. A state appeals court overturned the first conviction for violating the First Amendment, but affirmed the second. After a federal appeals court, citing *Griswold*, directed Eisenstadt to discharge Baird, Eisenstadt appealed to the Supreme Court.[47]

In *Griswold*, *Fanny Hill*, and *Loving*, the basic narrative of legal conflict was not in dispute. Some of the justices disagreed with the ruling or the reasoning of the lead opinion, but they did not challenge what were presented as "the facts." In *Eisenstadt*, the basic narrative was in dispute, primarily because of ambiguities about whether the woman given contraception was married. According to Brennan, the federal appeals court described the woman as unmarried, but "there is no evidence in the record about her marital status." This did not stop the majority from striking down the state law for violating the equality rights of the unmarried. Douglas joined Brennan's opinion, but separately argued that there was a First Amendment basis for deciding the case, since Baird had essentially been arrested for giving a speech. Writing for himself and Blackmun, White concurred in the judgment but not the majority opinion because "no proof was offered as to the marital status of the recipient" and therefore there was "no reason for reaching the novel constitutional question whether a State may restrict or forbid the distribution of contraceptives to the unmarried." Instead, citing *Griswold*, they argued that the state had not provided a compelling public health rationale for restricting the access of married people to vaginal foam. In essence, the four justices who endorsed Brennan's opinion took a step beyond *Griswold*; the two who signed White's did not; and one, Burger, argued that *Griswold* did not apply because *Eisenstadt* concerned "dispensing a medicinal substance without a licence."[48]

If a narrow majority of four took a step beyond *Griswold*, what was the step they took? The key passage in Brennan's opinion downplayed the extent to which *Eisenstadt* departed from *Griswold*. According to Brennan, "If under *Griswold* the distribution of contraceptives to married persons cannot be prohibited, a ban on distribution to unmarried persons would be equally impermissible. It is true that in *Griswold* the right of privacy in question inhered in the marital relationship. Yet the marital couple is not an independent entity with a mind and heart of its own, but an association of two individuals each with a separate intellectual and emotional makeup. If the right of privacy means anything, it is the right of the individual, married or single, to be free from unwarranted governmental intrusion into matters so fundamentally affecting a person as the decision whether to bear or beget a child." In using equal protection arguments to extend the rights of married couples to the unmarried, the first sentence made the rights of the latter dependent on and derivative of the rights of the former. Married people had privacy rights that included access to contraception, whereas unmarried people had such rights because they could not be discriminated against on the basis of marital status.[49] The third and fourth sentences more securely established that single people had autonomous privacy rights, but only ruled out "unwarranted" government action and did not make clear how far the right of privacy extended beyond reproduction.

Further confusing matters, in two passages Brennan denied that the Court had reached any firm conclusions about the fundamental privacy rights of the unmarried. In one, he argued that the Court need not decide whether the law infringed on "fundamental freedoms under *Griswold*" because "the law fails to satisfy even the more lenient equal protection standard." In the other, he declared that "we need not and do not . . . decide" whether the law could be upheld as a morality-based prohibition of contraception because "whatever the rights of the individual to access to contraceptives may be, the rights must be the same for the unmarried and the married." These passages grounded the ruling in an equality argument, rather than a privacy argument.[50]

Brennan's reference to the "more lenient equal protection standard" signaled that the Court was striking down the law not because it interfered with fundamental rights or relied on a suspect classification, which would have triggered strict scrutiny. Instead, the Court was using the test it generally applied in cases involving non-fundamental rights and non-suspect classifications, which involved asking whether the law served a reasonable state interest and whether there was a rational relationship between the law and the interest. Brennan's opinion discussed three asserted state interests: deterrence of nonmarital sex, promotion of public health, and deterrence of immorality (with "immorality" referring to contraception itself). In each case, the Court did not say that these were not reasonable state interests. Instead the Court emphasized that there was not a rational relationship between the law and these interests. According to Brennan, for example, the state claimed that the law's purpose was to "promote marital fidelity" and "discourage premarital sex," but the law allowed married people to have access to contraceptives "without regard to whether they are living with their spouses or the uses to which the contraceptives are to be put." Moreover, the majority did not believe that the state would regard "pregnancy and the birth of an unwanted child" as an appropriate punishment for fornication, and the law did not regulate the distribution of contraceptives "to prevent . . . the spread of disease." Brennan added, "Even conceding the legislature a full measure of discretion in fashioning means to prevent fornication . . . , we . . . cannot believe that . . . Massachusetts has chosen to expose the aider and abetter who simply *gives away* a contraceptive to 20 times the 90-day sentence of the offender himself."[51] All of this rested on the assumption that laws against nonmarital sex were constitutional.[52]

Notwithstanding the rhetoric and reasoning used by the justices, some commentators have argued that *Eisenstadt* is best understood as recognizing the rights of the unmarried to have sex. If the Court affirmed the birth control rights of the unmarried, they say, surely this indicates that the justices were recognizing the rights of the unmarried to have sex for purposes of pleasure rather than reproduction. Otherwise, some say, the Court would have found it legitimate for states to expect the unmarried to abstain from sex if they wanted to avoid reproduction.[53] There is a certain logic to this position, and *Eisenstadt* may have made it easier for the unmarried to have sex for pleasure without reproductive consequences. But for the reasons outlined above, this was not the logic of the justices, who distinguished between laws that criminalized nonmarital sex, which remained constitutional after *Eisenstadt*, and laws that criminalized nonmarital birth control, which were now unconstitutional. The *Eisenstadt* majority made this distinction, and individual justices in the majority made this distinction in cases decided before and after *Eisenstadt*.

Thus *Eisenstadt* is best regarded as a heteronormative reproductive rights decision, not an egalitarian or libertarian sexual rights decision. And as was the case with *Griswold*, *Fanny Hill*, and *Loving*, *Eisenstadt* had classed, gendered, and racialized meanings. Like Goldberg in *Griswold*, Brennan quoted the *Olmstead* dissent that referred to "the right most valued by civilized man," which invoked the classed, gendered, and racialized discourse of "civilization." Like Douglas in *Griswold*, Brennan used *Barrows*, the Court's decision on racially restrictive covenants, to establish the standing of Baird. According to Brennan, *Barrows* demonstrated that "one who acted to protect the rights of a minority" had standing to defend the rights of "the minority itself."[54] In addition, the arguments presented on behalf of Baird included statistics on the high rates of nonmarital reproduction among Blacks (said to be more than twice as high as among whites in Massachusetts) and referred to "the whole social problem of our nation with respect to the poor unwanted child and the welfare mother." Presumably influenced by this type of evidence, Douglas's concurring opinion emphasized that Baird's speech discussed "overpopulation in the world" and "the large number of abortions performed on unwed mothers." Brennan's majority opinion included a passage from the federal appeals court ruling that had argued, "To say that contraceptives are immoral as such, and are to be forbidden to unmarried persons who will nevertheless persist in having intercourse, means that such persons must risk for themselves an unwanted pregnancy, for the child, illegitimacy, and for society, a possible obligation of support." Unwanted pregnancy, illegitimacy, welfare, and overpopulation had classed, gendered, and racialized connotations in this period. In this context, the rhetoric and reasoning of *Eisenstadt* were marked by classed, gendered, and racialized anxieties about the reproductive sexual behaviors of the unmarried.[55]

Roe (1973)

Roe provided another opportunity to define the parameters of the right to privacy, and once again the Court affirmed the special and privileged status of reproduction within its heteronormative doctrine. In *Roe*, the Court declared that there were fundamental privacy rights at stake in decisions about abortion, but a woman's right to abortion was not absolute since the state had legitimate interests in promoting public health and protecting "potential life." Women's privacy interests and the medical judgments of their physicians were declared preeminent in the first trimester. These had to be balanced against the state's compelling interests in public health in the second trimester, when abortions were said to pose more of a risk to the pregnant woman. In the third trimester (after the point of fetal "viability"), the state's interests in protecting "potential life" became compelling. In striking down the Texas abortion law, the Court affirmed a right of reproductive, not sexual, privacy.[56]

The Court that initially considered *Roe* in 1971 consisted of the seven *Eisenstadt* justices, but by the time the decision was announced in 1973 they had been joined by Rehnquist and Powell. The majority opinion, which was authored by Blackmun and endorsed by six other justices, presented a narrative of conflict between the pseudonymous Jane Roe, an "unmarried and pregnant" woman, and the state of Texas, represented by Dallas County district attorney Henry Wade. Texas prohibited the provision or procurement of an abortion, with an exception if the abortion was necessary to save the life of a pregnant woman. According to Blackmun, similar statutes existed in most states, though they varied in the exceptions permitted.[57]

Blackmun set aside the case of James Hallford, a doctor charged with breaking the Texas law, on the grounds that his case was still pending in state court. He also set aside the case of a childless married couple, the pseudonymous John and Mary Doe, who had health-related reasons for wanting to avoid pregnancy. (This Mary Doe should not be confused with the Mary Doe of *Doe v. Bolton*, a Georgia case considered alongside *Roe*.) According to Blackmun, their claims were "speculative" since "their alleged injury rests on possible future contraceptive failure, possible future pregnancy, possible future unpreparedness for parenthood, and possible future impairment of health." As for Roe, because she had been pregnant in 1970 when the case was filed in Texas but was no longer pregnant when her appeal reached the Supreme Court, Blackmun argued that the Court had to set aside its usual practice of only adjudicating cases that present an actual controversy at the time of review because the short duration of pregnancy and the length of time necessary for appeals meant that this was the only way to determine the constitutionality of abortion statutes.[58]

Writing for the majority, Blackmun argued that in the past the Court had "recognized that a right of personal privacy, or a guarantee of certain areas or zones of privacy, does exist under the Constitution." Citing a long line of cases, including *Griswold*, *Loving*, and *Eisenstadt*, Blackmun concluded, "This right of privacy . . . is broad enough to encompass a woman's decision whether or not to terminate her pregnancy." Disputing the notion that this right was "absolute," however, Blackmun wrote that "a State may properly assert important interests in safeguarding health, in maintaining medical standards, and in protecting potential life." On this basis, the Court ruled that in the first trimester, "the abortion decision and its effectuation must be left to the medical judgment of the pregnant woman's attending physician." In the second, the state could "regulate the abortion procedure in ways that are reasonably related to maternal health." In the third, the state could "regulate, and even proscribe, abortion except where it is necessary . . . for the preservation of the life or health of the mother."[59]

The majority opinion was explicit not only in declaring that the right to abortion was not absolute but also in stating that the right to privacy was not absolute. According to Blackmun, the Court's precedents had made it clear that "the right has some extension to activities relating to marriage . . . , procreation . . . , contraception . . . , family relationships . . . , and child rearing and education." Now the Court was declaring that this right was "broad enough" to encompass abortion. But according to Blackmun, "It is not clear to us that the claim asserted by some *amici* that one has an unlimited right to do with one's body as one pleases bears a close relationship to the right of privacy previously articulated in the Court's decisions. The Court has refused to recognize an unlimited right of this kind in the past." Here Blackmun cited two cases (*Jacobson*, a 1905 decision concerning vaccination, and *Buck*, a 1927 decision concerning sterilization) that affirmed the state's legitimate interests in public health, safety, and welfare. On the one hand, Blackmun's language suggested that the right of privacy was not a right to do with one's body as one pleases. On the other hand, the language implied that the right of privacy *was* a right to do with one's body as one pleases, but that this right was limited. Either way, privacy rights could be overridden. And if there was a limited right to do with one's body as one pleases, Blackmun's formulation did not make it clear whether this was a sexual or a reproductive right. In the absence of clarifying language, the constellation of activities mentioned by the Court seemed to revolve around marriage and reproduction, not sex.[60]

In several passages, the Court referenced sexual rights more directly. According to Blackmun, the appellant argued that the constitutional basis of her right to terminate her pregnancy was "the concept of personal 'liberty' embodied in the Fourteenth Amendment's Due Process Clause" or the "personal, marital, familial, and sexual privacy said to be protected by the Bill of Rights or its penumbras." This passage is sometimes used to suggest that the Court recognized a right of sexual privacy in *Roe*, but Blackmun was describing the arguments of the appellant, not announcing the Court's conclusions. When the Court subsequently presented its views on the nature of privacy, it referred to "marriage" and "family" but not sex. In another passage, Blackmun wrote, "It has been argued occasionally that these laws were the product of a Victorian social concern to discourage illicit sexual conduct. Texas, however, does not advance this justification in the present case, and it appears that no court or commentator has taken the argument seriously. The appellants and *amici* contend, moreover, that this is not a proper state purpose at all and suggest that, if it were, the Texas statutes are overbroad . . . since the law fails to distinguish between married and unwed mothers." Some commentators have read this passage as meaning that the Court rejected the notion that states had a legitimate interest in discouraging illicit sex, but here, too, Blackmun was describing arguments, not announcing conclusions. A third passage dealt with the reasons for setting aside the case of Mary and John Doe. According to Blackmun, their claim was based on "an alleged 'detrimental effect upon [their] marital happiness' because they are forced to 'the choice of refraining from normal sexual relations or of endangering Mary Doe's health through a possible pregnancy.'" Blackmun responded, "This very phrasing of the Does' position reveals its speculative character." On this basis Blackmun concluded that the Does lacked standing, but his reasoning disregarded the issue of "refraining from normal sexual relations," which was not speculative.[61]

In contrast, when Douglas dissented in a 1971 abortion case, *Vuitch*, he wrote, "Abortion touches intimate affairs of the family, of marriage, of sex, which in *Griswold* . . . we held to involve rights . . . which are summed up in 'the right of privacy.'" The only other justice who came close to affirming a right of sexual privacy in this period was Marshall, who did so in *California v. LaRue* (1972). In this case, the Court upheld state liquor control regulations that prohibited certain forms of sexually explicit entertainment in licensed bars and clubs, including some that did not meet the Court's definitions of obscenity. In a dissenting opinion footnote that cited *Griswold*, Marshall declared, "I have serious doubts whether the State may constitutionally assert an interest in regulating any sexual act between consenting adults."[62]

Roe was a limited ruling not only because it balanced a woman's privacy rights against the interests of the state and "potential life," but also because privacy rights were conceptualized as reproductive, rather than sexual.[63] Like *Griswold*, *Loving*, and *Eisenstadt*, *Roe* also reflected and contributed to developments in class, gender, and race relations. As chapter 3 discusses, even the name of the case, which helped keep hidden from public view the details of Norma McCorvey's life, relates to the complexities of class, race, gender, and sexual politics. As for the rhetoric and reasoning of the lawyers, several briefs emphasized the large numbers of "unwanted" and "illegitimate" children and stated that many of these children were born to poor women, women on welfare, black women, and teenagers. At the very outset of his opinion, Blackmun declared that "population growth, pollution, poverty, and racial overtones tend to complicate . . . the problem" of abortion. Blackmun also referred to "the distress, for all concerned, associated with the unwanted child" and "the additional difficulties and continuing stigma of unwed motherhood." Blackmun was expressing concern for "the pregnant woman" and her family, but this type of sentiment led some to accuse abortion liberals of advancing race- and class-prejudiced agendas.[64]

As for the "facts" considered by the Court, Blackmun provided few details about Jane Roe, but in the linked Georgia case the Court noted that Mary Doe had three children, two in foster care and one in the process of being adopted "because of Doe's poverty and inability to care for them." Blackmun also wrote that Doe's "husband recently abandoned her" (though later they "reconciled"), that she was now living with "her indigent parents and their eight children," and that she had been a "mental patient" at a state hospital. On the one hand, Blackmun expressed sympathy for the classed and gendered aspects of Doe's difficult situation. On the other, his opinion left the impression that this was the type of woman who should not only have *access to* abortion, but who should *have* an abortion.[65]

The Court also offered classed, gendered, and racialized arguments in its long discussion of the history of abortion. In this part of his opinion, Blackmun emphasized that "the restrictive criminal abortion laws in effect in a majority of States today . . . derive from statutory changes effected, for the most part, in the latter half of the 19th century." But as he challenged the notion that restrictive abortion laws had a longer and more continuous history in the United States, he adopted the ethnocentric practice of privileging European and U.S. history. Blackmun's historical survey began with the Persians, Greeks, and Romans; proceeded through Christian theological and canonical law; continued with English common and statutory law; and turned finally to "American law." Conceptualizing abortion rights within a narrow Western civilization framework that privileged particular cultural, religious, and national histories, the opinion implicitly deemed other histories of abortion less relevant or irrelevant. Blackmun also surveyed the history of religious perspectives on abortion, but limited his discussion to Jews and Christians. The Court discussed abortion rights in an ethnocentric, Judeo-Christian historical framework.[66]

The Court also used a sexist framework that promoted the dominance of men rather than a feminist framework focused on the rights of women. As was typical in the 1970s, the Court used the term "man" in ways that, on the one hand, referred to all people, and, on the other, referred more specifically to those classified as male. In this context, Blackmun's opinion referred to the history of "man's attitudes" toward abortion and the "development of man's knowledge" about when life begins. Blackmun repeatedly referred to the pregnant woman as the "mother," despite the fact that motherhood was precisely what many abortion-seeking women were rejecting, avoiding, or deferring. As for the doctors who performed abortions, Blackmun emphasized "his" rights to practice medicine more than the rights of the pregnant woman. In one passage, the Court concluded that during the first trimester "the attending physician, in consultation with his patient, is free to determine, without regulation by the State, that, in his medical judgment, the patient's pregnancy should be terminated." Summarizing its findings, the Court declared that in this stage of pregnancy "the abortion decision and its effectuation must be left to the medical judgment of the pregnant woman's attending physician." In this formulation, the pregnant woman was not even given a consultative role; the decision seemed as if it were the doctor's alone to make. More generally, the Court set aside the arguments of those in *Roe* who emphasized women's autonomy and women's empowerment, though the decision would later be claimed as a feminist victory.[67]

THE COURT'S MOST SIGNIFICANT rulings on birth control, obscenity, interracial marriage, and abortion in the period from 1965 to 1973 reflected and produced a classed, gendered, and racialized doctrine of heteronormative supremacy. In these decisions, the Court used specific, careful, and deliberate language that recognized special rights and privileges for a constellation of heteronormative activities revolving around marriage, family, reproduction, and the home. In case after case, the Court signaled that laws against adultery, cohabitation, fornication, homosexuality, and prostitution remained constitutional. Many conservative critics denounced the Court for opening the door to libertarian sexual freedom and radical sexual egalitarianism. Many liberal supporters celebrated the Court for establishing progressive sexual precedents. But careful readers of the Court's decisions knew that the justices would subsequently have to reject the logic of *Griswold*, *Fanny Hill*, *Loving*, *Eisenstadt*, and *Roe* if they wanted to adopt a libertarian and egalitarian doctrine of sexual citizenship.

2 : Consistent Conservatism in *Boutilier*

In the 1967 *Boutilier* case, the Court acted in accordance with its heteronormative doctrine when six of nine justices upheld a 1952 federal law authorizing the Immigration and Naturalization Service (INS) to exclude and deport aliens "afflicted with psychopathic personality," a phrase the INS and the Court understood to refer to "homosexuals." Insofar as the rights of psychopaths were severely circumscribed in the United States, *Boutilier* had important implications for everyone classifiable as homosexual, but especially for aliens.[1]

Boutilier was not the Court's first gay rights case. In *ONE* (1958), five justices rejected a lower court's obscenity ruling against a homophile magazine, and in *Manual* (1962) six justices overturned the Post Office's designation of three male physique magazines as obscene. Then in *Rosenberg* (1963), five justices vacated a ruling that had upheld the deportation of a "homosexual" alien. The meaning of *ONE*, however, was unclear since the magazine featured neither erotic photographs nor sexually explicit prose and the Court did not explain its reasoning. *Manual* was also ambiguous, since one justice concurred without comment and three did so on procedural grounds. As for *Rosenberg*, the basis of this ruling was the claim that George Fleuti's return to the United States from a one-day trip to Mexico in 1956 did not constitute re-entry and therefore Fleuti's entry date was in 1952, before the psychopathic personality law took effect. These rulings did not indicate that "homosexual" and "heterosexual" speech would be judged by the same standards or that "homosexual" and "heterosexual" immigrants would be evaluated by the same criteria. Then in *Mishkin* (1966), the Court indicated that materials designed for and disseminated to sexual "deviants" would be judged by special standards and that its obscenity tests could be revised when the existing ones did not yield the results desired.[2]

In other cases before *Boutilier*, the justices reviewed antigay lower court rulings and either declined to accept the appeals for argument or issued summary dismissals. This occurred in several immigration cases highlighted below, as well as *Kameny* (1961), *Shields* (1961), *Williams* (1963), and *Caplan* (1963), which upheld the firing of government employees based on evidence of homosexual conduct. *Womack* (1961) and *Darnell* (1963) affirmed obscenity convictions in cases involving materials said to describe, depict, or promote same-sex sex. The Court also declined to hear appeals of sodomy and sodomy-related convictions in *Poore* (1964), *Chamberlain* (1966), and *Robillard* (1966). The justices did not announce their substantive conclusions in these cases, but they allowed conservative lower court rulings to stand.[3]

Although *Boutilier* was not the first gay rights case considered by the Court and not the first accepted for oral arguments, it merits careful consideration. *ONE* and *Rosenberg* included oral arguments, but in *Boutilier* the Court produced substantive majority and minority opinions. In addition, *Boutilier* was decided in the middle of the period in which the Court was announcing liberalizing decisions on birth control, obscenity, interracial marriage, and abortion. Examining *Boutilier* helps reveal how the justices distinguished between the issues raised in *Griswold*, *Fanny Hill*, *Loving*, *Eisenstadt*, and *Roe* and the ones raised in *Boutilier*, thus exposing the scope and limits of the Court's heteronormative doctrine.

Boutilier also merits attention because it concerns immigration law. U.S. immigration laws and practices not only determine who may enter U.S. territory lawfully and who may become eligible for U.S. citizenship, but also which groups within the country are identified as the most desirable citizens. U.S. immigration law has helped form and regulate class, racial, and religious hierarchies by favoring white Christians from northwestern Europe and Canada, and this has intersected with the formation and regulation of gender and sexual hierarchies through provisions and practices that favored heteronormative families. Immigration law is also important because the Court has been very deferential to the legislative and executive branches in this area. For instance, while the justices have asserted their prerogatives strongly in free-speech cases, they have been reluctant to challenge legislative and executive authority to determine who may enter the country and become a citizen. Rulings by the Court have granted resident aliens some but not all of the rights held by U.S. citizens; the congressional power to regulate the country's borders is generally regarded as pre- or extra-constitutional, meaning that the rights provisions of the Constitution do not necessarily apply. The Court's liberalizing rulings positioned homosexuals as second-class U.S. citizens, but *Boutilier* positioned alien homosexuals as ineligible for U.S. residency and citizenship.[4]

Before *Boutilier*

In the late nineteenth and early twentieth centuries, Congress passed laws that denied entry to aliens who were "mentally defective," aliens who had been convicted of "crimes of moral turpitude," and aliens who were "persons of constitutional psychopathic inferiority." In some contexts, these and related statutes were interpreted to apply to those who had committed illegal acts such as adultery, bigamy, cohabitation, cross-dressing, fornication, prostitution, public sex, rape, same-sex sex, sex with minors, and sodomy. These statutes were also used against those classified as particular types of persons, including homosexuals, inverts, prostitutes, transvestites, and people with sexually transmitted diseases. Meanwhile, Congress passed legislation that favored individuals who were migrating or reuniting with heteronormative Anglophone, Christian, white families from northwestern Europe or Canada.[5]

The 1952 Immigration and Nationality Act revised the language that excluded "persons of constitutional psychopathic inferiority" so that aliens "afflicted with psychopathic personality" were excludable. This reflected the rise of psychological models that de-emphasized "constitutional" (biological, hereditary, and congenital) explanations of sexual difference. The same legislation expanded the moral turpitude exclusion to cover those who had committed acts of moral turpitude, whether or not they had been convicted of crimes. According to William Eskridge's analysis of government data, 292 people were barred as "persons of constitutional psychopathic inferiority" from 1917 to 1924, 322 were barred under this category from 1937 to 1952, and 47 were barred as "psychopathic personality" aliens from 1953 to 1956. Margot Canaday's examination of immigration records and court cases suggests that early twentieth-century authorities more frequently targeted "gender/sex deviants" by denying entry to those likely to become "public charges" and those who had committed "crimes of moral turpitude," but in the 1950s and 1960s they began to favor the "psychopathic personality" exclusion. Eithne Luibhéid's study of sexual regulation at the U.S. border emphasizes the classed, gendered, and racialized aspects of sexual exclusion, noting that many "deviants" were affected in ways that would not be evident in official statistics or court cases.[6] This was true before and after 1965, when Congress passed new legislation excluding aliens with "sexual deviations."[7] (The same legislation replaced many racial exclusions and national quotas with less explicit forms of racialized regulation.) The "sexual deviation" exclusion was passed after Boutilier was first admitted to the United States in 1955, so the INS action to deport him was based on the claim that he had been excludable as a person "afflicted with psychopathic personality" at time of entry.[8]

Before *Boutilier*, U.S. appellate courts considered multiple gay-related challenges to immigration laws and practices, and some of their decisions were appealed to the Supreme Court. In *Babouris* (1960), *Ganduxe y Marino* (1960), *Hudson* and *Matos-Jordan* (1961), and *Wyngaard* (1961), the Court declined to consider appeals of rulings upholding deportation orders. These cases involved male plaintiffs convicted of public sex crimes, but in *Quiroz* (1961) the Fifth Circuit upheld the deportation of a female U.S. permanent resident from Mexico on the grounds that she was a homosexual and as such was afflicted with psychopathic personality.[9]

In the early 1960s, several appellate courts ruled in favor of "gay" defendants in exclusion/deportation cases. In *Fleuti* (1962), the Ninth Circuit considered the case of a Swiss citizen who had become a U.S. permanent resident in 1952, before the psychopathic personality exclusion was adopted, but who had taken a daytrip to Mexico in 1956, after the new legislation took effect. Responding to the INS claim that Fleuti was deportable because he had participated in homosexual acts before and after 1956 (his record included two public sex convictions), the Ninth Circuit ruled that the term "psychopathic personality" was void for vagueness. According to the vagueness doctrine, a statute violates the due process clause if its language fails to provide comprehensible warnings about proscribed conduct. The Ninth Circuit ruled that the law failed to warn Fleuti that "continuance of homosexual practices," which in his case was said to be "a matter of choice," might lead to deportation. When the Supreme Court considered the INS's appeal (now called *Rosenberg* because the Court lists the appellant's name first), it sidestepped the issue of vagueness and instead ruled 5–4 in favor of Fleuti based on the claim that his date of entry was 1952. In 1966, the Ninth Circuit was less sympathetic to the petitioner in *Tovar* when it upheld a decision by the Board of Immigration Appeals that an alien convicted three times of committing lewd vagrancy in public restrooms was not eligible for suspension of deportation because he was not a "person of good moral character." In the same year, however, the Ninth Circuit invoked the vagueness doctrine in *Lavoie*, which overturned the deportation of a U.S. permanent resident from Canada who admitted to homosexual and heterosexual conduct before entry and who had pled guilty to a charge of lewd and indecent conduct in a San Francisco Woolworth's store. When the Second Circuit issued a contrary 2–1 ruling in *Boutilier*, the Supreme Court saw a conflict between lower court decisions. Perhaps because *Boutilier* did not involve an alien convicted of a crime, the Court decided to accept this case for argument and hold *Lavoie* and *Tovar* for later consideration.[10]

Boutilier

In *Boutilier*, the Court wrestled with four questions: (1) did Congress intend to exclude and deport all homosexual aliens through the psychopathic personality provisions of the 1952 Immigration and Nationality Act? (2) did the Act's Public Health Service (PHS) certification procedures require medical authorities to defer to legal definitions or legal authorities to defer to medical definitions? (3) was the phrase "afflicted with psychopathic personality" unconstitutionally vague? and (4) were aliens to be classified as "afflicted with psychopathic personality" on the basis of homosexual conduct or character?

The justices in the majority (Black, Clark, Harlan, Stewart, Warren, and White) were influenced most directly by Judge Irving Kaufman, who authored the Second Circuit's 2–1 ruling against Boutilier, and Solicitor General Thurgood Marshall, who signed the government's briefs against Boutilier. Kaufman had worked in the 1940s for Attorney General Tom Clark, who authored the Court's ruling against Boutilier, but he is best known as the judge who presided over the espionage conspiracy trial of Julius and Ethel Rosenberg in the 1950s and sentenced the two to death.[11] Marshall, one of the nation's preeminent civil rights lawyers, served as President Johnson's solicitor general before his appointment to the Court. Marshall's signatures on the government's briefs do not necessarily mean that he participated actively in the litigation, and during this period Johnson and his advisors may have been testing Marshall as they considered whether to appoint him to the Supreme Court. Nevertheless, Marshall could have intervened in the *Boutilier* litigation in various ways, and the fact that this champion of civil rights allowed his name to be associated with the government's strongly antigay positions is noteworthy.[12]

Since this chapter focuses on the Supreme Court, this is not the place for a detailed discussion of Kaufman's ruling and Marshall's briefs, but several passages in Kaufman's opinion provide a useful introduction to some of the central issues in *Boutilier*. Kaufman's final footnote responded to a passage in Judge Leonard Moore's dissenting opinion that cited sexologist Alfred Kinsey's claim that "'at least 37 per cent' of the American male population has at least one homosexual experience." According to Moore, labeling all aliens with such experiences as excludable would be "tantamount to saying that Sappho, Leonardo da Vinci, Michelangelo, Andre Gide, and perhaps even Shakespeare, were they to come to life again, would be deemed unfit to visit our shores." Kaufman replied, "The dissent's parade of distinguished histori-cal personages allegedly possessing homosexual attributes does not detract one iota" from the fact that Congress meant to exclude homosexuals. "There is little doubt that some of these eminent gentlemen would be excludable." Kaufman then concluded, "While the house of horrors erected by our dis-senting brother stimulates the imagination and arouses our sympathy, it is largely irrelevant. Congress studiously avoided turning this into a medical problem and did not authorize immigration officials to conduct a detailed psychiatric examination into the nature, frequency and variety of a particular homosexual's acts; rather, it enacted a clear-cut rule of law: it determined that pre-entry homosexual behavior was to be a ground for exclusion." Horrified by what his "brother" had "erected," which had "stimulated" and "aroused" his sympathy, Kaufman apparently missed the fact that Sappho, the female poet of ancient Greece, was not exactly a gentleman. What was central for Kauf-man was a "simple fact of life": Congress meant to exclude "homosexuals."[13]

Kaufman's claim that "pre-entry homosexual behavior was to be a ground for exclusion" is significant when placed alongside some of his other argu-ments. In the very first words of his opinion, Kaufman declared, "Although a relatively young segment of contemporary society prides itself on its readi-ness to cast off conventional and tested disciplines and to experiment with nonconformance and the unorthodox merely to set out its contempt for tradi-tional values, certain areas of conduct continue to be as controversial in mod-ern and *beau monde* circles as they were in bygone and more staid eras." This passage, like the one that referred to homosexual "behavior," conceptualized homosexuality as a type of "conduct." Yet only pages later, Kaufman argued that the law "was never designed to regulate *conduct*; its function was to ex-clude aliens possessing certain *characteristics*." On one level he was contradict-ing himself, but on another he was using conduct as proof of character. This is what the Court did as well.[14]

Clark's majority opinion presented a narrative of legal conflict between Clive Michael Boutilier, a Canadian national who was first admitted to the United States at age twenty-one in 1955, and the INS, which initiated depor-tation proceedings after Boutilier's application for citizenship led the PHS to classify him as afflicted with psychopathic personality at time of entry. As was typical in Court rulings, the first section of the majority opinion offered a his-torical account of the case. Presented as sets of incontrovertible facts, these accounts were strategic narratives that selected, arranged, presented, trans-formed, and erased data from the record to begin building a case for the deci-sion.[15]

Clark's account supported the decision in six principal ways: (1) it presented critical legal "facts" about Boutilier, the INS, and the PHS; (2) it indicated that the behavioral evidence of Boutilier's "homosexual relations" constituted proof of his identity as "a homosexual"; (3) it suggested that Boutilier was a particularly undesirable homosexual and therefore a particularly undesirable immigrant; (4) it also suggested that Boutilier was a relatively respectable homosexual and that the ruling therefore applied to all homosexuals; (5) it implied that Boutilier's opponents and supporters agreed that he was a sexual deviate and a homosexual; and (6) it concluded that the only two questions remaining were "whether the term 'psychopathic personality' included homosexuals and if it suffered illegality because of vagueness."[16]

The first section began by describing Boutilier as an alien who first entered the United States in 1955 and last entered in 1959. This located Boutilier's entries in the period between the passage of the 1952 psychopathic personality provision and the 1965 sexual deviation amendment, which distinguished this case from *Rosenberg*. Clark then mentioned that Boutilier's "mother and stepfather and three of his brothers and sisters live in the United States." U.S. immigration statutes generally privileged the family members of U.S. citizens and residents, but the psychopathic personality exclusion did not. This information thus did not serve a formal legal purpose, but it helped create meaningful impressions. On the one hand, it gestured sympathetically toward depicting Boutilier as a member of a heteronormative family living in the United States. On the other, it invoked a standard trope of the pathologizing homosexual family narrative by hinting at an absent biological father. Even the sympathetic gesture proved to have negative implications, suggesting as it did that all homosexual aliens—no matter the nature of their family ties in the United States—were subject to exclusion and deportation.[17]

Clark then moved on to a discussion of Boutilier's citizenship application, noting that in 1963 Boutilier "submitted to the Naturalization Examiner an affidavit in which he admitted that he was arrested in New York in October 1959, on a charge of sodomy, which was later reduced to simple assault and thereafter dismissed on default of the complainant." Clark did not mention that Boutilier's partner in this incident was seventeen years old or that Boutilier acknowledged engaging in anal and oral sex during this encounter. These details were included in a draft by Clark's clerk, but the opinion still conveyed the impression that Boutilier had engaged in criminal, homosexual acts. By using the terms "assault" and "complainant," the opinion also turned what Boutilier claimed was mutually consensual into something that seemed more sinister (though legal experts may have understood that in many jurisdictions "simple assault" refers to nonconsensual touching). At the same time, by underscoring the fact that Boutilier had not been convicted of a crime, not mentioning the complainant's age, and not specifying the sex acts, Clark set the stage for a ruling that would cover all aliens classifiable as homosexual.[18]

Clark next noted that in 1964, "at the request of the Government," Boutilier submitted an affidavit that "revealed the full history of his sexual deviate behavior." The pleasant-sounding reference to the government "request" could have been described as an interrogation, without Boutilier's lawyer present, by INS investigator James Sarsfield. As for the reference to "sexual deviate behavior," this conflated the language of the 1952 Act, which did not refer to sexual deviation, and the 1965 amendment, which did. Clark summarized the "full history" as follows:

> His first homosexual experience occurred when he was 14 years of age, some seven years before his entry into the United States. Petitioner was evidently a passive participant in this encounter. His next episode was at age 16 and occurred in a public park in Halifax, Nova Scotia. Petitioner was the active participant in this affair. During the next five years immediately preceding his first entry into the United States petitioner had homosexual relations on an average of three or four times a year. He also stated that prior to his entry he had engaged in heterosexual relations on three or four occasions. During the eight and one-half years immediately subsequent to his entry, and up to the time of his second statement, petitioner continued to have homosexual relations on an average of three or four times a year. Since 1959 petitioner had shared an apartment with a man with whom he had had homosexual relations.

This conveyed the impression that some features of Boutilier's sexual conduct had remained stable over time. Over more than thirteen years he had engaged in homosexual acts three or four times a year, which suggested that his homosexuality was not a momentary episode or a passing phase. Other features of Boutilier's sex life apparently had changed. For instance, Clark's account suggested that after an initial "passive" experience Boutilier had become "active." Clark did not explain what he meant by "passive" and "active" participation, but most readers likely would have assumed that this referred to whether Boutilier had been the sexual initiator or penetrator.[19]

Clark's summary left out or modified several related details mentioned by the Second Circuit. For instance, Kaufman had described Boutilier's first sexual encounter as "involuntary," which implied that he had been victimized.[20] Clark also left out or modified several details highlighted in other case documents. In his 1963 affidavit, Boutilier claimed that he "ceased to continue homosexuality" after his 1959 arrest, and the examiner who questioned him in 1963 reported that Boutilier "stated that he began to practice homosexuality after his entry in the United States but since he was arrested he has ceased the practice." The 1964 affidavit, in contrast, acknowledged pre-entry and post-arrest homosexual experiences. Presumably the Court accepted the latter as the "truth." Boutilier also claimed in the 1964 affidavit that in his first sexual encounter a married man (approximately forty years old) whose bed he was sharing during a hunting trip "tried to put his penis in my rectum" and "didn't succeed but a flow of sperm came from his penis on my clothing." Boutilier did not indicate whether he regarded this experience as voluntary or involuntary, but Montague Ullman, a psychiatrist whom Boutilier's lawyers arranged for him to see, wrote in a letter submitted to the lower court that Boutilier "was apparently seduced by an older man." What for Ullman was seduction and for Kaufman was involuntary became "passive" for Clark. Ullman also wrote that until 1959 Boutilier's sexual experiences were "mostly with older men," who "usually initiated" the encounters, and Boutilier "never sought out homosexual contacts or relationships." As for types of sex, Boutilier's 1964 affidavit indicated that in "all" of his same-sex sexual experiences (after the first) he received "blowjobs" and did not give them, and the only mention of anal sex (after the first) referred to the encounter for which he was arrested. Clark's account thus ignored conflicting evidence about Boutilier's sexual history and created the impression that Boutilier had become an active homosexual before he entered the United States and remained one after entry.[21]

Clark also suggested that after engaging in a mix of heterosexual and homosexual sex in Canada, Boutilier had been exclusively homosexual in the United States. In fact, Boutilier's 1964 affidavit indicated that he had engaged in "sexual relations with a woman" three or four times in Canada, but he was not asked about post-entry heterosexual activities. The only other case file document that referred to Boutilier's heterosexual conduct was the psychiatric report by Ullman, which used an ambiguous tense in claiming that Boutilier "has had sexual interest in girls and has had intercourse with them." Ullman's letter stated that Boutilier "moves from homosexual to heterosexual interests as well as abstinence with almost equal facility."

Clark's summary proceeded to suggest that after engaging in anonymous public sex in Canada, Boutilier began to have cohabitational sex in the United States. Clark did not say that Boutilier stopped having anonymous public sex, but by identifying 1959 as the year of his arrest and the beginning of his cohabiting relationship with a man identified in the 1964 affidavit as Eugene

O'Rourke, he implied that Boutilier's conduct had changed in this way. This impression was supported by additional evidence in the 1964 affidavit, which referred to two anonymous sexual encounters in a Halifax public park; sex in 1959 in an undisclosed New York location with the seventeen-year-old, whose name Boutilier claimed not to know; sex two to three times a year with O'Rourke beginning in 1959; and one additional 1963 sexual encounter in the apartment of another man whose name he claimed not to know. To the extent that Boutilier stated that he consistently had same-sex sex three to four times a year, the affidavit suggested something not mentioned by Clark: that Boutilier and O'Rourke were cohabitants who occasionally, but not exclusively, had sex with each other. Clark also did not mention related information supplied by Ullman: that Boutilier had "abandoned all sexual practices within the past several months because of his annoyance and disgust with the problems these activities have brought about" and "moved back to living with his mother and stepfather."[22]

Having presented a selective account of Boutilier's sexual history, Clark explained that the 1964 affidavit was submitted to the PHS. Four days after Boutilier was questioned by INS investigator James Sarsfield, PHS senior surgeon Paul G. Smith and PHS medical director Maria Sarrigiannis certified that Boutilier was "afflicted with a class A condition, namely, psychopathic personality, sexual deviate" at time of admission to the United States. On this basis, the INS began deportation proceedings. Boutilier's initial appeal was heard by Special Inquiry Officer Ira Fieldsteel, who ordered Boutilier's deportation in 1965. According to Clark, the officer found that "no serious question . . . has been raised either by the respondent [petitioner here], his counsel or the psychiatrists [employed by petitioner] . . . as to his sexual deviation."[23]

Fieldsteel and Clark may not have regarded them as serious, but Boutilier's supporters had raised questions about how to classify Boutilier's behavior and character and whether "sexual deviation" was the appropriate term. Boutilier's lawyer Blanch Freedman, in her appearance before Fieldsteel, seemed at one point to accept the claim that Boutilier was "a sexual deviate" and noted that "in this case sexual deviation is homosexuality." But the letters from Edward Falsey and Montague Ullman, Boutilier's two psychiatrists, did not use the term "sexual deviation"; Freedman modified her language in later proceedings; and Boutilier never referred to "sexual deviation." Clark also stated that Fieldsteel "found that both of petitioner's psychiatrists 'concede that the respondent has been a homosexual for a number of years but conclude that by reason of such sexual deviation the respondent is not a psychopathic personality.'" Here, too, Fieldsteel misrepresented what Boutilier's psychiatrists said and Clark repeated the mischaracterization. Neither psychiatrist used the term "sexual deviation." Falsey wrote that Boutilier "explained quite frankly that he has been homosexual," but the psychiatrist neither endorsed nor rejected this self-description and he did not say that Boutilier has been "a" homosexual or that Boutilier "is" homosexual. Ullman referred to Boutilier's homosexual "contacts," "relationships," "interests," and "orientation," but never labeled him "a homosexual." This was a meaningful distinction insofar as Kinsey and other sexologists had argued that the term "homosexual" should be used for behaviors rather than persons. Boutilier's advocates emphasized this point, and his psychiatrists carefully avoided suggesting otherwise.[24]

Clark concluded his review of the case history by noting that "the issue before the officer was reduced to the purely legal question of whether the term 'psychopathic personality' included homosexuals" and whether it was illegal "because of vagueness." This formulation, which dismissed a set of other issues discussed in chapter 5, was the organizing principle for the remainder of the opinion, which took up each of these two issues.[25]

Clark's second section focused on the legislative intent of Congress in 1952 and the applicability of the statute to "homosexuals." When the meaning of statutory language is in question, the Court often refers to legislative intent, despite the difficulties associated with this mode of reasoning. Sometimes the justices have assessed intent on the basis of evidence about the goals of a statute's author or a committee that developed the legislation, even though Congress might have voted for passage and the president might have signed the bill for different reasons. In addition, legislation originating in one session is sometimes passed after an election, meaning that legislators who expressed their intentions in discussing the bill are not necessarily serving when it passes, and new legislators have not necessarily expressed their intentions. For legislation vetoed by the president and passed through a two-thirds vote of the House and Senate, which was the case for the 1952 Immigration and Nationality Act, the intentions of super-majorities become relevant. Moreover, later congresses sometimes retain old legislation for new reasons. Legislation also typically incorporates both substantive intentions related to goals and procedural intentions related to implementation. Sometimes substantive and procedural intentions work at cross-purposes, raising questions about how to choose between them.

Clark concentrated on the substantive intentions of the committees that proposed the statute, ignoring the procedural intentions of the committees and the substantive and procedural intentions of Congress as a whole. While claiming to discuss the intentions of Congress, Clark only provided evidence of committee intentions, and he only considered substantive intentions about the exclusion of homosexuals, not procedural intentions about who was to evaluate aliens and how they were to do so. Clark's conclusion that Congress intended to exclude "homosexuals" may have been reasonable, but one of the questions raised by Boutilier's defenders was whether Congress meant to exclude everyone who had ever engaged in same-sex sex. There were contexts, including the military, in which policymakers made such distinctions, and immigration officials sometimes did so as well, which the government's lawyer acknowledged in the oral arguments (as is discussed below). Boutilier's advocates also emphasized that the procedural intent was to have PHS doctors conduct examinations to determine whether individual aliens were afflicted with psychopathic personality, which had not been done in Boutilier's case.[26]

Clark began this section by declaring, "The legislative history of the Act indicates beyond a shadow of a doubt that the Congress intended the phrase 'psychopathic personality' to include homosexuals such as petitioner." According to Clark, in 1950 a Senate Judiciary subcommittee concluded that "the purpose of the provision against 'persons with constitutional psychopathic inferiority' will be more adequately served by changing that term to 'persons afflicted with psychopathic personality'" and "the classes of mental defectives should be enlarged to include homosexuals and other sex perverts." What Clark characterized as "the resulting legislation" included one clause referring to "psychopathic personality" and another referring to "homosexuals or sex perverts." Clark did not comment on the dropping of the word "other" and the resulting difference between the report's language, which suggested that homosexuals *were* perverts, and the proposed legislative language, which did not. But he did note that in a new congressional session, the "homosexuals and sex perverts" clause was eliminated, which he explained with an excerpt of the Senate Judiciary Committee report on the new bill: "The Public Health Service has advised that the provision for the exclusion of aliens afflicted with psychopathic personality or a mental defect which appears in the instant bill is sufficiently broad to provide for the exclusion of homosexuals and sex perverts. *This change of nomenclature is not to be construed in any way as modifying the intent to exclude all aliens who are sexual deviates.*" Here Clark presented solid evidence that the committee's intent was to exclude sexual deviates, but he did not address whether or how the PHS or the Senate committee distinguished between homosexuals, sex perverts, and sexual deviates. Nor did he address whether the legislators who voted for the psychopathic personality provision understood it to apply to homosexuals.[27]

Clark then examined the intentions of the House in 1952, though his evidence derived exclusively from a 1952 House Judiciary Committee report. According to Clark, the report demonstrated that the committee accepted the PHS recommendation "that 'psychopathic personality' should be used . . . as a phrase that would exclude from admission homosexuals and sex perverts." He also wrote that the committee adopted the PHS's 1951 report, which "recommended that the term 'psychopathic personality' be used to 'specify such types of pathologic behavior as homosexuality or sexual perversion.'" On the basis of this and the Senate evidence, Clark declared, "We, therefore, conclude that the Congress used the phrase 'psychopathic personality' not in the clinical sense, but to effectuate its purpose to exclude from entry all homosexuals and other sex perverts." The PHS again seemed to distinguish between homosexuals and perverts, but Clark's conclusion (by inserting the word "other") subsumed the former under the latter. Moreover, while Clark suggested that the committees had been influenced by the medical perspectives of the PHS and had adopted a medical term, he insisted that Congress had not used "psychopathic personality" in a "clinical" sense but simply wanted to exclude "homosexuals and other sex perverts." The significance of this became clear later, but here he emphasized that Congress intended to exclude all homosexuals.[28]

What did the PHS report say? In a section on "psychopathic personality," the PHS noted:

> Although the term "psychopathic personality," used in classifying certain types of mental disorders, is vague and indefinite, no more appropriate expression can be suggested at this time. The conditions classified within the group of psychopathic personalities are, in effect, disorders of the personality. They are characterized by developmental defects or pathological trends in the personality structure manifest by lifelong patterns of action or behavior, rather than by mental or emotional symptoms. Individuals with such a disorder may manifest a disturbance of intrinsic personality patterns, exaggerated personality trends, or are persons ill primarily in terms of society and the prevailing culture. The latter or sociopathic reactions are frequently symptomatic of a severe underlying neurosis or psychosis and frequently include those groups of individuals suffering from addiction or sexual deviation. Until a more definitive expression can be devised, the term "psychopathic personality" should be retained.

Clark did not mention that the PHS acknowledged that the phrase "psychopathic personality" was "vague," as this would have supported the vagueness argument. The opinion also did not excerpt the passage referring to "persons ill primarily in terms of society and the prevailing culture," which was an unusually transparent acknowledgement of the normalizing functions of psychological and psychiatric classifications. Nor did he refer to what Kaufman acknowledged in a footnote: "Dr. Paul G. Smith who signed the certification of Boutilier's condition as a 'psychopathic personality' testified [in another case] that modern psychiatric theory does not espouse the proposition that a sexual deviate is *ipso facto* a constitutional psychopathic inferior or a psychopathic personality." What Clark instead found useful was the PHS's link between "psychopathic personality" and "sexual deviation," even though this passage did not refer explicitly to homosexuality and did not classify all sexual deviates as psychopaths.[29]

The other relevant portion of the PHS report came under the heading "Sexual perverts":

> The language of the bill lists sexual perverts or homosexual persons as among those aliens to be excluded from admission to the United States. In some instances considerable difficulty may be encountered in substantiating a diagnosis of homosexuality or sexual perversion. In other instances where the action and behavior of the person is more obvious, as might be noted in the manner of dress (so-called transvestism or fetishism), the condition may be more easily substantiated. Ordinarily, a history of homosexuality must be obtained from the individual, which he may successfully cover up. Some psychological tests may be helpful in uncovering homosexuality of which the individual, himself, may be unaware. At the present time there are no reliable laboratory tests which would be helpful in making a diagnosis. The detection of persons with more obvious sexual perversion is relatively simple. Considerably more difficulty may be encountered in uncovering the homosexual person. Ordinarily, persons suffering from disturbances in sexuality are included within the classification of "psychopathic personality with pathologic sexuality." This classification will specify such types of pathologic behavior as homosexuality or sexual perversion which includes sexual sadism, fetishism, transvestism, pedophilia, etc.

This was the passage to which Clark was referring when he argued that Congress accepted the PHS recommendation to delete the explicit reference to "homosexuals and sex perverts" because they would be covered under the "psychopathic personality" exclusion. But did the material that followed the heading "Sexual perverts" intend to distinguish between sexual perverts and homosexuals or discuss them as equivalent? The PHS may have been using the terms interchangeably, but some of the language suggests that the PHS conceptualized sexual perversion and homosexuality as distinct. Nor did this passage make clear that all perverts and homosexuals were "psychopathic." Notwithstanding these ambiguities, the Court's decision was based on the conviction that the PHS meaning was clear, that the committees understood this meaning, and that the intentions of Congress were discernable.[30]

Having presented the majority's conclusion about the legislative intent to exclude all homosexuals, Clark proceeded to argue that Boutilier was a homosexual. According to Clark, "Petitioner stresses that only persons *afflicted* with psychopathic personality are excludable" and "this, he says, is 'a condition, physical or psychiatric, which may be manifested in different ways, including sexual behavior.'" In response, Clark stated that "petitioner's contention must fall by his own admissions." The key evidence was that "for over six years prior to his entry petitioner admittedly followed a continued course of homosexual conduct." On this basis, the PHS certified Boutilier as afflicted with psychopathic personality. Moreover, "petitioner admitted being a homosexual at the time of his entry." Clark concluded, "The existence of this condition over a continuous and uninterrupted period prior to and at the time of petitioner's entry clearly supports the ultimate finding."[31]

In this paragraph, Clark took Boutilier's lawyers' words out of context and reversed their analysis of the relationship between conduct and character. Boutilier's lawyers had written that "being 'afflicted' can relate only to a condition, physical or psychiatric, which may be manifested in different ways, including sexual behavior." Their next sentence, however, reads, "But it necessarily implies a condition that is medically ascertained—not by a rubber-stamp certification as was done here, but by a professional examination."[32] Clark addressed this issue at the end of his opinion, but here he used the lawyers' words to argue that "conduct" proved "condition," when they had indicated that a "condition" might be manifest in "conduct." While the lawyers' formulation was based on the notion that a person afflicted with psychopathic personality might engage in certain types of sexual conduct, Clark argued as though they had acknowledged that certain types of sexual conduct constituted proof of affliction with psychopathic personality.

Clark's depiction of Boutilier's sexual conduct was also meaningful in this context. In his 1964 affidavit, Boutilier had said that after having same-sex sex in a Halifax public park at about age sixteen, he had same-sex sex in Nova Scotia over "the next six or seven years," before entering the United States. Boutilier's account, however, contained chronological contradictions: born in September 1933, Boutilier was sixteen years old in 1949–50 and he entered the United States in June 1955 at age twenty-one, five years after the first Halifax episode. In oral arguments, Freedman tried to correct the mistake, noting that "actually it was only five years." Clark's claim that Boutilier "followed a continued course of homosexual conduct" for "over six years" prior to entry was in accordance with the details of Boutilier's sexual history only if Clark was including his "passive" experience at age fourteen. As for the reference to the existence of Boutilier's condition over a "continuous and uninterrupted" period prior to entry, Clark conveyed the sense that Boutilier had been "a homosexual" no matter the activities in which he was engaged: at work, at play, while having heterosexual sex, and at the moment he crossed the border. Immutability was a defining feature of the homosexual condition conceptualized in this passage.[33]

Had Boutilier admitted that he was "a homosexual at the time of his entry"? In his 1964 interrogation, Boutilier was asked detailed questions about his sexual activities in Canada and the United States, but not about whether he had been "a homosexual" when he entered the United States. The closest he came to using such language came toward the end of the interview, when Sarsfield asked why he had been classified 4-F by the Selective Service in 1957. The transcript indicates that Boutilier replied "I'm homosexual." If this was recorded accurately, Boutilier used "homosexual" as an adjective, not a noun, but Sarsfield immediately modified the construction, asking "Did they just accept your statement that you're a homosexual?" Boutilier responded, "After filling out the forms and asking the questions I was sent to see a psychiatrist and as a result I'm classified 4-F." Sarsfield asked, "You mean one of the questions on the form asks whether or not you are a homosexual and you answered Yes?" Boutilier responded, "Yes." At most, Boutilier had affirmed that he was "a homosexual" in 1957, two years after he entered the United States and in the context of a legal obligation to register for military service. He was interrogated in 1964, when the United States was escalating its involvement in the Vietnam War.[34] Yet according to Clark, Boutilier "admitted being a homosexual at the time of entry."

Having disposed of the questions of whether Congress intended to exclude all homosexuals and whether Boutilier was a homosexual, Clark turned in his third and final section to the issue of vagueness. According to Clark, Boutilier claimed that the statute "did not adequately warn him that his sexual affliction at the time of entry could lead to his deportation." Actually, Boutilier's lawyers had argued that the statute, because it used the phrase "afflicted with psychopathic personality," did not warn him that homosexual conduct in the United States could lead to deportation. But after mischaracterizing the argument, Clark nevertheless responded that the statutory exclusion "never applied to petitioner's conduct after entry" and "imposes neither regulation of nor sanction for conduct." He continued, "The petitioner is not being deported for conduct engaged in after his entry into the United States, but rather for characteristics he possessed *at the time of* his entry. Here, when petitioner first presented himself at our border for entrance, he was already afflicted with homosexuality. The pattern was cut, and under it he was not admissible." The issue of vagueness thus turned on the question of whether homosexuality should be conceptualized as condition or conduct. Favoring the former, Clark treated homosexuality as if it were a defining feature of individual identity, an innate and immutable essence of the self. Rejecting the latter, he did not acknowledge that nonhomosexuals might engage in homosexual acts or that sexual identities and acts might not correspond in expected ways. The government's lawyers had acknowledged that nonhomosexuals might engage in homosexual acts, writing in one of their briefs, "There may indeed be cases where it is difficult to determine whether—and in precisely what sense—an individual should be deemed homosexual within the intent of the statute. Such might be the case of an individual who had had only a few, isolated homosexual experiences and did not regard himself as homosexual." For the justices in the majority, however, sexuality functioned like a pattern for making clothing: once the fabric was cut, no major alterations were possible.[35]

The issue of vagueness also turned on the question of whether homosexuality should be conceptualized as a medical or legal category, and now the significance of Clark's earlier rejection of the notion that Congress used "psychopathic personality" in "a clinical sense" became clear. According to Clark, "It may be, as some claim, that 'psychopathic personality' is a medically ambiguous term. . . . But the test here is what the Congress intended, not what differing psychiatrists may think. It was not laying down a clinical test, but an exclusionary standard which it declared to be inclusive of those having homosexual and perverted characteristics." This also made clear the significance of Clark's earlier focus on substantive rather than procedural intent, since it provided him with a way to emphasize the congressional intent to exclude homosexuals and ignore the intent to have PHS medical experts make the determinations.[36] In effect, the Court was affirming the supremacy of the state over science, acknowledging that legislators may have used psychiatric language and given medical doctors a role to play in policy administration, but concluding that medical doctors employed by the state must defer to political decisions. Clark's final paragraph offered two additional reasons to reject the claim that Boutilier was "entitled to medical examination." According to Clark, "Since he is not an 'arriving alien' subject to exclusion, but a deportable alien within an excludable class—who through error was permitted entry—it is doubtful if the requirement would apply. But we need not go into the question since petitioner was twice offered examination and refused to submit himself. He can hardly be heard to complain now. The remaining contentions are likewise without merit."[37]

In short, once a homosexual, always a psychopath, no matter what a medical expert might say. Before addressing the issue of the medical examination, Clark explained, "We do not believe that petitioner's post-entry conduct is the basis for his deportation order. . . . We find no indication that the post-entry evidence was of any consequence in the ultimate decision of the doctors, the hearing officer or the court. Indeed, the proof was uncontradicted as to petitioner's characteristic at the time of entry and this brought him within the excludable class. A standard applicable solely to time of entry could hardly be vague as to post-entry conduct." Three drafts of Clark's opinion, the first of which has been attributed to a clerk, reveal significant modifications in the passages that dealt with post-entry evidence. The second draft, for example, included a line indicating that Boutilier's "last [homosexual] act was some four months prior to the [1964] statement." On the third draft, this line was crossed out, with an explanatory handwritten note in the margins: "Since we are deporting for *pre*-entry conduct and the dissent will say it's really *post*, perhaps this should be left out!" Similarly, the second draft stated that Boutilier admitted he was a homosexual "prior to entry as well as subsequently," but in the third draft this was crossed out and a handwritten comment noted, "We just set out his admission and I think should refer to *post*-entry conduct as little as possible." The third draft deleted six other references to Boutilier's post-entry homosexual conduct but added a new sentence: "The petitioner is not being deported for conduct engaged in after his entry into the United States, but rather for characteristics he possessed *at the time of* his entry." Another sentence in the second draft, which denied that post-entry conduct "played any part" in the deportation order, was modified in the third to deny that post-entry conduct was "the basis" for deportation. Two other sentences in the second draft were deleted in the third: "Certainly his conduct during the four years between these entries was probative of his characteristics at the time of his second entry. The evidence of subsequent years was merely cumulative having to do with homosexual activity with his male roommate in an apartment." The successive drafts clarified Clark's reasoning, but they also covered up the extent to which the deportation was based on post-entry evidence.[38]

If the post-entry evidence was of no consequence, why did the PHS, the special inquiry officer, and the Second Circuit majority devote so much attention to Boutilier's post-entry history? Moreover, had Boutilier not been arrested for post-entry conduct and not volunteered information about post-entry conduct, how would his characteristics at time of entry have come to the attention of the INS? For the majority, the post-entry evidence was relevant not because of what it indicated about Boutilier's U.S. life, but because of what it revealed about his character when he crossed the border. From this perspective, post-entry conduct merely confirmed pre-entry character since homosexuality was an immutable condition.

In her insightful discussion of immigration cases in the period leading up to and including *Boutilier*, Canaday describes the "emancipatory" and "repressive" effects of legal conceptions of homosexuality as an immutable condition. According to Canaday, "Asserting that homosexuals were defined by legal-political rather than medical categories . . . gave the state a way to win these cases, but . . . licensed a concept of the homosexual individual as potential citizen. And as much as the courts' rulings during these years envisaged the homosexual as a kind of anti-citizen, some who found themselves defined by the law as homosexual (as well as the lawyers and jurists who supported them) would redeploy these concepts." Canaday concludes, "The courts, the Congress, and the INS probably had little idea that they were lending authority to a burgeoning gay rights movement that continues to this day to base its claims on a legal-political conception of homosexuals as potentially good citizens. But at the same time, gay rights movements cannot themselves escape the ambivalent legacy of fixing homosexuality as identity and thereby surrendering themselves to regulation by state authority." Chapter 5 discusses this in relation to the homophile movement, but here it is worth noting that the Court first wrote about homosexuals in these ways in obscenity cases. In *Manual* (1962), Harlan and Clark referred to "homosexuals." In *Mishkin* (1966), Brennan referred to homosexuals as "a clearly defined deviant sexual group." The Court's template for conceptualizing homosexuals as a "legal-political" group did not position homosexual aliens as potential citizens but imagined homosexual citizens as potential audiences for obscenity.[39]

The Court's template for conceptualizing homosexuals in legal-political terms was also racialized. According to Clark's *Boutilier* opinion, "It has long been held that the Congress has plenary power to make rules for the admission of aliens and to exclude those who possess those characteristics which

Congress has forbidden. See The Chinese Exclusion Case." After citing *Chae Chan Ping*, an 1889 decision that upheld the Chinese Exclusion Act, Clark continued, "Here Congress commanded that homosexuals not be allowed to enter. The petitioner was found to have that characteristic and was ordered deported." In short, homosexual aliens were akin to Chinese aliens insofar as both were defined by characteristics rather than conduct. If Congress could exclude Chinese aliens, it could exclude homosexual aliens. The timing of Clark's invocation of *Chae Chan Ping* is striking. Congress had repealed the Chinese Exclusion Act in 1943 and abandoned the national origins immigration system in 1965, yet in 1967 six justices affirmed in *Boutilier* that Congress retained the power to exclude immigrants on the basis of characteristics including race and sexual orientation. The timing is also striking because by this time the Court regarded laws that classified U.S. citizens on the basis of race as "suspect," which meant they were subject to "strict scrutiny." *Boutilier*, however, did not concern the rights of a citizen, and while the Court found it helpful to make an analogy between a group defined by racial characteristics and a group defined by sexual ones, it distinguished between forms of discrimination that were subject to "strict scrutiny" and forms that were not.[40] If the Court helped construct the homosexual as a potential citizen, it paradoxically did so while simultaneously constructing the homosexual as an excludable and deportable alien.

On the most basic level, *Boutilier* declared to "homosexual" aliens and other aliens who had engaged in same-sex sex that they were not eligible for U.S. citizenship and were not welcome on U.S. land. For these people, the denial of U.S. citizenship was potentially or effectively literal. *Boutilier* also delivered powerful messages to U.S. citizens. The Court had previously announced in *Griswold* that marriage conferred special privacy rights on U.S. Americans and in *Fanny Hill* that community-based majorities had special privileges in relation to sexual speech. Soon the Court would declare in *Loving*, *Eisenstadt*, and *Roe* that some citizens could claim other special marital and reproductive rights. Having referred to the constitutionality of laws against homosexual conduct and having imposed discriminatory restrictions on homosexual speech, the Court now declared in *Boutilier* that homosexuals could be defined by the state as a class of individuals afflicted with psychopathic personalities. If the state could do this, what was to prevent it from doing anything that was viewed as "legitimate" state action in relation to psychopaths, including disfranchisement and institutionalization? And if the state could define consensual sexual activities as psychopathological, what was to prevent it from doing the same with heterosexual forms of adultery, cohabitation, fornication, and sodomy?

Along similar lines, what was to prevent the state from taking activities classifiable as "private" (and therefore protected) and conceptualizing them as "secret" (and therefore unprotected)? In contrast to the dissents and the arguments of Boutilier's advocates, Clark's opinion did not once use the terms "private" or "privacy" in relation to Boutilier's conduct. There are several possible reasons for this: Boutilier (in this case) was not charged with a crime related to private conduct; the *Griswold* opinions suggested that homosexuality was not protected by the right of privacy; and excludable aliens did not have recognized privacy rights. There were moments, however, when Boutilier's opponents invoked the closely related concept of secrecy, a major preoccupation of Cold War U.S. culture. The 1951 PHS report expressed concern about the "considerable difficulty" that "may be encountered in substantiating a diagnosis of homosexuality," but worried less about "other instances where the action and behavior of the person is more obvious, as might be noted in the manner of dress." According to the PHS, "ordinarily, a history of homosexuality must be obtained from the individual" because the individual could "cover up" his affliction. Moreover, in some cases homosexuality was so secretive that even the individual himself could be "unaware" of it. The PHS observed that "the detection of persons with more obvious sexual perversion is relatively simple," but "more difficulty may be encountered in uncovering the homosexual person." Kaufman, when defending Boutilier's "delayed exclusion," expressed similar concerns when he wrote that "without the provision, an imprimatur would be placed on deception of immigration officials at time of entry." One of the government's briefs for the Supreme Court also dealt with this issue, declaring that "the vagueness doctrine is not a device to enable an individual afflicted with a condition that if discovered would have barred his admission to this country so to conduct himself as to avoid making his condition known to the administrative authorities." In short, what might otherwise be called homosexual "privacy" was thought to be dangerous insofar as it might allow deceptively respectable homosexuals to enter the country. This suggests one possible way of thinking about court rulings and legal arguments that conceptualized privacy and homosexuality as mutually exclusive: privacy was a positive public good when claimed by married heterosexual citizens, but a negative, secret evil when used by homosexuals. Homosexual aliens were not just excluded from the privileges of privacy; they were subject to the demands of compulsory publicity.[41]

Boutilier sent a meaningful message to U.S. citizens that the homosexuals among them were only entitled to claim rights of second-class citizenship because they had been born in the United States or had been naturalized under false pretenses. Homosexual citizens were far from alone in receiving this type of message, as many members of ethnic and racial minorities, poor people, people with disabilities, and people with physical or mental illnesses knew the same was true for them. For these groups, citizenship in all of its political, social, and sexual dimensions was far less secure than it was for those in the dominant culture who would have been welcomed as first-class U.S. citizens had they not been born in the United States.

Inside the Court

The 6–3 decision against Boutilier appeared to represent the views of a solid majority of the justices, but the Court very nearly decided the other way. According to notes in the justices' papers, when the justices met to cast their preliminary votes, Warren sided with Boutilier. Black indicated that he was inclined to vote against Boutilier but would change sides if the majority voted the other way. After Douglas, Brennan, and Fortas spoke in favor of Boutilier and the other justices against him, it became clear that Boutilier had fallen one vote short. As the senior justice in the majority, Black assigned Clark to write the opinion. Warren, who disliked 5–4 decisions because he thought they weakened the Court's authority, later changed his vote, resulting in the 6–3 ruling. Boutilier lost three justices who voted liberal in *Griswold* and conservative in *Fanny Hill* (Clark, Harlan, and White), two who voted conservative in *Griswold* and liberal in *Fanny Hill* (Black and Stewart), and one who voted liberal in both *Griswold* and *Fanny Hill* (Warren).[42]

Given their earlier votes in cases dealing with sexual matters, Clark's and White's *Boutilier* votes are not surprising. Both had endorsed heteronormative reasoning in *Griswold*; voted against obscenity in the trio of 1966 cases; and favored the deportation of Fleuti in *Rosenberg*. In *Rosenberg*, the Court initially voted 5–4 against Fleuti, and as the senior justice in the majority, Clark assigned Goldberg to write the opinion. But after Goldberg changed his vote, Clark wrote a forceful dissent. Black likely tapped Clark to write the *Boutilier* opinion because Clark's earlier position now had majority support.[43]

Harlan's vote is also not surprising. Harlan had voted with the more liberal justices in *Ginzburg*, but with the more conservative ones in *Rosenberg*, *Fanny Hill*, and *Mishkin*. Harlan's obscenity votes reflected his distinctive conclusion that the Constitution constrained federal censorship more than state censorship. His vote against Boutilier was consistent with his vote in *Rosenberg* and his comments in *Griswold* about the constitutionality of laws against homosexuality.

Stewart, Black, and Warren were the swing votes in *Boutilier*, as they were in many rulings on sexual matters. Stewart voted with the more conservative justices in *Griswold*, but later accepted it as a legitimate precedent. He tended toward the free-speech side in obscenity cases, but voted against Fleuti in *Rosenberg*. Stewart was among the most active justices during the *Boutilier* oral arguments, and some who witnessed them thought he might vote against the INS. In one exchange with Boutilier's lawyer Blanch Freedman, Stewart said he thought her position was that the word "homosexual" was "an adjective and not a noun" and that "there is no issue in this case as to his having engaged in some homosexual acts" but "it doesn't necessarily follow that he . . . falls under that admission." Later Stewart asked Freedman a question more sympathetic to the government's position. After confirming that homosexual acts were criminal in New York, Stewart asked, "There is no reason to suppose that the criminal law is any less a deterrent, is there, than the threat of deportation?" Stewart was challenging Freedman's argument that Boutilier, with fair warning, could and would have refrained from homosexual activities.

Stewart's questions for Nathan Lewin, the government's attorney, seemed sympathetic to Boutilier. Challenging Lewin's characterization of the appeal, Stewart asserted that Boutilier's claim was not only that the statutory phrase "afflicted with psychopathic personality" was "not sufficiently specific": "It's that it's not sufficiently accurate. It doesn't say what you say Congress intended to say." Later, when Lewin claimed that "it wasn't even contested as to whether he really was a 'homosexual' to the extent that that word has meaning," Stewart responded, "To the extent that that word may have meaning, but may have no meaning. He'd engaged in heterosexual acts and he'd engaged in homosexual acts, both." In another exchange, Stewart asked whether the "sexual deviation" language of the 1965 immigration statute referred to a condition or to conduct. Lewin responded, "We think it refers to a condition." Stewart interrupted: "It could be read either way." Lewin replied, "Well, it does say afflicted. . . . One can hardly be afflicted by what he'd done in the past." Stewart replied, "It's rather an odd meaning."

Stewart also pressed Lewin on whether the INS ever used the "psychopathic personality" exclusion in nonhomosexual cases. Lewin replied in the affirmative, but later Stewart asked, "What other people have ever been excluded under this?" When Lewin admitted he did not know, Stewart continued: "Isn't it only homosexuals and people who have engaged in homosexual conduct?" After Lewin said again that he did not know, Stewart said,

"Is it your position that this is a code word meaning people who have engaged in homosexual conduct or is this a broad and definable class within which fall such people." Lewin responded, "We think it's a broad and definable class." Stewart continued, "Yes, but then if we find that only people who have engaged in homosexual conduct have been excluded, then it isn't a broad class." Hedging his bets, Lewin replied that "they may have been the only ones who were, in fact, excluded or deported," but then referred to the PHS manual's broad definition of psychopathic personality: "'These disorders are categorized by developmental defects or pathological trends in a personality structure with minimal subjective anxiety and little or no distress.'" Here Stewart could not resist, repeating back the last several words and declaring, "I should think that should cover about everybody. You as well." As laughter broke out, Lewin replied, "Well, that's all, of course, qualified by the introductory clause." Stewart continued: "There is a suggestion in the brief . . . that . . . it's only such people as this petitioner . . . who actually have been deported under this statutory language. And you can't tell me?" Lewin admitted, "I can't tell you. But I will supply an answer. I will find that out." Stewart replied, "I would be very interested."[44]

On 15 March, one day after the oral arguments, Marshall sent a letter to the Court with a copy of a memorandum by INS general counsel Charles Gordon, who explained that "our records do not include any breakdown." Gordon had made "informal inquiries" of the New York and Detroit offices of the INS and was told that "the 'psychopathic personality' charge has been used in situations other than those involving sexual perversion, but there is no information readily available as to the proportion of such cases." He continued, "Our general impression is that sexual perversion is the critical consideration in the preponderance of cases where the 'psychopathic personality' charge has been used," but he also mentioned a 1965 case involving "paranoid personality." Gordon also referred to a PHS manual that listed multiple conditions classifiable as psychopathic personality. Then he indicated that according to PHS figures on visa refusals in consular offices overseas, in fiscal year 1965 there were thirty-one psychopathic personality certifications. In the thirteen months after the effective date of the 1965 legislation there were seven certifications for sexual deviation and twenty-five for other types of psychopathic personality. Gordon also mentioned that from 1 March 1966 to 1 March 1967 the New York PHS office "issued 19 certifications for sexual deviation, 25 for schizoid personality and 7 for other categories under the 'psychopathic personality' classification." Nearly all of this information referred to the post-1965 era, so Stewart's question went unanswered. Nevertheless, Douglas's conference notes for Stewart read, "Insufficient notice for criminal stat—but notice is not important here, Congress intended to bar homos."[45]

Clark, White, Harlan, and Stewart had voted to uphold the psychopathic personality statute in *Rosenberg*, so their *Boutilier* votes were consistent with their earlier position. In contrast, Black and Warren had indicated when the justices met to discuss *Rosenberg* that they would affirm the Ninth Circuit's holding that the statute was unconstitutionally vague. According to Douglas's conference notes for *Rosenberg*, Warren was "not too sure" but "psychopathic personality means little, according to many doctors." As for Black, he stated that "due process and equal protection protects aliens as well as citizens, deportation is a penalty and this should be treated as a criminal law is treated, too vague." Later, after Goldberg switched sides in *Rosenberg*, Black and Warren joined his majority ruling, which focused on the technical issue of Fleuti's entry date. Four years later, Fortas had replaced Goldberg, which meant that if Fortas joined the four justices who had been willing to strike down the psychopathic personality statute in *Rosenberg*, that position would command a majority. Fortas did take that position, but Black and Warren now abandoned their earlier stance.[46]

Black had voted with his more conservative brethren in *Griswold*, but with his more liberal colleagues in *Rosenberg* and the trio of 1966 obscenity cases. According to Douglas's conference notes for *Boutilier*, Black concluded: "stat can be construed either way—psychopathic personality means sexual deviate—if majority think homos are not included, he'll not dissent—but he votes to affirm." Fortas's notes for Black read, "'Psychopathic personality' means precisely sexual deviation. May not dissent if Court goes other way."[47]

Warren sided with his more sexually liberal brethren in *Griswold*, *Fanny Hill*, and *Rosenberg* but with the more conservative justices in *Ginzburg* and *Mishkin*. Journalists Joyce Murdoch and Deb Price claim that "the fact that Chief Justice Warren didn't assign any of the three opinions written in homosexual cases during his tenure is an indication of how little a role he played in shaping the court's posture toward homosexuality." Warren may have not assigned these opinions, but this does not mean he did not play a key role. He was the only justice who voted with the majority in *Griswold*, *Fanny Hill*, *Ginzburg*, *Mishkin*, and *Boutilier*. Given Black's offer to switch positions, Warren's vote was significant in *Boutilier*.[48]

Not much is known about the development of Warren's thinking about *Boutilier*. One clerk had encouraged the chief justice to accept *Boutilier* for argument, emphasizing that "the statutory language afforded no warning and is, therefore, unconstitutionally vague." Later, the same clerk wrote, "The administrative determination of deportability seemed to be based quite substantially on petr's post-entry conduct. In that posture, an adequate warning that sanctions might flow from certain conduct was necessary. And the use of the term 'psychopathic personality' did not afford such a warning inasmuch as the only expert testimony was to the effect that (1) the term did not necessarily encompass homosexuality and (2) petr in particular was not a psychopath." According to Brennan's notes, Warren voted to "reverse on statutory meaning and not on vagueness." Douglas's notes on Warren read, "Reverses — does not rest on vagueness — Congress spoke meaningfully but in a medical sense — a homo might or might not be psychotic — very little of the conduct antedated his entry." This was in March, but after Clark began circulating drafts of his opinion in April and one day after Douglas circulated the first draft of his dissent, Warren switched his vote. Warren may have been convinced by Clark's opinion. He may have switched sides because he disliked 5–4 rulings. He may have been troubled by the dissent. And he may have been influenced by the heteronormative reasoning of *Griswold*, *Fanny Hill*, *Ginzburg*, and *Mishkin*.[49]

Dissents

Brennan, Douglas, and Fortas dissented in *Boutilier*, but in other cases they helped develop the Court's heteronormative doctrine. The *Boutilier* dissents thus can help clarify the meaning of the heteronormative decisions. As it turns out, the dissents, while supporting Boutilier's appeal, contained profoundly antigay rhetoric and reasoning. In this respect, Brennan, Douglas, and Fortas contributed to the attitudes that produced the *Boutilier* ruling. Boutilier won their votes, but the contents of their dissents suggest that the Court's antigay consensus was unanimous.

Four years before *Boutilier*, Brennan played an important role in revising Goldberg's draft opinion in *Rosenberg*. According to Douglas's *Rosenberg* conference notes, Goldberg initially took the position, "He's more than a homosexual — he has such a dominant sex drive that he performed publicly — he was a psychopath in the conventional sense — relies on Natl/Immig statute as applied." After Goldberg changed his mind, he drafted an opinion that ruled in favor of Fleuti but noted, "Congress unquestionably has the power to exclude homosexuals and other undesirables from this country." Brennan, in a flattering letter that referred to Goldberg's "splendid job," suggested that he "delete the words 'homosexuals and other.'" "Congress unquestionably has the power to exclude undesirable aliens," Brennan wrote, "but I think it may be, at least medically, a matter of doubt whether homosexuals necessarily fall into the category of undesirable aliens. In any event, I'd rather not put us on record as deciding that." Goldberg accepted the suggestion. The justices who endorsed Goldberg's opinion thus avoided, for the time being, the question of whether homosexuals were undesirable aliens, though Brennan's intervention suggests he had doubts.[50]

Four years later, Brennan was in the minority in *Boutilier*. According to Douglas's conference notes, Brennan agreed with Warren before Warren changed his mind. Instead of signing Douglas's opinion, however, Brennan wrote separately in a one-line statement that he was dissenting "for the reasons stated by Judge Moore." This was more significant than it seemed; Brennan was expressing respect for the opinion of a lower court judge but distancing himself from a fellow justice's dissent. Moore had argued that "both the procedure and the statutory interpretation used by the immigration authorities . . . are not only offensive to, but, in my opinion, completely lacking in, due process." According to Moore, Boutilier's rights had been violated because he had not been examined by the PHS and "greater procedural safeguards are constitutionally required in cases of deportation than in cases of exclusion." Moreover, Moore could not "impute to Congress an intention . . . to cover anyone who had ever had a homosexual experience," given the large population this would cover and the fact that "so broad a definition might well comprise more than a few members of legislative bodies." At most, the intent was to exclude those "with a long-lasting and perhaps compulsive orientation towards homosexual or otherwise 'abnormal' behavior," and to have "skilled psychiatrists" make judgments on a case-by-case basis. Moore then stated that, if this was the intent, Boutilier "had no way of knowing that 'psychopathic personality' meant what Congress intended it to mean."[51]

Moore (and thus Brennan) sided with Boutilier, but his opinion contained elements with troubling implications for sexual equality. In several passages, Moore highlighted Boutilier's positive qualities, which challenged popular stereotypes but suggested that homosexuals without these attributes might not merit equal treatment. In his first sentence, Moore referred to the deportation of "a young man who . . . has worked hard and gainfully . . . , who is respected in his work, and most of whose close relatives . . . reside in this country." Later Moore argued that "the most adverse conclusion . . . is that petitioner engaged in sexual activity on a quite infrequent basis with both men and women" before entering the United States. Moore also wrote that his "sexual deviation" had not "put him in repeated conflict with the authorities" and "his homosexual activities before and after his entry into this country" were "consensual acts between adults, almost always in private places."

Moore proceeded to emphasize, "Had the petitioner known that sexual deviation at the time of entry would be automatic grounds for exclusion, there is considerable reason to believe that he could have modified his behavior so that he could not be considered a deviate at the time of entry. He was young, intelligent, and responsible." Then Moore quoted a passage from the letter by psychiatrist Ullman, who had written, "His sexual structure still appears fluid and immature so that he moves from homosexual to heterosexual interests as well as abstinence with almost equal facility. His homosexual orientation seems secondary to a very constricted, dependent personality pattern." In this passage, Ullman reproduced the stereotype of homosexuals as immature and dependent. In the end, Moore concluded that Boutilier was being deported for a condition "which he probably would have been able to correct had he had any reasonable warning." Moore appeared to accept the notion that homosexuality was in need of correction, and Brennan seemed to agree.[52]

In several passages, Moore was more direct about which types of homosexuals might be excludable. As mentioned above, his dissent indicated that the term "sexual deviate" referred to a person with a "long-lasting and perhaps compulsive orientation towards homosexual or otherwise 'abnormal' behavior." Citing *Flores-Rodriguez* (1956), Moore wrote that "the courts have said that those afflicted with 'psychopathic personality' are 'individuals who show a life-long . . . tendency not to conform to group customs, and who habitually misbehave so flagrantly that they are continually in trouble with the authorities.'" According to Moore, Boutilier's behavior stood in contrast to the behavior of Flores-Rodriguez, who engaged in "blatant exhibitionist solicitation in public." Moore was accepting a sexually discriminatory standard because, after all, a long-lasting and compulsive orientation to heterosexual behavior and a history of engaging in heterosexual solicitation in public would not have been held against an alien. He also did not seem to recognize that homosexuals were commonly thought to "show a life-long . . . tendency not to conform to group customs" and to "habitually misbehave so flagrantly that they are continually in trouble with the authorities," which meant that, by his own definition, they were classifiable as psychopaths.[53]

Moore's dissent contained another troubling implication. In the course of defending Boutilier, Moore repeatedly deferred to the expertise of science, medicine, and psychiatry. Criticizing Kaufman for claiming that the PHS provided "'its expert views,'" Moore wrote that this "suggests a careful and particularized analysis by distinguished psychiatrists." But, as Moore noted, "nothing could be further from what actually happened" since the PHS did not examine Boutilier. Later Moore wrote that "Congress contemplated an inquiry in each case, to be performed by skilled psychiatrists." Moore also relied on the opinions of psychiatrists, who wrote that Boutilier did not have a psychopathic personality. Moore advanced these arguments in defense of Boutilier, but according to his logic Boutilier might have been excludable if PHS doctors had examined him or if private psychiatrists had testified that as a homosexual he was psychopathic. Moore and Brennan appeared willing to place the fate of homosexual aliens in the hands of medical doctors, a group that for decades had tended to view homosexuality as a form of mental illness.[54]

As for Fortas, he participated in *Boutilier* just months before FBI officials met with him to discuss allegations that he had engaged in homosexual acts. In the oral arguments, Fortas was the most active justice. After Freedman began by emphasizing constitutional issues, Fortas cut in: "Are you relinquishing the possibility that we might decide this just on the basis of an incorrect construction and application of the statute?" Freedman responded, "Oh no, sir." Fortas continued, "Because it is not your argument, is it, that the phrase psychopathic personality is . . . so at large that it has no discernable medical meaning?" Freedman answered, "On the contrary," noting that the phrase had a "describable" and "ascertainable" meaning, and agreed with Fortas's next characterization of her argument, "that the Service and the court below went contrary to that reasonably ascertainable and definite meaning in this particular case." Fortas seemed to be encouraging Freedman to recognize that she might have a better chance of winning on statutory grounds. This would leave the psychopathic personality exclusion in place but overrule the INS's application of the law in Boutilier's case.

Fortas's other major exchange with Freedman was less sympathetic. Interrupting her argument that the government did not have "an adequate standard or criteria to determine whom the label homosexual covers," Fortas asked, "Is there an issue about that? . . . There is no dispute that this man was a homosexual prior to entry." When Freedman tried to reply with reference to medical evidence, Fortas cut in again: "I'm not talking about medical evidence. I'm talking about the legal issue. Was that legal issue presented?" Freedman replied, "There is no contest that he admitted certain acts. There is no contest that he described himself when he was asked, 'Do you consider yourself a homosexual?'" But she insisted, "Whether or not someone is a homosexual is something that can only be . . . described medically. And that has never been done in this case."

In exchanges with Lewin, Fortas seemed critical of the government's arguments. After Lewin claimed that Congress viewed homosexuality as a pathological condition and wanted homosexuals to be excluded, Fortas asked, "What makes you say that's so clear in the legislative history?" Noting that he had noticed the government's reliance on the PHS report, Fortas said, "It certainly is arguable that what the Service said is that ordinarily, or frequently, people who are engaged in sexual deviation are psychopathic personalities. I really had a little trouble finding an unequivocal statement." After Lewin described the PHS recommendation, Fortas insisted that there were "two possible inferences": either Congress wanted to exclude all people who had "engaged in sexual deviation" or Congress wanted to exclude all people "who had engaged in sexual deviation *and* who were psychopathic personalities." Lewin replied by referencing the PHS statement that "the classification of psychopathic personality . . . will specify such types of pathologic behavior as homosexuality or sexual perversion." Fortas declared that the statement was "clear as mud." Referring to the PHS discussion of "sociopathic reactions," which were "frequently symptomatic of a severe underlying neurosis or psychosis and frequently include those groups of individuals suffering from addiction or sexual deviation," Fortas argued that "if you remember your rules of logic" this was not the same thing as saying that "persons suffering from addiction or sexual deviation are always included in the group." When Lewin replied that the PHS was saying that "if you use the word psychopathic personality you will cover everyone whom you intended to cover by the words homosexuals or sex perverts," Fortas replied, "It is also possible to read this to mean something that I take from the briefs here is more consonant with medical science, which is that some persons engaged in homosexual activities may be in the category of psychopathic personality. Some may not." Admitting that the PHS recommendation "is subject to differing constructions," Lewin then emphasized that "more relevant, we think, is what the . . . congressional committees understood the Public Health Service to mean."

Fortas's response shifted the topic to statutory interpretation: "You think that sexual deviants and persons who have engaged in homosexual acts are synonymous." Lewin replied in the negative, adding that the INS did not think this way either: "It's quite clear, we think, from the reported cases and from all the cases that we know of that . . . they don't consider one or sporadic acts of homosexuality as being sufficient. . . . In . . . *Matter of P* . . . , the Board of Immigration Appeals quite clearly noted that the fact that an individual performs a homosexual act does not immediately classify him as a homosexual." The INS standard "is not one that sweeps across the board to anyone who has committed a single or very sporadic homosexual acts in his lifetime, but to one who, as this petitioner did, engaged in it as a regular practice."

Later Fortas returned to legislative intent, this time to ask whether Congress expressed its intentions with arbitrary language that was at odds with the "medical dictionary definition" of "psychopathic personality." Lewin replied that this was right with one qualification: "We're not making that argument, but we also don't necessarily believe that it's wrong. We're saying it's a matter of dispute among psychiatrists. . . . Congress had before it, or could have had before it, various psychiatric opinions and it apparently chose one." He continued, "If today it turns out that that's wrong, or the weight of psychiatric opinion is to the contrary, that does not, we think, invalidate the statute or make it totally inapplicable. We just think it's Congress's choice among expert opinions as to which view it wants to take." In other words, Congress could ignore the weight of scientific opinion as long as it could find an expert who supported its view.[55]

In light of these exchanges, it is not surprising that Fortas sided with Boutilier. Douglas's conference notes for Fortas record that "as [Fortas] reads Public Health it says that ordinarily a homo is a psycho but many are not." This was not exactly a ringing endorsement of sexual equality. Later, after Douglas circulated a draft of his dissent, Fortas wrote that he would join it if Douglas removed an "offensive appendix," discussed below, which Douglas proved willing to do.[56]

Like Brennan and Fortas, Douglas sided with Boutilier but relied on anti-gay language and logic. Douglas's opening paragraph focused on the vagueness of the statutory language, declaring, "The term 'psychopathic personality' is a treacherous one like 'communist' or in an earlier day 'Bolshevik.' A label of this kind when freely used may mean only an unpopular person. It is much too vague." This was not an accidental analogy: Douglas had disagreed strongly with Kaufman's decision in the Julius and Ethel Rosenberg case and now he was disagreeing strongly with him in *Boutilier*. Later Douglas argued that the term "is much too treacherously vague," that the PHS "admits that the term is 'vague and indefinite,'" and that "'psychopathic personality' is so broad and vague as to be hardly more than an epithet."[57]

On the issue of congressional intent, Douglas first argued, "It is common knowledge that in this century homosexuals have risen high in our own public service—both in Congress and in the Executive Branch—and have served with distinction. It is therefore not credible that Congress wanted to deport everyone and anyone who was a sexual deviate, no matter how blameless his social conduct had been nor how creative his work nor how valuable his contribution to society." Douglas also wrote that he agreed with Moore that "the legislative history should not be read as imputing to Congress a purpose to classify under the heading 'psychopathic personality' every person who had ever had a homosexual experience." Here Douglas quoted Moore's summary of Kinsey's statistics, his line about distinguished homosexuals in history, and his comment about the number of legislators who could be classified as homosexual. In footnotes, Douglas supplied additional figures from Kinsey and excerpts of a 1935 letter by Freud that stated that "many highly respectable individuals of ancient and modern times have been homosexuals, several of the greatest men among them." Another footnote reviewed the legislative history, pointing out that the statute "provided for exclusion of '[a]liens afflicted with psychopathic personality,' but did not provide for exclusion of aliens who are homosexuals or sex perverts." The note concluded that "the term 'afflicted with psychopathic personality' was used in a medical sense and was meant to refer to lifelong patterns of action that are pathologic and symptomatic of grave underlying neurosis or psychosis."[58]

Douglas also dissented on due process grounds: "If we are to hold, as the Court apparently does, that any acts of homosexuality suffice to deport the alien, whether or not they are part of a fabric of antisocial behavior, then we face a serious question of due process. By that construction a person is judged by a standard that is almost incapable of definition." At this point Douglas referred to the "wide range" of definitions for "psychopathic personality" and concluded, "Caprice of judgment is almost certain under this broad definition. Anyone can be caught who is unpopular, who is off-beat, who is nonconformist." Douglas continued, "We deal here also with an aspect of 'liberty' and the requirements of due process. They demand that the standard be sufficiently clear as to forewarn those who may otherwise be entrapped and to provide full opportunity to conform. . . . The Court seeks to avoid this question by saying that the standard being applied relates only to what petitioner had done prior to his entry. . . . *But at least half of the questioning of this petitioner related to his postentry conduct.*" In addition, Boutilier was "entitled to a hearing."[59]

Finally, Douglas argued that "the fact that he presently has a problem, as one psychiatrist said, does not mean that he is or was necessarily 'afflicted' with homosexuality." After providing excerpts of the letters from Boutilier's psychiatrists, Douglas concluded, "I cannot say that it has been determined that petitioner was 'afflicted' in the statutory sense."[60]

The Douglas-Fortas dissent, like Brennan's, sided with Boutilier but used language that contributed to the legal institutionalization of heterosexual supremacy. On the one hand, Douglas challenged the notion that sexual transgression could be equated with mental illness. In one section, Douglas included an excerpt from Kinsey's 1948 study, which had argued,

> The impression that such "sexual irregularities" as "excessive" masturbation, pre-marital intercourse, responsibility for a pre-marital pregnancy, extra-marital intercourse, mouth-genital contacts, homosexual activity, or animal intercourse, always produce psychoses and abnormal personalities is based upon the fact that the persons who go to professional sources for advice are upset by these things. It is unwarranted to believe that particular types of sexual behavior are always expressions of psychoses or neuroses. In actuality, they are more often expressions of what is biologically basic in mammalian and anthropoid behavior, and of a deliberate disregard for social convention. Many of the socially and intellectually most significant persons . . . have socially taboo items in their sexual histories.

On the other hand, when Douglas focused on homosexuality specifically, his language was different. In various places, Douglas referred to the work of experts who regarded homosexuality as immature, narcissistic, and dysfunctional. Citing a 1949 scholarly essay by Henderson, Douglas wrote, "Those 'who fail to reach sexual maturity (hetero-sexuality), and who remain at a narcissistic or homosexual stage' are the products 'of heredity, of glandular dysfunction, [or] of environmental circumstances.'" Summarizing the 1944 conclusions of Abrahamsen, Douglas noted, "The homosexual is one, who by some freak, is the product of an arrested development." A clerk recommended deleting these passages, but Douglas declined to do so. Along similar lines, the Freud letter quoted by Douglas asserted that homosexuality is "produced by a certain arrest of sexual development." These may have been relatively sympathetic points, calling for medical rather than legal intervention, but they were not egalitarian. And while the references to great gays in history challenged stereotypes, they ran the risk of endorsing special exceptions for extraordinary aliens while leaving in place discrimination against ordinary ones. Douglas also mentioned that homosexuals had served in the executive and legislative branches of government, but avoided suggesting the same about his own judicial branch.[61]

Douglas's references to Boutilier also contained negative comments about homosexuality. The psychiatric assessment of Boutilier by Falsey, which was reproduced by Douglas, claimed, "From his own account, he has a psychosexual problem but is beginning treatment for this disorder." This doctor diagnosed Boutilier as having a "Character Neurosis." Douglas also included excerpts of the assessment by Boutilier's other psychiatrist, Ullman, who described Boutilier as a "dependent, immature young man" with "a very constricted, dependent personality pattern." Douglas concluded, "'Afflicted' means a way of life, an accustomed pattern of conduct. Whatever disagreement there is as to the meaning of 'psychopathic personality,' it has generally been understood to refer to a consistent, lifelong pattern of behavior conflicting with social norms without accompanying guilt." In essence, Douglas was suggesting that as long as an alien's homosexuality did not become a lifelong pattern or a consistent way of life, as long as it did not conflict with social norms, and as long as there was guilt, it should not be grounds for exclusion.[62]

Like Brennan, Douglas and Fortas were also willing to place the fate of "homosexual" aliens in the hands of scientific experts. The Douglas-Fortas dissent included extensive excerpts, summaries, and citations from a variety of expert sources, including Freud (1935), Kinsey (1948), Cleckley (1941), Guttmacher and Weihofen (1952), Noyes (1948), Curran and Mallinson (undated), Guttmacher (1953), Tappan (1957), Henderson (1949), Abrahamsen (1944), Caldwell (1941), and Lindman and McIntyre (1961). Douglas marshaled evidence from these sources to support his conclusions, but the median date of the scholarship cited here was 1948, nearly twenty years before *Boutilier*, and only one work cited was less than a decade old. This was a period of significant change in scientific, medical, and psychiatric perspectives on homosexuality and one that witnessed the collapse of the overwhelming antihomosexual consensus, yet Douglas relied on older works that were more antigay than were the materials cited by Boutilier's defenders. Douglas concluded, "The informed judgment of experts is needed to make the required finding. We cruelly mutilate the Act when we hold otherwise. For we make the word of the bureaucrat supreme, when it was the expertise of the doctors and psychiatrists on which Congress wanted the administrative action to be dependent." Douglas may have been rejecting bureaucratic supremacy, but he was embracing scientific supremacy, and science did not have a strong record of support for sexual equality.[63]

Finally, had Fortas not asked Douglas to remove the draft appendix, Douglas might have included additional antigay material. The first draft of the appendix reproduced a May 1967 *New York Times* article by Murray Schumach titled, "On the Third Sex," which began by announcing that Columbia University had recently become the first U.S. college "to issue a charter to an organization seeking equal rights for homosexuals." This "brought a few rays of sunshine to the twilight world that alternates between the furtive and the flagrant." According to Schumach, while New York homosexuals "still find plenty of evidence of discrimination, hostility and harassment," the situation was improving. One local official was quoted as saying that "a guy can mince down the street with marcelled blond hair and if he doesn't bother anyone it is not illegal." Schumach then noted, "Ironically, like any other group in process of assimilation, the homosexuals who think they are moving toward equality resent the lurid displays of others." Schumach also wrote that homophile leaders referred to improved job opportunities in "advertising, publishing, clergy, teaching and, of course, show business, dress designing, decorating and hairdressing," but some worried that "as corporations become even larger . . . , they tend to place greater stress on conformity." The article concluded with the words of homophile activist Randolph Wicker, who stated, "Things are getting better, in New York anyhow, but none of us is ever going to see the day when we are treated as humans."[64]

Douglas's motives in including the appendix are unclear, and he may have wanted to force his brethren to read the article without intending to use it. The politics of the appended text are also unclear. On the one hand, the article seemed sympathetic to the fight for homosexual equality. On the other hand, it referred to homosexuals as a "third sex"; reproduced stereotypes of gay life as furtive and flagrant; criticized male homosexuals who were feminine or lurid; and reinforced the association of male homosexuals with theatrical and feminized occupations.

Perhaps even more ambiguous were Douglas's intentions in adding to subsequent drafts a footnote at the end of the appendix that quoted from a 1956 book, *Homosexuality: Disease or Way of Life*, by the intensely antihomosexual psychoanalyst Edmund Bergler:

> For nearly thirty years now I have been treating homosexuals. . . . If I were asked what kind of person the homosexual is, I would say: "Homosexuals are essentially disagreeable people, regardless of their pleasant or unpleasant outward manner. True, they are not responsible for their unconscious conflicts. However, these conflicts sap so much of their inner energy that the shell is a mixture of superciliousness, fake aggression, and whimpering. Like all psychic masochists, they are subservient when confronted with a stronger person, merciless when in power, unscrupulous about tramping on a weaker person. The only language their unconscious understands is brute force. What is most discouraging, you seldom find an intact ego (what is popularly called 'a correct person') among them."

Was Douglas endorsing this view, seeing in Bergler's comments a sympathetic perspective that did not hold homosexuals responsible for their situation and called for medical rather than legal intervention? Was he offering it as an illustration of Wicker's point that "none of us is ever going to see the day when we are treated as humans"? Did Fortas want the appendix eliminated because he objected to Schumach's article or the Bergler material? Did either account for Brennan's rejection of Douglas's dissent or Warren's vote switch? None of these questions can be answered definitively, but it is noteworthy that Douglas circulated Bergler's work without condemnation.[65]

After *Boutilier*

After *Boutilier*, the Court did not accept another lesbian, gay, or bisexual rights case for oral arguments for seventeen years. This does not mean the Court did not take positions on sexual freedom and equality. As discussed in chapter 1, the Court's heteronormative doctrine was reaffirmed in obscenity, birth control, and abortion cases in the years from 1967 to 1973. Meanwhile, after deciding *Boutilier*, the justices dealt with two other gay immigration cases, rejecting the appeal of *Tovar* and vacating the Ninth Circuit's liberal ruling in *Lavoie*. In a set of additional lesbian, gay, and bisexual cases appealed to the Court from 1967 to 1973, the Court denied *cert* or dismissed appeals, effectively or explicitly affirming conservative lower court judgments. In *Inman* (1968), the Court declined to consider an appeal of a lower court ruling affirming a Miami ordinance prohibiting liquor licensees from knowingly employing, serving, or permitting the presence of homosexuals in their establishments. In *Talley* (1968), the Court denied *cert* in an appeal of disorderly conduct convictions for same-sex kissing in a gay bar. In additional *cert* denials, *Adams* (1970) permitted the Defense Department to deny security clearance to a man based on evidence of homosexual conduct, and *Schlegel* (1970) allowed the army to fire a civilian employee for engaging in homosexual conduct. *McConnell* (1972), another *cert* denial, allowed a university to withdraw a job offer to a man who acknowledged his homosexuality and promoted gay rights in public. *Baker* (1972) dismissed an appeal of Minnesota's decision to deny marriage licenses to same-sex couples. Two rulings in 1972 (a *cert* denial in *Buchanan* and a dismissal in *Crawford*) and two in 1973 (dismissals in *Connor* and *Canfield*) effectively sustained the constitutionality of state laws banning sodomy and crimes against nature and the application of these laws in cases involving same-sex sex. Finally, in *Wainwright* (1973) the justices ruled that Florida's "crime against nature" statute was not unconstitutionally vague because "these very acts had long been held to constitute 'the abominable and detestable crime against nature.'"[66]

Many commentators have claimed that the Court's rulings in *Griswold*,

Fanny Hill, Loving, Eisenstadt, and *Roe* established basic principles of sexual rights that have, over time, been extended to cover more and more groups and activities. According to this perspective, these liberal rulings were useful precedents that helped establish an advanced foundation of sexual citizenship within U.S. law. *Boutilier* has not fit comfortably within this framework, both because it did not concern the rights of U.S. citizens and because the Court ruled against the rights of "homosexuals." For these and other reasons, *Boutilier* is not well known. Yet when *Boutilier* is examined alongside *Griswold, Fanny Hill, Loving, Eisenstadt,* and *Roe,* all of these rulings begin to look quite conservative and the Court's doctrine of heteronormative supremacy comes into clearer view.

PART 2 : *Activists and Advocates*

3 : Liberalization's Lawyers

The Supreme Court can be criticized or celebrated for its doctrine of heteronormative supremacy, but to understand how the justices came to validate the doctrine it is important to recognize that they did not invent it on their own. Some scholars adopt biographical or macrohistorical methods to interpret the Court's decisions. This chapter and the next two are microhistorical. They concentrate on the most direct and immediate influences on the Court: the strategies and arguments used by the activists and advocates who worked on these cases.

Did the litigants and lawyers who were victorious in *Griswold*, *Fanny Hill*, *Loving*, *Eisenstadt*, and *Roe* encourage the justices to privilege heteronormative sexual expression or did they endorse a more egalitarian doctrine? The second possibility is tempting for those who support the outcomes of these cases and those who admire these reformers. This chapter resists that temptation, arguing instead that liberals and leftists helped the Court develop its doctrine of sexual inequality. Over and over again, they told the justices that rulings in their favor would not necessarily disturb heteronormative laws.

In reaching this conclusion, this chapter does not criticize the political wisdom or legal effectiveness of these reformers. They were working within a legal system that encourages cautious and conservative argumentation. It is difficult to convince the Court to overturn laws and practices, and these advocates succeeded in part because they assured the justices that their arguments were respectful of the Constitution, consistent with legal precedents, and compatible with the tenets of heteronormative supremacy. Tactically, it may have made sense to condemn nonmarital sex and reproduction. Strategically, it may have been smart to select cases and develop arguments that deferred to the prevailing politics of respectability. This chapter criticizes these advocates for using arguments that undermined sexual freedom and equality, but it does so with a realistic, perhaps cynical, acknowledgment that doing otherwise would have reduced their chances of winning important victories.

Griswold

The *Griswold* ruling recognized constitutional rights of marital privacy, but most of the justices suggested that laws against nonmarital sex remained constitutional. Was this the position promoted by the advocates who fought for birth control rights in this case?

By the time *Griswold* reached the Court, the birth control movement had a long history of using conservative rhetoric and reasoning. Linda Gordon's work demonstrates that while the fight for birth control in the early years of the twentieth century was led by socialist, anarchist, and feminist radicals who emphasized the needs of working-class women, in the 1920s the movement developed a less radical agenda that reflected the priorities of medical professionals and middle-class women. Beginning in the 1940s, the movement identified "planned parenthood" as its goal and married couples as the ideal planners. David Garrow, who has examined the decades of legal struggles that culminated in *Griswold*, shows that while some birth control advocates were supporters of sexual freedom, by the 1950s, key movement leaders had decided to initiate test cases that would focus on the rights of married women and their doctors.[1]

Griswold was not the first litigation based on this strategy, but it proved decisive. Shortly after the Court dismissed *Poe* (1961), an earlier birth control case, on the grounds that Connecticut was not enforcing its law (which was not true), Estelle Griswold, the executive director of the Planned Parenthood League of Connecticut (PPLC), developed plans to open a clinic in New Haven. Lee Buxton, a professor at Yale University Medical School, served as the medical director of the clinic. As Garrow points out, the clinic's policies were consistent with those of the Planned Parenthood Federation of America (PPFA), meaning that unmarried women would not "knowingly" be accepted as patients unless they were engaged to be married and were referred by members of the clergy. According to Gordon, "Planned Parenthood steadily refused to serve the unmarried, as did many doctors, but young women claimed to be engaged and to be seeking contraception in preparation for marriage, and there was a traffic in borrowed wedding rings." Deliberately wanting to provoke a response, PPLC opened its clinic on 1 November 1961 and on the next day held a press conference at which PPLC lawyer Fowler Harper declared, "I think it would be a state and community service if a criminal action were brought. I think citizens and doctors alike are entitled to know if they are violating the law." After a local conservative filed a complaint, two police detectives proceeded to the clinic. According to one of the detectives, the staff "seemed to welcome the intrusion."[2]

At a subsequent visit, the detectives asked for the names of at least two women who had received information and supplies. Griswold mentioned Joan Forsberg, a graduate of Yale Divinity School, the wife of a Christian minister, and the mother of three children. Griswold also identified Rosemary Stevens, who was a Yale graduate student and the wife of a Yale professor. Having emigrated from England, Stevens and her husband were not U.S. citizens and told Harper they "would not want to be deported if they had to testify." According to Garrow, Harper "laughingly volunteered that he would happily take that case to the U.S. Supreme Court." This proved unnecessary, as the alien status of Stevens was ignored in the legal proceedings. When Forsberg was interviewed by the police, she declared, "I shall be very happy to see the time when information about birth control is legally made available to all married women in this state." Stevens initially told a detective that "this opportunity should be made available to all women," but the detective asked, "'Don't you mean *married* women?'" Stevens "reluctantly" agreed and later commented, "I still feel badly about that."[3]

On 10 November, Griswold and Buxton were arrested and the clinic's services suspended. Several days later, the police requested additional patient names and Griswold obliged with Marie Tindall, who was married to a social worker. Forsberg and Stevens were white; Tindall was black. No direct evidence suggests that Griswold or her lawyers took race into consideration when complying with the police requests, but they may have believed that judges would be predisposed to side with married white women or favor birth control for black women. There is no uncertainty about whether they took marital status into consideration; the litigation strategy required the involvement of married women. Griswold and Buxton's lawyer Catherine Roraback could then argue in state court that the statute represented an "extreme invasion of the privacy of the marital relation." Along similar lines, when "CBS Reports" featured the case several months later, Harper was shown declaring, "One of the most intimate and sacred relations of life is the relation of a man and his wife in the privacy of their home. And when the long arm of the law reaches into the bedroom and prohibits a man and his wife doing what they want to do, and what medical advice suggests that they do, it seems to me that this is a merciless invasion of the freedom and liberty of the citizens of this country."[4]

As they developed their litigation strategy, Griswold and Buxton's lawyers, working with Planned Parenthood and the ACLU, decided that an *ami-cus* brief by a Catholic organization would strengthen their defense of marital privacy. This would rebut the presumption that Catholics were invariably opposed to birth control. In 1963, ACLU executive director John Pemberton wrote to Northwestern University law professor John Coons about the idea of having "a group of prominent Roman Catholic lawyers" submit a brief. Coons thought this was "a stroke of genius" and a "damn clever idea." According to Coons, "such a brief could have a significant 'political' effect" and would say to the Court, "'Look it's O.K.—we won't be mad if you make a sensible decision.'" Pemberton subsequently helped persuade the Catholic Council on Civil Liberties to submit a brief.[5]

Consistent with the planned strategy, the briefs submitted by Griswold and Buxton's advocates emphasized repeatedly that the central question was whether the state law violated marital rights. For instance, the jurisdictional statement by Harper, who initially represented Griswold and Buxton, and the Planned Parenthood brief by Morris Ernst and Harriet Pilpel identified this as the critical question. The briefs then established the fact that the clinic served married people. For example, Thomas Emerson and Catherine Roraback, who represented Griswold and Buxton after Harper died, argued that the clinic's purpose was to assist "married persons" and that the charges were based on the provision of birth control to "married women."[6]

Having highlighted these questions and facts, the advocates argued that the statute violated marital rights. According to Harper, the law "deprives married women in Connecticut of their liberty and their privacy, as protected by the Fourth, Fourteenth and Ninth Amendments." In support of his position, Harper cited *Meyer*, which had declared that "the term 'liberty' includes freedom 'to marry, establish a home, and bring up children.'" Emerson and Roraback observed that "although the boundaries of this constitutional right of privacy have not yet been spelled out, plainly the right extends to unwarranted governmental invasion of (1) the sanctity of the home, and (2) the intimacies of the sexual relationship in marriage." Like Harper, they emphasized that "the interest of married spouses in the sanctity and privacy of their marital relations involves precisely the kind of right which the Ninth Amendment was intended to secure." They also asserted that "of all relations with other people, marital relations are the most private."[7]

The *amicus* briefs similarly emphasized marital rights. For the American Civil Liberties Union (ACLU) and the Connecticut Civil Liberties Union (CCLU), Rhoda Karpatkin, Melvin Wulf, and Jerome Caplan argued that "marriage and the family" were "the ultimate repository of personal freedom" and "the power vested in husband and wife to conduct the affairs of their family free of state interference is virtually plenary." For the Catholic Council, Robert Fleming noted that "the nature of marriage and conjugal union presuppose[s] a degree of privacy for spouses basically inconsistent with such state intervention." Planned Parenthood asserted that "the state cannot . . . dictate to husbands and wives what they may and may not do in their marital relations" and that "Connecticut (like all other states) recognizes and declares the right of married persons to sexual relations."[8]

The advocates relied on more than just abstract arguments about privacy and liberty; they also highlighted the dangers of restricting access to birth control. Here, too, they selected their examples carefully, highlighting the dangers faced by married couples. Harper pointed out that birth control was "frequently necessary to the health of married women" and "avoids the long recognized ill effects of prolonged or permanent abstinence from marital relations." Emerson and Roraback discussed several examples in which life, health, and welfare were affected by access to birth control. One involved a married woman for whom "a further pregnancy 'would be exceedingly dangerous.'" Another concerned a married couple who had produced "three abnormal children" with "genetic" problems that contributed to early deaths. A third dealt with a married couple whose four children had died because of "blood factor incompatibilities." Emerson and Roraback concluded that the law placed women "in the position of risking serious injury or loss of life or, through abstinence, sacrificing the right to enjoy one of the most cherished aspects of the marriage relationship." On this latter point, they emphasized that experts had linked abstinence within marriage to "neuroses," "frustration," "anxiety," "tension," "extra-marital relations," and "divorce." Although many of these arguments applied to nonmarital situations, the advocates avoided calling attention to these implications.[9]

More generally, the *Griswold* advocates insisted that their arguments did not apply to nonmarital relationships, and in some instances they implicitly or explicitly endorsed laws against birth control for unmarried people and laws against nonmarital sex. This was a matter of concern for some of the lawyers who participated in consultations about the litigation. The ACLU had long opposed restrictions on the dissemination of birth control information and in the 1950s adopted a policy statement rejecting laws against the prescription, sale, or use of birth control. In *Griswold*, however, the ACLU planned to emphasize marital rights. In May 1964, San Francisco attorney Lawrence Livingston wrote to Melvin Wulf after reviewing drafts of the ACLU's briefs: "The thing that bothers me is that the law may be held unconstitutional as to married couples and, by inference, constitutional as to everybody else. To me this is nonsense." Several lawyers discussed taking a more radical position. In January 1965, Pilpel noted in a memorandum, "We considered the possibility, in connection with the privacy point, of including the ALI [American Law Institute] proposal about sexual behavior in private between consenting adults. Tom [Emerson] does not wish to take this on in his brief but would be delighted if we would mention it since he thinks a number of the judges might find it persuasive." Several months earlier at an ACLU conference, Pilpel had argued in favor of rejecting laws against consensual adult homosexuality, and the conference had voted to declare that the ACLU should support the American Law Institute proposal to decriminalize "sexual behavior between consenting adults in private." In the end, however, none of the *Griswold* briefs referenced the ALI proposal, which might have compromised the marital privacy strategy.[10]

According to Harper's jurisdictional statement, "These laws are not narrowly drawn. They are not restricted to their presumed purpose which is to prevent meritricious [*sic*] relations between unmarried persons. They are also applicable to married spouses and thus they 'burn down the house to roast the pig.'" He also noted that the laws "do not attain the desired results of preventing licentious relations between unmarried persons" because contraception could be obtained legally if the purpose was disease prevention. Emerson and Roraback similarly observed that "the statutes, considered as an effort to protect public morals by discouraging sexual intercourse outside the marital relation, are not reasonably designed to achieve that end." The implication was that just as it would be acceptable to roast the pig without burning down the house, it was acceptable to criminalize nonmarital sex as long as marital rights were protected.[11]

Some of the justices questioned Emerson about the distinctions he was making between married and unmarried women. After he noted that "the law makes no distinction between married and unmarried women, but our objection to it, essentially, goes only to the application to married women," Justice Black asked, "Why wouldn't it be a denial of equal protection of the laws to draw such a distinction?" Emerson replied that "it might be," but added, "There are differences between married and unmarried women for purposes of legislation in this area. So that the mere fact of distinction would not necessarily be a denial of equal protection." After the discussion turned to disease prevention, Justice Brennan asked, "Wouldn't you have had a rather compelling equal protection argument?" Emerson replied, "There are differences between married [and] unmarried persons, and between the use of devices for preventing conception and the use for preventing disease, and it's conceivable that the State legislature could validly make discrimination between them in some situations." Other justices also questioned Emerson about this, but he insisted that the case concerned marital rights.[12]

On the general subject of morals legislation, Emerson and Roraback argued that the standard for applying the due process clause should be as follows: "(1) the moral practices regulated by the statute must be objectively related to the public welfare, or (2) in the event no such relationship can be demonstrated, the regulation must conform to the predominant view of morality prevailing in the community." As an example of a law that would meet the first standard, they mentioned, without explanation, "a statute prohibiting prostitution." Their main point, however, was that "if the legislature cannot establish that the law promotes the public welfare in a material sense, it cannot enforce the morality of a minority group in the community upon other members of the community." To support this position, they referenced the Court's obscenity decisions, which endorsed the use of "community standards" and thus implied that state laws could not "enforce on the entire community moral principles not conforming to the predominant view of morality." They then cited various indicators of public attitudes to show that Connecticut's law did not "reflect the dominant moral opinion of the community." Planned Parenthood further substantiated the claim that "there is a national community consensus which . . . recognizes the imperative need for responsible family planning." While some of the evidence suggested that public support for birth control extended beyond marital contexts, the briefs did not call attention to this, emphasizing instead the overwhelming level of support for the rights of married couples. The implication of this argument was favorable for marital privacy but dangerous for forms of sexual expression that lacked majority support.[13]

In a few instances, *Griswold*'s advocates addressed sex laws more directly. In the course of making a point about the First Amendment, Harper, Emerson, and Roraback cited a 1959 ruling that held that a state could not "forbid the advocacy of conduct (in this instance adultery) which it could validly make a crime." Laws against adultery were constitutional, according to this formulation, even if laws banning pro-adultery speech were not. The advocates also suggested that states could pass laws aimed at discouraging nonmarital sex if they were reasonably designed to achieve that goal and did not interfere with marital rights. Emerson and Roraback declared explicitly that "the statutes could accomplish their objective by simply prohibiting the use of such devices in extra-marital relations." They also complained, with respect to prohibiting birth control use by married people, that "the situation is the same as if, in order to discourage adultery or fornication, Connecticut prohibited all sexual relations." Along similar lines, they wrote, "Nor is it necessary that the statutes sweep so broadly to achieve this aim of discouraging extramarital relations. Alternatives are available. Connecticut has statutes against adultery, fornication and lascivious carriage." They also noted, "Nor is it an answer to say that other statutes, dealing with fornication, adultery, homosexuality and the like, raise the same issues of privacy. We are not concerned with those statutes here. In any event, Mr. Justice Harlan disposed of the argument in *Poe vs. Ullman* when he said: 'Adultery, homosexuality and the like are sexual intimacies which the State forbids altogether, but the intimacy of husband and wife is necessarily an essential and accepted feature of the institution of marriage.'"[14] In *Griswold*, birth control advocates promoted special rights for married couples.

Fanny Hill

As discussed in chapter 1, the Court tended to divide into three factions in obscenity cases in this period, and in most instances the centrist plurality determined the outcome by voting with either the free-speech libertarians or the anti-obscenity conservatives. Did the lawyers who defended *Fanny Hill* pitch their arguments to the free-speech faction and try to convince some of the others to extend First Amendment protection to sexual materials? Or did they pitch their arguments to the centrist plurality by accepting sexual censorship while denying that *Fanny Hill* was obscene? Convinced that the latter offered the best chances for success, *Fanny Hill*'s advocates encouraged the Court to adopt discriminatory obscenity tests.[15]

Legal struggles over sexual censorship began long before *Fanny Hill* reached the Court. Over the course of the twentieth century some free-speech advocates opposed all sexual censorship, but most leading civil libertarians focused on ending the classification of abortion and birth control materials as obscene, restricting the reach of obscenity laws so that only specific types of materials could be banned, and extending protection to materials with artistic, intellectual, literary, or political value. In the 1950s and 1960s, the ACLU endorsed the "clear and present danger" test for sexual censorship. In the context of U.S. history, this position was relatively liberal since prosecutors would find it difficult to prove a "clear and present danger." But adoption of this test would allow prosecutors to define "danger" in ways that reinforced sexual inequality.[16]

Charles Rembar and Edward de Grazia, who argued significant obscenity cases in this period, later published books on the subject. Their work shows that while some anticensorship advocates may have been sexual egalitarians, leading First Amendment lawyers adopted strategies that contributed to the development of the Court's heteronormative doctrine. Rembar and de Grazia are more sympathetic to the Court's liberalizing decisions, but like hostile witnesses who help the opposing side, their books can be used to show that liberal advocates encouraged the justices to condone sexual inequality.[17]

Rembar's *The End of Obscenity* traces its author's role in defending *Lady Chatterley's Lover*, *Tropic of Cancer*, and *Fanny Hill*. The respectable publishers of these books—Grove for the first two and Putnam for *Fanny Hill*—anticipated that they would have to defend these works in court. They made strategic decisions about which books to publish, thought carefully about when and where to publish, and consulted with lawyers before proceeding. Rembar's goal was to convince the Court to adopt the principle that a book could not be suppressed "if it had merit as literature." He writes that he succeeded by developing an interpretation of *Roth* that accepted the illegal status of obscenity but insisted that materials with "value" were not obscene. To win his cases, he then just needed to show that these works had value. One danger of this approach was the implication that materials lacking the qualities of the works he defended also lacked value. In defending *Lady Chatterley's Lover*, for instance, Rembar made use of literary critic Malcolm Cowley's testimony that the book was valuable because it advocated "sexual fulfillment in marriage." Although Rembar later insisted that he defended the novel "not on the ground that it promoted morality, but rather that it presented a view on the subject," his account shows that he took pains to highlight the novel's heteronormative message.[18]

Other aspects of Rembar's pre–*Fanny Hill* arguments also contributed to the development of discriminatory obscenity tests. In defending *Lady Chatterley's Lover* and *Tropic of Cancer*, Rembar emphasized the respectability of the publishers, the mainstream media advertising, the good press reviews, and the positive assessments of critics. In the case concerning *Lady Chatterley's Lover*, Rembar's witness Cowley observed, "There are writers who are men of distinction and men of conviction and they deserve a great deal more liberty than third-rate talents." When challenging the claim that the novel appealed to prurient interests, Rembar argued that "normal sexual interest was not prurience." Later, when commenting on an anticensorship decision in a male physique magazines case, Rembar criticized Justice Harlan's opinion because it "did not consider the effect of the magazines on young men of unformed and ambivalent character." Rembar insisted that "this is not to say (or deny) that the magazines should have been suppressed," but he did not express similar concern about comparable representations of women.[19]

Rembar was hired by Putnam to defend *Fanny Hill* in several states, but the case that reached the Supreme Court began in 1964 in Massachusetts, where the state's attorney general successfully petitioned a state court to declare the book obscene. As Rembar developed his arguments, he grew concerned about how the ongoing *Ginzburg* and *Mishkin* litigation might affect his case. He later wrote that "the material Ginzburg had mailed was not, in itself, sufficient for conviction," but "the way Ginzburg had sold his publications created a problem." As for Mishkin, "his books were trash," and he "gave the impression of the inveterate commercial pornographer that the Chief Justice pictured in *Roth*." Rembar's efforts to distinguish *Fanny Hill* from *Ginzburg* and *Mishkin* contributed to the anti-obscenity decisions in the latter two cases.[20]

In *Fanny Hill*, Rembar did not argue that obscenity was protected by the First Amendment; instead he tried to show that this particular novel was not obscene. In his jurisdictional statement, Rembar asserted that the Court had formulated three tests of obscenity and "a book must fail by all of these tests before it may be suppressed." He then argued that *Fanny Hill* did not appeal to prurient interest, was not patently offensive, and was not "utterly without redeeming social importance." In his appellant's brief, Rembar explained that the novel did not appeal to prurient interests because "it is not morbid or unhealthy in its appeal to the normal adult," and "its candor is within the limits set by contemporary community acceptance." The novel failed to meet the second test because "it is elegant and decorous, the very opposite of the patently offensive." As for adhering to the third standard, "apart from its intrinsic values, [the book] occupies a significant place in the development of the novel, and has interest as social history." In his reply brief, Rembar emphasized that his arguments did "not mean that there is nothing in book form upon which anti-obscenity legislation may operate." In the oral arguments, he stated, "We do not say that any book can now be published." He also asserted, "There is no such thing in our opinion as valuable obscenity. Obscenity is worthless trash. That is its definition constitutionally."[21]

In making these arguments, Rembar not only countenanced sexual censorship but also condoned sexual discrimination. For instance, his language about prurience privileged the perspectives of "normal" adults and adopted "community acceptance" as a critical element. Perhaps the most negative implications for sexual equality arose from the ways in which Rembar defended the "value" of *Fanny Hill*, which he did by emphasizing the novel's moral qualities. When cross-examining the state's only expert witness, a Catholic school headmaster, Rembar asked about Fanny's early sexual encounter with a woman: "Do you recall, Dr. Collins, that the heroine, thinking back on this incident, refers to it as foolery and resolves to have no more such experiences?" Rembar also got Collins to acknowledge that Fanny ends up married to "the same young man with whom she had her first sexual experience." Rembar later submitted a review by J. Adams, who noted that *Fanny Hill* "emphasizes the fact that the sex relation, when informed by love, rests on a higher level than when it is a purely animal reflex." Rembar also submitted an article by V. S. Pritchett that claimed that the author viewed "old whores" as "hardened" but "young ones" as "rescuable . . . through the experience of love." Among the witnesses called by Rembar was Harvard's John Bullitt, who testified that the novel presented "the education of a young woman in a moral life."[22]

Rembar's experts emphasized not only that Fanny embraces heterosexual marriage and love but also that she rejects homosexuality and flagellation. Fred Stocking of Williams College described "the flagellant episode" as a "depraved" experience from which Fanny learns. He also noted that she reacts to "a homosexual encounter" with "anger and disgust." Norman Holland of the Massachusetts Institute of Technology observed that "Cleland is using the various sexual acts in the novel to trace the moral progress of his heroine. . . . The watching of the homosexuals, the masochists, the encounter with the sailor and so on, all of these fall farther and farther away from her ideal relationship with Charles. Then, at the end of the novel, she . . . comes back to sex with love." Ira Konigsberg of Brandeis University testified, "The homosexual incident is held up with scorn. . . . The same can be said of the whipping. . . . These acts of sexual perversion are there to be juxtaposed to the acts which are partaken in sexual health."[23]

Rembar distilled the significance of these comments. His jurisdictional brief emphasized Fanny's "affirmation of the superiority of sex-in-love to the merely lustful" and concluded that "the principal sexual interest of *Memoirs* is a normal heterosexual interest." In the main brief, Rembar noted that "the narrator condemns sexual deviation and holds it up to scorn." In his reply brief, Rembar distinguished *Fanny Hill* from the gay-oriented magazines considered in *Manual*, to which "the words 'propriety' and 'good taste' cannot possibly be applied." In his supplemental brief, Rembar objected to the characterization of *Fanny Hill* as a "lesbian" novel. According to Rembar, "There are early lesbian incidents in *Memoirs* . . . but Fanny soon rejects 'this foolery from woman to woman.'" These were effective arguments for *Fanny Hill*, but they did damage to the struggle for sexual equality.[24]

When *The End of Obscenity* was published in 1968, Rembar minimized the negative implications of the 1966 obscenity rulings. He acknowledged that "many people (myself included) felt there were aspects of Ginzburg's trial that seemed unfair and the five-year jail sentence was grotesque," but he concluded, "For freedom of expression, March 21, 1966, was a very good day. The pandering rule would send Ginzburg to jail, but its future as an inhibiting force on speech and the press would be negligible. The acceptance of the value test would give writers and publishers a freedom they had never before enjoyed." As for *Mishkin*, Rembar's comments left the impression that the case was correctly decided. Two decades later, in a new edition of *The End of Obscenity*, Rembar made it clear that he supported censorship in specific circumstances. The "law of obscenity," he observed, "ought to be exercised more." He specifically endorsed banning the sale of obscenity to children, restricting public displays of and advertisements for pornography, and acting against obscenity when acting against related illegal conduct was not feasible. Recognizing that some readers might be surprised by this, Rembar insisted that his position had not changed. He offered this parallel: "It needed a President who was Republican to make the peace in Korea; a Democrat would at the time have been reviled as soft on Communism." Similarly he contended that "more of a hearing may be gained for the argument that anti-obscenity statutes have some valid use if the position is presented by one who helped cut down the scope and force of those same statutes." In the 1960s and 1980s, Rembar believed there was an advantage in having an anti-censorship lawyer argue against obscenity.[25]

Loving

In *Loving*, the Court declared that marriage was a fundamental right and that it could not be denied on the basis of race. What did the *Loving* advocates say or imply about sexual rights?

Loving was the culmination of centuries of efforts to circumvent, reform, and repeal laws against interracial marriage. Most of these efforts utilized socially sanctioned discourses of marriage, family, love, and freedom. Interracial marriage advocates rarely challenged the special rights and privileges associated with marriage; they wanted interracial couples to have access to these rights and privileges. Some challenged laws against interracial sex, but many implicitly or explicitly supported nonracial laws against nonmarital sex. In fact, some argued in favor of interracial marriage precisely because nonmarital sex was illegal, which meant that the only way for interracial couples to have legal sex was to marry. Many also supported interracial marriage because this was the way that interracial couples could fulfill the reproductive ideal, which treated only the children of married couples as "legitimate."[26]

In the early twentieth century, the most significant organized opposition to miscegenation laws came from the NAACP and ACLU. According to Peggy Pascoe, in this period the NAACP feared that a campaign against miscegenation laws might damage its efforts to challenge segregation. But when public scandals about interracial relationships led many states to consider adopting new restrictions in the 1910s and 1920s, the NAACP launched a largely successful campaign to defeat the new measures. Pascoe notes that NAACP activists were particularly effective when they "framed their campaign against miscegenation [laws] as a defense of marriage and a plea for the protection of womanhood." Their arguments "worked in tandem with conventional morality, strengthening the power of marriage by cracking down on illicit sex."[27]

In the 1930s, the ACLU joined the NAACP in opposing miscegenation laws, but in this decade and the next, neither organization went to court to overturn the remaining state laws. Renee Romano and Alex Lubin show that during and after World War II, the NAACP challenged military officials who denied black soldiers permission to marry white women overseas. Meanwhile, the Japanese American Citizens League (JACL) began to provide support for U.S. servicemen who confronted obstacles when they tried to marry Japanese women. Going to court to overturn miscegenation laws was another matter. Peter Wallenstein writes that in this period "no national organization was prepared to give serious support" to litigation challenging the constitutionality of state laws against interracial marriage. In the 1940s and 1950s, the NAACP provided behind-the-scenes assistance to lawyers who requested help in challenging miscegenation laws, and some local branches took more public steps, but the national office generally counseled strategic patience. When asked, the NAACP declared its opposition to these laws, but litigation was "a low priority" because of the potentially negative consequences for its desegregation campaigns. The NAACP's concerns were shared by a majority of the justices, who voted against hearing a challenge to Alabama's antimiscegenation law just after Brown was decided in 1954 and then dodged a challenge to Virginia's antimiscegenation law in 1955 by claiming that the case record was incomplete.[28]

While the NAACP counseled patience, other organizations pressed forward. In 1948, a lawyer affiliated with the Catholic Interracial Council of Los Angeles won Perez, a California Supreme Court ruling that struck down that state's antimiscegenation law. In the 1950s, immigration lawyer David Carliner persuaded the ACLU to get more involved as he litigated *Naim*. Ham Say Naim, a Chinese sailor, had married a U.S. citizen classified as white, but after she obtained an annulment on the grounds that Virginia prohibited marriages between whites and Asians, Naim's application for an immigrant visa was in jeopardy, so he had an interest in challenging the antimiscegenation law. Carliner convinced the ACLU to support the litigation, and the American Jewish Congress, the Association of American Indian Affairs, the Association of Immigration and Nationality Lawyers, and the JACL provided assistance. Carliner lost the case, but his work led to the ACLU's active involvement in miscegenation cases at a time when the NAACP was more hesitant. Significantly, Carliner argued in *Naim* that "the power of a state to punish adultery and fornication between persons of different races stands on a different footing than any asserted power to prohibit interracial marriages." According to Carliner, "The right to marry is admittedly a fundamental liberty; a right to fornicate is not."[29]

As the ACLU became more involved in interracial marriage cases, its leaders thought carefully about strategy. According to political scientist Chang Moon Sohn, in the late 1950s the ACLU's Rowland Watts encouraged attorneys around the country to identify possible miscegenation test cases. Citing correspondence between Watts and University of Utah law professor Sanford Kadish, Sohn reports that "Criteria for a good test case were: (1) criminal prosecution is better than a proceeding in *mandamus* or an annulment proceeding; (2) a white husband and non-white wife combination is better than vice versa; (3) a white-Indian or a white-Oriental combination is better than a white-Negro combination; (4) a couple with a standing in the community is better than a couple without it; and (5) a case from a Western state or a border state is better than a case from the deep South." These criteria reflected a gendered, racialized, and class-based politics of respectability that avoided challenging the most deeply ingrained social prejudices about interracial relationships. The JACL's version of this was to try to find "a test case involving a war bride from Japan or Korea." Pascoe emphasizes that both groups "tried to distance their arguments on behalf of the 'right' of interracial marriage from the smoldering stigmas that surrounded interracial sex."[30]

By the early 1960s, the NAACP, the ACLU, and others were willing to assist litigants in challenging laws against interracial sex and marriage. The NAACP led the effort in *McLaughlin*, which succeeded in 1964 in overturning Florida's law against interracial cohabitation, while the ACLU led the effort in *Loving*.[31] The *Loving* litigation began in 1963, but the central facts of the case occurred five years earlier, when twenty-four states still banned specific types of interracial marriage. In 1958, Richard Loving and Mildred Jeter, residents of a rural Virginia community in which interracial relationships were common, traveled to Washington, D.C., to marry. Under Virginia law Loving was "white," Jeter was "colored," and therefore the two could not marry, leave the state to marry, or live together in the state as a married couple. (Jeter claimed that she was "part negro and part Indian," but was generally described in court and in the media as "colored" or "negro.") The Lovings returned to Virginia after their wedding and began living at the home of Mildred's parents. Six weeks later, they were awakened in the middle of the night by police, who arrested and jailed the couple. Richard was released after one night; Mildred was released after several days. After a trial, the judge sentenced them each to a year in jail, but suspended the sentences for twenty-five years if they left Virginia and did not return together or at the same time. The Lovings moved to Washington, D.C., and had three children. They apparently visited their Virginia families frequently and over time became less cautious about being seen together. In 1963, wanting to move back to Virginia and influenced by the civil rights movement, Mildred wrote a letter to U.S. Attorney General Robert F. Kennedy requesting assistance. Kennedy declined to intervene but put the Lovings in contact with the National Capital Area Civil Liberties Union, which referred the couple to Bernard Cohen, an ACLU cooperating attorney. Cohen agreed to represent the couple and was soon joined by another ACLU-affiliated lawyer, Philip Hirschkop. As the case developed, other ACLU lawyers, along with lawyers representing the NAACP, the NAACP Legal Defense Fund, the JACL, and the National Catholic Conference for Interracial Justice (NCCIJ), supported the litigation.[32]

The lawyers who defended the Lovings made two principal arguments, both based on the Fourteenth Amendment. First, antimiscegenation laws violated the due process clause because the right to marry was fundamental and could not be denied without legitimate justification and fair process. Second, these laws violated the equal protection clause because they discriminated on the basis of race. In support of the first, the jurisdictional statement by Cohen, Hirschkop, Carliner, and Melvin Wulf noted that marriage is a "fundamental and natural right." The statement also included excerpts from *Griswold* that emphasized "'the right of privacy in marriage.'" The appellant's brief by Cohen, Hirschkop, Wulf, Carliner, William Zabel, Arthur Berney, and Marvin Karpatkin referred to the right to marry as "even more fundamental than the right of students to attend an integrated public school." For the JACL, William Marutani and Donald Kramer observed that "freedom in marriage concerns one of the most basic and fundamental rights." The NAACP brief described marriage as a "civil right," while the NAACP Legal Defense and Educational Fund called the right to marry "a protected liberty under the Fourteenth Amendment." A brief by the NCCIJ, the National Catholic Social Action Conference, and a set of sixteen Catholic bishops and archbishops from southern states declared that antimiscegenation laws violated constitutional rights of privacy, marriage, and religion.[33]

These advocates did not just present the right to marry in abstract terms; they also highlighted specific "rights and benefits" that were "contingent upon the marital relationship." According to the jurisdictional statement, the Lovings and similar couples were "prohibited from establishing a family abode and raising their children in places where they and their family have often been long established." Moreover, the statement noted that "their children live under the stigma of bastardy" and the Lovings are "prejudiced in their right to certain tax, insurance, social security, and workman's compensation benefits; to bequeath or inherit property; to certain criminal defenses, and other benefits and privileges." The implication was that it was acceptable to grant special rights and privileges to married people and their children.[34]

The briefs acknowledged that the state had a legitimate role to play in regulating who could marry whom. Same-sex marriage was not addressed, but the main brief asserted that "the right to marry is not an absolute right and a State may restrict it in certain circumstances, for example, by imposing reasonable age and health limitations and prohibiting incestuous or polygamous marriages." The key issue was whether a restriction had a "reasonable relationship" to "a legitimate legislative purpose." According to the NAACP brief, "prohibition of marriages of feeble-minded persons or of persons with communicable diseases" was "supported by demonstrable scientific knowledge that such marriages present a potential danger to society through physically or mentally ill offspring." The Catholic brief acknowledged that "marriage is subject to *some* control by the state" and referenced a decision allowing states to regulate "the age at which the parties may marry." The brief also discussed a decision that upheld a state ban on plural marriage because polygamy was linked to "the patriarchal principle" and "despotism" and therefore was a "danger to the 'principles on which the government of the people . . . rests.'" Bans on polygamy were also justified on the basis of studies showing that polygamy "may be harmful to the family members." In other words, marriage might be a fundamental right, but the state could justify restrictions based on legitimate concerns about health and harm. The briefs did not deal with the ways these arguments could be deployed against people with disabilities, people with diseases, and same-sex couples. Nor did they address the patriarchal, despotic, and harmful aspects of monogamous marriage.[35]

In the oral arguments, the justices pressed Bernard Cohen on these issues. When one justice asked whether "a state could forbid marriage between a brother and a sister," Cohen replied, "We have conceded that the State may properly regulate marriages," and he specifically mentioned laws against polygamy. According to Cohen, antimiscegenation laws were based on "race," which was "arbitrary and capricious," but other restrictions might be justifiable. One of the justices replied, "Some people might think, with reason, that it's arbitrary and capricious to forbid first cousins to marry." Cohen responded by saying that the burden would be on the appellant to show that this was "arbitrary and capricious," whereas in a racial discrimination case the burden was on the state. Marutani also addressed this issue, asserting that the state could restrict marriage based on "consanguinity, mentality, age, and number of spouses" because these restrictions applied "to all races." For Cohen and Marutani, race was an inherently suspect classification whereas various other classifications were not.[36]

The briefs did not say much about laws against sex, but in a few instances they offered arguments that presumed such laws were constitutional. The jurisdictional statement's claim that the Lovings were "prohibited from establishing a family abode" in Virginia rested on the assumption that the state's cohabitation law was constitutional. This was made more explicit in the main brief, which stated that because the state viewed the marriage of the Lovings as void they were vulnerable to prosecution for "cohabitation" and "fornication." The main brief also argued that antimiscegenation laws "perpetuate and foster illicit exploitative sex relationships" between white men and black women. This was because such laws deprived black women in relationships with white men of the status and protection that came with marriage. This was true, but it reinforced the notion that nonmarital relationships were "illicit" and that women in such relationships were not entitled to the rights and privileges of married women. The JACL brief noted that in *McLaughlin* the Court confirmed that "even though the Florida statutory prohibition involved 'concepts of sexual decency ... dealing ... with extramarital and premarital promiscuity,'" the law was unconstitutional because it constituted invidious racial discrimination. In contrast, the law challenged in *Loving* "seeks, not to deter sexual promiscuity or such similar opprobrious activity but rather the noble and necessary goal common to all persons—'marriage and procreation.'"[37]

As several of these passages suggest, the marital ideal put forward in the briefs was monogamous, heterosexual, and reproductive. When they repeatedly invoked the reference in *Meyer* to the right to "marry, establish a home and bring up children," they were not just delineating three independent rights; they were prescribing a particular sequential ideal. When they referred to "illegitimate" children living under the "stigma of bastardy," they elevated marital over nonmarital reproduction. Marutani and Kramer claimed that "freedom in marriage concerns one of the most basic and fundamental rights of the individual, rooted, indeed, in one of man's biological drives." Assuming that the drive was sexual, this formulation privileged marital over nonmarital sex. They went on to cite the claim in *Skinner* that "'marriage and procreation are fundamental to the very existence and survival of the race,'" a formulation that linked procreation, which was necessary for species survival, to marriage, which was not. Citing *Buck* and *Skinner*, the Catholic brief declared, "Whatever may be said of the power of the state directly to deny to individuals the exercise of procreative powers on account of mental deficiency . . . or habitual criminality . . . , the state is without power directly or indirectly to inhibit its citizens in the exercise of such powers solely on account of their race." According to the brief, antimiscegenation laws denied interracial couples "the right to beget children," which was "one of the chief lawful rights in marriage." The marital ideal put forward in the briefs was reproductive and the reproductive ideal was marital.[38]

Eisenstadt

In *Eisenstadt*, the Court ruled in favor of reproductive rights for the unmarried. Did the advocates encourage the Court to recognize sexual rights for the unmarried?

After *Griswold*, many birth control activists shifted their energies to the struggle for abortion rights, but many continued to work on improving access to contraception. Having emphasized reproductive rights for the married in *Griswold*, the ACLU soon began challenging birth control laws and practices that discriminated against the unmarried. In 1966, for example, ACLU executive director John Pemberton wrote to the director of the federal government's Office of Economic Opportunity to complain that its "prohibition on the distribution of funds for contraceptive aid to unmarried women or women living apart from their husbands" violated the equal protection clause.[39]

Although the ACLU and PPFA were committed to birth control reform, *Eisenstadt* was not initiated by either. William Baird was a dedicated birth control and abortion rights activist with what Garrow describes as "a highly developed taste for publicity" and contentious relationships with other movement leaders. In 1965, he was arrested for breaking a New York law banning the distribution of contraceptives by anyone other than specified health professionals. The charges were soon dropped, but in 1966 he was arrested for displaying contraceptives in New Jersey. That state's supreme court overturned the conviction, but meanwhile Baird was in the news again for picketing a PPFA event in New York to protest the "excessive fees" charged at PPFA clinics. As Garrow points out, "Baird's demonstration certainly did not endear him to his ostensible allies within Planned Parenthood."[40]

In March 1967, Boston University students invited Baird to give a lecture on their campus and Baird announced that during his visit he would challenge a state law banning the display or distribution of contraceptives, with an exception for doctors who provided contraception to married women. In April, Baird spoke to an audience of 1,500–2,500 in a lecture hall rented by the campus chapter of Students for a Democratic Society. According to Garrow, student activist Raymond Mungo introduced Baird by announcing, "We are here to test the legal aspects of the birth control and abortion laws in the state." A state senator had called for Baird's arrest if he broke the law and seven policemen were present in case that occurred. Toward the end of his lecture, Baird announced that he would distribute a list of abortion providers outside the United States and packages of contraceptive foam. After calling on the police to "do their duty" and telling the audience that "the only way we can change the law is to get the case into a court of law," Baird invited those who wanted the foam to come forward. About twenty people did so, Baird handed packages to several women, and others helped themselves. Baird later told the *Boston Globe* that he had "arranged ahead of time with a young 19-year-old student" to give her a can of foam. ACLU lawyer James Hamilton assisted Baird as he was arrested and released on bail.[41]

While students organized a legal defense fund, the Civil Liberties Union of Massachusetts (CLUM) informed Baird that it had not decided whether to represent him. CLUM eventually affirmed its willingness to help, but Baird concluded that the support lacked the "necessary vigor." Baird later told the *Globe* that CLUM's lawyers had said "they would refuse to defend him if he kept on talking about the law." The Planned Parenthood League of Massachusetts (PPLM) also distanced itself, asserting that the state law did not interfere with rights to use and talk about contraception. According to a *Boston University News* editorial, "the national 'population control lobby'" went "out of its way to dissociate itself from Baird." Comparing PPFA to "'mainstream' civil rights groups," the editorial accused the group of "being defensive about its own entrenched position, its own hard-won 'respectability,' and its own bloated bank accounts." Baird asserted that Planned Parenthood was motivated by its "vested business interest." He explained, "When you have a $12 million monopoly and your executives get over $20,000 a year, and along comes Baird with a cheap way, a new way, and can really reach the poor . . . well. We're the only group in the country saying come to me, single or married, and I will help you." According to former PPFA president Loraine Campbell, Baird was "a thorn in our flesh" and was "always talking about abortion under the aegis of birth control, when we were trying to avoid the issue of abortion." Admitting that he had done "more good than harm" she noted that "every forward step in history requires its nuts." In the meantime, local lawyer Joseph Balliro agreed to represent Baird. CLUM later submitted an *amicus* brief when Baird's appeal was heard by the state supreme court, and the ACLU, the PPFA, and their local affiliates submitted briefs to the Supreme Court. After the case's importance became clear, national population control leaders convinced Baird to replace Balliro with former U.S. senator Joseph Tydings. In the end, Balliro submitted the main brief, Tydings and David Rutstein submitted a supplemental brief, and Tydings handled the oral arguments.[42]

Beyond the ambivalent help he received from birth control and civil liberties groups, Baird also had some support from the organized women's movement. In the second half of the 1960s, a revived feminist movement began to claim birth control and abortion as important women's issues. In 1967, the National Organization for Women (NOW) endorsed abortion law reform, and a few years later several New York members urged NOW to submit an *amicus* brief in *Baird*. NOW declined to do so, but Human Rights for Women, founded in 1968 in part to support "litigation involving rights of women under the law," did. Baird's relationship with the women's movement was contentious, however, and in 1972 he complained in a letter to *Playboy* that "not one feminist group" responded to his request for an *amicus* brief when he was arrested for corrupting the morals of an infant at a birth control lecture. According to Baird, while the Playboy Foundation supported his efforts, "I and other males were banned from speaking at equality rallies because of our sex," and NOW founder Betty Friedan told reporters, "'It's been rumored that Bill Baird is a CIA agent.'"[43]

While Baird was a strong advocate of reproductive rights, he expressed ambivalence about nonmarital sex. On the one hand, in 1965 Baird led a campaign against a New Jersey county welfare director's plan "to bring morals [fornication] charges against unwed mothers on welfare seeking aid for dependent children." On the other hand, when asked in 1967 about his "position on the moral implication of birth control," Baird told a reporter, "I will say to my own children, try to reserve this for marriage. I believe in the responsibility and the privilege of intercourse which is best reserved for marriage. But as a realist, I know this doesn't happen."[44]

The main arguments used by Baird's advocates focused on reproductive rights as these related to rights of life, health, and privacy. Balliro declared, "We are ... concerned with a fundamental right older than the Bill of Rights— older and more cherished even than the marriage relationship. We concern ourselves here with the right to health, to social and economic well-being and, indeed, the right to life itself." The PPFA brief by Pilpel and Nancy Wechsler stated that "the right of access to medical services for contraception is a fundamental right." Representing Human Rights for Women, Sylvia Ellison argued that the law "denies single women due process of law in that it arbitrarily invades the privacy of their lives with no reasonably related benefit to health, safety, morals, or the general welfare." The ACLU/CLUM brief by Melvin Wulf, Lawrence Sager, and John Robertson emphasized that the Constitution protects "the right of free personal choice—of autonomy—over one's own body" and this "encompasses the right of individuals to decide whether or not to prevent conception."[45]

Baird's advocates also argued that the state was discriminating on the basis of marital status, sex, and class, which violated the equal protection clause. Timing was critical here, as the briefs were submitted in the period when the Court was beginning to consider whether sex classifications, like race classifications, were "suspect" and subject to strict scrutiny. Later in the 1970s, a majority of the justices would agree to treat sex classifications as "quasi-suspect," meaning that laws that treated men and women differently had to serve important state interests and there had to be a substantial relationship between the law and those interests. This intermediate scrutiny standard fell between strict scrutiny, under which the law had to serve compelling state interests and be narrowly tailored and necessary to serve those interests, and minimum scrutiny, under which the law had to serve legitimate state interests and have a rational relationship to those interests. The Court continued to use minimum scrutiny for most types of discrimination, and this was the standard used by the Court in *Eisenstadt* when it ruled that the law violated the equality rights of the unmarried.[46]

Eisenstadt was considered by the Court before the justices developed the intermediate scrutiny standard and the advocates did not argue the case in these terms. On behalf of PPLM, Roger Stokey and Stephen Weiner approvingly cited the conclusion of the Court of Appeals, which ruled in favor of Baird, that the law was "grossly discriminatory" because it required doctors to treat married and unmarried women differently. The Human Rights for Women brief declared, "The statute denies single women the equal protection of the law in that . . . it discriminates against them in favor of married women. . . . Although society favors marriage, *a woman should not have to marry in order to exercise fundamental human rights*." Some of the briefs argued that the law violated equal protection because it discriminated against the poor. Pilpel and Wechsler explained that "poor women irrespective of their marital status are faced with an often insurmountable obstacle to access to contraception because they are unable to obtain a physician's services." As for discrimination against women, Pilpel and Wechsler claimed the law "imposes a harsh penalty on women who violate the laws against fornication by putting them at risk of unwanted pregnancy, health hazards and the birth of illegitimate children, yet their male partners, equally guilty of fornication, are not burdened by forced conception." The Human Rights for Women brief asserted that the law discriminated against single women "in favor of single men." According to the brief, "Although the statute is also intended to prevent single men from access to contraceptives, the effect on them is about as meaningful as a law denying them maternity leave. That is, the effect on single men is nil, while the effect on single women is drastic."[47]

As they made these arguments, Baird's defenders had much to say about nonmarital reproduction, which they presented as unfortunate. The PPFA brief observed that "the effects of out-of-wedlock pregnancies and births" were "disastrous." If the woman did not have an abortion or get married, "the costs to her, to the illegitimate child and to society are incalculable." The brief asserted that, for the unwed mother, "the likelihood of becoming a school dropout, economically dependent, poverty stricken and trapped is obvious." There were also "adverse effects upon the health of the unmarried mother and her child." Balliro discussed the "tragic consequences" of illegitimacy, which included maternal and infant mortality, social stigma, "handicaps" in "physical development," damaged health, and "maternal hatred." Human Rights for Women observed that "unwanted children" suffered from child abuse as well as "juvenile delinquency, failure in school, drug addiction, and mental illness."[48]

As for nonmarital sex, Baird's supporters presented a complex set of arguments. After emphasizing life, health, and privacy, Balliro declared, "This is not to say that the legislature has no right to regulate morals, any more than the court in *Griswold* was saying that the legislature could not proscribe an act directly and reasonably related to that purpose. We concede the desirability of regulation that will enhance morals and diminish sexual promiscuity." Referring to the argument that "the unmarried should not fornicate and the married shall adhere to their vows," Balliro wrote that "we have statutes providing punishment for those and related misadventures, and those statutes are not under attack here." Balliro noted that "we accept, for this day, any direct statutory proscription on enumerated sexual behaviors," but he was unwilling to accept the notion that the state wanted to "permit the ills of unwanted pregnancies" and "venereal disease" to "spread unchecked *among those who indulge in illicit sexual intercourse.*" Moreover, if the goal was to promote morality, which was "a noble purpose," Balliro observed that it was "difficult to see that our birth control statutes validly accomplish that end."[49]

In the end, Balliro returned to the arguments made by Griswold's defenders to distinguish between legitimate and illegitimate morals laws. According to his brief, "moral purposes are more easily understandable in the direct prohibition of fornication, adultery and other statutes where the sexual act is of direct consideration," but the moral principles invoked in this case were "not subject to objective evaluation." Asserting that the "constitutional standard for applying due process in cases where the legislature seeks to promote public morals requires that the *specific* moral practice . . . regulated by the statute must be objectively related to the public welfare," Balliro argued that "in the event no such relationship can be demonstrated, the regulation must at least conform to the predominant view of morality prevailing in the community (the proscription of fornication, adultery, etc.)." Balliro defended this position by citing the Court's opinions in obscenity cases. Then he argued that the Massachusetts law was not "objectively related to the public welfare" since contraception was available for disease prevention, married people could obtain contraception for extramarital purposes, and there were no serious health risks associated with contraception. As for community values, Balliro asserted that "it is not necessary to condone immorality in order to recognize that the predominant, prevalent present day thinking is opposed to the damning, devastating and tragic consequences that result from the proscription of contraceptives to the wayward."[50]

The PPLM brief was less direct in its comments on sex laws. Like Balliro's brief, it argued that there was no rational relationship between the law and the goal of discouraging extramarital sex. As for fornication, the brief noted that it was a misdemeanor with a maximum ninety-day penalty whereas the maximum penalty for breaking the anticontraception law was five years. If the goal was to deter fornication, the penalties for it would be more severe. These arguments rested on the assumption that penalizing nonmarital sex was constitutional.[51]

Three of the briefs gestured more favorably in the direction of sexual rights, but qualified their support. According to Ellison's Human Rights for Women brief, *Griswold* recognized "the right of privacy in matters pertaining to marriage, family and sex" and a federal court in *Roe* affirmed "the right to engage in sexual intercourse without unwanted pregnancy free from governmental intrusion." Ellison also cited a California ruling that stated, "The Griswold case makes it clear that private sexual relations are beyond the purview of the state." A footnote referenced the American Law Institute's model penal code, which recommended decriminalizing "'all sexual practices not involving force, adult corruption of minors, or public offences.'" Ellison's argument was libertarian and feminist: "We disagree with Appellant that there does not exist a right of single persons to sexual relations without unwanted pregnancy . . . and we believe that denial of this right works a particular hardship on single women." Ellison nevertheless noted, "We are not advocating 'free love.' We are simply saying that the law should not restrict what is a matter of individual and very personal choice." She also wrote that the state "should be commended for its concern in safe-guarding the morals and chastity of the single people," but "such concern is not compelling enough to adversely affect the right of single women to sexual relations free of unwanted pregnancy." In these passages, a feminist and libertarian defense of sexual freedom deployed heteronormative rhetoric about morality and chastity.[52]

The ACLU/CLUM brief also tried to have it both ways. In the spring of 1971 John Robertson submitted a draft of the brief to Melvin Wulf. One section argued that while the state had a legitimate interest in promoting morality, the birth control law did not serve the goal of preventing nonmarital sex. The draft insisted that its argument "does not entail the conclusion that all laws regulating extra-marital sex are invalid." According to Robertson, "analysis may indeed show that birth control laws serve no compelling state interest, but that fornication, adultery and similar laws are so central to public morality that an unmarried person's liberty is justifiably infringed." Elsewhere the draft mentioned "prohibitions against public intercourse, incest, seduction of minors, and perhaps bans on fornication, adultery and certain sexual perversions" as examples of valid laws that served compelling state interests. Several weeks later, Wulf replied with concerns about this section. "I would not even suggest that laws against fornication or adultery might not be unconstitutional. Not as far as the ACLU is concerned!" Robertson responded:

I do not see how it is possible to argue that the aspect of privacy or liberty at issue here is *absolute* and in no circumstances may be limited. Such an argument leads to the position that all restrictions on sexual activity, including prohibiting distribution of birth control pills except by doctors or incest, are unconstitutional. . . . It will be a major victory for civil liberties (and open the door to a frontal attack on other morals legislation) if the court in *Baird* finds that [the statute] infringes a fundamental right of privacy/liberty to engage in sex. Recognizing that this right may be limited in cases of "compelling state interest" in no way depreciates the right, but merely brings it in line with the current law on fundamental rights. Indeed, much—if not the whole-battle—is to be gained by applying this analysis to private, consensual sexual activities. In most cases the state will not be able to carry the burden of establishing a "compelling," as opposed to a cognizable, state interest. . . . On the fornication and adultery point, I merely wanted to distinguish those statutes from [the birth control statute] in order to make clear that the court in deciding *Baird* is not necessarily deciding those cases as well. . . . A fundamental right—compelling state interest analysis here will pave the way to attacking other sex regulations, and lead, I believe, to their eventual invalidation. *Baird* is an essential step in the demise of a whole range of morals legislation, but depends on the court's recognition that a *fundamental right* is at stake. Page 12 is perhaps too easy on adultery-fornication laws in making this point. In any case, I think this distinction must be made, but don't object to restating it so that we do not appear to be favoring such regulations.[53]

This exchange suggests that Robertson and Wulf did not want their brief to condone laws against fornication and adultery (and perhaps other sex laws). But what did their brief actually say?

On the one hand, the brief declared that "the area of activity which has been the most prominent beneficiary of the constitutional tradition of individual autonomy is that concerning marriage, the family, and sexual relationships." *Griswold* affirmed that "the sexual intimacies of man and wife are correctly considered to be private matters" and "subsequent decisions" interpreted *Griswold* as "establishing a right of sexual privacy which extends to both married and single men and women." Citing a lower court ruling in a Texas sodomy case, the brief insisted that "the notion that a state has a legitimate interest in adjusting the sexual morality of its citizens is itself open to serious question."[54]

On the other hand, the brief qualified its support for sexual freedom and equality. "Whatever the ultimate reach of the right to sexual privacy," the brief declared, "it surely encompasses the right of individuals to decide whether or not to prevent conception." This placed reproductive rights in a privileged position in the universe of sexual rights. The brief then adopted an ambivalent position on laws against nonmarital sex. After dismissing the notion that the purpose of the law was to deter nonmarital sex, the brief observed, "If the State does have a secure basis for a proscription of fornication it is the interest in reducing the birth rate of illegitimate children. The Massachusetts law accomplishes just the reverse." This provided the state with an argument in favor of its fornication law. Then the brief stated that if it is "assumed" that "sexual morality can plausibly be considered a goal of the legislation, and that such a goal is permissible," this "could validate a statute making fornication illegal" but not a law against contraception. The brief concluded, "If the State has any interest and place in defining sexual morality, it can do so with its criminal laws directly." The brief presented these arguments in conditional form, acknowledging the legitimacy of sex laws only if certain assumptions were accepted. But the repeated invocation of these conditional claims provided the justices with a way to strike down the law without abandoning the tenets of heteronormative supremacy.[55]

Like the ACLU/CLUM brief, Pilpel and Wechsler's PPFA brief hedged its bets. On the one hand, the brief argued that "this Court has acted on numerous occasions to protect from state interference the rights of the individual in matters relating to marriage, the family and sex." On the other hand, Pilpel and Wechsler offered arguments that implicitly or explicitly condoned state laws against sex. Their first argument was that the Massachusetts law violated the right to life because it "places many women at risk of serious injury, and in some cases even death, if they violate the law prohibiting fornication." They made a similar argument about extramarital sex, noting that "while those who do this may be violating the law, they have not given up their constitutional rights with respect to medical treatment and with respect to having children." In other passages, Pilpel and Wechsler provided the justices with ways to preserve the constitutionality of sex laws. At one point they declared, "Regardless of whether the state has a valid interest in regulating consensual sexual activity, it can have no valid interest in forcing people to have children or in denying them medical services in the area of contraception." At another point they stated, "Whatever interest Massachusetts may legitimately have in regulating sexual conduct cannot justify the ban on contraception for the unmarried." Several pages later, they noted that "it is not necessary for the decision of the present case to rule on the constitutionality of state laws proscribing fornication and adultery." Addressing laws against nonmarital sex, they insisted that adultery "is not deterred by this law since married persons have access to contraceptives irrespective of whether or not they engage in illicit relationships" and "the state may take steps against fornication without adopting the essentially totalitarian rule of forcing women to bear illegitimate children if they fail to observe those laws." They concluded, "If Massachusetts is truly concerned with deterring fornication and adultery, it can deal with these offenses by means of the statutes which directly proscribe that conduct." Baird's advocates thus presented a range of arguments about the constitutionality of sex laws, but if the justices wanted to recognize the birth control rights of the unmarried without acknowledging the rights of the unmarried to have sex, Baird's advocates provided them with ways to do so.[56]

Roe

In *Roe*, the Court adopted a compromise position, rejecting restrictive antiabortion laws but also opposing "abortion on demand." Did Roe's advocates present arguments that supported or undermined the pursuit of sexual freedom and equality?

Abortions in the early stages of pregnancies were legal in the first decades of U.S. history, but this changed in the mid-nineteenth century when various states enacted restrictive laws. By the mid-twentieth century, the states permitted abortions only in exceptional circumstances (typically when necessary to save the lives of pregnant women), and the vast majority of women who had abortions did so illegally. Support for abortion law reform came from the overlapping ranks of birth control activists, population control experts, medical professionals, civil libertarians, advocates for poor people and people of color, and feminists.[57]

Abortion rights activists pursued their goals in various ways. Some helped women circumvent anti-abortion laws. Some campaigned for legislative reform, which in the 1960s led ten states to eliminate some restrictions on abortion (most commonly for women whose lives or health were endangered, women whose pregnancies resulted from rape or incest, and women carrying fetuses with what were deemed "grave physical or mental defects"). More states lifted restrictions in the early 1970s. Meanwhile, beginning in the early 1960s and with increased confidence after *Griswold*, leading reformers concluded that a Supreme Court ruling would be necessary to overturn anti-abortion laws across the country.[58]

A complicated network of individuals and organizations participated in strategy discussions about abortion reform. One milestone occurred in 1959, when the American Law Institute (ALI) voted to support limited abortion law reform (in cases of rape or incest, substantial risks to women's physical or mental health, and fetal "defects"). As Leslie Reagan points out, "The ALI consciously avoided challenging the sexual norms that forbade sex outside of marriage and that treated pregnancy and childbearing as punishment for sexually active unmarried women. The idea of allowing pregnant unmarried women to have abortions provoked a storm. . . . The motion to allow abortions in cases of illegitimacy did not receive a second." In the 1950s and early 1960s, Planned Parenthood and the ACLU rejected calls to endorse abortion rights, but in the second half of the 1960s both changed their positions. An ACLU statement adopted in 1969 asserted that "a woman has a right to have an abortion . . . prior to the viability of the fetus." Part of the statement addressed "the oft-heard contention that removal of criminal sanction on abortion will undermine the morality of our youth and open the door to promiscuity." According to the ACLU, this was "an understandable concern," but "the primary impact of the laws would seem to fall not on the unmarried and potentially promiscuous teenager . . . but on the married woman with an established family." Meanwhile, in the late 1960s the American Medical Association endorsed reform, as did various liberal and radical feminist groups. Local, state, and national abortion rights groups, including the Association for the Study of Abortion (ASA) and the National Association for Repeal of Abortion Laws (NARAL), also were key advocates.[59]

In the late 1960s and early 1970s, abortion rights advocates pursued multiple court cases. For example, the California Committee for Therapeutic Abortion (CCTA) and the southern California ACLU affiliate assisted Dr. Leon Belous, who had been convicted of violating a state law for referring a woman to an unlicensed abortion provider. In *Belous* (1969), the California Supreme Court ruled that the state law allowing abortions only if they were necessary to preserve the pregnant woman's life was unconstitutionally vague. Also in 1969, the James Madison Constitutional Law Institute (which hired Roy Lucas to coordinate abortion litigation), the ACLU, the ASA, the Center for Constitutional Rights, and the Women's Health Collective challenged New York's abortion statute in a set of cases that became moot in 1970 when the state repealed some of its restrictions. Meanwhile, Lucas helped persuade a federal judge in Washington, D.C., to rule in *Vuitch* (1969) that the district's anti-abortion statute, which permitted abortions necessary for the preservation of the mother's life or health, was unconstitutionally vague. This decision was reversed by the U.S. Supreme Court in 1971, though the Court emphasized that the health exception had to be defined broadly and Vuitch's conviction was later voided. In 1970, abortion rights advocates helped Dr. Sidney Babbitz win a federal district court ruling that overturned Wisconsin's anti-abortion statute. In the same period, Minnesota reformers assisted Dr. Jane Hodgson after she was indicted for aborting a fetus damaged by rubella. Activists affiliated with Georgia Citizens for Hospital Abortions and Georgia's ACLU and Planned Parenthood affiliates developed a test case involving Sandra Bensing, who had failed to navigate the state's abortion approval process. This case, *Doe v. Bolton*, would eventually be considered alongside *Roe* by the U.S. Supreme Court.[60]

The litigation that culminated in *Roe* began in Texas. After Dr. James Hallford was indicted in 1969 for violating the state's abortion law, lawyers Roy Merrill and Fred Bruner contacted Lucas, the ASA, NARAL, and the ACLU for assistance. Meanwhile, a group of feminist activists at the University of Texas–Austin began focusing on abortion and referring women to extralegal abortion providers. After consulting with lawyer Sarah Weddington, they began to think seriously about developing a test case. (Two years earlier, when she had been an unmarried twenty-two-year-old law student, Weddington had traveled to Mexico for an abortion, but she did not reveal this to her abortion rights allies until years after *Roe* was decided. When she did, she emphasized that she had been celibate until she and her future husband "were talking about getting married.") Weddington discussed the idea of a test case with lawyer Linda Coffee and the two agreed to look for a woman with an unwanted pregnancy. Weddington later wrote that "several women who came to the referral project for information indicated they would be happy to help, but they were all at an early stage of pregnancy and had the money to get a prompt abortion." One possibility emerged in 1970, when Dallas attorney Henry McCluskey contacted Coffee about Norma McCorvey, an unmarried woman with an unwanted pregnancy. Coffee had recently helped McCluskey in his work on *Bachelor*, a Texas sodomy case; McCorvey later learned that McCluskey was "gay, like me, but deeply in the closet." After meeting Coffee and Weddington, McCorvey agreed to serve as the plaintiff in a case challenging the Texas law. Around the same time, Marsha King, a Dallas abortion rights activist with health conditions that made pregnancy inadvisable, offered herself and her husband David as plaintiffs. A short time later, Merrill, Bruner, Weddington, and Coffee combined their cases, which allowed them to argue on behalf of an unmarried woman, a married couple, and a medical doctor.[61]

Norma McCorvey became Jane Roe in part because she and her lawyers believed that abortion was a private matter and they wanted to spare McCorvey negative publicity. They may have shared the common view of abortion as shameful and embarrassing. But McCorvey also became Roe because her lawyers were concerned that various features of her life, which could more easily be exposed if her real name was used, might damage their chances.

McCorvey, who describes herself in a 1994 autobiography as "half Cajun and part Indian," had a difficult childhood, did not complete high school, and spent several years in reform school. As a young adult, she was often poor and unemployed. A survivor of physical, sexual, and emotional abuse by family members, sexual partners, and Catholic nuns, she had alcohol and drug problems and struggled with depression. She had married and divorced, had a history of sexual relationships with men and women, and had worked and socialized in lesbian and gay bars. McCorvey had gotten pregnant and given birth twice before, and in both instances she lost custody of her children. When she became pregnant again, she asked her doctor for an abortion, but he explained that abortions were illegal, encouraged her to put the child up for adoption, and referred her to a lawyer. When the lawyer asked McCorvey if the pregnancy was a result of rape, she lied and said yes, hoping that abortions were permitted in such situations. When he asked about the rapist's race, she avoided answering. Later the doctor told her that the lawyer had said he could not help because the child was "probably of mixed race and would be hard to place with white parents." After trying unsuccessfully to self-abort, McCorvey contacted McCluskey, the second lawyer recommended by her doctor, and he put her in touch with Coffee and Weddington. At this point, McCorvey was still in her first trimester and hoped to have an abortion, but Coffee and Weddington claimed they did not know where she could get one. They warned her about the dangers of illegal procedures and convinced her to become their plaintiff. McCorvey writes that she initially told Coffee and Weddington that the pregnancy was the result of rape, but Weddington told her this would not matter since the law did not make an exception for rape. Weddington explains, "I was not going to allege something in the complaint that I could not back up with proof. Also, we did not want the Texas law changed only to allow abortion in cases of rape." McCorvey recalls that when she asked when she would be able to have her abortion, Weddington replied, "When the case is over, if we've won." McCorvey asked when that would be; Weddington reportedly replied that it was "impossible to tell." In a 1976 interview, Weddington claimed that after the federal district court ruling, "We had to face the decision of whether . . . we should make arrangements for her to go outside the state to try and get an abortion. . . . She chose to carry the pregnancy to term because at that point the law regarding abortion was in a nebulous enough state that we were afraid that the Supreme Court, if it wanted to, could duck the issue by saying that it was moot because she had been able to get an abortion." According to Weddington, "We explained all that to Jane Roe and told her if she wanted to go, we would help her. But I think even then, she had in some ways a sense of the historic proportion of the case." By the time the Court ruled in her favor, McCorvey had given birth and McCluskey had arranged for the child's adoption.[62]

McCorvey has expressed admiration for her lawyers and pride in her role, but also resentment about the fact that Weddington did not tell her about her own abortion, direct her to an abortion provider, or inform her that the litigation would likely not conclude before it was too late for an abortion. Indeed, if McCorvey had found the referral service that Weddington was assisting, she likely would have had the abortion she wanted. In a 1994 interview, McCorvey complained, "I didn't know until two years ago that she had had an abortion herself. . . . When I told her then how desperately I needed one, she could have told me where to go for it. But she wouldn't because she needed me to be pregnant for her case. I set Sarah Weddington up on a pedestal like a rose petal. But when it came to my turn, well. Sarah saw these cuts on my wrists, my swollen eyes from crying, the miserable person sitting across from her, and she knew she had a patsy." More generally, McCorvey criticizes abortion rights activists for regarding her as "an embarrassment." According to McCorvey, she did not "fit many people's idea of a historical role model," partly because she was a lesbian, partly because she was not "a gentle woman," and partly because she was not "sophisticated." These resentments likely contributed to McCorvey's alliance with anti-abortion activists in the late 1990s.[63]

Long before this occurred, the briefs supporting Jane Roe, John and Mary Doe (the pseudonyms for the Kings), and James Hallford presented multifaceted arguments about the rights of unmarried women, married couples, and medical doctors. The jurisdictional statement and the main and supplemental briefs focused on rights of privacy and liberty, rights of life and health, and rights to practice medicine. According to the jurisdictional statement, the Court ruled in *Griswold* that "a husband and wife are constitutionally privileged to control the size and spacing of their family by contraception" and except in Massachusetts "authorities have uniformly held the *Griswold* rationale applicable to litigants who had not entered into the marriage contract." In *Belous*, the California Supreme Court recognized the "fundamental right of the woman to choose whether to bear children" and in *Roe* a federal district court concluded that the Texas statutes "deprive single women and married couples of their right . . . to choose whether to have children." The statement also emphasized that the laws interfered with the "marital relations" of the Does and threatened Mary Doe with serious harm to her health.[64]

According to the main brief, "The law abridges rights emanating from the First, Fourth, Ninth, and Fourteenth Amendments to seek and receive health care, to privacy and autonomy in deciding whether to continue pregnancy, and, as to physicians, to administer medical care." To support its claims about health care, the brief emphasized that having an abortion posed less of a risk to a woman's health than bearing a child and that for women like Mary Doe the differences were even more significant. To support the argument about privacy and autonomy, the brief referenced *Griswold* and *Loving* and concluded that "if the concept of 'fundamental rights' means anything, it must surely include the right to determine when and under what circumstances to have children." The main brief also elaborated on the claim that the law interfered with the marital relations and rights of the Does and made two additional arguments: the law was unconstitutionally vague in the guidance it provided to physicians and it imposed unconstitutional burdens of proof on physicians.[65]

The *amicus* briefs expanded on these arguments and made several additional ones. Harriet Pilpel and Nancy Wechsler's brief for the PPFA and the American Association of Planned Parenthood Physicians noted that earlier decisions, including *Griswold*, established "the fundamental nature of the rights of the individual in areas relating to marriage, the family and sex." Pilpel and Wechsler also emphasized "the woman's right to life and to needed health services and her physician's right to practice medicine." For the American College of Obstetricians and Gynecologists, the American Psychiatric Association, the American Medical Women's Association, the New York Academy of Medicine, and a group of 178 physicians, Carol Ryan argued that the Texas laws violated the rights of doctors to practice medicine, the rights of patients to medical treatment, and the privacy rights of women. On the latter point, the brief declared, "The freedom to be the master of her own body, and thus of her own fate, is as fundamental a right as a woman can possess. The Texas statute . . . is the most severe and extreme invasion of her right to privacy. She is forced to function as a baby factory for an unwanted child." This was a "gross invasion by the state into a pregnant woman's physical autonomy."[66]

While the main brief mentioned women's rights in passing and the medically oriented brief emphasized the rights of women in one section, two other briefs were more fully and forcefully feminist. One was produced by Nancy Stearns for New Women Lawyers, the Women's Health and Abortion Project, and the National Abortion Action Coalition. According to Stearns, laws against abortion "deny to women their right to control and direct their lives and bodies as protected by the Fourteenth Amendment's guarantees of life and liberty." This was a variation on the arguments made by others, but Stearns made two additional points. She contended that insofar as women bore "the disproportionate share" of the "burdens and penalties of pregnancy, child birth and child rearing," laws against abortion denied women's equality rights. In addition, Stearns argued that because "carrying, giving birth to, and raising an unwanted child can be one of the most painful and longlasting punishments that a person can endure," laws that "condemn women to share their bodies with another organism against their will, to be child breeders and rearers against their will," violated the Eight Amendment's prohibition on "cruel and unusual punishment." A second feminist brief by Joan Bradford for the California Committee to Legalize Abortion, the South Bay Chapter of NOW, Zero Population Growth, and two individual women argued that anti-abortion laws "violate the Thirteenth Amendment by imposing involuntary servitude."[67]

The briefs defended abortion rights, but used heteronormative language about marriage and reproduction. Working with precedents such as *Griswold* that granted special rights to married couples, several briefs privileged the married Mary Doe's rights over the unmarried Jane Roe's. The jurisdictional statement declared that "the substantive question presented is whether a State may enact a felony statute to punish a physician, a woman, and her husband" for an abortion. The statement asserted that "a husband and wife are constitutionally privileged to control the size and spacing of the family by contraception." A footnote extended the argument to cover unmarried women, but the language was explicit about the privileges of married couples. The statement's second argument, which emphasized that the law interfered with the "marital relations" of the Does, did not mention Roe at all. The main brief made several arguments that applied equally to Mary Doe and Jane Roe, but several applied only to Doe. At one point, the brief stated that "the importance of the institution of marriage and of the family has long been recognized by this Court." After citing *Skinner*, *Poe*, and *Griswold*, the brief declared, "Associated with the right to marry is the right to have children, if one chooses, without arbitrary governmental interference." This section concluded that the Texas statute "has a maximum destructive impact upon the marriage relationship." Underscoring this point, the brief included an excerpt of an article by retired justice Tom Clark, who had written, "Abortion falls within that sensitive area of privacy—the marital relation."[68]

The briefs also privileged marital reproduction. The main brief emphasized that one of the reasons Roe wanted an abortion was "the social stigma attached to the bearing of illegitimate children." Several briefs offered statistics about "unwanted" and "illegitimate" children and stated that many of these were born to poor women, women on welfare, Black women, and teenagers. Discussing the unmarried woman, Stearns observed that "she may be forced to become a welfare recipient" and fall into the "cycle of poverty." The PPFA brief pointed out that "childbirth may be dangerous or unsuitable" for a variety of reasons, one of which was that "the pregnancy may occur in a teenager out of wedlock." Pilpel and Wechsler referred to the "incalculable" costs to the unmarried pregnant woman, her "illegitimate" child, and society. All of this contributed to a larger public discourse that favored marital over non-marital reproduction; none of it suggested that unmarried women deserved equal treatment.[69]

As for sexual rights, the Roe briefs presented mixed messages. Several passages encouraged the Court to reject laws that interfered with sexual rights. The main brief referred approvingly to the California ruling in Belous, which had referred to the Court's "repeated acknowledgment of a 'right of privacy' or 'liberty' in matters related to marriage, family, and sex." Planned Parenthood highlighted "the fundamental nature of the rights of the individual in areas relating to marriage, the family and sex." The feminist brief by Stearns emphasized the sexual rights of women, declaring, "Man and woman have equal responsibility for the act of sexual intercourse. Should the woman accidentally become pregnant, against her will, however, she endures in many instances the entire burden or 'punishment.'" The brief also observed, "Forcing a woman to bear a child against her will is indeed a form of punishment, a result of society's ambivalent attitude towards female sexuality. The existence of the sexual 'double standard' has created the social response that when a woman becomes pregnant accidentally, she must be 'punished' for her transgression, particularly if she is single." The brief concluded that "by denying women the right to abortion the state is punishing her for her sexual activity with the equivalent of long-term imprisonment and giving her an indeterminate sentence of life with an unwanted child." These statements were based on a feminist vision of sexual freedom, liberty, and equality.[70]

At the same time, the briefs qualified their support for sexual rights. For instance, the arguments that privileged the rights of Mary Doe over those of Jane Roe were based in part on the notion that married couples had special sexual rights. Responding to the argument that the Does lacked standing, the jurisdictional statement insisted that the case was not hypothetical because of the impact of the laws on "marital relations." The main brief explained that the Does "face the choice of refraining from normal sexual relations or of endangering Mary Doe's health through a possible pregnancy." The brief continued, "It is not their right to end an unwanted pregnancy at present that is being violated by the statute, but rather, the right to engage in normal marital relations with the assurance that should contraception fail, Mary's health would not be endangered." No comparable arguments were put forward about the sexual rights of Roe or other unmarried women.[71]

The most direct comments about sex laws were made as the briefs wrestled with the interests claimed by the state, which focused on protecting public health, promoting morality, and defending human life. Responding to the claim that the abortion laws promoted morality, the main brief argued that "the availability of adultery and fornication statutes to enforce strictures on sexual behavior" meant that the abortion laws were "overly broad" because they applied to married couples. This became more clear when the brief highlighted the Court's conclusion in *Griswold* that "the statute could not be justified as a device to discourage pre-marital or extra-marital relations, for it had the same impact on marital relations." The brief then declared, "The Texas abortion law operates identically. No distinction is made between married and unmarried women, and married women who seek abortion are not required to reveal whether they were impregnated through a lawful marital relation. The Texas statute, if explained as a deterrent to illegal sexual conduct, is unconstitutionally overbroad for failing to make these distinctions. Moreover, if the state desires to discourage certain sexual conduct, it may enforce laws prohibiting adultery and fornication." The main brief also insisted that "no evidence exists that limited access to abortion curtails promiscuity." These points were based on the assumption that the state's interest in promoting heteronormative sexual morality was legitimate.[72]

Along similar lines, Planned Parenthood noted that "any asserted state interest in enforcing morals by forbidding abortions, on the theory that this would prevent illicit sexual conduct, scarcely merits discussion." First, PPFA argued that "neither Texas nor Georgia draws any distinction between pregnancies occurring within the marriage relationship and those outside it." The brief then pointed out that "narrowly drawn statutes exist or may be devised for the purpose of deterring sexual misconduct." The idea of punishing "illicit intercourse" with "unwanted pregnancy" was "monstrous" and "there is no reasonable basis for believing that illegal sexual behavior has been or will be deterred by proscribing abortion." This section of the brief concluded by insisting that "any interest in deterring fornication or adultery cannot be deemed sufficiently compelling to justify the interference worked by these statutes on the rights of women (including married women pregnant by their husbands) and the rights of their physicians."[73]

The feminist briefs joined the others in making these types of arguments. According to Stearns, "As for the use of abortion laws to ensure the community standards of morality, it should be clear from this Court's decision in *Griswold* . . . that such an argument is not constitutionally sufficient." Insofar as the law affected married women, the state could not claim that its goal was to discourage nonmarital sex. Bradford noted that "it is often argued that restrictions on abortion discourage sexual promiscuity . . . and thus enhance 'public morality.'" However, Bradford contended that "there is no evidence that a prohibition on abortion deters 'immoral conduct' or even non-marital sex." After reviewing the *Eisenstadt* ruling, which rejected the notion that "deterrence of pre-marital sex may reasonably be regarded as the purpose of the Massachusetts law," the brief concluded, "A prohibition on abortion without limitation to specifically criminal conduct (e.g., fornication, adultery, prostitution) sweeps too broadly, prohibiting abortion for unwanted pregnancy occurring in marriage." The brief also declared, "What is the woman's crime? . . . Is her crime that of having engaged in a sexual relationship? If the relationship occurred within marriage, no crime is involved." The feminists who submitted briefs in *Roe* presented distinctive arguments based on women's rights, but joined their allies in offering arguments that could be used to overturn abortion restrictions while retaining laws against sex.[74]

ROE, LIKE THE OTHER RULINGS discussed in this chapter, has often been portrayed, criticized, and celebrated as a "sexual freedom decision." Chapter 1 showed that there is little support for this view in the opinions of the justices. This chapter has shown that there is little support for this view in the work of the activists and advocates responsible for bringing these cases to and through the courts. Working within a conservative legal system, liberal and leftist lawyers in *Griswold*, *Fanny Hill*, *Loving*, *Eisenstadt*, and *Roe* used strategies and developed arguments that encouraged the justices to affirm special rights and privileges for heterosexual, marital, and reproductive forms of sexual expression. Whether or not they believed in sexual freedom and equality, their strategies and arguments helped the Court develop its doctrine of heteronormative supremacy.

4 : Boutilier's Defenders

Liberal and leftist advocates supported the development of the Supreme Court's heteronormative doctrine in *Griswold, Fanny Hill, Loving, Eisenstadt,* and *Roe.* They also contributed to the antigay language and logic of *Boutilier.* In part, this can be attributed to the constraints of the legal system, but it also reflects the influence of heteronormative ideas on, and the strategic choices made by, Boutilier's supporters.

Three sets of advocates fought for Boutilier. Blanch Freedman, a leftist immigration lawyer affiliated with the American Committee for the Protection of the Foreign Born (ACPFB), served as his primary attorney. Although Freedman and her comrades had battled immigration authorities for decades and *Boutilier* was not their first case to reach the Court, it may have been their first to deal with homosexuality, a subject long treated with ambivalence by the left. Boutilier's second set of advocates worked through the Homosexual Law Reform Society, a new organization in the homophile movement. By the mid-1960s, this movement had been defending the interests of homosexual citizens for nearly two decades but rarely focused on aliens. Boutilier was also supported by the ACLU and the New York Civil Liberties Union (NYCLU), both of which had years of experience fighting for the rights of immigrants and homosexuals, but did not fully embrace sexual freedom and equality. This chapter introduces Boutilier's advocates; the next shows that their arguments were marked by profound ambivalence about homosexuality.

By the mid-1960s, there was a long history of conflict and cooperation between leftists, libertarians, and homophile activists in the United States. Before World War II, communists, socialists, and anarchists often joined forces with civil libertarians, many of them leftists, to oppose violations of free speech and due process rights. In the Cold War years, however, many leftists disdained the patriotic pieties of civil libertarians and criticized the ACLU's involvement in anticommunist campaigns and the defense of fascists. Civil libertarians, in turn, often distanced themselves from leftists accused of endorsing violence, advocating revolution, or promoting totalitarianism. In the 1940s, the ACLU began purging communists from its ranks and supporting anticommunist crusades.[1] Meanwhile, the U.S. homophile movement was founded in the early 1950s by former communists, and homophile activists counted ACLU lawyers among their most important allies. But the homophile movement became strongly anticommunist in the mid-1950s, and in the 1960s some homophile activists criticized the ACLU's positions on sexual matters. And while anarchists had a long tradition of supporting sexual liberation, many socialists and communists regarded homosexuality as a form of bourgeois decadence and treated sexual politics as a distraction from class struggle.[2] In *Boutilier*, leftists, libertarians, and homophiles had different agendas, but worked together in an extraordinary coalition. Paradoxically, they all contributed to the Court's conservative decision.

Boutilier's advocates used great legal skills and savvy strategic politics in selecting their case, developing their arguments, and presenting them to the Court. In Boutilier, they had a long-time U.S. resident who could be portrayed as a member of the country's dominant racial, linguistic, and religious groups; a son and brother who was part of a heteronormative and patriotic family; a worker who conformed to ruling-class values; and a petitioner whose sexual history and gender presentation were minimally transgressive. In the Immigration and Nationality Act of 1952, Boutilier's advocates had a law with an ambiguous legislative history, unclear definitions of key terms, and procedural provisions open to conflicting interpretations. In the scientific experts whose views they emphasized, the advocates had the support of influential cultural authorities. Despite all of this, they knew it would be difficult to convince the Court to reverse or make an exception to its heteronormative doctrine, and Boutilier's primary lawyers were obliged to represent his interests and not necessarily those of the movements supporting his litigation. If this meant condoning social hierarchies, endorsing dominant values, or relying on experts whose fields were responsible for the pathologization of homosexuality, at least Boutilier's advocates could know they were fighting hard for their client. They hoped their arguments would yield a positive ruling and a useful precedent.

Unfortunately for Boutilier, this is not what occurred. Instead of helping Boutilier win, the strategy of emphasizing his positive qualities reproduced the conservative politics of respectability and led the Court to conclude that all homosexual aliens, no matter how respectable they were, could be excluded and deported. The arguments that minimized Boutilier's same-sex sexual experiences implied there was something undesirable about homosexuality and contributed to a ruling suggesting that any homosexual activity was sufficient to justify exclusion or deportation. The description of homosexuality as a variable behavior rather than a fixed characteristic encouraged the Court to view it as a choice that one could resist and discouraged the justices from considering identity-based arguments. The advocates' deference to expertise condoned the Court's acceptance of antigay scientific perspectives and prompted the justices to underscore the state's authority over science. Acknowledging these effects need not lead to the conclusion that Boutilier's advocates, in their historical circumstances, made unwise choices; rather, it helps reveal how their choices and circumstances interacted.

Radical Immigration Advocacy

Boutilier's primary lawyers brought to his case the skills and strategies they had developed over decades of fighting on behalf of immigrants, leftists, workers, and women. Robert Brown served as Boutilier's lawyer in 1959 when he was charged with sodomy, but there is no evidence that Boutilier consulted a lawyer in 1963 when he applied for citizenship and revealed information about his arrest. In January 1964, he was interrogated by an INS investigator without a lawyer present. At some point in this period, Boutilier contacted Brown, who arranged for him to see psychiatrist Edward Falsey. Falsey apparently met twice with Boutilier during the period when he was having difficulty with his citizenship application. Nearly a year later, the INS ruled that Boutilier was subject to deportation; he was notified on 4 February 1965.[3]

Sometime in the next few weeks, Blanch Freedman began acting as Boutilier's attorney. Brown likely referred Boutilier to Freedman because she was a well-known immigration lawyer and her Manhattan office was near his. Freedman represented Boutilier at an INS hearing on 8 March and arranged for him to see psychiatrist Montague Ullman on 30 March. Ullman was not an expert on homosexuality, but had known Freedman's brother in the U.S. military during World War II. When Freedman wrote Ullman to confirm Boutilier's appointment, she noted, "I would very much appreciate your reading the enclosed extract from the Court's opinion in a similar case. The alien's statement and criminal court record in that case was considerably more damaging than what obtains in the Boutilier case." She was probably referring to *Rosenberg* and trying to influence Ullman's assessment. With assistance from Brown and her husband David, Freedman acted as Boutilier's main advocate for the next several years.[4]

Born Blanch Laven in New York City in 1908, Freedman was the child of Russian Jewish immigrants. According to her brother, she was the only woman in her graduating class at St. John's University Law School. He also writes, "She was a most attractive blonde and all the young congressmen and judges wanted her to clerk for them but she didn't like their politics. Instead, she later married a red radical." In 1940, the Freedmans had a son, Michael, who later became a professor of anthropology.[5]

Whether Freedman was a member of the Communist Party is not clear, though she certainly lived in the milieu of the left. Her brother indicates that he was a party member and believes the Freedmans were once denied passports because of their association with him. Michael Meeropol, the son of Julius and Ethel Rosenberg, recalls that he and Michael Freedman went to the same summer camp in the 1950s. Gay activist and writer Allen Young, related by marriage to the Freedmans, remembers Blanch as a socialist and a vegetarian. A 1952 obituary for Freedman's law partner Carol King states that King denied being a Communist Party member. Another law partner, Gloria Agrin, later denounced the "cowardly" role played by the Party in the trial of the Rosenbergs, whom the U.S. government executed in 1953 after they were convicted of spying for the Soviet Union. Freedman's brother remembers Blanch as "first and foremost a caring lawyer and also an activist . . . of the best kind— never a zealot, pragmatic, and always open but with an inbred, strong, keen sense of justice and fairness."[6]

By the time Freedman began serving as Boutilier's lawyer, she was well known for her advocacy on behalf of workers, women, leftists, and immigrants. In the 1930s and 1940s, she was active in the Women's Trade Union League, eventually becoming the organization's executive secretary. She also got involved with the ACPFB, which was founded in the 1930s and targeted by the U.S. Subversive Activities Control Board in the 1950s. In a high-profile 1949 case supported by the ACPFB, Freedman defended thirty-seven aliens threatened with deportation to Pakistan.[7]

In the late 1940s and 1950s, the Freedmans defended various victims of the Red Scare. In a 1950 Supreme Court case, David helped defend the General Secretary of the U.S. Communist Party, who unsuccessfully challenged his conviction on contempt charges for refusing to appear before the House Committee on Un-American Activities. David also represented the *Daily Worker*, the National Lawyers Guild, and the Independent-Socialist Party.[8]

In the late 1940s, Blanch formed a law partnership with King, who had a long career defending immigrants, union leaders, leftists, and African Americans, including the Scottsboro Boys. In a Second Circuit case decided in 1951, King and Freedman unsuccessfully defended a Finnish national subject to deportation because he had concealed a prior conviction in England. In another Second Circuit case decided the same year, they unsuccessfully defended a Greek national subject to deportation because of past membership in the U.S.

Communist Party. After King died, Freedman took charge of *Gordon*, which concerned a Finnish-born Canadian citizen subject to deportation because of past membership in the U.S. Communist Party.[9] Around this time Freedman formed a law partnership with Agrin, who helped defend the Rosenbergs. The judge who sentenced the Rosenbergs to death was Irving Kaufman, who later wrote the Second Circuit opinion against Boutilier.[10]

Over the next few years, Freedman and Agrin worked on various immigration cases while also representing the ACPFB and the Joint Anti-Fascist Refugee Committee. In 1953, they unsuccessfully argued before Kaufman in *Radzie*, which dealt with the denaturalization of a man found to have made false statements about his communist party membership. In 1954, Freedman argued her first case before the Supreme Court, winning *Barber*, which overturned the deportation of a man born in the Philippines who had been convicted of assault and burglary in California and Washington. According to the Court, the man had moved to the U.S. mainland before the Philippines gained independence from the United States and therefore could not be deported for crimes committed "after entry." In 1955, Freedman and Agrin again argued before the Supreme Court, this time winning *Nukk*, which challenged the supervision requirements imposed on fourteen communists and former communists on parole while awaiting deportation.[11]

Freedman's work on these and other cases exposed her to the morals provisions of U.S. immigration law. In 1956, Freedman and Agrin won *Dickhoff*, a district court decision making an alien who had belonged to the Communist Party in 1929–30 eligible for suspension of deportation. U.S. authorities had claimed that Freedman's client was ineligible because a divorce he obtained in Mexico was invalid, which meant he was committing adultery with his second wife and therefore was not "a person of good moral character." The district court overturned this decision, arguing that just as another court had held that Congress could not have meant to authorize the deportation of aliens who "accidentally, artificially, or unconsciously" joined an organization "of whose platform and purposes they have no real knowledge," in this case "Congress could not have intended to authorize the wholesale deportation of aliens who, accidentally, artificially, unknowingly, or unconsciously in appearance only, are found to have technically committed adultery."[12]

In the late 1950s, Freedman continued to argue immigration and border control cases. In 1957, she and Agrin represented African American scholar-activist W. E. B. DuBois after the State Department refused to renew his passport unless he signed an anticommunist statement. In 1959, the Freedmans and Agrin won *Siminoff*, a Second Circuit case concerning restrictions placed on the movements of seven deportable communists not yet expelled. Then in 1960, Freedman filed an ACPFB brief in *Niukkanen*; in this case the Supreme Court upheld the deportation of a Finnish national who had come to the United States as an infant and was accused of having belonged to the Communist Party in 1937–39.[13]

Freedman's name does not appear in any Supreme Court or Court of Appeals decisions between *Niukkanen* in 1960 and *Boutilier* in 1966–67. Nevertheless, her earlier participation in cases involving immigrants and leftists influenced her *Boutilier* strategies and arguments. To begin with, when she argued *Boutilier* she was appearing before judges and justices who had encountered her before, and they likely associated her with cases involving immigrants and leftists. As other scholars have noted, homosexuals were often seen as communists in the 1950s and 1960s, communists were often seen as homosexuals, and both were seen as secretive subversives who threatened the nation. As Douglas's *Boutilier* dissent made evident when it drew parallels between the targeting of communists and the targeting of homosexuals, these links were activated in *Boutilier* and Freedman's presence helped activate them.[14]

Beyond this, Freedman's defense of Boutilier drew on her knowledge of the bureaucracy of border control, the mechanisms of deportation and exclusion, the provisions of immigration law, and the vulnerabilities of working-class immigrants. In many respects, Freedman's *Boutilier* arguments were based on the templates of her earlier arguments defending leftists and immigrants. When she challenged the government's interpretation of the legislative intent of the "psychopathic personality" provision, she was making the kind of argument she had made about the legislative intent of other immigration statutes. When she highlighted Boutilier's frank admission of homosexual acts, she was distinguishing his case from those of aliens accused of making false statements. When she emphasized Boutilier's family ties in the United States, she was doing what she had done when defending other immigrants. When she denied the contention that pre- or post-entry homosexual conduct constituted proof of homosexual character at time of entry, she was making the kinds of chronological and conceptual distinctions she had made when arguing on behalf of ex-communists. When she argued that the vagueness of the psychopathic personality statute left aliens ignorant about proscribed conduct, she was using the type of argument that had convinced the courts to make exceptions for aliens who "unknowingly" joined the Communist Party or committed morals offenses. When she avoided arguing that there was a right to be a homosexual or engage in homosexual conduct, she was doing what she had done when she had avoided arguing that there was a right to be a communist or engage in subversive conduct. In these and other ways, the defense of leftists and immigrants influenced *Boutilier*'s defense.

Homophile Advocacy

One of the lessons Freedman had learned from her earlier legal work was the importance of forming alliances. Toward the end of 1966, she contacted Norman Leonard, the lawyer representing Gerald Lavoie, whose gay-related deportation case reached the Supreme Court around the same time that Boutilier's did. Leonard told Freedman, "I guess that the court is simply going to sit on my case until it disposes of yours. I do not think that there is anything I can do except possibly examine your brief. . . . My client appears to be less interested in the problem than does yours, and I think that, if he has to, he would go back to Canada without much concern."[15]

Freedman also reached out to the homophile movement. In part, the motivation was financial. In February 1965, Freedman billed Boutilier $500, which he paid off in monthly installments. At some point in 1966, Boutilier was fired from his job after his case was publicized. By January 1967, Freedman's total expenses on *Boutilier* approached $3000; this included a $550 fee for filing the Supreme Court writ, $1000 for printing costs, and $1000 for her services. Boutilier paid more than $1100, but that left nearly $2000 outstanding. After the Second Circuit ruled against Boutilier in 1966, Freedman contacted the homophile movement.[16]

The earliest homosexual rights groups in the United States were formed in the early twentieth century, but these were small and short-lived until the 1950s, when the Mattachine Society, One, and the Daughters of Bilitis were established. By the mid-1960s, the movement included organizations in all regions of the country and had thousands of supporters. Homophile activists organized discussion groups, sponsored lectures and conferences, distributed literature, and published newsletters and magazines, including *ONE*, *Mattachine Review*, and the *Ladder*. They cultivated alliances with other movements and organizations, provided information and advice to individuals in need, spoke to community groups, promoted positive media representations, criticized discriminatory policies and practices, and challenged those who viewed homosexuality as a sin, crime, or disease.[17]

From its earliest days, the homophile movement regarded legal reform as important. In the 1950s and 1960s, homophile periodicals reported extensively on the progress of sex-law reform in the United States and elsewhere. In the 1950s, several homophile law reform groups, including the Los Angeles Mattachine Legal Chapter, which became the National Association for Sexual Research (NASR), were established. According to *ONE*, NASR had an "elaborate program for legal defense, law reform and general research" and was active for five years.[18]

Agreement on the importance of law reform did not mean there was consensus about how to promote legal change. In some contexts, homophile activists emphasized public education, believing that adjustments in social attitudes were necessary before legal change could be achieved. In other contexts, they promoted involvement in electoral and party politics, lending support to sympathetic politicians, encouraging dialogue with candidates, and mobilizing voters. Homophile activists also lobbied federal, state, and local officials. Influenced by the civil rights movement, homophile militants in the mid-1960s began to organize demonstrations, pickets, and sit-ins to publicize their cause and accelerate the pace of change. Homophile groups also pursued reform through the courts, and this became a favored strategy in the 1960s.

Although the movement regarded legal reform as important, it did not focus on immigration law. The decriminalization of private homosexual acts by consenting adults was the movement's highest priority, if one is to judge by the frequency with which it was discussed in the homophile press. In the 1960s, achievement of this goal in Illinois and Connecticut received extensive coverage in the gay and lesbian press. Homophile groups targeted legal reform in five other areas: (1) liquor control and police practices, (2) employment discrimination, (3) military policies and practices, (4) obscenity law enforcement, and (5) sex offender and sexual psychopath laws. This last area used the same key term as the psychopathic personality immigration statute, but the homophile movement paid little attention to immigration law until *Boutilier*. The lawyer who argued *Rosenberg*, the first gay immigration case accepted for argument by the Supreme Court, was Hiram Kwan, an Asian American attorney who identified as straight and had no known connections to the homophile movement.[19]

In discussing law reform, many homophile activists qualified their support for sexual liberalization. Proposals to decriminalize private homosexual acts by consenting adults were routinely accompanied by clarifying statements that supported laws against public sex, sexual violence, sex with minors, incest, and prostitution, though opinions were more divided on prostitution. Many activists made it clear that, while they were opposed to the unfair application of obscenity laws, they did not reject anti-obscenity laws. Determined to show they were advocating responsible reform, homophile activists frequently highlighted the sex laws they favored.

Homophile disinterest in immigration law can be linked to two assumptions shared by many activists: that the movement was of and for U.S. citizens and that the Constitution, if properly interpreted, protected the rights of homosexuals. Evidence of the first assumption is ubiquitous in the homophile press. "We are citizens of this country," declared an open letter to a U.S. Senator that was published in *Mattachine Review* in 1955. "Every citizen" is entitled to civil rights, insisted the Mattachine Board of Directors shortly thereafter. This type of rhetoric was used despite the fact that U.S. homophile groups included members who were not U.S. citizens; the homophile press prided itself on its international readership; and homophile media regularly published letters from aliens inside and readers outside the United States.[20]

The movement's disinterest in immigration law can also be linked to its faith in the Constitution. Homophile activists routinely promoted the notion that the rights of homosexuals were protected by the Constitution, not pausing to acknowledge that, as interpreted by the courts, the Constitution offered limited protection to homosexual aliens. In 1959, Daughters of Bilitis (DOB) founder Del Martin observed that homosexuals "are citizens of these United States and as such are entitled to those civil rights set forth under the provisions of our Constitution." In 1961, DOB president Jaye Bell wrote that "the only rights we want are those given to us as a whole people under the United States Bill of Rights." If these and other comments are any indication, it scarcely occurred to most homophile activists that the Constitution might be a deeply flawed document that failed to protect gay and lesbian rights in general and the rights of gay and lesbian aliens in particular.[21]

Influenced by their beliefs about the Constitution and the examples of the civil rights and civil liberties movements, homophile activists followed, funded, and fought a variety of court cases. Perhaps the movement's greatest success in the 1950s was its victory in the *ONE* obscenity case, and the homophile press provided extensive coverage of many other obscenity cases. A second set of cases that drew intense homophile interest concerned gay bars and other commercial establishments. In 1959, for example, the DOB assisted a lawyer who filed an *amicus* brief in a successfully appealed San Francisco bar case. In the early 1960s, a Mattachine legal defense fund aided those charged with frequenting a disorderly house in San Francisco, and Pan-Graphic Press, which was affiliated with Mattachine, printed the main brief in another California bar case. A third area of interest consisted of cases dealing with sexual and gender conduct, where important victories were registered in several lower courts.[22]

Emboldened by the victories in *ONE*, *Manual*, and *Rosenberg*, some activists began arguing for increased use of court-based strategies. In 1963, a letter published in *ONE* urged the movement to "study the possibility of setting up a test case which might reach the U.S. Supreme Court." More specifically, "Two adults accompanied by a friendly attorney could go and confess to committing a 'crime against nature' in the privacy of their home." In 1964, homophile leader Frank Kameny "advocated . . . that already existing legal channels, including the U.S. Supreme Court, be more widely used." Later the same year, Kameny argued at a homophile conference that "one good court case or court decision will go farther than a dozen radio appearances." He "urged that discriminatory laws and regulations be tested in the courts and that cases be encouraged, even rigged up if necessary." After noting that "judicial means are more practical, since legislatures are tied in too closely with the prejudices we're fighting," Kameny observed, "The Negro went to the courts and Southerners still don't like him. He nevertheless now has his basic rights. . . . The changes in attitude will accommodate themselves to what constituted authority hands down."[23]

At the same conference, David Carliner, who had worked on the *Naim* interracial marriage case and later co-authored the ACLU *Boutilier* brief, urged the movement to pursue court-based strategies. According to a summary of Carliner's comments, "Arguments about morality and attempts to influence votes are fruitless tactics for homophile groups. . . . We must distinguish between what the courts will do and what the Congress will do. . . . The courts . . . are very sensitive to demands for rights in the due process field. One way of getting to the Supreme Court is through conflicting decisions obtained in the various circuit courts. Most landmark cases in the Supreme Court have been the result of deliberate legal strategy." Three lawyers on a panel with Carliner agreed. According to one, "Brick by brick, and stone by stone, the law is built. The homosexual is consigned to slow and piecemeal progress. Start with the easiest inroad: change in and enlargement of procedural rights in cases of dismissal for homosexuality." According to the second panelist, "Attitudes in the courts toward homosexuality are now more realistic and civilized, and the prognosis for change is favorable." The third lawyer noted, "Only recently have enlightened and courageous defendants been willing to give their lawyers the opportunity to push the courts into rulings which would help build a defense for the position of the homosexual. Homophile groups can lend support to these defendants." Kameny then asked if the panelists were "willing to form a board to look into the possibility of a coordinated, multi-attorney approach to planned legal strategy." After a positive response, Carliner noted that "the NAACP has raised a legal defense fund" and Kameny "proposed that such a plan be the first order of business for the new Board."[24]

Over the next few years, Mattachine Washington took the lead in litigation challenging government employment discrimination.[25] Meanwhile, California homophiles also turned to the courts. According to a 1964 issue of *Mattachine Review*, Mattachine Los Angeles contributed money to promote "the complete revamp of California's penal code"; San Francisco's League for Civil Education raised $3,000 in gay bars to support litigation; and the Tavern Guild in San Francisco provided legal services to gay bars. After a New Year's Ball sponsored by the Council on Religion and the Homosexual in San Francisco was raided by police in 1965, the Council successfully fought back in court. In 1966, several homophile groups went to court after the California State Fair denied them permission to sponsor a booth. Gay lawyers Evander Smith and Herb Donaldson, who were active in the homophile movement, defended gay rights in several California cases. In 1966, Smith appealed *Smayda*, an "oral copulation" ruling, to the Supreme Court, which denied *cert*.[26]

Over time, court-based strategies gained more support. Toward the end of 1965, an article in *ONE* highlighted the importance of its Supreme Court victory. Criticizing the movement's recent emphasis on demonstrations, the article noted that gay and lesbian press reports "seem to imply that this struck some great blow for homophile freedom, and there is much mention of how the pickets dressed." Complaining that "we are told less about their specific accomplishments than about those white shirts and ties," *ONE* observed, "It might be wondered if these enthusiasts are aware that a U.S. Supreme Court decision creates 'case law' which is binding upon the Courts of all the States. It is as if all of the legislatures had in that particular matter acted favorably." At a 1965 conference, psychoanalyst Ernest van den Haag "urged the homophile organizations to do what Negro groups have done successfully — they should get test cases in the courts and try to get the laws against homosexual acts invalidated." In 1966, Ernestine Eckstein, an African American member of the NAACP, DOB New York, and Mattachine New York, observed in the *Ladder*, "I don't find in the homophile movement enough stress on courtroom action. I would like to see more test cases." Later in 1966, a DOB conference panel concluded that "legal improvements" were "far more likely . . . to be made through judicial processes than by State legislatures" because the courts were "freer from inhibiting political pressures."[27]

Freedman thus contacted the homophile movement at a moment when it had become interested in pursuing court cases, but not necessarily ones that concerned immigration. On 21 July 1966, she spoke by telephone with Dick Leitsch, the president of Mattachine New York. The following day, she wrote to request assistance: "The constitutional questions on appeal and the outcome of this litigation (although of immediate and paramount importance to Mr. Boutilier) are of wide concern and far transcend the personal interests of my client. Involved is the basic issue of due process of law to which everyone including the hapless alien is entitled. There is also the important matter of statutory interpretation of the term 'afflicted with a psychopathic personality' which has been construed by the lower courts and the government to automatically and arbitrarily embrace all homosexuality irrespective of the existence of any pathology." According to Freedman, Boutilier had "carried the cost of these proceedings thus far alone" but was "not financially circumstanced to continue." After describing how costly the appeal would be, she wrote, "For one whose income is very modest the burden is much too great." Appealing for help, she stressed that she had less than a month to file her petition.[28]

Freedman wrote to Leitsch in a period when Mattachine New York became involved in several significant cases. These included *Robillard*, a police entrapment case rejected for consideration by the Court on the same day it accepted *Boutilier*; a federal court challenge to U.S. Customs, which was blocking the importation of magazines with nude male photographs; a state court challenge to the use of vagrancy laws against drag queens; and several gay bar cases. In March 1967, Leitsch wrote to a friend that his group had been asked to file a brief in defense of "a nice lesbian in Poughkeepsie" who was "up for deportation back to Denmark." Leitsch explained, "She's been here twenty years, has had several lovers. According to the government's own brief . . . , she never outraged public decency in any manner. They held a hearing and decided to throw her out because she's a 'psychopathic personality.' Fearing an adverse ruling . . . in *Boutilier*, they changed this, and said she was not psychopathic. Instead, they're tossing her out as a person of 'poor moral character.'" Leitsch continued, "We've been asked to file *amicus* (another five or seven hundred dollars—where is it coming from?), but there's a complication. Not only do we face the necessity of proving that private, consenting lesbian activities . . . can be moral, we must also counter previous court rulings which have held that 'good moral character is conduct which measures up as good among the average citizens of the community in which the applicant lives, or is conduct that conforms to the generally accepted moral conventions current at the time.'" Leitsch also wrote about Mattachine's success in persuading the New York Supreme Court to rule that the State Liquor Authority (SLA) could not revoke the licenses of bars "simply because homosexuals gather" in them, but complained that the SLA had begun targeting bars that permitted same-sex dancing.[29]

Shortly after Freedman contacted Leitsch, he informed her that Mattachine would raise funds for *Boutilier* and invited Freedman to speak at the group's August meeting. Freedman's sister remembers going to a "big gay meeting where Blanch was the speaker" and says that Freedman later remarked, "'Everyone is so loving to me. They must think I'm a lesbian.'" Mattachine's fundraising flier, titled "A Great Society or a Straight Society," invoked the name of Lyndon Johnson's liberal program, reprinted an article about the Second Circuit decision against Boutilier, and observed that "the issue at stake is basically whether the homosexual has a place in the 'Great Society.'" For Mattachine, the "main issue," which was "whether the term 'psychopathic personality' includes homosexuality," was "far more pressing than whether Mr. Boutilier remains in the United States." Like Freedman's letter, Mattachine's flier suggested that the importance of Boutilier's case transcended his personal interests; in fact, the flier placed the interests of the movement over and above the interests of Boutilier.[30]

Mattachine, however, did not turn over any funds to Freedman. In January 1967, Freedman complained to Leitsch that this was "not quite fair or proper" given that "funds were solicited ... and moneys have been received by you for this purpose." In June, Mattachine New York's newsletter reported that the group had raised $3600 for its bar cases but said nothing about *Boutilier*. Then in December, several months after *Boutilier* was decided, Leitsch referred to the case when responding to a man writing in "desperation" because a gay friend was "about to be deported to France." Leitsch took partial credit for *Boutilier*, claiming that "MSNY recently participated in a challenge to this before the U.S. Supreme Court." He observed, "Unfortunately, we lost, but I will admit that the case was built on rather shaky grounds, and was not exactly an ideal test-case." Mattachine may have decided against funding *Boutilier* because of the "shaky grounds," though this seems like a retrospective evaluation. What may have been more significant was that in late 1966 Freedman accepted an offer of assistance by the Homosexual Law Reform Society (HLRS). Once she took this step, political conflicts and personal enmities between the leaders of Mattachine New York and HLRS contributed to Mattachine's withdrawal of support.[31]

HLRS was established in 1966 by the Philadelphia-based Janus Society. Under the leadership of Clark Polak, Janus did many things that other homophile groups did, but it also struck out in new directions, most significantly by publishing *Drum* magazine, which integrated homophile militancy, sexual liberationism, and gay pornography. According to advertisements for the magazine, first published in 1964, "*DRUM* presents news for 'queers,' and fiction for 'perverts.' Photo essays for 'fairies' and laughs for 'faggots.'" Aspiring to be "a gay *Playboy*, with the news coverage of *Time*," *Drum* promoted homophile sexual liberation through male physique photographs, campy comic strips, playful parodies, naughty news, pro-gay features, and pro-sex editorials. Within months of its founding, *Drum*'s readership was larger than that of all other homophile publications combined; within a few years its circulation was 15,000 per issue. Polak also established Trojan Book Service and Beaver Book Service, which became major producers and distributors of gay and straight pornography.[32]

Many homophile leaders attacked Janus and *Drum*, fearing that sexual liberationism would provide ammunition for movement enemies. In February 1965, East Coast Homophile Organizations (ECHO), a regional federation, expelled Janus. Asserting in a draft of a letter to Polak that "the ACLU, while defending the right of *Playboy* to be published, would not publish a *Playboy*-type of magazine," ECHO argued that "controversial, unconventional, and unusual ideas and positions have far higher probability of being listened to and accepted, if presented within the framework of, and clothed with the symbols of acceptability, conventionality, and respectability." Leitsch observed privately that he was "exceedingly aware that *Drum* was selling well," but complained that "it contains nothing likely to reach the public." He concluded, "If we're in business to entertain, then let's go whole hog and provide drag shows, muscle movies, gay bars, dances and orgies!" Mattachine Washington editorialized against "magazines which contain both articles of serious homophile interest and photographs of naked teenage boys," which "bolster the public's erroneous image of the homosexual as a child-molesting sex fiend." At a conference in 1966, Kameny declared, "This is the homophile movement—we are not fighting for sexual freedom."[33]

In response, Polak indicted the "comic-opera gulf between the unrealistic homophile movement and the realities of homosexual life," criticized the movement's "anti-homosexual disdain," and attacked movement publications for "groveling obsequiousness." Drawing on the black power critique of civil rights "Uncle Toms," Polak assailed groups that cared only about "'good' homosexuals," which he labeled "Aunt Maryism." In contrast, Polak argued for a broad agenda of sexual liberation, writing at one point to *Time* and the *New Republic*: "However egregious the laws against the love that dare not speak its name, we must not lose sight of the prohibitions that effectively class the sub-

stantial majority of the adult population as sex criminals. The sodomy statutes
. . . make certain acts married heterosexuals enjoy with their spouses equally
illegal, and when this is added to the weight of the abortion, birth control,
obscenity, prostitution, adultery, fornication, and cohabitation laws, we are
hard put to find any citizen free of legal anti-sexualism." Polak did all of this
while fighting obscenity charges, a problem that escalated after *Ginzburg* and
Mishkin prompted the Department of Justice to conclude that he would be
"an ideal target for a test case" to affirm that "commercial advertisements are
not protected by the first amendment."[34]

Many of Polak's projects defied the politics of respectability, but he also
poured his profits into legal battles, often fought with respectable tactics. In
1963, he declared, "Last on my list of projects but first on my personal mind
is legal reform. . . . This is an area where we need professional advice and
lots of money, and for these reasons, must be held in secondary position for
the time being." One year later, Polak wrote to the Janus board of directors
that *Drum*'s success meant that Janus could now afford "to finance other long
term projects." Rhetorically asking, "Should we assume a more militant role in
bringing about law reform?" Polak answered, "Yes, with care." He concluded,
"I recommend an investigation of the procedure necessary to put us into a
position of forcing the recalcitrant legislators into action. Perhaps the best
policy will be to leave things alone, or to attempt to bring actions in several
states so that the Supreme Court will be forced to make an adjudication or to
initiate action on corollary issues such as the Negro did in gaining the decision
that Negros cannot be indicted by a Grand Jury that systematically excluded
them from service. Are there homosexual parallels?"[35]

Toward the end of 1964, Janus began discussions about forming "a new organization along the lines of the Homosexual Law Reform Society" in Great
Britain. A few months earlier, Janus's magazine had published a letter from
the secretary of the British HLRS, who noted that "we are not an organization
of homosexuals, but a broad-based national society supported by many eminent people." Shortly thereafter Polak announced the formation of the Janus
Society Advisory Board, which was "patterned after the Homosexual Law Reform Society and the Albany Trust" in Great Britain. Among the "prominent"
people who joined the board were attorneys Gilbert Cantor (author of the
HLRS *Boutilier* brief) and Spencer Coxe (executive director of the Greater
Philadelphia ACLU).[36]

Initially Janus's litigation plans were blocked by lack of money. In February
1965, the Janus newsletter reported that "Tropic of Crabs," a sexually explicit
parody of Henry Miller's *Tropic of Cancer*, had been removed from a recent

issue of *Drum*. According to Polak, "Since we were not currently in a position to support litigation in the courts, it was best to avoid possible controversy." Polak continued, "Any indictment against CRABS would have been thrown out of Federal courts, but the road there is paved with solid gold." Polak, however, had not given up. In April, *Drum* reported on Max Doyle, a "transvestite" sentenced to twenty to thirty years on a sodomy charge in North Carolina. After a court ordered Doyle released because his right to counsel had been violated, Polak observed, "Doyle's case brings home the need for appeals of sodomy convictions. . . . If the states do not bring their own houses in order, others will do it for them."[37]

Around this time, Janus acquired the necessary financial resources. Significant fundraising began with an anonymous $6000 donation in 1965; according to *Drum*, "a substantial portion of the fund is being reserved to help finance future court cases." In July 1965 (one month after *Griswold* was announced), the Janus newsletter predicted that "the really important progress recorded for the homophile cause will ultimately stem from the courts." Shortly thereafter, Polak wrote in *Drum* that *Griswold* had bolstered his confidence and shifted his focus: "Law reform will not be effectuated through the State Legislatures" since "few elected legislators are willing to risk a brand as one who advocates perversion." Polak wrote that for this and other reasons, "We see the solution within the Federal Court system, with the Supreme Court as the final voice. The Connecticut birth control decision points the way—invasion of privacy. Clear appreciation of the value of Church-State separation is another." In November 1965, Polak wrote that Janus had raised $10,000 and "we are now looking for court cases to support." One possibility was an obscenity case involving a Massachusetts male physique photographer. A second concerned "Virginia's apparent negligence to care for and protect a man jailed on sodomy" who "ended up being blinded in one eye with temporary paralysis in his left side." The following month, the Janus newsletter mentioned two other possibilities: one concerned a Pennsylvania bar that had lost its license for "the alleged serving of alleged homosexuals"; the other dealt with a New York lesbian blackmailed by a coworker.[38]

Plans for HLRS, which came to fruition in 1966, reflected the development of a strategic politics of respectability whose effectiveness depended upon keeping legal reform projects institutionally separate from, though financially dependent on, pornographic enterprises. In January 1966, Polak wrote in *Drum*, "Reform of state laws through revisions from the individual state legislatures is simply out of the question. . . . The solution to the homosexual's legal problems rests in overthrowing the sodomy laws through appeals on constitutional grounds." Meanwhile, Janus hired lawyers to investigate two gay bar license revocations in Pennsylvania and advised two men that their arrests for "solicitation for an unnatural sex act" in Ohio were invalid because the state law had been struck down in 1965. In February 1966, *Drum* indicated that Janus was exploring the possibility of supporting Models Studio in Massachusetts in an obscenity appeal, but in September Polak announced that the results in *Fanny Hill*, *Ginzburg*, and *Mishkin* had led Janus to reconsider. At a national conference in August, Polak declared, "It is time for the movement to cease to hide behind names like Mattachine. . . . We are in the process of changing our unfortunate choice [the Janus Society] to the Homosexual Law Reform Society." He also emphasized that law reform was an instrument of broader social change: "What laws are we attempting to reform? Criminal sanctions? Hardly. The chief oppression faced by the homosexual is the cultural tone which says 'I despise you.'" In September, Polak announced that the Janus Society would be broken up into three parts: Drum Publishing Company, Janus Trust ("a non-profit, tax deductable charity"), and HLRS (for "the coordination of law reform efforts throughout the United States").[39]

Over the course of 1966, 1967, and 1968, Janus and HLRS supported court battles across the country. HLRS provided assistance in cases involving blackmail in Pennsylvania, public sex in Ohio, and bar licenses in Florida. In the bar license case, *Drum* reported in 1968 that the Supreme Court in *Inman* "refused to review a lower court decision that held that a Miami ordinance that forbids homosexuals to congregate in, be employed by, or be served in a bar . . . was constitutional." Also in 1968, HLRS established a Delaware branch that lobbied the state legislature to eliminate consensual sodomy and loitering to solicit sex from the state's criminal code. Speaking about this to a reporter, Polak made it clear that his goal was broader social change: "Almost all discussions of homosexuals begin with the assumption that homosexuality is somehow undesirable. It is our contention that homosexuality is not in any way undesirable. It is on a par and equal to, but certainly not superior to, heterosexuality."[40]

In 1968, a front-page story in the *Wall Street Journal* on homophile legal reform described HLRS as "one of the more active legal aid groups" and reported that the group spent $5,000 on court cases in 1967 and "set aside another $25,000 for future litigation." Polak was quoted as saying, "Until recently, the only court cases we got involved in were the ones we couldn't avoid. . . . Now we are very much concerned with initiating litigation." He also observed, "There's no shortage of lawyers to argue cases for homosexuals. . . . Volunteer heterosexual lawyers are the backbone of our movement. It's very similar to the early days of the civil rights movement when the strongest supporters were the whites."[41]

HLRS's greatest success came in a New Jersey gay bar case in 1967. In January 1966, *Eastern Mattachine Magazine* reported that Mattachine New York, DOB New York, and Janus were raising money to support litigation by Val's, an Atlantic City bar. The magazine predicted "a long drawn-out legal battle, culminating in a U.S. Supreme Court case." While "unfortunate" for the bar, this was thought to be "fortunate" for "the homosexual community," since "a favorable ruling by the U.S. Supreme Court (and such appears almost inevitable, if we can get the case there) would firmly establish the homosexual's freedom of assembly in every state." Moreover, the magazine hoped that "the 'legalization' of gay bars would establish a precedent" and the case could be "as important to the homophile movement as the school-desegregation case was to the Negro rights movement."[42]

In February 1966, *Drum* reported that after the bar appealed to Janus for help, "it was quickly determined that this particular case offered great possibilities as a further delineation of the right of the homosexual to assemble, and the Society responded with a cash contribution of $1,000." Norman Oshtry, a lawyer who advised Polak, Janus, and *Drum*, represented Val's, while other lawyers represented One Eleven Wine and Liquors and Murphy's Tavern in linked cases. In March 1967, *Drum* explained why HLRS was supporting *Val's*: "In this case, there are no allegations of overt homosexual conduct and the charges are solely that homosexuals congregated at Val's. The other two cases allege at least kissing between two males and attempting to have the court differentiate between the issue of public homosexual sex-expression and that of the right and desirability of homosexual association might prove difficult."[43]

In the end, the New Jersey Supreme Court ruled unanimously that homosexuals had the right to assemble in bars, absent evidence of "overtly indecent conduct" or "public displays of sexual desires manifestly offensive to currently acceptable standards of propriety." Several months later, *Drum* reported on the victory in *Val's*, but expressed concern about the "unfortunate tone" of the decision, which was "underscored by a separate and concurring opinion that warned homosexuals that as long as they were 'well-behaved' the Court had extended them its protection, but that 'they may not engage in any conduct which would be offensive to public decency. A tavern should not provide an arena for men kissing each other on the lips, etc.'" Although HLRS may have contributed to this "unfortunate tone" when it distinguished between *Val's* and the other cases, *Drum* concluded, "It will remain for future cases to establish the homosexual's right to participate in various types of quasi-sexual behavior publicly to the same degree that similar behavior is found acceptable among heterosexuals."[44]

While HLRS remained in the background in *Val's*, its involvement in *Boutilier* could not be missed. On 15 November 1966, eight days after the Supreme Court accepted *Boutilier* for argument, Polak wrote to Freedman that the ACLU's Melvin Wulf had suggested he contact her: "The question of psychopathology and homosexuality is actually one of our specialties and we might submit an *amicus* brief on this point, if you felt it could be beneficial to the case. We would also be willing to support the case financially." Polak's interest in psychopathology rather than immigration was consistent with his movement's longstanding focus on the rights of citizens and its longstanding struggle against the classification of homosexuality as a mental illness. Polak and Freedman spoke by telephone in the next several days, and then Freedman wrote an enthusiastic letter indicating that the brief would be "most welcome" and have "impact in enlightening the Court." She finished off by noting, "We greatly appreciate your offer of financial assistance. The fact is that the situation is desperate."[45]

By the time Freedman posted her letter, Polak had already swung into action, sending her a check for $500, telling her that he had begun making contacts about the HLRS brief, and asking questions: "Would it be beneficial to have non-medical professionals, such as religious leaders, sociologists, criminologists, etc., sign our brief? . . . Would medical professionals who feel homosexuality is a 'disturbance,' but not pathology, who would be willing to sign the brief with reservations be beneficial?" Freedman acknowledged his contribution "with gratitude." In response to his queries, she wrote, "I have serious reservations about the last question but prefer to think about it carefully." Here one of the most sexually radical leaders of the homophile movement was considering the strategic use of antigay testimony, while his straight ally expressed reservations. The relationship between Freedman and Polak is particularly striking given the fact that Freedman was a socialist who dedicated much of her life to defending the rights of anticapitalists while Polak was a businessman who dedicated much of his life to the pleasures, profits, and politics of pornography.[46]

Freedman likely did not realize that in accepting help from HLRS she was jeopardizing her support from Mattachine New York. In late 1966, Leitsch mentioned *Boutilier* in a memorandum to other homophile leaders: "MSNY has been involved in this case from the very beginning, though we understand another homophile organization has now joined us." Polak responded privately: "One small correction. . . . We have not 'joined (you). . . .' We have agreed to finance the case and have already contributed many hundreds of dollars to it. Any assistance, as you note, would be appreciated, though we are certainly capable of carrying the financing alone." Leitsch shot back that this "comes as quite a surprise" and "the first mention of your name that we heard in connection with this matter came early last week when Mrs. Freedman casually mentioned that you were going to contribute." He added, "I was personally gratified to learn that Janus was finally going to put some of its reputedly large profits from Drum into something of value for the homosexual community. . . . If you are assuming all costs of the Immigration case, I will suggest to our Board and to Mrs. Freedman that we contribute no more."[47]

Meanwhile, Janus and HLRS began raising consciousness about *Boutilier*. In December 1966, *Drum* reported (inaccurately) that "for the first time since 1964" the Supreme Court had agreed to hear a case concerning homosexuality. The magazine claimed, "The case will have ramifications affecting a significant percentage of America's homosexuals." *Drum* noted that while "the specific issue is quite narrow," the Court's decision might "weaken—or strengthen—the Federal government's stand that homosexuals are unacceptable as Federal employees." This formulation presented federal employment discrimination as more important than immigration discrimination. Along similar lines, Polak's letter inviting scientific experts to submit statements for the HLRS brief declared, "The HLRS feels that the most be made of this immigration case even though the point at issue is tangential to the central homosexual civil liberties questions."[48]

According to Freedman's records, HLRS contributed at least $750 toward her *Boutilier* expenses. Three other homophile groups also provided financial support: DOB–New York; Personal Rights in Defense and Education (PRIDE), which was based in Los Angeles; and the National Legal Defense Fund (NLDF). The Fund, proposed at the National Planning Conference of Homophile Organizations in 1966 and incorporated in San Francisco the following year, was another example of the homophile movement's turn to court strategies. According to the *Ladder*, "The attorneys and founders of the NLDF believe that some, if not all, penal code reform can most easily be achieved through the judicial process." After Freedman wrote to request the Fund's assistance and explained that the costs were "prohibitive for a worker to carry alone," the NLDF sent $350, offered to consider additional contributions, and thanked her for her efforts.[49]

While various homophile groups supported Boutilier's appeal, Gilbert Cantor, with help from Polak, produced the HLRS brief. Born in 1929, Cantor was a Harvard-trained lawyer who had served in the army and the Pentagon. By the 1960s, he was a partner in a Philadelphia law firm with a specialty in estates and trusts. Cantor also authored *The Barnes Foundation* (1963), *The Ten Best Ways to Save Estate Taxes* (1978), *How to Totally Avoid Estate Taxes* (1980), and *The Lawyer's Complete Guide to the Perfect Will* (1984). Married with two children at the time of *Boutilier*, he later remarried and had two more children. Not much is known about what led Cantor to begin working with the homophile movement, but he was an active member of the Congress of Racial Equality and the Greater Philadelphia ACLU; he worked on a significant Pennsylvania obscenity case in the 1960s; and he later worked on and wrote about abortion rights, transsexual rights, women's rights, war tax resistance, the decriminalization of drugs, and the abolition of the criminal justice system.[50]

According to a 1968 *Wall Street Journal* article, Cantor first became involved in gay and lesbian rights cases in 1964. He was quoted as saying, "'Good representation ought to be available to anyone . . . and I admire their willingness to assert their rights as citizens rather than acting as members of an underground society.'" In 1965, Cantor secured an injunction against Philadelphia's Penn Center Inn, which had canceled a room reservation for a Janus lecture at the last minute. According to Polak, "Cantor's quiet, masterful handling of the preliminary discussions with the opposition lawyer was sufficient to force a complete capitulation." Cantor also represented a federal employee dismissed from her position based on her homosexual orientation.[51]

Cantor approached the writing of the *Boutilier* brief with a set of convictions derived from his experiences in civil rights, civil liberties, and homophile movements and his exposure to mid-twentieth-century philosophy, psychology, sociology, and legal studies. About a year before becoming involved in *Boutilier*, Cantor received a standing ovation when he presented an address titled "Anticipations—Legal and Philosophical" at a homophile conference in New York. In noteworthy respects, the address anticipated the arguments he made in *Boutilier*.[52]

The first section of Cantor's speech urged the homophile movement to consider with care and caution the strategies used by the civil rights movement. "In these times," he declared, "it appears that all liberal causes tend to analogize themselves to the Negro freedom movement and to emulate it." According to Cantor, similarities between the black and homophile movements "facilitate that identification," but it was important to recognize "the similarities and the differences." Each of these movements represented "a minority group whose members are the subjects of prejudice and the victims of discrimination," and both "raise for the dominant group the specter of sexuality and sensuality which threatens the repressive system." Nevertheless, discrimination against blacks was worse in housing, education, and employment, except for federal employment and with the caveat that the comparative gay advantage required "constant concealment." Cantor argued that there were also "differences in public sympathy," in part because "the majority group in society does not have the consciousness of guilt toward the homosexual which has been developed toward the Negro." As a result, he contended that in some respects "the homosexual is treated worse." Cantor explained, "It is not a crime to be a Negro or to live as a Negro, although the Negro and the white are not always equal before the law. It is not regarded as a sin to be a Negro, though some regard the Negro as frequently sinful. And it is not considered an illness to be a Negro, although the condition of the Negro easily leads to emotional maladjustments." In addition, he claimed that "the whole society, including its economy," is "based on the great desirability and joy of heterosexual love and sex." The implication was that homosexuals challenged the dominant social order in ways that blacks did not. Given these differences, the homophile movement could not use direct action and expect "a public response similar to the response to direct action in the Negro freedom movement." Cantor then observed, "Perhaps the heterosexual participants or friends of the Homophile movement can help to avoid these miscalculations by bringing a dual or a different perspective to bear." Positioning himself as a heterosexual ally of the homosexual cause with an implied parallel to his position as a white ally of the black freedom struggle, Cantor encouraged the homophile movement to think strategically about its models.

In the second section of his speech, Cantor made predictions. "In law," he argued, "the trend is clear and the result is certain." He said these were "brutal times," but there was "something to the contrary in the air," and this was evident in rulings about "the right of accused persons to counsel, the right to a prompt hearing, and various other aspects of what we call due process." In all of this, Cantor saw "a clear humanitarian, libertarian trend, a concern for the rights and the dignity of the individual as against the power of his government." Reforms championed by the homophile movement were thus "inevitable." He predicted that in due course "homosexual acts between consenting adults will not be regarded as crimes"; police entrapment "will not be tolerated"; and fair employment practices will be introduced. Questions about employment in "sensitive positions" would "fade out in time." Military reform would occur, but "full acceptance" by the military was "not to be expected." As for "homosexual marriage and the adoption of children by homosexual couples," these were "not worth discussing." "The principal objective," which was "the abolition of sanctions imposed for sex acts between consenting adults," might occur through the legislative process or through constitutional litigation based on privacy arguments. According to Cantor, "Sodomy, fornication and adultery laws have never been challenged on Constitutional grounds in the Supreme Court. . . . In an appropriate case I suggest that this be put forward."

The third part of Cantor's speech addressed the factors that would contribute to the conceptual changes necessary for law reform to occur. The first factor was legal reform itself, which would encourage conceptual change. The second was psychiatric reform, which was raising questions about the pathological nature of homosexuality. The third factor was an increase in "public knowledge" about homosexuality, which was based on "increased scientific knowledge." Homophile groups could contribute to this, but Cantor warned that "homophile organization members ought to remember that they . . . represent the 'square' homosexuals, just as the Negro freedom movement organizations represent the square Negro." In both cases, the "square" reformer "believes in organization, in negotiation, in the manners and morals and techniques of the dominant culture." According to Cantor, just as "we discover in Watts, California, that the hip Negro has nothing to do with the square Negro," homophile activists "must not assume that the square homosexual speaks for the 'other' . . . homosexual." Again invoking the civil rights movement, Cantor urged activists to recognize the limitations of the politics of respectability.

Cantor's concluding remarks asked, "Where does the homosexual fit into the scheme or program of a Great Society?" The homosexual, he asserted, had a role to play in confronting one of the "greatest problems" of the century: "the universal spread of a drab uniformity." Acknowledging that he was relying on "gross generalizations," Cantor argued that the homosexual would continue to represent "taste, humor, sensuality, othermindedness, diversity and individuality, in a society where these things will be in ever-decreasing supply." Noting that "the idea of a Great Society springs directly from the Greek experience," Cantor observed that the homosexual could help the Great Society integrate the "Appollonian" [sic], which was concerned with intellect, art, order, and justice, with the "Dionysian," which was concerned with "the sensual, the voluptuous, the wild." The "great symbolic function of the homosexual" was to pose the question of "how maleness and femaleness are to be lived" and to answer this question "in the rediscovery of the body, and of pleasure." Cantor did not make this particular argument in his *Boutilier* brief, but other aspects of his 1965 homophile conference speech prefigured his arguments in *Boutilier*.

Cantor's *Boutilier* arguments were also anticipated in his article, "How Black Is Black?" which was published in Philadelphia's *Legal Intelligencer* in July 1966. The article concerned litigation strategies that could be used against Girard College's policy of admitting only white students, which derived from the terms of Stephen Girard's will. Cantor argued that while the policy could be challenged as a form of discrimination prohibited by the Fourteenth Amendment, there might be a better way to gain a favorable result. To make his point, Cantor imagined a policy that prohibited the admission of witches and then explained that such a policy could be challenged under estate and trust law. First, in special circumstances trustees were permitted to commit "judicious breaches of trust." Second, the prohibition could be struck down as "whimsical and capricious." Third, a court could hold that "witchcraft is not deserving of judicial recognition" because witches did not exist. Cantor then argued that "a 'white man' or a 'Negro' is as mythical a character as a witch." To support this notion, Cantor described ambiguities and inconsistencies in state and federal definitions of racial groups. Then he turned to anthropological studies, which indicated that "there is not now and never was a white race or, for that matter, a black race or a yellow race." Cantor concluded that Girard's policy could be challenged based on "the rejection of racial identification as a valid concept for governmental determination or enforcement." Just a few months later, Cantor argued in *Boutilier* for the rejection of sexual classifications as a valid concept for governmental determination or enforcement.[53]

Just as Freedman's *Boutilier* briefs were influenced by her earlier work defending leftists and immigrants, Cantor's *Boutilier* brief was influenced by his earlier work defending homosexuals and blacks. His main argument addressed whether homosexuality was psychopathological. Challenging the classification of homosexuality as a mental illness was a central mission of the homophile movement, and ultimately these efforts led to the American Psychiatric Association's declassification of homosexuality as a mental illness in 1973.[54] On this issue, the success of the HLRS in obtaining statements by experts was based on the movement's long history of dialogue with, and often its deference to, scholars. When the HLRS brief incorporated the statements of experts who denied that homosexuality was psychopathological but expressed negative attitudes about homosexuality, it was following a model developed in earlier years. The use of such expert statements challenged the classification of homosexuality as a mental illness, while allowing the movement to present itself as neutral, objective, and scientific. The homophile movement also occasionally offered a more radical critique of psychiatry, and Cantor's brief made this argument as well.

The HLRS brief also was influenced by the homophile movement's use of two types of arguments about the nature of homosexuality. In many contexts, homophile activists depicted homosexuality as an innate feature of individual identity and portrayed homosexuals as a minority group defined by same-sex sexual orientation. These depictions allowed activists to analogize the struggles of homosexuals and blacks and insist that homosexuals should not be oppressed on the basis of a condition over which they had no control. What is often forgotten in criticisms of homophile movement identity politics, however, is that in other contexts the movement emphasized that homosexuality was a universal potential for everyone. From this perspective, homosexuality was best conceptualized in behavioral terms and the human population could not be divided into mutually exclusive groups of homosexuals and heterosexuals. The movement often misrepresented the work of sexologist Alfred Kinsey to claim that 10 percent of the population was homosexual, but it also invoked Kinsey's arguments about the behavioral nature of homosexuality and the problems of classifying people as homosexual or heterosexual. This position also allowed activists to link the struggles of homosexuals and blacks, as Cantor did when he adapted his argument against racial classifications to make an argument against sexual classifications.

On this issue, the homophile movement influenced Freedman's arguments in a general sense but also in a very specific contribution made by Kameny. In 1965, Mattachine Washington and other homophile groups picketed the Civil Service Commission headquarters as part of their campaign against federal employment discrimination. After years of refusing to meet with homophile representatives, the Commission relented in late 1965 and Mattachine was encouraged to submit a formal statement. In February 1966, the group received a reply from Commission Chairman John Macy. In one passage, Macy referred to Mattachine's "fundamental misconception": "We do not subscribe to the view, which indeed is the rock upon which the Mattachine Society is founded, that 'homosexual' is a proper metonym for an individual. Rather we consider the term 'homosexual' to be properly used as an adjective to describe the nature of overt sexual relations or conduct." About a year later, Kameny wrote to Freedman, explaining that Polak had loaned him a copy of her "excellent" *Boutilier* brief. After noting that the government "rests its case upon the existence . . . of a condition of homosexuality," Kameny pointed to Macy's letter "explicitly denying that the term homosexual can be used to describe a person or a condition, and averring that the term can be used only to describe acts." Kameny concluded, "Two agencies of the Government are taking opposite positions, as suit their particular purposes of the moment." The same could have been said of the homophile movement. Kameny also suggested that Freedman do something with the word "afflicted." Some homosexuals, he argued, "may well be afflicted," but "many others may well not be afflicted but merely neutrally have—or, if you want to go all the way, be blessed with—the condition." He concluded that Congress "meant only to exclude those homosexuals whose homosexual condition is an affliction." Freedman used Kameny's suggestion about conflicting government claims in her reply brief.[55]

Finally, the HLRS brief was influenced by the homophile movement's strategic politics of respectability. Cantor and Polak both understood homosexual law reform to be part of a larger campaign for sexual law reform, but in the HLRS brief, Cantor did not link his arguments to larger points about sexual freedom, discuss the liberatory function of homosexuality in a repressive society, or promote the integration of the Apollonian and Dionysian. Presumably, he believed these arguments would not be well received by the Court. He instead depicted homosexuals as healthy and respectable. That this was a strategy rather than an article of faith is suggested by the many other contexts in which Cantor and Polak offered more sexually radical arguments. In *Boutilier*, they chose to make arguments derived primarily from homophile discourses of scientific expertise, sexual behaviorism, and social respectability.

Libertarian Advocacy

Around the time that Freedman contacted Mattachine New York about *Boutilier*, she also reached out to the ACLU.[56] This was a moment of transition in the ACLU's approach to lesbian and gay rights. Historians have tended to accept the claim made in the group's 1957 policy statement on homosexuality (and repeated in the 1960s) that the ACLU was "occasionally called upon to defend the civil liberties of homosexuals." The group's involvement was much more extensive than this implies. Although the ACLU declined a request for help in the *ONE* case, in the 1950s and 1960s the ACLU and its affiliates defended gay and lesbian rights in numerous cases and contexts; ACLU representatives spoke at many homophile meetings, conferences, and lectures; and the homophile movement came to view civil liberties groups as valued allies.[57]

This occurred despite the limitations of the 1957 statement, which declared, "It is not within the province of the Union to evaluate the social validity of laws aimed at the suppression or elimination of homosexuals. We recognize that overt acts of homosexuality constitute a common law felony and that there is no constitutional prohibition against such state and local laws on this subject as are deemed . . . to be socially necessary or beneficial. Any challenge to laws that prohibit and punish public acts of homosexuality or overt acts of solicitation for the purpose of committing a homosexual act is beyond the province of the Union." On the subject of government employment discrimination, the ACLU statement was only slightly more supportive: "Homosexuality is a valid consideration in evaluating the security risk factor in sensitive positions. We affirm, as does Executive Order 10450 and all security regulations made thereunder, that homosexuality is a factor properly to be considered only when there is evidence of other acts which come within valid security criteria." Several other passages were more supportive. In one paragraph, the ACLU declared, "Homosexuals, like members of other socially heretical or deviant groups, are more vulnerable than others to official persecution, denial of due process in prosecution, and entrapment. . . . These are matters of proper concern for the Union." There was no mention of immigration and ACLU statements on immigration did not mention homosexuality.[58]

Homophile groups had mixed responses to the ACLU statement. In 1957, the *Ladder* reprinted it and commended the ACLU for its "fine work." *Mattachine Review* reprinted it with an introduction that declared, "We believe that the serious interest of ACLU in matters of civil rights and due process of law merit the praise of Mattachine members and friends." *ONE* published excerpts, but asked, "Would it be within the province of the Union to evaluate the social validity of laws aimed at the suppression or elimination of Negroes, Jews, or Jehovah's Witnesses? Of course it would. Then why not homosexuals?" Over the next several years, some homophile activists and civil libertarians criticized the ACLU policy. At a DOB convention in 1960, Albert Bendich, staff counsel for the northern California ACLU affiliate, declared that he "disagreed with the ACLU that there was no constitutional basis for challenging sex laws." ACLU chapters in Southern California, New York, Philadelphia, and Washington, D.C., pressured the national organization to revise its policy.[59]

In the early 1960s, Frank Kameny criticized the ACLU for its arguments in a gay immigration case. Kameny had learned from an ACLU annual report that "the Immigration Service had failed to prove its case that an admitted homosexual, defended by the ACLU of Northern California, was a homosexual at the time of his 1958 entry." In 1962, Kameny, writing as an ACLU member, asked the ACLU why this "devious" approach was adopted, "rather than a direct challenge." ACLU Associate Director Alan Reitman responded by sending Kameny the 1957 statement and noting, "I expect that the Union in the coming years will be more actively involved in this area." Kameny's reply labeled the statement "unfortunate" and asked, "Is this still, unchanged, the policy of the ACLU?" Reitman indicated it was, but also forwarded a letter he had written recently to the Colorado-based Homosexual Voters Advisory Service, which stated that ACLU staff had been discussing homosexual law reform and "planned to present the issue to one of our committees, if the Supreme Court upheld our position . . . in the Connecticut birth control cases [*Poe*]." Reitman explained, "The Court refused to deal with the constitutionality of this issue, but a new test is on its way to the Supreme Court [in *Griswold*]. Once we have the high court's opinion in this area, we will be in a better position to determine our policy on the civil liberties aspect of a variety of sexual practices, including homosexuality." In 1963, Reitman urged the executive director of the Greater Philadelphia ACLU to attend an upcoming homophile conference "since I imagine we will be doing some work in this field in the near future, as soon as the Supreme Court gives us some guidelines in the birth control case."[60]

Critics of the 1957 statement were not willing to wait. At a 1964 ACLU conference, Harriet Pilpel, who had spoken at a homophile conference titled "New Frontiers in the Law" the year before, urged the group to challenge laws against abortion and homosexuality. At the same ACLU conference, the National Capital Area CLU attacked antihomosexual federal employment discrimination. The conference endorsed two recommendations. First, the "ACLU should support standards set forth in the American Law Institute proposal that no sexual behavior between consenting adults in private be made subject to criminal sanctions." Second, "The National Capital Area CLU position paper opposing the federal practice of excluding homosexuals from government employment should be referred to the national Board for study along with reconsideration of the Board's 1957 statement."[61] The ACLU, however, was experiencing rapid growth and change in this period, and the adoption of a new statement on homosexuality ended up taking three years. The lawyers who prepared the ACLU/NYCLU *Boutilier* brief thus acted in the absence of clear organizational directives.

Having been asked to review the 1957 statement, the ACLU Board of Directors referred the matter to its Due Process Committee. By the time the committee began its work in 1965, *Griswold* had been decided. *Griswold*'s influence on the ACLU discussions is suggested by Reitman's reply to a 1966 letter from the Texas Student League for Responsible Sexual Freedom, which asked about laws against fornication, homosexuality, and miscegenation. After noting that the ACLU was reviewing its policies on these subjects, Reitman added, "What the Supreme Court will do in dealing with laws concerning sex is a matter of pure speculation. Certainly the *Griswold* opinion . . . was a pace-setting decision. But the Court looks at the facts of each individual case; the facts of the *Griswold* case dealt with a physician prescribing contraceptives. . . . This is not to say that the Court will not strike down laws punishing various kinds of sexual activity, but to indicate that what the Court decides often depends on the particular case."[62]

In November 1965, the Due Process Committee recommended that the ACLU adopt a new four-paragraph statement on homosexuality. According to the first paragraph, "No sexual behavior between consenting adults in private should be made the subject of criminal sanctions." The paragraph, however, also noted that challenges to laws against "public acts of homosexuality or overt acts of solicitation for the purpose of committing a homosexual act" were "beyond the province of the Union." The next two paragraphs repeated the 1957 statement's language about "official persecution, denial of due process in prosecution, and entrapment." The fourth paragraph contained new language about employment discrimination: "Persons who are presently practicing homosexuals in their private lives should not, ipso facto, be barred from government service. However, homosexuality may be a relevant factor in considering whether a person is suitable for a job in certain sensitive areas, including not only in those in the national security area, but those outside this area such as the job of job corps counselor. Only active and presently practicing homosexuals could be barred in these circumstances. But even in such cases the burden of proof should be on the government."[63]

Over the next two years, the ACLU Board of Directors and Due Process Committee discussed various components of the policy statement, including the passages addressing (or not addressing) public sex, sexual solicitation, sex with minors, and commercialized sex. There was also debate about the validity of the government's use of homosexuality as a basis for employment discrimination and the question of whether the language on employment discrimination should distinguish between public and private sex and between present and past conduct. Another topic of discussion was whether the statement should focus on homosexual conduct or address consensual sex more generally, and, if it addressed the latter, how to deal with adultery and incest. In the end, the Board voted to accept, with minor modifications, the Due Process Committee's recommendation that "(1) Homosexuality *per se* should not bar from government employment persons who are presently practicing homosexuals in their private lives. (2) The burden is always on the government to show the relevance of homosexuality to qualification for a particular job." The Board also agreed that "private sexual conduct, whether homosexual or heterosexual, of any person, male or female, involving adults should not bar that person from government employment *per se*." Final drafting was left to the ACLU staff.[64]

When the new ACLU statement was announced in August 1967, it differed significantly from the drafts circulated in 1965 and 1966. What accounts for the delay and the changes is unclear, but perhaps the ACLU decided to wait for the *Boutilier* decision. The statement began with three paragraphs that referenced British law reform, American Law Institute proposals, and Illinois penal code revision. These paragraphs mentioned "the growing recognition of the right of privacy" and "the belief that 'the right to be left alone,' free of government interference or restraint, is a cherished element of man's existence." The next three paragraphs addressed sexual conduct laws and police practices. On the one hand, the statement declared that "the right of privacy should extend to all private sexual conduct, heterosexual or homosexual, of consenting adults" and condemned "entrapment by special police squads" and "the use of 'peep holes' and other devices for secret surveillance of public rest rooms." The statement also criticized "police, license officials, and other government administrative personnel" who "continually subject homosexuals to a variety of pressures, in bars, parks, night clubs, and other places." On the other hand, the statement noted that "the state has a legitimate interest in controlling, by criminal sanctions, public solicitation for sexual acts" and "sexual practices where a minor is concerned." According to the ACLU, "the public has the right to be free from solicitation, molestation and annoyance in public facilities and places," and "protection against adult corruption of minors is a proper interest of the state."

The final four paragraphs discussed employment discrimination. The Civil Service Commission policy was described as "discriminatory, unfair, and illogical," and the statement argued that "private homosexual conduct, like private illicit heterosexual conduct, should not be an automatic bar to government employment." Again defining the limits of its position, the ACLU added that "if a homosexual employee becomes an irritating force by making sexual advances on the job which interferes with his or her performance or a fellow worker's performance, then the normal Civil Service procedures governing work performance can be invoked." The ACLU also noted that "in certain jobs there may be a relevancy between that job and a person's private sexual conduct," but "the burden of proof should be placed on the government" and "the government should be restricted to evidence only of present homosexual conduct or conduct so recently in the past that it is clear that the job applicant or employee is presently practicing homosexual conduct."

Significantly, the statement did not discuss immigration law, though *Boutilier* influenced it in indirect and direct ways. The insistence that only recent and present homosexual conduct was relevant in government employment cases may have been indirectly influenced by *Boutilier* insofar as the government claimed it was deporting Boutilier on the basis of evidence from the distant past. More direct influence from *Boutilier* is evident in one of the paragraphs addressing employment discrimination, which included an excerpt of Douglas's *Boutilier* dissent that referred to the "common knowledge" that "in this century homosexuals have risen high in our own public service—both in Congress and in the Executive Branch and have served with distinction."[65]

Leading homophile activists criticized the new statement. In September 1967, Kameny thanked the ACLU for sending him a copy. While he noted that his comments should not be interpreted "as a strong criticism of an excellent statement," he raised two objections. First, "In what conceivable jobs could homosexuality, or a person's private sexual conduct, generally, legitimately be a factor?" Second, "This question of solicitation needs *much* more careful examination." According to Kameny, "In the context of homosexuality, the term solicitation often conjures up images of some sort of crude, men's-room scene." He reasoned, however, that "such solicitations can be anything from a glance to a conversation in a bar" and are "parallel to those made frequently on a heterosexual basis." Agreeing that "there must be some sort of limits placed upon public solicitation," Kameny argued that they "should not differ one iota for homosexuals and for heterosexuals." He concluded by drawing a parallel with the ACLU's "conservative handling of the matter of prostitution, which is, after all, merely a matter of a private business arrangement between two consenting adults." According to Kameny, "There is no rational distinction, after all, between a woman's hiring out her hands for stenography or her genitals for intercourse." Reitman thanked Kameny for his letter, noted that "there was some feeling that in certain government positions involving contact with young people it might be appropriate to consider whether homosexuals should be employed," and added that the solicitation language "does need more careful examination, particularly as I have just learned that the police in many communities are skipping over laws barring homosexual practices and using anti-solicitation laws."[66]

Reitman had learned this from Polak, who wrote a critical response on the day the new ACLU policy was announced. In 1965 and 1966, Polak was in regular contact with ACLU Legal Director Melvin Wulf, who represented Janus when U.S. Customs blocked the importation of several allegedly obscene magazines. Now Polak was disappointed. He had hoped the ACLU statement would suggest "truly meaningful law reform." Unfortunately, the statement "comes oh so close—but yet, oh so far—from that mark." Polak's main objection concerned the language about solicitation. Noting that an earlier ACLU draft had accepted the constitutionality of laws against "improper" public solicitation, Polak complained that the new policy omitted the word "improper," which "almost totally negates the 'liberalization' of removing sodomy from the purview of the criminal law." He concluded that "half-way reform will result in more homosexuals being convicted of more crimes."[67]

Meanwhile, the ACLU was also developing new positions on two other issues raised by *Boutilier*: the rights of immigrants and the rights of the mentally ill. In the early twentieth century, the ACLU had argued that "no person should be refused admission to the United States on the ground of holding objectionable opinions," that no one should be deported on the basis of past or present membership in an organization, and that no one should be denied citizenship "because of the expression of radical views, or activities in the cause of labor." In the 1950s, the ACLU modified its position, noting that laws denying permanent residence and citizenship to members of communist, fascist, and other totalitarian parties were acceptable. In the early 1960s, as Congress discussed immigration reform, the ACLU advocated major changes. In testimony before House and Senate subcommittees in 1964–65, the ACLU's David Carliner called for a ten-year statute of limitations for conduct-based deportations, arguing that resident aliens "who have engaged in deportable conduct in the distant past should be freed from the threat of banishment and exile." In addition, children admitted for permanent residence before their fourteenth birthdays should not be deportable and "a person's color, race, nationality, or ancestry" should not be relevant "in determining whether he is worthy to live in America." The testimony did not specifically address the psychopathic personality provision.[68]

As for the rights of the mentally ill, this was also a topic of ACLU interest, though not necessarily in relation to immigration or homosexuality. In the early twentieth century, the organization had begun defending the rights of those classified as mentally ill, and in the 1940s the ACLU established the Committee on the Rights of the Mentally Ill. In the 1960s, the ACLU adopted a position against involuntary commitments of people with mental illnesses except in cases of danger to self or society. In 1968, the NYCLU established the Mental Health Law Project (also referred to as the Civil Liberties and Mental Illness Litigation Project), which fought for the rights of the institutional-ized. In the 1970s, the Mental Health Law Project won *Donaldson*, a landmark decision against the involuntary institutionalization of nondangerous people. In the same decade, however, Thomas Szasz, a prominent critic of psychiatry, challenged the ACLU's "disastrous history of uncritically accepting the concept of 'mental illness,' whose 'treatment,' by imprisonment, is then casually delegated to the psychiatric profession." For Szasz, the ACLU's acronym should be understood to stand for "the American Civil Lunacy Association — an association for the defense of lunacy, the privileged territory of the psychiatric mafia." In this context, it is noteworthy that at the time of *Boutilier* the ACLU had not criticized the classification of homosexuality as a form of mental illness or the deportation of aliens classifiable as mentally ill.[69]

In short, by 1967 the ACLU had a long history of defending the rights of homosexuals, immigrants, and the mentally ill, but also a long history of being criticized for its ambivalent positions on these issues. The ACLU had limited experience dealing with the intersection of these issues in cases involving alien homosexuals subject to deportation as psychopaths. In theory, the ACLU/NYCLU *Boutilier* brief could have derived its arguments from earlier litigation involving homosexuals, immigrants, and the mentally ill. For the most part, however, the brief focused on one issue: whether the term "afflicted with psychopathic personality" was unconstitutionally vague. In passing, the brief's introduction made a more forceful argument, urging the Court to reject the use of immigration statutes to deport aliens on the basis of nondangerous conduct.

The lawyers who signed the ACLU/NYCLU *Boutilier* brief were ACLU board member David Carliner, ACLU cooperating attorney Burt Neuborne, NYCLU general counsel Nanette Dembitz, and NYCLU staff counsel Alan Levine. Decades later, Neuborne recalls that he wrote the first draft and that it was his first Supreme Court brief. At the time, he was a Wall Street lawyer who did volunteer work with the ACLU; soon thereafter, he took a full-time job with the NYCLU. Levine, another Wall Street lawyer, began working for the NYCLU in the 1960s after a transformative experience with the Lawyers Constitutional Defense Committee, an ACLU-affiliated group that defended southern civil rights protesters. When asked recently about *Boutilier*, Neuborne writes, "My sense is that we would write a very different brief today, one that challenged the right of the government to use sexual orientation as a reason for deportation. My recollection is that we wrote a much narrower brief, seeking to challenge the phrase 'psychopathic personality.'" He adds, "I looked at the precedents and decided that vagueness was the only way to assemble 5 votes on that Supreme Court. The vagueness concept was being effectively used by the Supreme Court to shield civil rights demonstrators. . . . Today, I would link the vagueness argument with a substantive challenge to the government's power—but in those days, the idea had not yet ripened." Neuborne does not think any of the ACLU/NYCLU lawyers who worked on *Boutilier* were gay or lesbian.[70]

Neuborne and Levine began their civil liberties careers in the context of the 1960s and had limited Supreme Court experience before *Boutilier*. In contrast, Dembitz and Carliner began their careers in the context of the Great Depression, World War II, and the Red Scare and had substantial Supreme Court experience. Dembitz, a cousin of Justice Louis Brandeis, had worked for the National Labor Relations Board and the Justice Department in the 1940s, but resigned from the latter after the Court upheld the internment of Japanese Americans during World War II. She served as NYCLU volunteer general counsel from 1955 to 1967 and in that capacity defended several people who refused to answer the questions of the House Committee on Un-American Activities. She also helped challenge the requirement by the Subversive Activities Control Board that the Communist Party register as a communist action organization. Dembitz's work on *Boutilier* was likely influenced by her use of vagueness arguments in earlier cases and her membership from 1964 to 1967 on Planned Parenthood's national board.[71]

While Neuborne, Levine, and Dembitz, based in New York, had limited experience with homosexual cases, Carliner, based in Washington, D.C., had been an active defender of lesbian and gay rights. Like Freedman, Carliner was the son of Jewish immigrants and had ties to the left. Like Cantor, Carliner served in the U.S. military during World War II. Born in 1918, Carliner was expelled from the University of Virginia Law School after an arrest for distributing communist literature; he later earned his law degree from National University in Washington, D.C. An immigration expert who began arguing cases before the Supreme Court in the 1950s, Carliner led the National Capital Area Civil Liberties Union in the 1960s and authored the first edition of *The Rights of Aliens: The Basic ACLU Guide to An Alien's Rights* in the 1970s. Several of his earlier Supreme Court cases raised issues related to *Boutilier*. In *Marcello*, an unsuccessful 1955 appeal, Carliner represented a Tunisian man ordered deported for a conviction under the Marijuana Tax Act despite the fact that the conviction occurred before the passage of the relevant immigration statute. According to the Court, "the prohibition of the *ex post facto* clause does not apply to deportation." In 1956, Carliner successfully helped defend Tom We Shung, a Chinese alien who in 1947 sought admission to the United States under the War Brides Act; Shung claimed he had been fathered by a member of the U.S. armed forces. Then in 1957, Carliner lost *Lehmann*, which upheld the deportation of an Italian man who, after entering the United States as a stowaway, had been convicted twice of blackmail, which was classified as a crime of moral turpitude. This was another case in which the Court held that Congress could make aliens deportable for crimes that were not grounds for deportation at the time they were committed. Also in 1957, Carliner lost *Klig*, a D.C. Circuit decision that upheld the deportation of a Russian-born Canadian citizen who had been a member of the Communist Party of Canada from 1929 to 1932.[72] As discussed in the last chapter, Carliner also played a significant role in two interracial marriage cases: *Naim*, which concerned an alien subject to deportation when his interracial marriage was invalidated, and *Loving*.

Carliner was an early supporter of homosexual law reform. In fact, *Boutilier* was not Carliner's first gay immigration case. In 1960–61, Carliner helped represent Robert Wyngaard, a citizen of Holland who came to the United States as a permanent resident in 1948. In 1955, Wyngaard was convicted of "frequenting or loitering about any public place and soliciting men for the purpose of committing a crime against nature or other lewdness." On this basis, he was ordered deported for having been convicted of a "crime of moral turpitude." In 1961, the D.C. Circuit rejected the argument that the federal district court should have convened a three-judge panel to determine whether the phrase "crime involving moral turpitude" was "unconstitutionally vague." Carliner petitioned the Supreme Court to hear the case, but was turned down.[73]

In the next several years, Carliner became more involved in homosexual law reform. Beginning in 1963, he worked with Kameny on several employment discrimination cases. As mentioned above, in 1964 he encouraged the homophile movement to pursue court cases. Beginning in 1964, he helped pressure the ACLU to modify its 1957 statement on homosexuality. Then in 1965, he successfully defended Bruce Scott, a former Labor Department employee who reapplied for a position but was rejected on grounds of homosexual "immoral conduct." In *Scott*, the D.C. Circuit Court ruled that the Commission "must at least specify the conduct it finds 'immoral' and state why that conduct related to 'occupational competence or fitness.'" Responding to the government's claim that Scott was a homosexual who had engaged in homosexual conduct, the court stated that these were "vague labels" and had "different meanings for different people." In 1965 and 1966, as a member of the ACLU Board of Directors, Carliner played an active role in the development of the new statement on homosexuality.[74] Of the four lawyers who signed the ACLU/NYCLU brief, Carliner had the most expertise in immigration and homosexual law reform.

For reasons that remain unclear, there were disagreements within the ACLU/NYCLU about the contents of its *Boutilier* brief. On 11 January 1967, Polak wrote to Freedman to inform her that he was about to file the HLRS brief and to ask, "What is the story on the ACLU's brief?" After receiving a copy of the HLRS brief, Freedman replied: "Both you and Mr. Cantor are to be congratulated. It is a very fine document and I hope that you will be able to get added use out of it. The ACLU are just about ready to file their brief now! It appears that there was a difference of opinion between the author of the original brief and the person in charge of the New York office. Their brief was rewritten."[75] Neuborne and Levine do not recall what the difference of opinion was and the draft has not been found, but it is possible that the dispute was related to the brief's introductory comment challenging deportations based on nondangerous, private, and consensual sexual conduct, a point not fully discussed or developed.

The final version of the ACLU/NYCLU *Boutilier* brief was influenced by the earlier work of civil libertarians in several legal arenas. ACLU/NYCLU lawyers had used the vagueness doctrine in cases involving communists, immigrants, civil rights activists, and homosexuals. Now they emphasized that the phrase "psychopathic personality" was vague and that Boutilier could not have known that homosexual conduct would put him at risk. Meanwhile, the ACLU had criticized U.S. deportation policies and practices; it was in the process of developing a position against the criminalization of private and consensual homosexual conduct; and it was working on the rights of nondangerous mentally ill people. In the *Boutilier* brief's introduction, these arguments were integrated to challenge deportations based on private, consensual, and nondangerous conduct.

In several specific respects, the ACLU/NYCLU brief was influenced by the earlier work of civil libertarians on homosexual and sex law reform. Just as the 1957 ACLU statement defended the due process rights of homosexuals while also accepting laws that aimed to "suppress" or "eliminate" homosexuals, the brief's vagueness argument emphasized Boutilier's due process rights while implying that a clear antihomosexual statute would be constitutional. The 1967 ACLU statement made distinctions between private and public sex, between consensual and nonconsensual conduct, and between adult sex and sex with minors; the *Boutilier* brief highlighted the "private" and "consensual" nature of Boutilier's adult homosexual conduct. In an earlier case, ACLU lawyers argued that the INS had not shown that an alien was homosexual when he entered the United States. Now ACLU/NYCLU lawyers argued that the INS could not use post-entry evidence to prove that Boutilier was homosexual when he entered the United States. In *Wyngaard*, Carliner defended an alien convicted of a public sex crime. In *Boutilier*, Carliner and his colleagues emphasized that Boutilier had never been convicted of a crime. In *Scott*, Carliner convinced a court that the terms "homosexual" and "homosexual conduct" were unconstitutionally vague. In *Boutilier*, Carliner and his colleagues tried to convince the Court that the term "psychopathic personality" was unconstitutionally vague. In many gay and lesbian cases, ACLU lawyers highlighted the respectability of their clients and invoked the authority of scientific expertise. In *Boutilier*, the ACLU/NYCLU brief emphasized Boutilier's positive qualities and cited the opinions of experts who denied that homosexuality was psychopathological.

The ACLU/NYCLU brief was also influenced by the prior work of civil libertarians on immigration law reform. The ACLU/NYCLU lawyers were familiar with the provisions and mechanisms of U.S. border control, distinctions between exclusion and deportation procedures, and the history of litigation concerning the rights of resident aliens. The ACLU had taken positions against immigration laws that discriminated on the basis of past or present objectionable opinions, radical views, labor activism, organizational memberships, race, color, nationality, or ancestry. In the early 1960s, the ACLU challenged deportations based on "crimes of moral turpitude" and conduct in the "distant past." None of this applied directly to *Boutilier*'s case, but these positions helped create the frameworks used by the ACLU/NYCLU to challenge Boutilier's deportation. Moreover, in emphasizing Boutilier's long U.S. residence, highlighting the INS's reliance on post-entry evidence, and focusing on Boutilier's procedural rights, the ACLU/NYCLU brief invoked arguments used in earlier immigration cases.

The influence of the ACLU's work on mental health reform on the *Boutilier* brief is less clear, which may reflect the fact that those who denied that homosexuality was a form of mental illness did not typically argue for gay and lesbian rights on the basis of arguments about the rights of the mentally ill. That said, when the brief discussed the meaning of the phrase "psychopathic personality," it referred to several state and federal cases that dealt with mental health issues, including cases related to involuntary commitments. The brief's emphasis on the nondangerous nature of Boutilier's conduct may have been influenced by the ACLU's developing position on the rights of the nondangerous mentally ill. In a similar fashion, the brief's argument against the use of the phrase "psychopathic personality" to regulate "non-conforming conduct" may have been influenced by the ACLU's developing position against institutionalizing nonconformists. The ACLU/NYCLU's *Boutilier* brief, like the briefs of Freedman and the HLRS, adapted arguments developed in very different contexts to defend a "homosexual alien."

IN AN AUGUST 2005 *New Yorker* article on the nomination of John G. Roberts Jr. to a position on the Supreme Court, Jeffrey Toobin claimed that "systematic legal efforts on behalf of gays began only in the nineteen-seventies, and the Justices didn't address the issue in a substantive way until the eighties." Toobin's view is all too common, even among experts in gay and lesbian history and politics, and it reflects the assumptions and attitudes that have marred popular interpretations of the gay and lesbian past, even among those sympathetic to the cause of sexual equality.[76] In the 1950s and 1960s, the homophile movement developed a Supreme Court strategy, raised significant funds to support that effort, created institutional vehicles to pursue litigation, and achieved significant victories and losses. Moreover, the homophile movement was not alone; homosexual rights litigation was supported by leftist lawyers such as Blanch Freedman and civil liberties lawyers affiliated with the ACLU. For better and for worse, the defense of Boutilier was influenced by the work of radical immigration advocates, homosexual law reformers, civil libertarians, and civil rights activists.

Boutilier's advocates used multifaceted legal arguments and rhetorical strategies when they argued his case before the Supreme Court. The main argument
made by Blanch Freedman, assisted by Robert Brown and David Freedman,
was that Boutilier's due process rights had been violated. First, while the 1952
Immigration and Nationality Act provided for the deportation of aliens afflicted with psychopathic personality, the law was administered as though it
provided for the deportation of aliens who engaged in homosexual acts. In
this respect, the law was unconstitutionally vague, making Boutilier vulnerable to arbitrary administrative decisions and depriving him of the right to be
informed that homosexual conduct could result in deportation. Second, there
was no scientific basis for the conclusion that homosexual conduct was necessarily indicative of psychopathological condition. Third, the legislative history did not support the conclusion that Congress intended to provide for the
deportation of all aliens who engaged in homosexual acts. Fourth, Boutilier
was never given a medical examination by the Public Health Service (PHS),
which was required under the law. Fifth, Boutilier was being deported on the
grounds that he had an excludable condition at time of entry, but much of the
evidence derived from post-entry conduct. Sixth, Boutilier was deprived of
the right to counsel during his INS interrogation. Freedman's arguments were
supported by *amicus* briefs from the HLRS and the ACLU/NYCLU. The HLRS
collected statements by more than thirty scientific experts who challenged
the notion that homosexuality was psychopathological. The ACLU/NYCLU
elaborated on the vagueness argument and extended the procedural points
to stress that Boutilier was not told that he had the right to refuse to answer
INS questions and was denied the right to present a competent defense at the
INS hearing. The ACLU/NYCLU also argued that deportations should not be
based on private, consensual, and nondangerous conduct.

Boutilier's defenders were knowledgeable and experienced advocates who
viewed themselves as supporters of gay rights and considered with great care
how they could best represent Boutilier's interests and the interests of the
movements mobilized on his behalf. Nevertheless, their work was marked

by profound ambivalence about sexual freedom and equality. The vagueness argument criticized the use of the psychopathic personality statute, but implied that a clearly antigay law would be constitutional. In addition, by emphasizing that Boutilier could have refrained from homosexual conduct had he known it would make him vulnerable, his advocates seemed to be arguing for the right to abstain from same-sex sex. The scientific argument challenged the notion that homosexuality was psychopathological, but suggested that if the government could find scientists who supported its views the INS interpretation would be acceptable. Moreover, much of the scientific evidence submitted by Boutilier's defenders challenged the notion that homosexuality was psychopathological but presented it as undesirable. The legislative history argument raised questions about congressional intent, but implied that Congress could order the exclusion and deportation of homosexual aliens if it wanted to do so. The post-entry evidence argument raised procedural objections about this particular case, but suggested that the use of pre-entry evidence was acceptable. None of the procedural arguments challenged INS authority to deport homosexual aliens if proper procedures were followed. All of the arguments that emphasized the minimal nature of Boutilier's homosexual conduct implied that homosexuality was undesirable. Their intentions were to help Boutilier. They used arguments that were consistent with recommended legal practice, and they may well have done the best they could, but Boutilier's defenders contributed to the Court's conservative ruling.

Legal Arguments

VAGUENESS

Freedman and Brown summarized the vagueness argument in their petition to the Court: "The term 'psychopathic personality' in the statute could not and did not forewarn petitioner that it would be interpreted to mean what the [Second Circuit] court now says it does. He had no warning when he sought admission; he had no warning during the years of residence." Freedman and Freedman's main brief pointed out that "first, the exclusion statute failed to apprise petitioner at the time of entry of what respondent now claims made him then excludable; second, it failed to apprise him that his post-entry sexual behavior could be made the basis for his expulsion."[1]

As they developed this argument, Boutilier's advocates made several distinct points, some of which worked at cross-purposes. For instance, at times they emphasized that the meaning of the term "psychopathic personality" was uncertain, but at other times they defined it in order to prove that Boutilier did not meet the definition. In one passage, Freedman and Freedman cited the words of two experts who regarded the term as "meaningless." In the expert letters appended to the HLRS brief, Ralph Elias wrote that the term was "unscientific" and "misleading" while Ray Evans declared that it "has long been considered inadequate." According to the ACLU/NYCLU brief, there was "no coherent definition" for "psychopathic personality" and even the PHS described the term as "vague and indefinite."[2]

Nevertheless, Boutilier's advocates proceeded to define the indefinite. According to Freedman and Freedman, "The term is a *medical one* and the statute has meaning and can be administered only if it is given a medical meaning. Vague as it is, it can only be defined medically." According to a *Webster's* definition they cited, "psychopathy" means "mental disorder." In an appendix to their brief, sex researcher Clarence Tripp pointed out that "the term 'psychopath' has lingered on in the language of medicine and psychology" and in one definition denotes "any kind of 'mentally deranged person' . . . or 'an eccentric and queer person, one near the border of mental disorder.'" The ACLU/NYCLU brief noted that a Minnesota court had construed "psychopathic personality" to mean "persons who, by an habitual course of misconduct in sexual matters, have evidenced an utter lack of power to control their sexual impulses and who, as a result, are likely to attack or otherwise inflict injury, loss, pain or other evil." The HLRS brief observed, "The term 'psychopathic personality' is a medical or psychiatric term; it has no other meaning. It involves some kind of mental disorder or disease." In the HLRS appendices, Clifford Allen defined psychopathy as "acting in an antisocial manner"; Ralph Elias wrote that "psychopathology . . . is correctly understood as difficulty in personal conduct or psychosocial problems"; Albert Ellis claimed that "psychopathic personality" referred to a person who is "seriously disturbed . . . in an antisocial manner, and who is driven by his disturbance to keep committing acts of a criminal or delinquent nature." Almost all of the HLRS statements denied that homosexuality was psychopathological, but most indicated that psychopathy was definable, and Tripp's definition linked the psychopathic and the queer.[3]

By the time they produced their reply brief, Freedman and Freedman were no longer arguing that the term was vague. In one passage, they wrote, "Resort to legislative history is necessary or meaningful only if the statute on its face is vague or ambiguous. This is not the case here. . . . If the statute is enforced as it reads, petitioner does not challenge it as 'vague' or unconstitutional." In oral arguments, Freedman declared that the term "psychopathic personality" is "not ambiguous"; it denotes "a medical condition" that is "fully defined in medical literature."[4]

There was a similar dynamic at play in the ways Boutilier's defenders dealt with definitions of homosexuality. After observing that "there is no definition of sexual deviate or homosexual in the statute," Freedman and Brown asked, "Who is a homosexual? If, as Dr. Kinsey estimated . . . , at least 37% of the American male population have had homosexual experiences, are they all people who would be excludable were they aliens seeking entry?"[5] Here, too, Boutilier's advocates used arguments that worked at cross-purposes, emphasizing that the term "homosexuality" was vague, but insisting that experts now agreed that it was a type of behavior. In the course of arguing that "psychopathic personality" and "homosexuality" were vague, they defined both and linked them together.

The vagueness argument also had ambivalent implications because it suggested that a clearly antihomosexual statute would be constitutional. This was one of many instances in which Boutilier's defenders made arguments that might help their client but hurt the homophile movement. Some of the briefs pointed out that the 1965 sexual deviation amendment had solved the vagueness problem, but could not be retroactively applied. After the ACLU/NYCLU challenged the notion that Congress had used "psychopathic personality" as a term "encompassing all forms of sexual deviation," it argued, "If that is what Congress actually intended, it is unfortunate that a more descriptive phrase such as 'sexual deviate' was not utilized. In fact, in 1965, Congress amended Section 212(a)(4) to include 'sexual deviation' as a ground for exclusion." This suggested that the psychopathic personality provision was unconstitutionally vague, but the statute referring to sexual deviation was constitutionally clear.[6]

In several instances, the vagueness argument seemed to become an argument for the right to abstain from homosexual conduct. Freedman and Freedman observed that the statute's vagueness deprived Boutilier of "the opportunity to refrain from homosexual practices." In oral arguments, Freedman pointed out that Boutilier's post-entry homosexual acts "may well have been avoided" and Boutilier "could have and in all probability would have refrained from such practices" had he known they would make him deportable. The ACLU/NYCLU applied this argument to the pre-entry period, citing a passage in the Second Circuit dissent that stated, "Had [Boutilier] known that sexual deviation at the time of entry would be automatic grounds for exclusion, there is considerable reason to believe that he could have modified his behavior so that he could not be considered a deviate at the time of entry."

With "reasonable warning," the ACLU/NYCLU contended that he "would have been able to correct" his "psychological condition."[7]

In other passages, the vagueness argument seemed to support favorable treatment for aliens whose homosexual conduct was minimal and aliens who also engaged in heterosexual sex. Freedman and Brown's petition complained that the government had not indicated whether the term homosexual "includes one who engages in both homosexual and heterosexual acts as the petitioner did, prior to entry; whether it applies to someone who has engaged in it once in his life, once a year, four times a year, or constantly; whether it means one who is compulsively drawn to such practices or includes one who is an experimenter or socially induced." Freedman and Freedman argued, "Neither statute nor regulation places limitations or guide lines on the kind of homosexual behavior thus characterized, so that it may include persons who also engage in heterosexual acts, and persons whose homosexual practices vary from rare or infrequent to those who engage in it continuously and flagrantly." It is difficult to imagine what it would mean to engage "constantly" or "continuously" in any form of sex, but these points were not favorable to those who had same-sex sex on a regular, open, or long-term basis. At one point, Freedman and Freedman mentioned that the Second Circuit in *Flores-Rodriguez* had used "psychopathic personality" to characterize "individuals who show a life-long and constitutional tendency not to conform to group customs, and who habitually misbehave so flagrantly that they are continually in trouble with authorities." They also cited a passage in Moore's *Boutilier* dissent that defined a "sexual deviate" as "someone with a long lasting and perhaps compulsive orientation towards homosexual or otherwise 'abnormal' behavior."[8] The vagueness arguments had the potential to help Boutilier, but showed the justices that even defenders of gay rights agreed that homosexuality was undesirable.

SCIENCE

The core of the science argument was that there was no legitimate basis for classifying homosexuality as psychopathological. As Freedman and Freedman stated, "It is the considered opinion of many psychiatrists that homosexual behavior is not necessarily an indication of psychotic disturbance." To support their position, they cited the works of numerous scientific experts who agreed that homosexuality was not intrinsically psychopathological: "Eminent psychiatrists beginning with Sigmund Freud" had made it clear that "indulgence in homosexual conduct" does not necessarily mean that one is "afflicted with psychopathic personality." The assumption that homosexuality is psychopathological was, they argued, "not rational," and "the extent of homosexual practices and its ubiquitousness alone is sufficient to negate it." Even PHS psychiatrists agreed: "Indeed, this opinion is shared by Dr. Smith, chief psychiatrist for the Public Health Service, the very physician who certified petitioner without examination to be a 'psychopathic personality.'" On this point, Freedman and Freedman cited Smith's testimony in *Matter of Anne-Lise Coppo* (1965), which had convinced the Second Circuit majority that Smith "does not espouse the proposition that a sexual deviate is *ipso facto* a constitutional psychopathic inferior or a psychopathic personality." The appended statement by Tripp asserted, "Explanations of homosexual behavior in terms of underlying 'degeneracy,' 'constitutional inferiority,' 'psychopathy' or 'psychopathic personality' are inappropriate and consequently have been abandoned by medical and social science."[9]

According to the HLRS brief, "There is widespread professional opinion that homosexuality *per se* does not indicate psychopathology." To support this conclusion, the brief discussed the findings of the British Wolfenden Commission, the studies of psychologists Evelyn Hooker and Joseph DeLuca, the work of sociologist Michael Schofield, and the positions taken by psychiatrist Judd Marmor and psychoanalyst Sigmund Freud. Then the brief explained that the HLRS had written to "prominent persons in the fields of psychoanalysis, psychiatry, psychology, sociology, anthropology and biology," asking each to outline their positions. Short excerpts of twelve responses from Marmor, Schofield, Harry Benjamin, Hendrik Ruitenbeek, Isadore Rubin, Paul Gebhard, Norman Reider, Ernest van den Haag, Ray Evans, Thomas Szasz, Lester Kirkendall, and Peter Bentler challenged the link between homosexuality and psychopathology. Then a complete set of twenty-nine responses was presented in an appendix; these included statements by Clifford Allen, Alfred Auerbach, Gordon Bermant, John Butler, George Corner, DeLuca, Bernard Diamond, Ralph Elias, Milton Diamond, Albert Ellis, John Hampson, H. Hediger, Margaret Mead, Clellan Ford and Frank Beach, Richard Michael, John Money, Leonard Olinger, and Martin Schein. Additional appendices reproduced a study by DeLuca, Freud's "Letter to an American Mother," and a compendium of expert opinions produced by the Mattachine Society of Washington, D.C. The overwhelming majority of the experts denied that homosexuality was intrinsically psychopathological.[10]

Unfortunately for Boutilier, his advocates, having deferred to science, opened the door to conflicting scientific perspectives. In an attempt to preempt the use of antigay evidence, the HLRS brief acknowledged that "the scientific data is not uniformly accepted by psychiatrists and psychoanalysts" and some experts "ignore the experimental data" or "question the methods." The brief posited that "the *assumptions* of psychoanalytic theory offer resistance to scientific data" and cited the claim of one expert that "all psychoanalytic theories *assume* that adult homosexuality is psychopathologic." These passages were preceded and followed by sections that highlighted the views of experts who denied that homosexuality was psychopathological, but the impression created was that science was divided.[11]

As far as the government was concerned, congressional intent was more important than scientific conclusions. In oral arguments, the government's lawyer, Nathan Lewin, stated, "It's a matter of dispute among psychiatrists.... Congress had before it, or could have had before it, various psychiatric opinions. It apparently chose one, and that's perfectly within the domain of the legislature. If today it turns out that that's wrong, or the weight of psychiatric opinion is to the contrary, that does not, we think, invalidate the statute." Scientific knowledge was not absolute, Lewin's position suggested, and Congress had the power to take sides in scientific disputes.[12]

Meanwhile, many of the cited experts denied that homosexuality was psychopathological but presented it as undesirable. Psychopathology was the key legal issue, but undesirability had the potential to swing votes away from Boutilier. Several of the experts linked homosexuality to childhood development problems. Freud's "Letter to an American Mother," reprinted in the HLRS brief and excerpted by Freedman and Freedman, asserted that homosexuality was "produced by a certain arrest of sexual development." In the main HLRS appendix, Elias wrote that "the early life of one with a homoerotic disposition was probably impaired," but it was possible for homosexuals to "transcend their handicaps." According to Auerback, "Homosexuality arises from distortions in the individual's psychosexual development. During the child's formative years the absence of a parent, overattachment to a parent, lack of identification or overidentification, and conscious or unconscious parental seduction have all proven to be important to the etiology of homosexuality." Auerback claimed that troubles arose for boys "when the father is weak, absent from the home or psychologically displaced by the mother," when "the father is tyrannical and abusive to the mother," when "either parent is blatantly promiscuous," or when "the mother's attitude is antisexual." For girls, troubles developed because of "the father's violence or alcoholic outbursts," a "domineering mother," or the "absence of a father." These experts joined the antihomosexual consensus.[13]

As some of these comments suggest, several HLRS experts presented homosexuality as a form of gender trouble. According to Butler, "In many instances, the person who practices homosexuality has been trained to assume the attitudes and behavioral patterns of the opposite sex." In his discussion of the "small percentage" of homosexual men who exhibit "effeminate traits," Auerback pointed out that "the effeminate male has a strong need to renounce his biological sex and a conscious or unconscious desire to identify with women and may develop, sometimes to an exaggerated degree, the characteristics such as voice, gestures, and gait that are associated with femininity." Tripp discussed effeminate "fairies" alongside other troubled homosexuals: "Any piece of behavior that is taboo, or that is under tight social regulation, may be 'thrown in the face of society' in the form of public displays by persons who . . . do not know how to respect the surface demands of the society in which they live. Other individuals who perfectly well know the limits of social decorum, such as various 'angry young men,' may choose to flaunt taboo behavior as a means of expressing social protest. And still other individuals . . . may be so personally disturbed by their own tendencies . . . that they push forward some distorted fragment of this misinterpretation as an element of their own identity—as seen, for instance, in the rare but dramatic display of the 'painted fairy.'" These "sometimes psychotic or neurotic manifestations" were not to be confused with those who "discreetly make similar sexual choices" and are "well-integrated socially." Such comments encouraged positive treatment of gender-conforming homosexuals but negative treatment of gender-transgressors.[14]

Other HLRS experts emphasized that the troubles of homosexuals were attributable to hostile social attitudes. According to a book by Schofield that was cited by Cantor, negative social attitudes toward homosexuality "create a stress situation" that can lead to "character deterioration" in some homosexuals, who then become "social casualties." Marmor pointed out, "I am not denying that the spectrum of personality distribution in homosexuals tends to be more heavily weighted toward neurotic patterns of behavior than is that of heterosexuals. This is inevitable in a society that makes such behavior ipso facto maladaptive." This meant that as long as dominant society continued to view homosexuality negatively, homosexuals would continue to suffer from psychological problems. Though intended as a way to promote changes in social attitudes, this argument supported the contention that homosexuals maladapted to present social circumstances were not desirable immigrants. This position also suggested that even if U.S. attitudes changed, antihomosexual attitudes elsewhere would continue to produce psychological problems in immigrants.[15]

To be sure, many of the HLRS experts extolled the virtues of extraordinary homosexuals. Freud's letter noted that "many highly respectable individuals of ancient and modern times have been homosexuals, several of the greatest men among them." According to Allen, "There is a strong probability that homosexuality is much more associated with genius rather than psychopathy." As examples he mentioned Michelangelo, Leonardo, Donatello, Bacon, Shakespeare, Marlowe, Byron, Shelley, Tennyson, Goethe, Rimbaud, Verlaine, Gide, Proust, Tchaikovsky, and Wagner. Money added, "Many extraordinarily accomplished people in all walks of life, who have much to contribute to the nation's advancement, would be excluded if all homosexuals are, de facto, excluded as psychopathic." According to Rubin, "A number of them are making highly significant contributions to the social and cultural life of our country; in past history, some emerged as intellectual or cultural leaders of eminence."[16]

Regretting the loss of the extraordinary was not the same thing as welcoming the ordinary. Some HLRS experts, while denying that homosexuality was intrinsically psychopathological, reached conclusions that were quite unfavorable toward homosexuals. For Auerback, "homosexuality is one of the most common psychological disorders." For Ellis, "fixed or exclusive homosexuality . . . may be and often is pathological." Ellis continued, "In our culture most individuals who are fixed homosexuals are neurotically or psychotically obsessed with homosexual behavior, and have a great fear of engaging in heterosexual acts. Many of them, as well, are quite compulsive in their homosexual behavior." He was convinced that "the vast majority" of homosexuals are "seriously disturbed individuals" and are "neurotic or psychotic." Perhaps the most unfavorable conclusion was reached by Bernard Diamond, who wrote: "I do not think that homosexuality is necessarily indicative of a 'psycho-neurosis.' I am not prepared to state that homosexuality, in itself, is not psychopathological. In other words, I do not subscribe to the theory that homosexuality can be 'normal.'" Not missing the opportunity to use his opponents' evidence against them, Nathan Lewin, after asserting in the oral arguments that Congress did not "fly in the face of psychiatric testimony when it said this is conduct which could be classified under afflicted with a psychopathic personality," added, "Some of the responses in the amicus brief of the Homosexual Reform League, we think, indicate that those who responded believe that maybe it could be categorized [as such]." The fact that these experts were cited in an *amicus* brief by homophile advocates may have been particularly damning, as it was unlikely that the justices would think of the

HLRS as biased against homosexuality.[17] In the end, Boutilier's advocates presented evidence that supported the conclusion that (1) scientific experts were divided on the question of whether homosexuality was psychopathological, (2) some experts believed it was, and (3) even those who thought otherwise viewed homosexuality and homosexuals as undesirable.

LEGISLATIVE INTENT

The third argument made by Boutilier's defenders focused on the intent of the 1952 legislation. On the one hand, legislative intent was irrelevant if the statute was unconstitutionally vague. As Freedman and Freedman observed, "Substantive due process demands that the statute involved give [the immigrant] adequate notice, without requiring him to read legislative histories or to probe the mind of the legislators." On the other hand, the legislative history did not support the conclusion that Congress intended to exclude and deport all aliens who engaged in homosexual conduct. Even if this was the substantive intent, the procedural intent was to have PHS doctors, using medical criteria, determine whether individual aliens were excludable.[18]

To challenge the contention that Congress wanted to exclude and deport all aliens who engaged in homosexual conduct, Freedman and Freedman argued that the government's interpretation was "predicated solely on a single reference in a Senate Report accompanying a bill which never became law." Moreover, the proposed Senate legislation listed both "aliens afflicted with psychopathic personality" and "aliens who are homosexuals or sex perverted," which implied that the Senate did not understand "psychopathic personality" to include "all homosexuals." In any event, Freedman noted that the final legislation derived from a House bill, and the House report "does not reflect the House Committee's understanding of the term 'psychopathic personality' to embrace all homosexual practices." A 1951 PHS report submitted to the House Judiciary Committee implied that the PHS only wanted to target "homosexuality and sex perversions that were pathologic and symptomatic of severe underlying neurosis or psychosis." The House committee "chose to have homosexuals considered within the framework of the term psychopathic personality—a medical term denoting a pathological condition." In short, some homosexuality was pathological, but some was not, and Congress did not necessarily intend to exclude everyone who had ever engaged in homosexual conduct. Freedman and Freedman also argued that Congress could not have intended to exclude all such persons, given evidence that a large percentage of the population engaged in homosexual conduct at some point in their lives.[19]

The arguments about legislative history challenged the notion that Congress intended to exclude anyone who had ever engaged in homosexual conduct, but conveyed the impression that Congress believed that many such persons were psychopathic. In addition, these arguments did not challenge the government's power to exclude and deport aliens on the basis of homosexuality if it wanted to do so. Freedman and Freedman's brief, for instance, cited a dissenting opinion in *Jordan* that stated, "We do not here question the power of Congress to define deportable conduct. We only question the power of administrative officers and courts to decree deportation until Congress has given an intelligible definition of deportable conduct." Along similar lines, when responding to the notion that "Congress can enact legislation after an alien's arrival that makes him deportable," Freedman and Freedman's reply brief declared, "The essential point is that while Congress can, Congress hasn't." Boutilier's advocates seemed to share the government's vision of Congress's power to discriminate against aliens on the basis of sexual conduct.[20]

MEDICAL EXAMINATION

Boutilier's advocates also argued that the legislative intent and statutory language indicated that aliens were to be classified as "afflicted with psychopathic personality" on the basis of PHS medical examinations. Since the PHS never examined Boutilier, the INS could not deport Boutilier on this basis. According to Freedman and Brown, in 1964 the PHS certified, without conducting or referencing a medical examination, that when Boutilier entered the country in 1955 he had been a psychopathic personality. Freedman and Freedman underscored the tenuous nature of the procedure by emphasizing that the PHS certified Boutilier only four days after he was interrogated by the INS and retrospectively diagnosed him as having had a condition nearly a decade earlier. Citing the Second Circuit dissent, which asserted that "Congress contemplated an inquiry in each case, to be performed by skilled psychiatrists," Freedman and Freedman argued that the INS violated the intent and terms of the statute. PHS doctors "signed their names to the certification as physicians," but "they were not performing a professional act; they were acting as clerks."[21]

On this issue, Boutilier's advocates responded to two points made by the government: that the statute did not require medical examinations for deportations, as opposed to exclusions, and that Boutilier had refused to be examined by the PHS. On the first, Freedman and Freedman emphasized that Boutilier was being deported for having been excludable at time of entry. This meant that the INS had to follow proper exclusion procedures: "The proof that petitioner was *excludable* requires at least the same proof that would have been required to *exclude* him." To conclude otherwise would lead to "the anomalous and incredible situation that a person who has lived here for ten years may be deported on a record on which he could not have been excluded." The principle involved here was the notion, generally accepted by the Court, that resident aliens had more rights than nonresident aliens seeking entry.[22]

As for Boutilier's refusal to be examined by the PHS, Freedman and Freedman argued that agreeing to an examination would have been "futile" since PHS regulations required its doctors to certify that Boutilier was a psychopathic personality, "irrespective of what their medical examination of him disclosed." Essentially, Freedman and Freedman were accusing the U.S. government of practicing what the United States accused the Soviet Union of doing: forcing medical doctors in general and psychiatrists in particular to follow the dictates of the state. Boutilier's advocates also emphasized that the only medical examinations of their client, those performed by private psychiatrists, concluded that he was not psychopathic.[23]

Just as the legislative intent argument did not challenge the power of Congress to provide for exclusions and deportations based on homosexuality, the medical examination argument did not challenge the authority of the PHS to certify that homosexual aliens were afflicted with psychopathic personality. Moreover, when Boutilier's advocates highlighted the conclusions of his private psychiatrists, they attacked the claim that he was psychopathological but still presented him as an undesirable alien. According to Falsey's report, "He is not psychotic. From his own account he has a psychosexual problem but is beginning treatment for this disorder. Diagnostically, I would consider him as having a Character Neurosis, believe that the prognosis in therapy is reasonably good and do not think he represents any risk . . . of decompensation into a dependent psychotic reaction nor any potential for frank criminal activity." Though Falsey intended to help Boutilier, his report presented Boutilier as having a psychosexual problem, a character neurosis, and a disorder requiring treatment. Ullman wrote, "What emerged out of the interview was not a picture of a psychopath but that of a dependent, immature young man with a conscience, an awareness of the feelings of others and a sense of personal honesty. His sexual structure still appears fluid and immature. . . . His homosexual orientation seems secondary to a very constricted, dependent personality pattern. . . . I do not believe that Mr. Boutilier is a psychopath." Ullman's report denied that he was a psychopath, but presented him as dependent and immature. In the course of criticizing the government for not following proper PHS examination procedures, Boutilier's defenders produced their own unfavorable diagnoses.[24]

Boutilier's advocates also argued that the legislative history and statutory language made it clear that, in order to deport an alien as a psychopathic personality at time of entry, the INS had to rely on evidence of a pre-entry condition. To the extent that Boutilier's deportation was based on post-entry conduct, it was not legitimate. Boutilier's advocates relied on two critical distinctions here. Chronologically, the INS had to prove that the affliction existed at the time of entry. Conceptually, the INS had to prove that Boutilier was afflicted with a condition. Freedman and Freedman asserted that "petitioner is being deported because he was involved in homosexual experiences after his entry," and there is "no statutory basis for deportation on such ground." The government claimed that "the statute aims at excluding *persons of certain characteristics*," but the INS "administered the act as relating to *persons who have engaged in certain behavior*." Freedman and Freedman concluded, "There is no evidence by respondent as to petitioner's psychological or physical *condition*. The evidence is only of his behavior, that is, of a number of homosexual experiences."[25]

To support their position, Boutilier's advocates challenged the credibility of the claim that Boutilier's post-entry conduct had not been decisive in his certification as a psychopath. Freedman and Brown argued that the notion that the PHS did not base its certification on post-entry practices was "inconceivable." Given Boutilier's "relatively meager" pre-entry sexual experiences, the post-entry acts "must have been decisive." Freedman and Freedman wrote that the post-entry conduct was used as "persuasive evidence" of his condition at entry. The ACLU/NYCLU brief declared, "It would be the purest fiction to suggest that pre-1955 behavior alone motivated the government in ordering Boutilier deported." Post-entry conduct was "a major factor" and the PHS certification "rested heavily" on post-entry activities.[26]

In making this argument, Boutilier's advocates again seemed to be arguing for the right to abstain from same-sex sex. At one point, Freedman and Freedman observed, "There is nothing in the certification of the Public Health Service's doctor or in the decision of the Special Inquiry Officer to indicate . . . if there would have been any difference in their conclusions had petitioner experienced but two homosexual acts per year prior to entry, or only one such act, or even none, so long as there was the testimony with respect to post-entry sexual behavior." The ACLU/NYCLU brief insisted that "it seems incredible to suggest . . . that, if Boutilier had lived a life of impeccable conventional morality between 1955 and 1964, the post-entry years, the government would have initiated its deportation proceedings." Boutilier's advocates were making these arguments to show that the INS had relied on post-entry evidence, but in effect they were defending the rights of aliens who committed no homosexual acts before entry or lived lives of "impeccable conventional morality" after entry.[27]

Boutilier's advocates cited several rulings in support of their position. Freedman and Freedman pointed out that in *Fleuti* the Ninth Circuit ruled that "while the post-entry conduct was not itself the ground of deportation, but was used as evidence of a pre-entry condition, the prejudice would be substantial." The court concluded that whether Fleuti would have been classified as a psychopathic personality based only on pre-entry evidence was "a matter of speculation" and "the fact that the examining officer chose to rely heavily upon post-entry behavior is some indication that a charge might not have been filed, or a finding entered, on pre-entry behavior alone." Freedman and Freedman also discussed the Second Circuit's ruling in *Powlowec*, which seemed to suggest that "post-entry testimony is permissible to establish an excludable condition at time of entry." They argued that the situation in *Powlowec* was "materially different," since the court was "dealing with an inherent, psychotic condition" and "the post-entry diagnosis was provoked by manifestations of mental derangement that could only be the reflection of a condition organic and constitutional."[28]

Boutilier's advocates were arguing about the type and timing of the evidence the INS used, but they were also making a point about the relationship between conduct and condition. On this issue, Freedman and Freedman's brief pounced on a contradiction in the Second Circuit opinion by Kaufman. In one passage, Kaufman stated that "the [psychopathic personality] provision was never designed to regulate *conduct*; its function was to exclude aliens possessing certain *characteristics*." In another passage, the opinion declared that Congress "determined that pre-entry *homosexual behavior* was to be a ground for exclusion." In their reply brief, Freedman and Freedman argued that the government's brief similarly "spoke of characteristics and behavior as if they were interchangeable." For the government, "a homosexual" is "anyone who has engaged in homosexual acts," and any such person is "afflicted with psychopathic personality." This "substitutes behavior or conduct for condition." Later in the brief, they complained that the INS was "very agile in jumping from behavior to condition to suit its argument."[29]

Boutilier's opponents may have been agile in jumping from behavior to condition, but his defenders were agile as well. In some passages, the condition Boutilier's lawyers claimed he did not have was "affliction with psychopathic personality"; in others, the condition he did not have was "homosexuality"; and in others there was no such thing as a "homosexual" condition. Freedman and Freedman argued that "homosexuality is a kind of behavior, evidently very wide-spread, and not the manifestation of a particular kind of person." According to Tripp's statement, "Kinsey and his associates . . . never once used it [homosexual] as a substantive noun, nor as an adjective, to describe persons." They spoke only of "homosexual acts, homosexual responses . . . , etc." Tripp continued, "To speak of a person as 'a homosexual' entails two troublesome distortions. (1) It amounts to classifying a person according to the sex of somebody else (the partner). (2) It implies that persons fall into categories of homosexual and heterosexual that are sharp enough to be used as classifications." After summarizing Kinsey's findings about the large percentage of the population that could not be classified as exclusively homosexual or heterosexual, Tripp highlighted Kinsey's conclusion: "'It would encourage clearer thinking on these matters if persons were not characterized as heterosexual or homosexual, but as individuals who have had certain amounts of heterosexual experience and certain amounts of homosexual experience.'" Making use of Frank Kameny's suggestion (discussed in chapter 4), Freedman and Freedman's reply brief pointed out that the Civil Service Commission had argued in a different context that "homosexual" was not "a proper metonym for an individual" but should be used as "an adjective to describe the nature of overt relations or conduct."[30]

Boutilier's advocates tried to emphasize that homosexuality was a type of behavior rather than a type of person, but many of the experts they cited used contrary language. The appended H L R S statements by Allen, Auerbach, Benjamin, Bentler, Butler, DeLuca, (Milton) Diamond, Ellis, Evans, Freud, Hampson, Hediger, Kirkendall, Marmor, Money, Olinger, Reider, Rubin, Ruitenbeek, and van den Haag freely discussed "homosexuals," "homosexual men," "homosexual women," "the homosexual," and "a homosexual." Some of the H L R S experts explicitly discussed homosexual identities or conditions. Money defined "homosexuality as a matter either of psychosexual identity (obligative homosexuality) or of transient opportunism in an otherwise heterosexual person (facultative homosexuality)." Schofield described homosexuality as "a condition which in itself has only minor effects upon the development of the personality." Auerbach emphasized Kinsey's conclusion that "4% of white males are exclusively homosexual throughout their lives." Allen noted that "about five per cent of the population is believed to be permanently homosexual." The impression that at least some people could be described as having a fixed homosexual orientation was strengthened by DeLuca's study of recent military inductees, which was reproduced in the HLRS brief. According to DeLuca, 95 percent of the men who were "currently engaged in homosexual activities" indicated that "they were determined to continue this way of life." The ACLU/NYCLU brief referred to Boutilier as a member of a "regulated class" and cited with approval a passage in the Second Circuit dissent that referred to his "psychological condition." The HLRS could not control the language used by its experts, any more than the ACLU could control the language used by the Second Circuit, and in general Boutilier's lawyers tried to use language that defined homosexuality as a type of behavior rather than a type of person. But insofar as homosexuality was generally conceptualized in both ways, it was difficult to be consistent. These passages worked at cross-purposes with the effort to define homosexuality as a type of behavior.[31]

The behavioral position offered Boutilier's defenders several strategic advantages. If homosexuality was conceptualized as a type of behavior, perhaps no one could be classified as having a homosexual condition. If homosexual acts were common, the notion that homosexuality was psychopathological was less credible, as was the notion that Congress intended to exclude and deport all aliens who engaged in homosexual conduct. If homosexuality was defined in behavioral terms, the government's failure to warn Boutilier seemed more troubling. If there was no such thing as a homosexual condition, then the only condition that mattered was "affliction with psychopathic personality," which could only be diagnosed through a medical examination. The behavioral argument was also reassuring to those who experienced moments of homosexual desire and to those who engaged in homosexual acts but did not want to think of themselves as having a homosexual condition, character, or identity.

The behavioral argument also had disadvantages. As Kinsey's work and Tripp's statement suggested, it was commonly believed that people could be classified as "homosexual" or "heterosexual." Kinsey, Tripp, and others challenged this belief, but if Congress in 1952 shared the popular view, perhaps the legislative intent was to exclude and deport all aliens classifiable as homosexual. If the Court shared this view, the justices might very well classify Boutilier as homosexual. Even if the Court accepted the notion that homosexual conduct could be distinguished from a homosexual condition, the justices might conclude that there was enough pre-entry homosexual conduct to justify classifying Boutilier as having a homosexual condition. This was the government's position when it argued, "There may indeed be cases where it is difficult to determine whether—and in precisely what sense—an individual should be deemed homosexual within the intent of the statute. Such might be the case of an individual who had had only a few, isolated homosexual experiences and did not regard himself as homosexual. There is no ambiguity on this score here, however."[32]

Meanwhile, the behavioral position made it difficult for Boutilier's defenders to make identity-based arguments. In a period in which discrimination based on national origin, race, and sex was being challenged on the basis of claims about fixed and involuntary identities, the behavioral arguments used by Boutilier's advocates required them to avoid making similar arguments to challenge discrimination based on sexual orientation. Homophile legal reformers did make identity-based arguments in other cases and contexts in the 1960s, but Boutilier's advocates did not. This may reflect the fact that this was an immigration case; Boutilier's defenders knew that the Court allowed Congress to discriminate on the basis of fixed identities at the nation's borders in ways supposedly not permitted inside the nation's borders. There were good reasons, in an immigration case, to define homosexuality as a type of behavior rather than a type of person. Still, the behavioral position limited the options of Boutilier's defenders.

LEGAL REPRESENTATION, SELF-INCRIMINATION, AND DUE NOTICE

In addition to highlighting the lack of a PHS examination, Boutilier's advocates made other procedural points. Freedman and Brown noted that Boutilier was "unrepresented by counsel" when he was "interrogated." Freedman and Freedman added, "Petitioner was not advised of his right to counsel or that he need not answer any or all of the questions put to him." The ACLU/NYCLU cited several cases to support the contention that "a permanent resident alien possesses the right to invoke the protection of the Fifth Amendment in connection with a deportation proceeding." The brief also argued that the statute's vagueness "deprived him of his constitutional right to receive clear notice of any charges against him," which in turn deprived him of the "opportunity to prepare and present an adequate defense."[33]

Boutilier's defenders may have made a mistake in not making these procedural arguments at an earlier stage. When the case reached the Supreme Court, the government's lawyers objected to the fact that these points had not been made in the lower courts. In addition, the government claimed that Boutilier was "fully advised of his rights" and was told that any statement he made "might be used against him." The government also insisted that this rule applied only to criminal proceedings and only those that occurred after 1964. In any case, these arguments did not challenge the power of Congress and the INS to order the exclusion and deportation of homosexual aliens if proper procedures were followed.[34]

PRIVATE, CONSENSUAL, AND NONDANGEROUS CONDUCT

Boutilier's advocates offered one final argument. In the introduction to its brief, the ACLU/NYCLU declared, "This Court should consider the vital question of the application of deportation statutes to conduct which does not endanger the public safety. Where conduct, like that in which petitioner was engaged, is private and consensual, without any act of aggression towards the community, no interest of the state is threatened." Freedman and Freedman's reply brief noted that "making private, consensual homosexual practices between adults the subject of oppressive legislation and ostracism is reminiscent of history's other witchhunts."[35]

None of Boutilier's advocates developed these points into arguments about the rights of aliens or the powers of Congress. No cases or precedents were cited in support of these assertions; no constitutional provisions were invoked; no philosophical discussions about human rights were offered. In this sense, these seemed more like legislative arguments about what Congress should do rather than judicial arguments about what Congress could do. Perhaps the advocates did not develop these points because the precedents (and especially *Griswold*) did not suggest that the Court would recognize a broadly formulated right of sexual privacy. Moreover, Boutilier's advocates did little to challenge widely held beliefs that homosexuality could never be private and consensual because it endangered public safety, threatened state interests, and was better characterized as secret, coercive, and aggressive. At best, this argument offered homosexuals equality in the private sphere and discrimination in the public sphere.

Rhetorical Strategies

DEFERENCE TO SCIENCE

In addition to making substantive legal arguments, Boutilier's advocates used rhetorical strategies to defend their client. Like the substantive arguments, the rhetorical strategies were marked by profound ambivalence about sexual freedom and equality. One rhetorical strategy—deferring to scientific expertise—has already been mentioned. This involved not only invoking works of science, but also promoting the superiority of scientific knowledge. This was done most explicitly in the HLRS brief, which used the work of Kenneth Boulding to proclaim, "'The growth of knowledge is one of the most irreversible forces known to mankind.' The advancement of civilization depends upon the gradual triumph of scientific knowledge over 'folk knowledge.'" According to Cantor, "This case is part of the struggle now taking place between the scientific image of homosexuality ... and the folk image." This placed Boutilier's defense on the side of modernity and progress, while also suggesting that victory was inevitable. As indicated above, however, the strategy of deferring to science had disadvantages as well, especially given the availability of antigay scientific claims. Moreover, at least one HLRS expert, Szasz, was a radical critic of science, devoting much of his career to challenging psychiatric knowledge. While most of the experts cited criticized bad science, some criticized science more generally, which had the potential to undermine the scientific basis of Boutilier's defense.[36]

POSITIVE QUALITIES

Boutilier's advocates also made strong efforts to emphasize their client's positive qualities. Their descriptions drew heavily on the reports of Boutilier's private doctors, which integrated elements of the standard psychiatric case history and the conventional immigration narrative. According to Falsey's report,

> Clive was the eldest son with an older sister, Phyllis, who is now 34, married with 8 children and living in Wellin [Welland], Ontario. A brother, Andrew, 28, is married with 2 children in New Jersey. Danny, 26, is married with one child, was in the U.S. Military Service. A sister, Roseanne, now 20, is married and is living in Brooklyn and the youngest brother, Paul, is 18 and makes his home with the patient's mother who is 49 and who is working as a practical nurse. Mr. Boutelier's [sic] father died in 1957 of heart disease.

Ullman's report stated,

> Boutilier comes from a family of six siblings raised on a small farm in Canada. He is the second oldest. A sister, aged 34, and a brother, aged 30, are in Canada. The others are all in the States. His three brothers are married. There is no history of any nervous and mental disorder in the family and no history of any sexual problems among any of his siblings. His father died eight years ago. His mother remarried and the patient is now living with his mother and stepfather. The patient recalls very little about his early years except that everyone had to work to maintain the farm. His own

schooling was interrupted at the age of thirteen so that he could contribute to the support of his family.

In their main brief, Freedman and Freedman noted that "with the exception of one sister and brother, his family of six siblings lives in the United States, as do his mother and stepfather, with whom he resides." Within the first few minutes of her oral arguments, Freedman declared, "He resides in New York City with his mother, who is a naturalized citizen, and his stepfather, also a citizen. His father is dead. And, in addition, he has a large family of married brothers and sisters who live in this country with their respective spouses and children." These portraits presented Boutilier as the child of a struggling farm family that had migrated in search of a better life, a good son and brother who made sacrifices to support his parents and siblings, a member of a productive, reproductive, and patriotic network of households, and a relative of U.S. citizens who contributed to national health and security. Boutilier's advocates were not making a legal argument that he deserved special treatment because the U.S. immigration system favored family unification and privileged the relatives of U.S. citizens, but they were attempting to harness the cultural power of family, immigrant, and patriotic values while challenging the notion that homosexuality was linked to familial and foreign pathologies.[37]

Designed to help Boutilier, this strategy had conservative implications. If from one perspective Boutilier was a member of a heteronormative family, from another he was the product of a troubled one. According to Ullman, "his father and mother fought a great deal" and "he felt very close to his mother and tended to take her side." There was no mention of divorce, but the evidence indicated that Boutilier's mother began living in the United States in 1956, three years before Boutilier's father died in Canada, and that she had remarried. The family narratives included several elements that were common in antigay psychological case histories, suggesting that Boutilier grew up as a mama's boy in a contentious household. This impression was strengthened when Boutilier's advocates highlighted his work as a health care attendant, which suggested that he was following in his mother's nursing footsteps. Moreover, to the extent that the strategy succeeded in presenting Boutilier as a member of a heteronormative family, it implied that homosexuals whose families did not conform to dominant cultural values deserved less than equal treatment. To the extent that Boutilier's advocates succeeded in convincing the Court that he was a member of a normative family but failed to win their case, the result was a decision against all homosexual aliens, no matter how respectable their families might be.[38]

Similar dynamics occurred when Boutilier's advocates presented him as honest, intelligent, hardworking, responsible, conscientious, and religious. All of these were positive qualities in general, but took on added meaning because immigrants and homosexuals were often said to lack these characteristics. Falsey observed that Boutilier spoke "frankly" about his homosexuality. According to Ullman, he was "cooperative" and had a "sense of personal honesty." Freedman and Freedman noted that Boutilier was "candid" and "frank." This not only depicted Boutilier as honest and open, but also allowed his advocates to distinguish his case from those of aliens who did not tell the truth (even though, as discussed in chapter 2, Boutilier initially denied having engaged in homosexual conduct). In a similar fashion, Falsey's description of Boutilier's "good intelligence" functioned not only to create a positive impression, but also to demonstrate that Boutilier met the immigration system's minimum intelligence requirements. "Intelligence" was also significant as Freedman and Freedman emphasized "the requirement that legislation be definite and certain so that men of common intelligence will know what conduct is being commanded or forbidden." Supporting this depiction of Boutilier, the ACLU/NYCLU cited a description of him as "young, intelligent, and responsible."[39]

Falsey's report addressed Boutilier's qualities as a worker: "This patient is working steadily as a building maintenance man. . . . Earlier he served as attendant and companion to a man who was mentally ill and the patient performed responsibly." Ullman observed, "Boutilier has made a good work adjustment in his country. . . . He is well liked, conscientious about his work and concerned with doing a very good job." Freedman and Freedman pointed out that Boutilier had worked "steadily" and was "at all times self supporting." Addressing his leisure time, Ullman reported, "His evenings are spent mostly at home. He occasionally goes bowling. He attends mass but otherwise does not go regularly to church." These comments conveyed favorable images of Boutilier while distinguishing his case from those of aliens who were excludable because they were likely to become public charges, aliens who were deportable because they were not self-supporting, and aliens who engaged in less respectable leisure activities. Moreover, the description of Boutilier as a mental-health care worker positioned him as someone who cared for the mentally ill, not as someone who was himself mentally ill.[40] These descriptions, while intended to help Boutilier's cause, also had conservative implications. The implications were not favorable to aliens who were not as honest, intelligent, hardworking, responsible, conscientious, or religious. And when the Court accepted these descriptions but upheld Boutilier's deportation, the implications were negative for all aliens classifiable as homosexual, no matter their positive qualities.

Boutilier's advocates also referenced his age, nationality, race, and sex. Ullman described him as a "white male." Freedman and Freedman depicted him as a "Canadian national, now thirty-three years old," who had been a "young man of twenty-one" when he entered the country. In oral arguments, Freedman's very first words, after the obligatory "if it pleases the Court," declared, "The petitioner is an alien of Canadian nationality." Perhaps no country received more favorable treatment within the U.S. immigration system than Canada, which was seen as a neighboring country with a predominantly white, Christian, and English-speaking population. The U.S. immigration system also favored young, able-bodied men, who were seen as less of a potential economic burden than others. Boutilier's advocates did not make formal legal arguments about these characteristics, but in referring to these facts they presented Boutilier in ways they hoped would be advantageous. Like the comments on family history and personal character, the invocations of Boutilier's age, nationality, race, and sex suggested that aliens without these traits should not receive equal treatment. Having highlighted these characteristics, Boutilier's advocates ended up contributing to a decision against all homosexual aliens, no matter their age, nationality, race, or sex.[41]

SEXUAL CHARACTER AND CONDUCT

Of particular importance to Boutilier's defense was the description of his sexual character and conduct. As far as pre-entry matters were concerned, Boutilier's advocates hinted at his sexual victimization as an adolescent; denied that he pursued homosexual encounters; minimized his homosexual conduct; emphasized the private, consensual, and nondangerous nature of his sexual activities; and highlighted his heterosexual experiences. They did not mention that Boutilier told an INS investigator that he had sex in a Halifax public park on at least two occasions. According to Ullman, "The patient was not aware of any feelings of difference or difficulties of any kind during his childhood. He had no sexual experiences until the age of sixteen when he was apparently seduced by an older man. There followed a period of sporadic occasional experiences, mostly with older men and usually initiated by them." Using an ambiguous tense, he also wrote, "The patient has had sexual interest in girls and has had intercourse with them on a number of occasions. He has at times become interested in a girl but develops acute anxiety and withdraws when the girl herself has expressed a serious interest." Freedman and Freedman stated that Boutilier "admitted having had homosexual experiences about three or four times a year from age sixteen until twenty-one, during which time he also engaged in heterosexual practices." They described the evidence of pre-entry homosexual acts as "meager" and "fragmentary" and the experiences as "sporadic" and "youthful." They noted as well that "petitioner testified that he had been heterosexual also." The appended statement by Tripp concluded, "Boutilier cannot be classed as either heterosexual or homosexual—particularly not at age 21 when these mixtures are especially common." The ACLU/NYCLU observed that Boutilier's sexual conduct was "private and consensual, without any act of aggression." His homosexual experiences were "irregular and consensual," and his behavior "never exhibited the slightest tendency to violence."[42]

Boutilier's advocates argued that post-entry evidence should not be used, but also emphasized that Boutilier's post-entry homosexual conduct was minimal, private, consensual, and nondangerous; he was never convicted of a sex crime; he established a long-term domestic partnership with another man; and he was capable of controlling his sexual impulses. Recently he had ended his long-term relationship, moved back in with his parents, and stopped having same-sex sex. They also implied, though there was no evidence in the record about this, that Boutilier's heterosexual conduct had continued in the post-entry period. According to Ullman, Boutilier's pre-entry pattern of occasional homosexual conduct "persisted" in the United States "until . . . about eight years ago when he moved in with a homosexual male with whom he remained for about seven years." He continued, "The patient never sought out homosexual contacts or relationships on his own and the occasion on which he was picked up was the only one in which he was involved with a minor." Ullman noted that "he has abandoned all sexual practices within the past several months because of his annoyance and disgust with the problems these activities have brought about." He also observed, "He moves from homosexual to heterosexual interests as well as abstinence with almost equal facility. . . . My own feeling is that his own need to fit in and be accepted is so great that it far surpasses his need for sex in any form." This suggested not only that Boutilier was capable of controlling his desires, but also that his desire to be a good immigrant ("to fit in and be accepted") was stronger than his desire for sex. Freedman and Freedman emphasized that Boutilier's post-entry homosexual conduct occurred "approximately three to four times a year." Elsewhere they mentioned that in the *Rosenberg* case, "the history of Fleuti's homosexuality covered 22 years, 1936–1959, with monthly indulgences and two convictions." Surely, they implied, the Court could not rule against Boutilier when it had ruled in favor of Fleuti. In addition, they asserted that Boutilier's homosexuality was under his control and the statute's vagueness deprived him of "the opportunity to refrain" from homosexual conduct, "which according to the statements of his doctors, he was well able to do." They declared, "There is nothing in the record to establish or even suggest that those experiences were compulsive in character and not merely a matter of choice." In oral arguments, when Freedman pointed out that Boutilier "in all probability would have refrained from such practices" had he known they would lead to trouble, she noted that this is what Boutilier had done after the deportation proceedings commenced.[43]

Boutilier's advocates could not ignore his arrest, but they worked to present this in the least damaging light. Freedman and Freedman pointed out, "He has never been convicted of a crime. However, in 1959 he was arrested at home on a charge of sodomy . . . , which was subsequently reduced to simple assault and ultimately dismissed for failure of the complainant to prosecute." The impression created was that the sex was consensual, the complainant had not felt aggrieved, and Boutilier was not caught having public sex. None of the briefs mentioned that the complainant was a seventeen-year-old minor. None mentioned the possibility that Boutilier had lied when he told the INS he did not know the name of the minor, though Freedman's notes hint that Boutilier knew his name was Gibson. None mentioned that Boutilier had been treated in the early 1960s for syphilis, which was recorded in Freedman's notes.[44]

The references to his sexual history attempted to present Boutilier in a favorable light, but activated conservative values. To begin with, there were negative implications about aliens who were exclusively homosexual or engaged in homosexual conduct on a regular basis. There were also negative suggestions about aliens who pursued homosexual liaisons in more active and public ways and aliens who did not form long-term domestic partnerships. The implications were also troubling for aliens convicted of sex crimes, including crimes involving adult, private, and consensual sex. Moreover, the presentation of Boutilier's sexual history contained elements that were consistent with popular antigay attitudes, suggesting that Boutilier had been damaged permanently when he was victimized sexually as a child, that he had phobias about heterosexual sex, that his pre-entry homosexual conduct was part of an adolescent phase, and that he lacked the normal male or human need for sex on a regular basis. These arguments also reproduced the idea that adult homosexuals preyed on minors, linked homosexuality to public sex and sex crimes, and suggested that homosexuals were incapable of forming successful long-term relationships.

As discussed above, Boutilier's advocates tried to depict homosexuality as a type of behavior rather than a type of person. Because of this they avoided referring to Boutilier as "a homosexual." This had the ambivalent political implications highlighted above, but Boutilier's advocates were also not entirely consistent. In a 1965 INS hearing, Freedman seemed to agree with Special Inquiry Officer Ira Fieldsteel's assertion that "there is no serious contest as to whether or not this respondent was a sexual deviate but only as whether he is a psychopathic personality." She also stated that "in this case sexual deviation is homosexuality." Freedman did not repeat these formulations in her briefs, but they were cited by the opposing lawyers.[45]

None of the briefs submitted by Boutilier's advocates mentioned that his 1963 affidavit stated, "I had admitted to the selective service board that I was a homosexual" or that he told an INS examiner in 1964, when asked why he was classified as 4F, "I'm homosexual." Boutilier's lawyers likely wanted to avoid highlighting anything that stated or implied that Boutilier thought of himself as having a homosexual identity. Falsey, however, noted that Boutilier "explained quite frankly that he has been homosexual." Ullman mentioned that Boutilier had "moved in with a homosexual male," which implied that some men did have homosexual identities and that Boutilier associated with one. Freedman and Freedman's brief avoided referring to Boutilier as "homosexual" or "a homosexual," but noted that "insofar as his sexual behavior prior to entry is concerned, petitioner testified that he had been heterosexual also." The "also" implied that Boutilier was "homosexual" and "heterosexual." The ACLU/NYCLU brief and the main text of the HLRS brief avoided referring to Boutilier as "homosexual" or "a homosexual," but the same cannot be said for the letter Clark Polak wrote to the experts whose statements were included in the HLRS appendices. Polak's letter, which was appended to the HLRS brief, began by observing that the INS "is attempting to deport an alien Canadian on the grounds that, as a male homosexual (the fact of his homosexuality is not contested by the defense) he is a 'psychopathic personality.'" If Boutilier's advocates were supposed to avoid referring to him as "a homosexual," this was a slip. But it also was an example of the tensions between Boutilier's defense, which was Freedman's priority, and the defense of gay rights, which was Polak's.[46]

This became an issue in the oral arguments. When Fortas questioned Freedman about whether the factual issue of Boutilier's homosexuality had ever been raised, she responded, "There is no contest that he admitted certain acts. There is no contest that he described himself, when he was asked, do you consider yourself a homosexual?" But she went on to argue that "whether or not someone is a homosexual is something that can only be described medically" and "that has never been done in this case." In this exchange, Freedman tried to insist on the behavioral model and the medical model, even going so far as to deny the legal import of Boutilier's description of himself as "a homosexual." But she also claimed that medical doctors could determine that a person was "a homosexual," which worked at cross-purposes with the argument that homosexuality was a type of behavior rather than a type of person. Freedman's position also sacrificed an important weapon in the arsenal of identity-based movements—the power of an individual to affiliate with a group—and turned this weapon over to medical science, which had been responsible for pathologizing homosexuality in the first place. One result was the strange spectacle of a case in which the proponents of gay rights denied, and the opponents of gay rights defended, the validity of homosexual self-description.[47]

VICTIMIZATION

Another rhetorical strategy involved emphasizing the many ways in which the law was victimizing Boutilier. According to Ullman's report, Boutilier was "extremely tense and anxious." The psychiatrist continued, "As soon as he began to speak and from time to time throughout the interview his eyes teared. His initial spontaneous outburst was to the effect that the proceedings against him over the past six years were forcing him to make bank loans and for the first time in his life he was unable to financially cope." After mentioning that Boutilier had "abandoned all sexual practices" because of his "annoyance and disgust" with his legal problems, he noted, "The patient's present difficulties obviously weigh very heavily upon him. He feels as if he has made his life in this country and is deeply disturbed at the prospect of being cut off from the life he has created." Along similar lines, when the briefs highlighted Boutilier's family ties in the United States and emphasized that he had lived in the country for approximately ten years, they implied that deportation would be highly disruptive. Freedman and Freedman noted that deportation would require Boutilier "to forfeit his residence and the opportunity to work and live in the United States." The ACLU/NYCLU referred to the "direct injury" that Boutilier would sustain; he had been "lulled . . . into believing that he was eligible for the benefits of residence, and, eventually, citizenship," and based on this he "left his native land." In their reply brief, Freedman and Freedman noted that had Boutilier known that his pre-entry experiences would "forever menace him," he might not have "uprooted himself from Canada and established his home and livelihood in this country."[48]

The briefs also discussed, in more general terms, the victimization of those who are deported. Freedman and Brown cited a 1963 ruling that referred to deportation as "the equivalent of banishment or exile." Freedman and Freedman mentioned "the drastic penalty and consequences that attend deportation." Their reply brief cited a case in which the Court referred to deportation as "a savage penalty." The rhetoric of victimization underscored the harm caused by the use of the statute. To the unsympathetic, however, these comments suggested that Boutilier was weak, unstable, dependent, and incapable of coping with adversity.[49]

ANALOGIES

To make and strengthen their arguments, Boutilier's advocates also used analogies that helped link the issues raised in this case to matters of settled law, customary practice, commonplace logic, or political consensus. The homophile movement most commonly invoked analogies based on race, religion, and sex. Homophile activists routinely analogized the oppression of "homosexuals" and the oppression of "Negroes," "Jews," and "women," hoping to benefit from the greater political strength of and popular sympathy for these groups. In *Boutilier*, however, these were not the primary analogies used, perhaps because they were not seen as promising in the context of the behavioral arguments or because discrimination on the basis of characteristics such as race and sex remained constitutional in the context of immigration.[50]

Analogies based on ethnicity, nationality, race, religion, and class were not entirely absent. The HLRS brief included an excerpt of a book by Szasz that claimed, "In the past, discrimination has been based chiefly on nationality, race, religion and economic status; today, there is a mounting tendency to base it on psychiatric considerations." In his appended statement, Szasz wrote, "What kinds of behavior are categorized as 'sick' is arbitrary in exactly the same sense as it is arbitrary to categorize one religion as 'true' . . . or one skin color as 'superior.'" In the Mattachine Washington materials appended to the HLRS brief, Eugene de Savitsch claimed that in "the majority of cases" homosexuals "are no more responsible for their condition than is a brunette for her hair or a Negro for his skin." This type of rhetoric was used to convince the Court to side with Boutilier, but Szasz's statement implied that national, racial, religious, and economic discrimination was no longer active, and this argument had conservative implications. So did the suggestion by de Savitsch that no one would choose to be "Negro" or homosexual, which was at odds with the politics of pride adopted by those who believed that "Black is Beautiful" and "Gay is Good." These comments also did not acknowledge that discrimination on the basis of nationality, race, religion and economic status was part of the history of psychiatry. Moreover, these formulations failed to recognize that each of these classification systems was sexed and gendered, as was evident in de Savitsch's assumptions that brunettes were female ("her hair"), "Negroes" were male ("his skin"), and homosexuals were neither or both ("their" condition).[51]

Boutilier's advocates relied more heavily on a different set of analogies. While de Savitsch compared homosexuals to brunettes, Freedman and Freedman distinguished between sexual orientation and hair color when challenging the notion that "there is some kind of recognizable human being that is a 'homosexual'—like one might recognize a 'red-head.'" In the HLRS appendices, Benjamin declared that homosexuality "is no more 'pathological' than an oddly-shaped ear, strikingly red hair or left-handedness." He also wrote, "'Must the individual homosexual be rejected?' . . . With similar justification we could ask whether a left-handed or a color-blind person should be rejected. All of these people exist, and they exist by no fault of their own." This implied that no one would choose to be homosexual, left-handed, or color-blind, thus suggesting that these were undesirable characteristics. These analogies also linked homosexuality to characteristics that were commonly believed to be fixed and innate, which had the potential to damage the effort to define homosexuality as a variable behavior.[52]

One analogy distinguished between good and bad forms of homosexuality by invoking good and bad forms of heterosexuality. After making the point that homosexuality was sometimes, but not invariably, associated with mental disorder, Tripp argued that "to confuse these sometimes psychotic or neurotic manifestations with examples of people who discreetly make similar sexual choices, but who are well-integrated socially . . . would be almost as serious as confusing rape with ordinary sexual intercourse." In the structure of this analogy, psychotic and neurotic homosexuality was like rape, whereas discreet homosexuality was like ordinary sexual intercourse. Moreover, the effectiveness of the analogy depended on rape being seen as rare; otherwise the risks of admitting homosexuals would be perceived as unacceptably large.[53]

As this example suggests, many of the analogies used by Boutilier's defenders activated negative associations. One of the excerpts of Kinsey's work included in Tripp's statement declared, "The incidence of tuberculosis in a tuberculosis sanitarium is no measure of the incidence of tuberculosis in the population as a whole; and the incidence of disturbance over sexual activities among the persons who come to a clinic is no measure of the frequency of similar disturbances outside of clinics." Kinsey was challenging studies that used clinical contexts as the basis for conclusions about the incidence of sexual disturbance in nonclinical populations, but the analogy linked homosexuality with a life-threatening disease. In the HLRS appendices, Milton Diamond declared that, in defining psychopathology, "we cannot depend only on a criteria of frequency of occurrence; individuals who parachute for a hobby may be rare in our society yet wouldn't necessarily be considered psychopathic." This, too, was intended to help Boutilier, but just as Kinsey's point linked homosexuality with disease, Diamond's linked it with a hobby many regarded as dangerous and self-destructive.[54]

In an analogous fashion, Boutilier's advocates established connections between homosexuality and alcoholism. In the HLRS appendices, Hampson wrote, "Just as *some* alcoholics may be 'psychopathic personalities' . . . , so too *some* homosexual persons may be 'psychopathic personalities.' But in neither case does this constitute a very large percentage of the total. . . . When law views all homosexuals as 'psychopathic personalities' it is guilty of using faulty logic. It is the same order of faulty logic as saying 'alcoholism occurs in businessmen therefore all businessmen are alcoholic.'" Hampson did not argue that just as a person who drinks alcohol is not necessarily an alcoholic, so too a person who engages in homosexual conduct is not necessarily a homosexual. Instead, he made the argument that just as not all businessmen are alcoholic, not all homosexuals are psychopathic. The first sentence, however, linked homosexuals and alcoholics.[55]

Freedman and Freedman also linked homosexuality with stealing. Kleptomania, they observed, was "the disease of stealing," and those who have the disease steal because they have an "irresistible impulse to steal." If Congress had passed a law excluding kleptomaniacs and administered the law in the way it was administering the psychopathic personality law, "respondent would exclude as 'kleptomaniacs' all persons who pilfer, shop-lift or steal without regard to whether such acts are 'irresistible' or 'in spite of all restraint.'" They concluded, "Obviously, not everyone who steals is a kleptomaniac. . . . Equally, not everyone who engages in a homosexual act is suffering from a psychopathic disorder." Freedman and Freedman did not use their analogy to argue that not all people who engaged in homosexual conduct could be classified as homosexuals. Rather, their point was that not all people who engaged in homosexual conduct could be classified as psychopathic. But the analogy positioned homosexuality as analogous to stealing. And just as many Americans would not favor the immigration of alcoholics, many would not favor the immigration of thieves.[56]

Other analogies linked homosexuality with masturbation and menstruation. In the appendix to Freedman and Freedman's brief, Tripp wrote, "Masturbation was thought for generations to be associated with mental disease because psychotic and mentally deficient persons were the ones seen doing it." Today, in contrast, Tripp argued there was knowledge that masturbation was practiced by "not less than 96 per cent of the entire American male population." He then argued, "Homosexuality has been subjected to approximately the same course of interpretation—from sharp taboo, to being associated with mental disease, to a general recognition of its commonplace frequency, and finally to its being seen as of small sociologic consequence." Along similar lines, Benjamin wrote that the notion that homosexuality is psychopathological "belongs in the medical wastebasket, with the rest of the errors and superstitions of an ignorant past." In his view, the notion "ranks with the 'toxicity' of the menstruating women, or the 'vice' and harmfulness of masturbation." In another HLRS statement, Olinger declared, "The tendency to regard homosexuality as an illness or pathology *per se* was unfortunately reinforced by the same kind of thinking that permitted masturbation to be conceived of as leading to mental illness." In the case of both homosexuality and masturbation, the statement held that "uncritical observers" used "primitive logic" in reaching conclusions on the basis of institutionalized or hospitalized patients. Boutilier's defenders hoped to demonstrate that old ideas about homosexuality, like old ideas about masturbation and menstruation, should be discarded. But the analogies also activated cultural anxieties about masturbation and menstruation.[57]

Boutilier's advocates also linked homosexuality with witchcraft, communism, promiscuity, and unemployment. As mentioned above, Freedman and Freedman argued that laws that targeted "private, consensual homosexual practices between adults" were "reminiscent of history's other witchhunts." In the HLRS brief, Cantor quoted his own previously published work when asserting that "once it is recognized, for example, that 'There neither are nor ever were witches . . . ,' the judicial labeling and punishing of people as witches must come to an end." In the aftermath of the Red Scare of the 1950s and in the wake of Arthur Miller's critique of McCarthyism in *The Crucible*, the witchcraft analogy implicitly linked the politics of antihomosexuality and the politics of anticommunism. The ACLU/NYCLU brief argued that "if 'psychopathic personality' may be construed to encompass consensual homosexuality, it may also be applied . . . to other forms of non-conforming conduct, such as promiscuity or unemployment." Boutilier's defenders were hoping that the Court would regard attacks on accused homosexuals as equivalent to attacks on accused witches and communists and would treat the deportation

of Boutilier as equivalent to the deportation of the promiscuous or the unemployed. It is likely, however, that many readers, including the justices, favored
excluding and deporting all of these groups.[58]

DEMOCRATIC VALUES

Boutilier's advocates also invoked abstract political, social, and cultural
values, including decency, democracy, and diversity. Tripp's appended statement included an excerpt from an essay by Szasz: "Why is homosexuality a
problem? Mainly because it presents, in sexual form, the classic dilemma of
popular democracy: How much diversity should society permit?" The HLRS
brief declared that "a decent society will not equate difference with deviance."
The HLRS also cited the words of John Stuart Mill: "'Such are the differences
among human beings in their sources of pleasure, their susceptibilities of
pain, and the operation on them of different physical and moral agencies, that
unless there is a corresponding diversity in their modes of life, they neither
obtain their fair share of happiness, nor grow up to the mental, moral, and
aesthetic stature of which their nature is capable.'"[59]

The HLRS experts also linked Boutilier's defense to abstract notions of justice, fairness, modernity, and affluence. Corner wrote that "it is a gross injustice to exclude a person otherwise eligible for residence in the United States
on this ground." Rubin declared that "any attempt to classify an individual
as a 'psychopathic personality' purely on the basis of the fact of his homosexuality" is "grossly unjust." Ellis observed that "many of our existing laws
against fixed homosexuality are antiquated and unfair." Also included in the
HLRS brief was a statement by Elias, who praised recent efforts to think about
homosexuality "openly and honestly," which was necessary for the United
States to "evolve as an affluent nation."[60]

In their main brief, Freedman and Freedman referenced "the fundamental idea of fairness and fairplay essential to the very concept of justice." In the
reply brief, they asserted that expecting Boutilier to have had "knowledge at
the time of his entry of something which may have come into being long after
is violative of every instinct of justice and fairness." On the issue of ex post
facto laws concerning aliens, the brief called for "fairness and justness" for
"all persons dwelling here under our constitution." In their final paragraph,
Freedman and Freedman declared that "this case presents an inherent question of ultimate morality."[61]

The briefs did not invoke the notion of equality, though the HLRS brief
did refer to a set of related concepts. Appealing to a court that prided itself
on the role it had played in challenging racial prejudice, discrimination, and

oppression, the brief condemned the treatment of Boutilier as prejudiced, discriminatory, and oppressive. In the HLRS appendix, Reider claimed that the practice of defining homosexuality as a form of psychopathic personality was "discriminatory." According to Marmor, classifying homosexuals as psychopathic personalities "is a clear indication of stereotyping based on social prejudice." In the final paragraph of their reply brief, Freedman and Freedman criticized laws that made "private, consensual homosexual practices between adults" the target of "oppressive legislation and ostracism."[62] In these passages, Boutilier's advocates tried to link the struggle for homosexual rights to the much more powerful struggles for the rights of oppressed racial, religious, and economic groups. However, most of Boutilier's advocates did not use this type of rhetoric, perhaps because the case concerned immigration law. And they did not invoke abstract notions of equality, perhaps because they thought that an argument for homosexual equality would not be well received.

In several instances, Boutilier's defenders referenced abstract Cold War values and comparative references to Cold War enemies. In the HLRS appendices, Elias asserted, "The strength of a free society is grounded in the opportunity it offers every one including those who fulfill themselves by dissent and deviation. As John Stuart Mill noted, stringent conformity produced the deterioration of the ancient and advanced culture of China." This implied that the United States would suffer the fate that had befallen China if the country did not respect dissent and deviation. In the HLRS brief, Cantor pointed to the danger of replicating the ways of the Soviet Union. According to Cantor, "The labeling of a person who commits homosexual acts as a 'deviant' and as a 'psychopathic personality' has to do with the preservation of society's dominant value system rather than with mental disturbance. It involves the abuse of psychiatric terminology for the purpose of social control. This is a step on the way to the 'therapeutic state.'" Later in the brief, Cantor explained the reference: "To permit this is to take a step in the direction of the 'therapeutic state,' which Dr. Szasz has described and which was dramatized in Ward 7 [an autobiographical novel by Valering Tarsis], a depiction of a Soviet 'lunatic asylum' which holds 6000 patients, only one of whom is a 'lunatic' and the rest are 'victims of their lot as Soviet citizens.'" Cantor then included a line from Ward 7: "'In fact, there were neither patients nor doctors but only jailers in charge of inconvenient citizens.'" Here Cantor deployed Cold War political rhetoric to defend Boutilier.[63]

In one instance, Cantor linked the defense of Boutilier with the struggles that led to the founding of the United States. After introducing his argument about "scientific" and "folk" knowledge, Cantor wrote, "James Otis in 1764 framed the same issue as between Parliament's laws and natural laws: 'There must be in every instance a higher authority, viz. God. Should an act of parliament be against any of *his* natural laws, which are *immutably* true, their declaration would be contrary to eternal truth, equity and justice, and consequently void.'" By implication, Congress and the INS were acting toward homosexuals just as the British Parliament had acted toward its American colonies, and the defense of homosexuality, so often labeled unnatural and antireligious, was now linked to the defense of natural law and religion. Cantor also referenced an even earlier episode in American history when invoking colonial-era witchhunts. Just a decade earlier, *The Crucible* had used the Salem witchcraft trials to challenge the anticommunist politics of McCarthyism. Now Cantor tried to use popular antipathy to anticommunist witchhunts to challenge the antihomosexual politics of immigration law.[64] Here, as elsewhere, Boutilier's advocates positioned themselves as defenders of traditional American values.

THE STRATEGIES OF Boutilier's advocates did not succeed in their primary goal to prevent Boutilier's deportation. They also did not achieve their other main objective, which was to establish a helpful precedent for the rights of immigrants and homosexuals. This is not to say that other strategies might have succeeded where these failed or that lawyers in other types of cases were more consistent, more effective, or more progressive. Boutilier's advocates were working within and against a set of challenging constraints. Liberal and leftist advocates in *Griswold* and *Fanny Hill* had encouraged the justices to develop a doctrine of heteronormative supremacy. The fact that *Boutilier* concerned an alien rather than a citizen only added to the difficulties. The arguments used by these advocates may well have represented Boutilier's best hope for success, though in the end they failed. Four decades later, it comes as no surprise to find that the Supreme Court's ruling against Boutilier was influenced by the conservative arguments made by his opponents. It is more surprising to see that the Court's decision was influenced by the arguments made by his defenders. Legal advocates, then and now, may be tempted to reach for every possible argument that can be mobilized to defend their clients, but arguments have implications, and the implications of the arguments used by liberals and leftists in *Griswold, Fanny Hill, Boutilier, Loving, Eisenstadt*, and *Roe* supported the doctrine of heteronormative supremacy.

PART 3 : *Readings and Readers*

The Supreme Court's heteronormative rulings had multiple authors, including the justices, their clerks, and the advocates who influenced the decisions. Paradoxically, readers of the Court's opinions also authored them. Like the Constitution itself, the Court's decisions only acquired meaning through interpretive reading processes. The justices could not fully control the ways in which their rulings would be read, especially when they used ambiguous language or inconsistent reasoning. Readers of the opinions became agents of change as they interpreted the Court's rulings in distinctive ways. Among the most influential readers of these decisions were journalists, judges, and scholars. Their comments about *Griswold*, *Fanny Hill*, *Loving*, *Eisenstadt*, and *Roe* can be examined as examples and vehicles of public reception, revealing how the rulings were interpreted by those who read them and how others were encouraged to interpret rulings they did not necessarily read for themselves.

Readers of the Court's opinions also authored them insofar as the justices were influenced by readings of their rulings. In a sense, this is what happened when pornographers tested the limits of the Court's obscenity rulings, when birth control and abortion advocates tested the limits of privacy rulings, and when interracial couples tested the limits of rulings on racial equality. Having read the relevant rulings or having hired lawyers who had done so, these readers authorized litigation involving the work of multiple authors and authorities. In addition, the justices paid attention to the work of journalists, judges, and scholars who read their rulings. At times, when the justices believed their words were being misread, they incorporated corrections and clarifications into later opinions. They also disagreed with one another about how to read their precedents, and these disagreements shaped the writing of subsequent opinions.

The justices in this period were quite concerned about how their rulings were being read. In 1973, for instance, after Warren Burger persuaded a majority of the justices to endorse more conservative obscenity tests, a Virginia county prosecutor announced that he would take action against newsstands that sold *Playboy*. Burger quickly distributed a memorandum to the other justices, insisting that he had never intended to allow officials to define *Playboy* as obscene. Six years later, the *New York Times* reported that Burger was concerned that lower court judges "might be misreading" recent decisions. Burger was quoted as saying, "'Maybe judges are reading newspaper reports of what we said' rather than the court's majority opinion," and he "implied that Washington reporters had misinterpreted some recent Court rulings." Several days later, the *New York Times* reported that Lewis Powell had stated at the American Bar Association's annual meeting that the Court was "'totally dependent on the media to interpret what we do'" since "'that's all the public knows about us.'" He then observed that "sometimes 'under the constraint of deadlines, we find that what is written appears to bear little relationship to what we did decide.'" In 1991, William Brennan addressed this subject in a *Playboy* interview. According to interviewer Nat Hentoff, Brennan "stressed his disappointment at the way the Court was covered by the press—at the inaccuracy of the reporting and the placing of decisions out of context." Hentoff continued, "He kept returning to the failures of the press, because although the Court makes decisions affecting millions of Americans, many have only the dimmest notion of the content of those decisions and of how they were arrived at. And that, he thinks, is the fault of the press." Even lawyers who won Supreme Court cases were critical of the press coverage. Sarah Weddington, who argued for abortion rights in *Roe*, recalls in her 1992 autobiography that she was "disappointed that so few of the journalists described the legal arguments accurately."[1]

In general, the journalists, judges, and scholars who wrote about *Griswold*, *Fanny Hill*, *Loving*, *Eisenstadt*, and *Roe* portrayed the rulings as more sexually libertarian and egalitarian than the texts of the decisions stated or implied. While the texts affirmed the special rights and privileges associated with normative marriage, reproduction, and heterosexuality, many in the public sphere presented the decisions as recognizing rights of sexual liberty and equality. Many readers translated the Court's language of marital and reproductive privacy into the language of sexual privacy. They often downplayed evidence suggesting that the Court accepted the constitutionality of laws against nonmarital sex. In discussing obscenity decisions, they typically highlighted the liberalizing rulings, focused less attention on the conservative ones, and depicted anti-obscenity outcomes as unusual exceptions, temporary errors, or legal anomalies. These readers generally presented sexual conservatism in the law as the work of lower courts and other branches of government, not the Supreme Court. Such readings tended to suggest that, with time, the Court would complete the process of sexual liberalization in the legal system. Sexual conservatives decried this process; sexual liberals celebrated it; but most agreed that this is what was happening.

As these readings circulated in the period from 1965 through 1973, much of the public came to believe that the Court had developed an expansive and expanding doctrine of sexual freedom and equality. When it later became clear, beginning in the mid-1970s, that the late Burger and early Rehnquist Courts did not read the precedents in this way, many concluded that the Court had reversed direction. The continuity of the Court's sexual conservatism across the second half of the twentieth century was overlooked, and instead the post-*Roe* Court was said to have been influenced by New Right politics. Eventually, this became the conventional wisdom promoted by leading historians of marriage, family, and sex.[2] In one further twist, in the first years of the twenty-first century the Court itself seemed to accept the conventional wisdom, interpreting the earlier decisions as more sexually libertarian and egalitarian than the texts of the decisions stated or implied. In this way, the readers of rulings in the late 1960s and early 1970s became the authors of decisions three decades later.

Mainstream Media

Mainstream newspaper and magazine coverage of *Griswold* presented conflicting messages, some of which highlighted the Court's emphasis on marital privacy and some of which suggested that the Court had developed a much broader privacy doctrine.[3] For example, while the *New York Times* made it clear in its front-page story that the Court had ruled that "married couples had private rights" and the subhead declared "7-to-2 Ruling Establishes Marriage Privileges," the headline, "High Court Bars Curbs on Birth Control; Finds Connecticut Law Invades Privacy," was less qualified. Readers of the headline, the first two paragraphs, and the news summary inside the paper might reasonably have concluded that the Court had struck down all birth control restrictions, and not just those affecting married couples. Not until the end of the story did the reporter observe that "lawyers were uncertain as to [the ruling's] effect on other birth control laws." Several days later, a *New York Times* column stated that "the Court keyed its decision to the contention that married couples have private rights" and acknowledged that the ruling "barely touched other state anti-contraceptive laws." But the headline declared more broadly, "Court Bans Birth Control Curbs." Without referring to marriage or marital privacy, a *Los Angeles Times* columnist declared that the Court "has now recognized birth control as constitutional." One year later, the *Washington Post*'s obituary for birth control advocate Margaret Sanger declared (inaccurately) that *Griswold* "struck down the Nation's last anti-contraceptive law."[4]

Except for excerpts of the opinions published in the *New York Times*, none of the newspaper's many articles about *Griswold* in the months following the ruling referred to the passages in which the justices suggested that laws against nonmarital sex were constitutional. Nor were these passages mentioned in the *Los Angeles Times* or *Washington Post*. Two years later, a *New York Times Magazine* article, after predicting that the Court "will strike down existing state laws which make practicing homosexuals criminals," noted that *Griswold* "supports this belief." Then in 1970, journalist Fred Graham wrote in the *New York Times* that *Griswold* raised "legal doubt about the state's authority to protect the public morals and welfare through laws against such evils as abortion, pornography, birth control and unmarried sex." According to Graham, the Court had decided that Connecticut's law violated the "'right of privacy' in sexual matters." He also claimed that *Griswold* meant that "the Government cannot reach the physical intimacies of sex" and the country was thus moving toward "the 'Danish' solution toward sex—a hands-off policy by the Government toward adults' sexual conduct."[5]

Other periodicals also presented conflicting messages about *Griswold*. *America* and *Christian Century*, for example, argued that the ruling honored marriage and protected married couples from coercive state-sponsored birth control programs. The *New Republic* noted that the Court held that a statute banning the use of contraceptives "could not stand in a state . . . that did not trouble to treat married couples at all differently from frolicking teen-agers." In contrast, when *Business Week* predicted that *Griswold* would result in increased sales for companies that produced birth control pills and devices, it did not reveal that the Court decision applied only to married couples. Nor did *Newsweek*, which reported that the Court "struck down a Connecticut law against contraception"; *U.S. News and World Report*, which contended that the Court overruled a law "prohibiting information about, and the practice of, birth control"; or the *Saturday Evening Post*, which said that the Court viewed the law as "an unconstitutional violation of privacy." An editorial in *Commonweal* quoted Douglas's argument that "we deal with a right to privacy older than the Bill of Rights," but did not include the rest of the passage, which made it clear that this referred to marital privacy. Many stories emphasized *Griswold*'s invocation of marital privacy, but many did not, which helped create the perception that the Court had developed an expansive sexual privacy doctrine.[6]

Some stories that acknowledged the references to marital privacy contributed to the sense that the doctrine was broader. An article in *Commonweal* emphasized "marital privacy," but also stated that the Court had "raised the long-mooted 'right to be let alone' to a new status." After noting that "by no means may their holding be stretched to cover every private act now proscribed by penal laws," the article pointed out that "radiations of this right [of marital privacy], going well beyond use of contraceptives, were indicated at various points by the majority justices." The *Christian Science Monitor* editorialized that the Court "upheld the right of marital privacy, thereby strengthening the right of privacy in general." The *Nation* referred to the "clear suggestion that the majority will recognize other forms of a general right to privacy." *Time* concluded, "Lawyers can now spend years happily fighting over just what else the new right of privacy covers." In these contexts it would have been illuminating to address the justices' comments about what was not necessarily covered by "the new right of privacy," but mainstream periodicals did not do so. *Life* magazine went one step further. After referencing Douglas's claim that "the 'right of privacy' in marriage is older than the Bill of Rights," an editorial observed that this right "may have an interesting future if the Court should apply it to such issues as wiretapping and homosexuality." Quite a few articles mentioned that future decisions would have to clarify what was covered by the doctrine of privacy, but none of the country's leading periodicals mentioned what the *Griswold* opinions said about laws against nonmarital sex.[7]

A noteworthy set of comments about *Griswold* appeared in *Playboy*. In general, *Playboy* was exceptional among periodicals in that it provided readers with many examples of the existence and enforcement of laws against adultery, cohabitation, fornication, obscenity, sodomy, and other sex crimes.[8] In the aftermath of *Griswold*, however, *Playboy* seemed convinced that the Court had not and would not uphold the constitutionality of such laws. The magazine first referred to *Griswold* in August 1965, when it published two letters poking fun at the prosecuting attorney's arguments. In an editorial reply, the magazine noted that the Court was "similarly unimpressed" and struck down the law. One month later, *Playboy* published several letters from readers outraged by the recent account of a man serving a one-to-ten-year sentence in a maximum security prison in West Virginia for a "crime against nature," which in his case consisted of consensual, heterosexual oral sex with a female high school student. One letter noted that the Supreme Court "is immune to pressures that frighten elected officials" and asserted that "the recent trend of its decisions certainly gives grounds for hope that it would invalidate these 'morality' laws en masse." Another letter expressed "outrage" about "archaic sex laws," wondered whether cases were ever appealed "to have such puritanical laws judged unconstitutional," and asked, "Doesn't freedom of sexual practice come under some aspect of the Constitution?" *Playboy* replied that "hopefully . . . the Supreme Court's recent decision invalidating Connecticut's antiquated birth-control law will establish a healthy precedent." Referring to the Court's conclusion that the law interfered with constitutionally protected "zones of privacy," *Playboy* asserted that "so, it would seem, do most state sodomy statutes." Neither the letters nor *Playboy*'s editorial comments addressed what the *Griswold* opinions said about laws against nonmarital sex.[9]

In November 1965, the latest installment of "The Playboy Philosophy" by Hugh Hefner referenced *Griswold* without mentioning the passages suggesting that laws against fornication, adultery, and homosexuality were constitutional. According to Hefner, nonpublic sexual acts between consenting adults should be free from interference by the state, and he criticized thirty-six state laws against fornication and fifteen state laws against cohabitation. In support of his position, Hefner observed that "this principle of privacy was the key consideration in a recent U.S. Supreme Court decision declaring Connecticut's anticontraceptive law unconstitutional." Along similar lines, R. Lucas, a Glasgow University law professor, noted in a 1966 letter to *Playboy* that "an abortion case, a fornication case, a sodomy case, an adultery case may well fall on receptive ears in the Supreme Court." Prodding *Playboy* to promote litigation, which Hefner was doing through the Playboy Foundation, Lucas wrote that "a brave doctor fought his unenlightened state for almost 20 years before *Griswold vs. Conn.* was decided." In a 1966 *Playboy* panel discussion of "religion and the new morality," Harvard professor James Luther Adams noted that *Griswold* held that "the use of contraceptives by married couples is in the realm of privacy" and asked, "Shouldn't this principle be extended, in restricted ways, to the homosexual behavior of consenting adults?" Later the same year, a *Playboy* article by Nat Hentoff discussed *Griswold* in similar terms, noting that the privacy doctrine "might be taken far enough to invalidate statutes punishing consensual sexual conduct among adults." Two years later, a letter by ACLU attorney R. Michael Gross asserted that "the broader question, not yet answered by the U.S. Supreme Court, is whether any state can prohibit sexual intercourse between consenting unmarried adults in private." Then in 1971, a *Playboy* article on the ACLU claimed that *Griswold* had become "the basis for a burgeoning legal doctrine that personal sexual practices are protected from government intrusion." This article, like the earlier ones, did not mention that a majority of the justices had signaled their rejection of such a broad formulation. The interpretations of *Griswold* that circulated in the public sphere diverged from the Court's interpretations.[10]

Mainstream media coverage of *Fanny Hill*, *Ginzburg*, and *Mishkin* captured more of the Court's ambivalence about sexual liberalization. Perhaps this reflects the importance the media attached to free speech, but it may also be attributed to the fact that the liberalizing decision in *Fanny Hill* was announced on the same day that obscenity convictions were upheld in *Ginzburg* and *Mishkin*. Nevertheless, there were revealing differences between the Court's language and the media's. For example, *Fanny Hill*, which overturned an obscenity decision because of "redeeming social value," and *Ginzburg*, which upheld a conviction based on commercial "pandering," received much more attention than *Mishkin*, which affirmed a conviction based on the "prurient" interests of "deviant sexual groups." In many stories, Ralph Ginzburg was depicted as a free-speech martyr who had received an unduly harsh sentence, whereas Edward Mishkin was ignored or portrayed as a sleazy profiteer who got what he deserved. Multiple articles on these rulings, in a wide range of publications, ignored *Mishkin*'s distinctive treatment of materials produced for sadists, masochists, fetishists, and homosexuals.[11]

Of the major periodicals that discussed *Mishkin*, some mentioned the references to sadomasochism, fetishism, and homosexuality, but others were more selective. Several depicted the Court as having ruled against sadistic and masochistic materials, but left out the references to homosexuality, lesbianism, and fetishism. Meanwhile, some of the *Fanny Hill* coverage implied that the decision had protected representations of same-sex sex, despite the Court's emphasis on the novel's condemnation of homosexuality. *Christian Century*, for example, argued that it was difficult to reconcile the ruling against Ginzburg with the ruling for *Fanny Hill*, which it described as including an episode depicting a "lesbian encounter." *Newsweek* published excerpts of the *Ginzburg* and *Fanny Hill* opinions, including one that referred to *Fanny Hill*'s representations of "lesbianism" and "homosexuality," which suggested that the rulings were pro-gay.[12] These articles downplayed the extent to which the Court had ruled against treating homosexuality and heterosexuality equally.

Most mainstream media stories about the obscenity rulings did not portray the decisions as completely liberal, and some warned that they represented a step toward the dystopian world of Big Brother in the novel *Nineteen Eighty-Four*. Many resolved the apparent contradiction between the notion that the Court was sexually liberal and the evidence of its sexual conservatism by presenting *Ginzburg* and *Mishkin* as anomalous errors, temporary aberrations, or short-term deviations. One *Playboy* letter about *Ginzburg* declared, "I regard the present U.S. Supreme Court as the best in history, with a real potential for greatness. But even the best can err." Ginzburg himself commented in a

Playboy interview, "We're moving very rapidly in the area of sexual liberalization.... I think it's only a backward step, not a major backward trend, and I'm convinced it's only a temporary backward step." Several years later, a letter from Ginzburg to *Playboy* commented on "vanishing obscenity restrictions" and declared that this "proves the adage that lust conquers all!" Meanwhile, an article in the *Atlantic* concluded that "in having come this far," the Court "is within sight, though it may still be facing in somewhat the wrong direction, of that brave land where so far Justices Black and Douglas have been the only inhabitants." While the article admitted that it was "impossible to predict" whether the majority would "join these two heroic voyagers," it declared that the "days of literary censorship" were "substantially over." The *National Review* predicted that *Ginzburg* "will be one of the final successful prosecutions of obscene material published in America." *Publishers Weekly* suggested that the rulings "may represent only temporary setbacks" and "it may be that in the long run, progress is achieved by taking two steps forward, one step back."[13]

Media comments in subsequent years extended these interpretations. After further obscenity rulings in 1967, the *New Republic* declared that "it appears that the Court has changed its attitude back again, simply leap-frogging Mr. Ginzburg." This indicated that "there is no new threshold after all, or if there was, it was there for Ginzburg alone." These decisions came at a moment when the U.S. government was using the pandering doctrine to take aggressive action against pornographers, including HLRS leader Clark Polak. After *Stanley* (1969) extended protection to the possession of sexual materials in private homes, some media stories presented the Court as having done much more. According to *Playboy*, *Stanley*'s "emphasis on the right of privacy will undoubtedly encourage attorneys to argue that laws prohibiting consensual sex acts between adults in private are also unconstitutional." The magazine noted that "the Court had already acknowledged a marital 'zone of privacy' in its 1965 birth-control decision; the new decision appears to enlarge that zone, thereby moving closer to a recognition that the law doesn't belong in the bedroom." In 1972, when *Playboy* reported that Ginzburg had begun serving his sentence, it noted that the ruling was based on a "pandering" doctrine "never before applied and rarely invoked since."[14]

As suggested above, in some instances the obscenity rulings were taken to be evidence that the Court had developed a doctrine of sexual freedom that covered both speech and conduct. Fred Graham wrote in the *New York Times* in 1969 that *Stanley* showed that "inroads are being made into the traditional assumption that the law can and should be used to police private sexual conduct." After discussing laws against fornication, adultery, homosexuality, and sodomy, Graham declared that "there have been growing indications that the law is recognizing a distinction between socially disapproved sexual activity that threatens public order and decency, and that which is purely a private affair." Acknowledging that "because the ruling turned on the free speech aspects of the case, it does not bear directly on the statutes that outlaw sexual conduct," Graham nevertheless argued that *Stanley* "enlarged the 'zone of privacy'" recognized in *Griswold*. He concluded that "at this time" the Court was unlikely to accept the notion that "'an adult has a fundamental right of privacy which allows him to choose his own form of sexual satisfaction, to be enjoyed within the privacy of his own home,'" but "that is the direction that the law seems to be taking." The following year, Graham acknowledged that recent liberal obscenity rulings in the lower courts could be reversed because of President Nixon's appointments. Still, he concluded that "the trend toward greater constitutional protection of private thought and conduct seems well established now, and is likely to continue."[15]

By 1972, Graham had adjusted his views. In an article headlined "Nixon Appointees May Change Supreme Court," he wrote that "important shifts in the authority of government to regulate obscene material . . . could be close at hand." The Court did adopt more conservative obscenity tests in 1973, but when Graham suggested that the four Nixon appointees might reverse the "consistent trend" in recent years in which the prosecution lost obscenity cases, he succumbed and contributed to historical amnesia about *Ginzburg*, *Mishkin*, *Darnell*, *Landau*, and *G.I. Distributors*. Several months later, a *Harper's* article by Paul Bender, who had argued the case against *Ginzburg*, challenged predictions made at the time of *Fanny Hill* that henceforth "virtually no literature would be forbidden as 'obscene.'" Still, according to Bender the Court might soon restrict the scope of obscenity prosecutions to situations "where materials are given or sold to children without parental consent or participation, and where sexual depictions are forced upon those who do not want to see them." He claimed that this might have "significant future legal consequences" since "obscenity legislation for 'consenting' persons is just the tip of an iceberg of adult 'morals' prohibitions." Noting that "the Court has thus far largely avoided direct constitutional confrontation with these statutes," Bender nonetheless predicted that "once the Court has faced the obscenity muddle, it may find it difficult to avoid moving on from there to require rationality in other 'moral' restrictions on individual liberty." The suggestion was that liberalization in obscenity law would lead to liberalization in sex law more generally. Bender's assertions came one month after the Court stated in *Roe* that it did not accept the notion that "one has an unlimited right to do with one's body as one pleases" and several months before the majority in *Paris* rejected "the proposition that conduct involving consenting adults only is always beyond state regulation."[16] The meanings of the Court's obscenity decisions changed as they circulated in the public sphere.

While the mainstream media were divided on the merits of *Griswold*, *Fanny Hill*, *Ginzburg*, and *Mishkin*, a more unified chorus of praise greeted *Loving*. For the most part, the mainstream media, like the Court, focused primarily on the holding that laws against interracial marriage violated the equal protection clause and secondarily on the holding that these laws, in restricting the freedom to marry, violated constitutional liberty and due process rights. In this respect, a *New York Times* editorial was unusual in emphasizing that the Court "affirmed that choosing a husband or wife lies in the inviolable area of personal freedom that government may not enter." More typical was the main news story in the *Times*, which highlighted the Court's conclusion that bans on interracial marriage violated equality rights. In future years, the Court and media would refer to *Loving* as a privacy case and link it to *Griswold*, but at the time, neither the Court nor the media did so, which encouraged readers to see *Loving* as a racial-equality decision.[17]

In general, the mainstream media did not discuss *Loving*'s conservative assumptions and implications. Almost none of the coverage mentioned the marriage restrictions that remained constitutional. These included minimum age requirements, rules about marriages within the same family, laws concerning people with disabilities, and customary prohibitions on same-sex marriage. Several stories revealed that a man whose 1967 marriage was Tennessee's "first" legal interracial union was later given a two-year prison sentence for bigamy. These accounts implicitly acknowledged that *Loving* left in place laws against plural marriage, but this was rarely emphasized. Most media stories also did not refer to the Court's assertion that marriage was "fundamental to our very existence and survival," a formulation based on a narrowly reproductive conception of marriage and a narrowly marital conception of reproduction. Stories that did cite this passage, including items in *Christian Century*, *Jet*, the *Los Angeles Times*, and *Playboy*, did not explore the conservative implications of the Court's language.[18]

In its coverage of *Loving*, the mainstream media also tended to avoid all mention of sex, though in many states one of the benefits of marriage was the right to have legal sex. Popular media discussions of *Loving* generally did not emphasize that miscegenation laws made interracial couples especially vulnerable to charges of fornication and cohabitation. Nor did they consider the issue of whether the Lovings had committed fornication or cohabitation before marriage or whether Richard had committed statutory rape, though later accounts suggest that the two began "courting" when Richard was seventeen years old and Mildred was eleven and that Mildred was pregnant when the two married.[19]

Instead, *Loving* was presented within narratives of love, romance, and family values. *Ebony* referred to the decision as "the high point of a great love story, a saga brimming with faith, determination, and undying devotion." Accompanying a photograph of the couple was a caption that read, "A look imparts the devotion that enabled Lovings to endure long fight." Multiple photographs of the couple's three children were published, but according to *Ebony*, they were not "aware of the suffering their parents endured." The magazine explained, "Their mother feels that 'this is the best way' and the father is dead set against getting his kids involved." This type of coverage presented the Court's decision as a victory for love.[20]

In an exceptional instance in which sex was mentioned in relation to *Loving*, the ruling was presented as a precedent that could have expansive implications. In a letter to the editor in *Playboy*, Richard Butler of San Francisco asserted, "This decision affirms a principle of American democracy: As long as the actions of individuals do not infringe on the liberty of others, the state has no right to interfere. When this principle is fully applied to sex and marriage, to communications, to food and drink and to all other aspects of private life, this will truly be the free country the founding fathers intended."[21] Recognizing that the principle had not yet been "fully applied to sex and marriage," the letter made it clear that there were limits to what the Court had done. But the principle in question, which encompassed sexual freedom, went well beyond, and arguably was quite distinct from, the principle affirmed by the Court.

The perception that the Court had already recognized rights of sexual freedom and equality may help explain the lack of media attention to *Eisenstadt*, which received far less coverage than had *Griswold*, *Fanny Hill*, *Ginzburg*, and *Loving*. *Eisenstadt*, one might argue, took a major step by extending birth control rights to the unmarried, but since the media had represented *Griswold* as overturning laws against birth control, *Eisenstadt* must not have seemed very significant. The *New York Times* buried its news story inside the paper, miscounted the vote, mischaracterized the concurrences, and reported that the case would have "minimal direct impact upon state laws." The *Progressive*, *Harper's*, and *U.S. News* each devoted one sentence to the case in more general articles on the Court. With the exception of *Playboy*, other major magazines provided no coverage of *Eisenstadt*.[22]

The limited media coverage of *Eisenstadt* meant that the ruling's qualifying language received limited exposure. Before the Court decided the case, *Ramparts* confidently asserted that "Baird is aware that if he wins his Massachusetts case, it will go a long way towards knocking out many of the fornication laws which discriminate against unmarried people." After the decision, the *New York Times* acknowledged that the majority "rejected the state's argument that the law was a proper exercise of the state's power to discourage fornication." But the story did not highlight the implication that fornication laws were constitutional. Along similar lines, the *Los Angeles Times* noted that Massachusetts had claimed that its birth control law "deterred fornication and protected public health," but the newspaper explained that the Court concluded that "the statute was riddled with exceptions making contraceptives available for use in premarital sexual relations and its scope and penalty structure failed to act as a deterrent." None of these articles discussed the majority's conclusion that, because the case could be decided on equal protection grounds, the Court need not decide whether the law infringed on "fundamental freedoms under *Griswold*." None examined the suggestion that laws against nonmarital sex remained constitutional.[23]

Instead, these stories promoted the notion that the Court, even in the Nixon era, was continuing to encourage sexual liberalization. In a letter published in *Playboy*, Baird wrote that "lawyers have told me that the decision in my case may provide a basis for nullifying anti–sex laws in general, such as those against abortion, fornication and sodomy." In comments about the decision cited by the *Washington Post*, Baird declared that this was "the first time the people have been granted freedom to deal with their own bodies." The *Progressive* observed that "the Nixon bloc seems likely to exercise its conservatism in the months ahead in several important areas that involve sexual attitudes: homosexuality, with its implication for the right to equal protection; obscenity, with its implications for the right to free speech; and abortion, which embraces woman's right to control her own body." Despite this prediction, the magazine concluded, "Yet even in matters involving sexual attitudes, the present Court has at times demonstrated the one greatest attribute of all past Supreme Courts — the ability to separate deeply ingrained personal attitudes from independent judicial reasoning. With only Burger dissenting, the (seven-man) Court overturned a Massachusetts statute which barred anyone but doctors and pharmacists from distributing contraceptives." *Eisenstadt* was taken to be a sign that the Court would not necessarily reverse the process of sexual liberalization. In *Harper's*, Paul Bender wrote, "The Court has recently seemed to recognize, in cases involving the distribution of contraceptive devices and information, that adults, whether married or unmarried, are constitutionally entitled to engage in private sexual relationships that do not harm others." This was an argument that most liberal advocates had avoided and the justices had never endorsed, yet Bender portrayed it as the meaning of *Eisenstadt*.[24]

In contrast to *Eisenstadt*, *Roe* was covered extensively by the nation's leading newspapers and magazines. In the 1960s and early 1970s, as religious communities, medical professionals, feminist activists, political parties, and legal reformers discussed abortion, and as state legislatures revised their abortion codes, the mass media devoted significant attention to abortion law. Beginning in 1969, when lower court abortion decisions began to assert that the Supreme Court had already recognized a constitutional right of sexual privacy, the popular media presented arguments for and against the new rulings, but did not express criticism, doubt, or skepticism about the accuracy of the lower court claims about what the Supreme Court had said about sex. For four years before the Court decided *Roe*, mainstream media stories about abortion cases suggested that it had already affirmed a constitutional right of sexual privacy.

In 1969, many media stories reported on the California Supreme Court's reference in *Belous* to "the Supreme Court's and this court's repeated acknowledgment of a 'right of privacy' or 'liberty' in matters related to marriage, family, and sex." Later that year, reports on *Vuitch* highlighted U.S. district court judge Gerhard Gesell's reference to "an increasing indication in decisions of the Supreme Court" that "a woman's liberty and right of privacy extends to family, marriage and sex matters." By reporting on and not challenging lower court assertions about what the justices had said, these periodicals contributed to the invention of a Supreme Court doctrine of sexual privacy.[25]

After the Court announced *Roe* in 1973, newspapers and magazines generally depicted the decision as one that balanced the privacy interests of women against the state's interests in public health and "potential life." In this respect, they showed that the Court had adopted a compromise position, rejecting both bans on abortion and "abortion on demand." Very few stories on *Roe*, however, captured the Court's emphasis on reproductive, as opposed to sexual, privacy. And very few cited the passages in Blackmun's opinion that suggested that the Court continued to accept the constitutionality of laws against nonmarital sex.[26]

Instead, the mainstream media depicted *Roe* as a sexual privacy decision. *Time*'s initial coverage claimed that "the basis for the court's ruling is a 1965 Supreme Court decision that struck down Connecticut's anti-contraception law and recognized for the first time a constitutional right to privacy in family, sexual and other matters." One week later, *Time* announced that *Roe* declared that the right to privacy "overcomes any state interest in using abortion statutes . . . to regulate sexual conduct." In this instance, *Time* confused a position the Court described with one it endorsed. Anthony Lewis observed in the *New York Times* that Blackmun's opinion "showed that earlier Supreme Court cases had identified a constitutional right of intellectual and physical privacy extending to sex and marriage." *Christian Century* reported that Roe "took her case to court on the grounds that her constitutional rights to privacy and liberty in matters related to family, marriage and sex were being denied." Another article in *Christian Century* criticized *Roe* for excluding "the claims of the unborn," but supported the argument that "any kind of private sexual behavior between or among consenting adults is none of the state's business (except possibly in the case of the masochist who desires the supreme ecstasy of being murdered)." The notion of a constitutional right to sexual privacy was treated with ambivalence by Roe's lawyers and was avoided or rejected by the justices, but in the mainstream media sexual privacy was a constitutional right recognized by the Supreme Court.[27]

An article in *America* may be considered one of several possible exceptions as it noted, "The Supreme Court did not base its decision on 'a woman's absolute right to control her own body,' but on a limited right of personal privacy that includes the choice to abort or give birth *except when a compelling state interest justifies a statutory limitation*." *Commonweal* also highlighted the reproductive features of *Roe*, pointing out that the "seeds" of the Court's conclusion were "explicit in a statement last year by the Court when it recognized 'the right of the individual, married or single, to be free from unwarranted governmental intrusion into matters so fundamentally affecting a person as *the decision whether to bear or beget a child*.'" More exceptional still were Susan Sontag's comments in *Partisan Review*. According to Sontag, "gaining the right to have an abortion—like the right to divorce and to purchase contraceptives legally and cheaply—will help conserve the present system of marriage and the family" and "reinforce the power of men." Sontag acknowledged that "these reforms do nevertheless correspond to the concrete, immediate needs of hundreds of millions of women" and the right to abortion "becomes a valuable demand . . . when taken as a step in a chain of demands, and actions, which can mobilize and move forward the awareness of large numbers of women." Highlighting the potential role of abortion reform in politicizing women, Sontag emphasized the conservative aspects of reform as well.[28] More generally, however, the nation's leading newspapers and magazines presented *Roe* as a sexual-freedom ruling.

Why the mainstream media represented the rulings in these ways is a difficult question to answer. The decisions were depicted as sexually liberal in the context of supportive, neutral, and critical comments, so the media representations cannot be dismissed as the products of liberal or anti-liberal bias. Several possible reasons are worth considering. First, some commentators may have relied exclusively on the majority or plurality opinions, which limited their ability to use concurring opinions, concurring judgments, and dissents to explicate the meanings of the rulings. Commentators also may have relied exclusively on the holdings, which limited their ability to use dicta—the non-essential parts of the opinions—to interpret the decisions. For instance, those who wrote about *Griswold* but read only Douglas's opinion, which was supported by a narrow majority of five, missed the fact that seven justices suggested in their concurring or dissenting opinions that laws against non-marital sex were constitutional. The multiple opinions help clarify what the majority meant by marital privacy, but some commentators ignored their contents. Second, some commentators who believed that the Constitution's language about liberty, freedom, and equality applied to sexual matters may have conflated what the Constitution said and what the Supreme Court said, reading the former into the latter. Third, after *Brown* in 1954, the media generally perceived the Court as a bastion of liberal values and may have developed a tendency to fit subsequent decisions within this interpretive framework, even though *Brown*, too, was a limited ruling. A fourth possibility is that periodicals supportive of liberalization tended to exaggerate the liberalizing nature of the rulings in order to celebrate and promote liberalization, while those opposed to liberalization tended to exaggerate the liberalizing nature of the rulings in order to condemn and discourage liberalization. Fifth, perhaps journalists and others who expressed themselves in the media continued to link sexuality so closely with marriage and reproduction that they viewed the Court's endorsement of marital and reproductive privacy as equivalent to an endorsement of sexual privacy. Regardless of the reasons, the result was that the meanings of the Court's rulings changed as they circulated in the public sphere. The Court's cautious recognition of marital, reproductive, and familial rights became an endorsement of sexual rights. One of the effects of this was to obfuscate and mystify the ongoing construction of a legal regime of heteronormative supremacy. This helped secure the allegiance of various classes of sexual criminals—including heterosexual adulterers, cohabitants, fornicators, and sodomites—to the dominant order with the false belief that their rights to engage in formerly proscribed sexual activities had been affirmed by the Court. Ultimately, this may have delayed and disrupted the building of a broad coalition of sexual criminals who could have worked together to achieve legal reform.

Gay and Lesbian Media

If the mainstream media tended to present the Court's decisions as though they had recognized rights of sexual freedom and equality, what about alternative media addressed to those classified as sexual criminals? In the 1950s, 1960s, and 1970s, lesbians and gay men were probably the best organized sexual criminals in the United States. Did newsletters, newspapers, and magazines that targeted this audience highlight the Court's sexual conservatism?[29]

Homophile press coverage of *Griswold* was preceded by more than a decade of brief references to and longer discussions of abortion, birth control, and sterilization. Much of the coverage was critical of legal restrictions on abortion and birth control, some of it expressed opposition to coercive sterilization programs, and there were also discussions about whether homosexuality should be conceptualized and promoted as a form of birth control. Some of the coverage focused on sex law reform. For example, in 1964 *Drum* reported on an international conference of jurists that adopted a resolution declaring that "adultery, fornication and homosexual behavior should not be prohibited by law," that "the distribution of birth control information and contraceptive devices should be regarded as criminal only if in violation of pornography or obscenity laws," and that there should be "possibilities for obtaining legal abortions." In 1965, an article in *Eastern Mattachine Magazine* criticized New York's failure to repeal a law against the dissemination of birth control information. The article concluded, "Homosexuals . . . stand little chance of being granted their fundamental human and civil rights by a Legislature so dominated by the antiquated theory that personal morality can be legislated."[30]

The homophile press paid little attention to *Griswold* as the case was making its way to the Supreme Court, but this changed after the final ruling was announced. In September 1965, Clark Polak declared in *Drum* that *Griswold*'s "invasion of privacy" argument "points the way" for sodomy law reform. Three months later, *ONE* mentioned *Griswold* in a report on a West Virginia heterosexual "crime against nature" case. After discussing *Playboy*'s extensive coverage of the case, *ONE* quoted a *Playboy* editorial statement that expressed the hope that *Griswold* could be used to challenge these types of laws. In 1966, *ONE* referenced *Griswold* when it reprinted a policy statement on sexual behavior adopted by the ACLU of Southern California. "The right to privacy in sexual relations is a basic constitutional right," the statement declared, and "each individual has the right to decide what kind of sexual practices he or she will or will not engage in, what technique will be used, and whether or not a contraceptive should be used." The ACLU affiliate continued, "This general statement is couched in terms of 'constitutional right' because of the recent decision of Justice Goldberg in *Griswold*. . . . Goldberg applied the ninth amendment to marital privacy and it could just as well be applied to the whole area of sexual conduct." Two years later, *Drum* referred to *Griswold* as a decision that endorsed the notion that "sex, the hetero kind at least, can be had for pleasure alone." According to *Drum*, those who favored less "official restraint of matters sexual" could "profit" from *Griswold*. Although the homophile press could have expressed concern about the negative references to homosexuality in the *Griswold* opinions, these were not discussed. *Griswold*'s sexually conservative formulation of the right to privacy became a beacon of sexual liberalization in the homophile press.[31]

In some instances, the gay and lesbian press's view began to change in the early 1970s, as it began to be clear that the Court was not necessarily going to interpret *Griswold* as a sexual freedom ruling. In 1971, Walter Barnett, a lawyer working on the *Buchanan* sodomy law appeal, cautioned in the *Advocate* that one of the problems confronted by lawyers interested in challenging sodomy laws is that "they all have to argue from analogy to recent decisions of the Supreme Court which announce rather novel constitutional doctrines in terms that are none too clear." Barnett explained that the *Buchanan* appeal rested on a "compelling analogy: If a state cannot constitutionally prohibit married couples form using contraceptives . . . , then it is reasonably certain that it can't prohibit them from engaging in oral-genital or anal-genital contact." But Barnett concluded that this was "small comfort to gay people," since "a state could promptly re-enact its statute to exclude married couples." This was a rare gay press acknowledgment that *Griswold* was a marital privacy ruling, rather than a sexual privacy ruling. But as we will see, after *Eisenstadt* in 1972, the gay and lesbian press again began referring to *Griswold* as a ruling with positive implications for sexual freedom.[32]

In the 1950s and 1960s, the homophile press devoted far more attention to rulings on obscenity, including many that did not refer to same-sex sex, than it did to rulings on birth control. The Court's 1958 decision in *ONE* was covered extensively, which is not surprising given that it provided the legal foundation for the continued existence of the homophile press. Although the papers of the justices reveal that the magazine won a narrow five-to-four decision, many gay and lesbian press reports claimed that the ruling was unanimous.

Homophile commentators apparently did not understand or did not wish to emphasize that in unsigned *per curiam* rulings the Court announced its decision without revealing the vote.[33]

The coverage of the *ONE* case proved to be an early instance of the homophile press's tendency to present courts as strong opponents of sexual censorship. In 1958, *Mattachine Review* noted that "in almost every obscenity court test" the books targeted by local authorities had been declared non-obscene. In 1960, *ONE* observed that "the nation's courts, all thru 1959, have been consistently clipping the censor's claws." In a review of developments from 1955 to 1962, *Mattachine Review* observed "greater 'freedom to read' in the English-speaking world, particularly in the U.S." The magazine claimed that the "pressure of the censors remains, but laws and courts progressively permit greater freedom." The gay and lesbian press highlighted the activities of anti-obscenity groups and authorities, but in general the courts were depicted as defenders of sexual speech.[34]

Homophile periodicals presented the Supreme Court in particular as an opponent of sexual censorship. In 1959, *ONE* reported on a Pennsylvania court that, "in defiance of the U.S. Supreme Court," had upheld obscenity convictions in a case involving two nudist magazines. In 1960, *Mattachine Review* stated that the League for the Abolition of Postal Censorship was challenging postal officials "who have declared that they must circumvent U.S. Supreme Court decisions." Also in 1960, *ONE* reported that the chief postal inspector had recently "gloated over a 1958 law 'that helps the department get around' Supreme Court limitations on obscenity prosecutions." In 1961, *ONE* observed that the governor of Texas had "signed into law still one more of those so-called anti-obscenity laws which in due time invariably wind up in the U.S. Supreme Court only to have the stuffing knocked out of them."[35]

Homophile press coverage of *Manual*, which concerned male physique magazines, promoted the notion that the Court was a protector of sexual speech. In 1962, *Mattachine Review* published a statement by H. Lynn Womack, the petitioner in *Manual*, who claimed, "The U.S. Supreme Court handed down a decision of some 41 pages which completely supersedes all previous obscenity decisions, greatly widens the standards for judging obscenity, lays down a national standard for judging materials for obscenity, and declares that the Postmaster General lacks any authority whatsoever for engaging in censorship." Womack asserted that the Court ruled that "physique magazines per se are not obscene" and "homosexuals are as much entitled to pin-ups as are heterosexuals." The following month, *ONE* likewise reported that the Court had ruled in *Manual* that three physique magazines were not obscene.

In contrast, the *Ladder*'s coverage emphasized the limited nature of the ruling. According to a summary of a presentation by an ACLU representative, "There were two Justices . . . who did voice the opinion that the magazines were not considered obscene. But the case was finally decided on another issue—that the Post Office Department had no right to censor—and was not decided on the obscenity issue." Even when the homophile press criticized the justices, it presented the Court as a defender of sexual speech. In 1965, *Drum* published an article by Polak titled "The Story Behind Physique Photography." Discussing *Manual*, Polak wrote that "the Supreme Court was unable to regard Womack's motives as anything other than 'sordid' nor the gay public as more than 'unfortunate,' but this case stands as one of the two most important homosexual court victories." The justices might be antigay, Polak suggested, but they opposed sexual censorship.[36]

Having presented the Court as a defender of sexual speech, the homophile press confronted the difficult task of explaining *Ginzburg* and *Mishkin*. Most gay and lesbian periodicals looked on the bright side. Ignoring earlier anti-obscenity rulings, Mattachine New York's newsletter reported that the Court "for the first time in its history upheld two lower court decisions which ruled that published material was obscene." After summarizing the rulings and highlighting *Mishkin*'s emphasis on the "prurient interest of perverted people—sadists, masochists, homosexuals, lesbians, fetishists, and so forth," the newsletter pointed out that "for those of us who deplore censorship of any kind on principle, these two Supreme Court decisions are discouraging." Still, the newsletter noted that "those of us who are tired of seeing lurid covers on reasonably respectable homosexual books may not be unreasonable in hoping that the Ginzburg decision may lead to book jacket designs (and advertising) which are more representative of content." In addition, Mattachine New York claimed, "There are . . . many books published (especially about lesbians) which, although they feature homosexuals and other sex variants as major characters, appeal in actuality to essentially heterosexual buyers. . . . If books of this kind can be called obscene under the Mishkin decision, it may be that their removal from the bookstands will make way for serious homosexual literature." This turned the Court into a promoter of better books for gay and lesbian readers.[37]

Other homophile magazines also found reasons to be hopeful. Commenting on the "shock waves of confusion" after the rulings in *Ginzburg* and *Mishkin*, ONE noted that "it is quite likely that the hysterical panic indulged in by some commentators . . . will gradually subside." The "principal ray of hope" arose from the number of concurring and dissenting opinions and the "withering sarcasm directed at the legal reasoning behind each of the three widely split decisions." This might be of little help to Ginzburg and Mishkin, but "narrow decisions are sometimes reversed the next time." *Drum* also found a way to express hope. According to a legal expert cited by the magazine, "If you accept the concept of legal obscenity, the court acted properly in *Mishkin*. Why should homosexuals and other so-called deviates be technically permitted to have hard-core pornography when heterosexuals are prohibited?" *Mishkin* was presented here as an egalitarian ruling. *Drum* also claimed that "the effect of the *Ginzburg*, *Mishkin* and *Fanny Hill* decisions has been virtually nil," partly because of "the total confusion surrounding the meaning of the decisions."[38]

Over the next several years, the gay and lesbian press sometimes seemed to forget about the Court's anti-obscenity rulings. In 1969, the *Ladder* referred to censorship as "almost non-existent," even as the *Advocate* and *Drum* were reporting on dozens of censorship cases around the country. In 1968, *Drum* noted that "the Court seems to be taking the position that something somewhere is probably obscene and that they would know it if they saw it, but they just haven't seen any real obscenity in a long time." In fact, the Court thought it had seen obscenity in *Womack* (1961), *Darnell* (1963), *Landau* (1967), and *G.I. Distributors* (1967), not to mention *Ginzburg* and *Mishkin*. A short time later, *Drum* reprinted a newspaper's assertion that "the courts have all but defined away the possibility of obscenity findings for printed matter." The same issue reprinted a story noting that "the Supreme Court, which had varied between permissiveness and indignation in handling recent appeals in obscenity cases, allowed the admission of thousands of Danish magazines featuring photographs of the nude male." This was a reference to *Potomac News* and *Central Magazine Sales*, but no mention was made of *G.I. Distributors*, decided one week earlier, in which the Court denied *cert* in an appeal of an anti-obscenity ruling that relied on *Mishkin*'s discussion of "deviant sexual groups." The coverage in *Drum* is particularly noteworthy because federal authorities were using *Ginzburg*'s language about "pandering" and *Mishkin*'s language about "deviant sexual groups" to pursue obscenity charges against Polak, the editor and publisher of *Drum*.[39]

In contrast to its regular invocation of *Griswold* and its extensive coverage of the 1966 obscenity rulings, the homophile press paid virtually no attention to *Loving*. Nor did the homophile press pay much attention to laws against interracial cohabitation or marriage. In a rare exception, in 1955 *ONE* observed that under North Carolina law "homosexuality, bestiality and miscegenation" were felonies while "fornication and adultery" were misdemeanors. In the stream-of-consciousness style often used in *ONE*, the magazine immediately thereafter observed that in Mississippi a Black man had recently been executed for allegedly raping a white woman while a white man had been sentenced to two years for allegedly raping a thirteen-year-old Black girl. In another exception, Mattachine New York's newsletter declared in 1967 that "we were downright shocked to learn that the Supreme Court had handed down, with some very nice decisions on miscegenation and electronic eavesdropping, the decision to uphold the deportation order of a Canadian immigrant on the grounds that homosexuality is included in 'psychopathic personality' in . . . the Immigration and Nationality Act." The decision in *Loving* relied on heteronormative logic, but Mattachine New York suggested that there was something inconsistent about the rulings in *Loving* and *Boutilier*.[40]

More generally, the homophile press ignored *Loving*, which in some respects is puzzling. In the 1950s and 1960s, gay and lesbian periodicals frequently mentioned laws against adultery, extramarital sex, fornication, incest, prostitution, public sex, rape, sex with minors, and sodomy, but not laws against interracial cohabitation or marriage. In many instances, the homophile press emphasized that laws criminalized heterosexual as well as homosexual sex and that both types of laws, when concerning consensual adult conduct in private, should be repealed. Sometimes the homophile press criticized the disparate treatment of homosexual and heterosexual crime. The homophile press often drew its own boundaries between sex laws that it favored (most commonly, laws against rape and sex with minors) and those it did not (most commonly, laws against fornication and sodomy). Laws against interracial cohabitation and marriage could have been discussed in these contexts, but they were not. This is noteworthy because the homophile press frequently invoked civil rights analogies and examples, occasionally featured articles that mentioned interracial homosexuality, and sometimes mentioned same-sex marriage.[41] Moreover, while the homophile movement was predominantly white, some homophile groups were led by people of color, quite a few included civil rights activists, and many had ethnoracially diverse memberships. Decades later, the interracial marriage analogy would be used by same-sex marriage proponents, but in the 1960s *Loving* did not receive much attention in the gay and lesbian press. This may reflect the particular ways in which the homophile movement invoked civil rights analogies, which were often based on the notion that the civil rights movement had already achieved full racial equality. In addition, the homophile movement may have been reluctant to link its cause to a struggle it perceived as unpopular. Moreover, much of the homophile movement may have regarded same-sex marriage as unobtainable or undesirable, making interracial marriage a subject of minimal interest. Finally, homophile disinterest in *Loving* may reflect the extent to which the case was perceived to concern racial equality rather than marital, reproductive, or sexual rights.

Five years later, when the Court announced its decision in *Eisenstadt*, a new generation of lesbian and gay periodicals had taken the place of the homophile press. In the new lesbian feminist press, *Eisenstadt* did not receive much attention, partly because birth control was not typically seen as a lesbian feminist issue and partly because minimal mainstream press coverage led many lesbian feminists to overlook the significance of the case. An exception was *Lesbian Tide*, which mentioned *Eisenstadt* in a 1972 article about a California ruling that struck down the state's law against oral sex. The case involved men and women accused of committing illegal acts during the making of a pornographic movie. According to *Lesbian Tide*, the ruling was based on the Court's recognition of "the right of marital privacy" and its recent conclusion that "a law directed only toward single persons, in that case a ban upon distribution of contraceptive devices, violates the rights of single persons under the equal protection clause." More generally, the lesbian feminist press ignored *Eisenstadt*.[42]

The *Advocate* provided extensive coverage of court cases in the early 1970s and paid close attention to those with implications for gay and lesbian rights. As is discussed in the next chapter, the gay and lesbian press grew increasingly concerned about the Court in the early 1970s as President Nixon's four appointees joined with other justices to turn away dozens of gay and lesbian rights appeals. *Eisenstadt*, however, raised the hopes of the *Advocate*. In 1972, the newspaper mentioned the case in an article about the California oral sex ruling. After emphasizing the judge's reliance on *Griswold* and *Eisenstadt*, the *Advocate* asserted, "By its implication that laws differentiating between married and single persons violate the 'equal protection' clause, *Eisenstadt* may also have much influence on other cases." The next issue included in-depth coverage of *Eisenstadt* under the headline "Equal Protection Ruling by Top Court May Aid Gay Rights." After asserting that the ruling "may have established precedents which will prove vital in future cases involving single persons, particularly Gays," the story noted that Nixon appointee Harry Blackmun had sided with the majority. Not mentioning the fact that Blackmun's concurrence, like White's, was based on the fact that the evidence was unclear as to whether the woman to whom Baird gave birth control was unmarried, the *Advocate* implied that the equal protection reasoning was endorsed by more justices than it was. Along similar lines, an article about a Wisconsin case asserted that *Eisenstadt* meant that "single persons have the same right of privacy as married persons." Then in 1973, the *Advocate* reported on a D.C. Superior Court decision overturning a local law against prostitution. After noting that the court also declared that "the statutory prescription against fornication, sodomy, and adultery engaged in by consenting adults is an unconstitutional invasion of the right to privacy," the story explained that the decision cited *Eisenstadt*, which the judge said involved "the same fundamental issue now before us," and *Griswold*, which the judge used to emphasize "the constitutional right of the individual to control the use and function of his or her own body." None of these articles mentioned *Eisenstadt*'s qualifying and limiting language. The *Advocate* transformed a reproductive rights decision into a sexual rights decision.[43]

By early 1973, the *Advocate* was expressing renewed concern about court-based strategies, but continued to promote the notion that the Court would do the right thing. In January, an editorial praised the formation of new homosexual law reform groups and noted that "what may eventually grow out of these efforts" is "something akin to the Homosexual Civil Liberties Union this newspaper has urged for a long time." The *Advocate* was convinced that "the new wave of anti-gay bigotry that is erupting . . . is . . . a last gasp that will . . . be swamped by a larger wave of a new humanity." A few weeks later, a lawyer challenging state laws against oral and anal sex was quoted in the *Advocate* as saying, "'Considering the general trend of the past 20 or 30 years in sexual matters, I would be surprised if these laws were still on the books in this country in the next five to 10 years.'" The lawyer acknowledged that "the courts are changing" and "the Nixon administration is very tough on this kind of thing," but when asked specifically about the Supreme Court he said, "I could not say that this court is a loser, not necessarily."[44]

The *Advocate* also presented *Roe* as a ruling with positive implications for sexual freedom and equality. A 1973 report on an Arkansas ruling that upheld that state's sodomy law noted that the Court, "in a series of rulings capped by its recent monumental decision striking down state abortion laws, has been widening and polishing the privacy doctrine." According to the newspaper, "A number of constitutional lawyers now feel that [the Court] will eventually strike down virtually all prohibitions on consensual sex." The following month, the *Advocate* reported on a D.C. Superior Court decision that ruled that the District's sodomy law could only be used in cases involving force or minors because "privacy in sexual activity is a fundamental right." According to the *Advocate*, the judge "cited several Supreme Court cases in which sexual activity is declared to be one of the matters in which there is a right to complete privacy," including "the recent decision involving abortion, and past decisions on contraception and possession of obscene material."[45]

In contrast, several lesbian feminist periodicals presented *Roe* as a significant but limited ruling. *Off Our Backs*, a feminist newspaper with significant lesbian content, reported in February 1973 that "what was won was only a significant first start in a continuing struggle for the right to choose." Emphasizing that the ruling in *Roe* permitted significant state restrictions on abortions in the second and third trimesters, *Off Our Backs* warned that the abortion rights movement would have to mobilize in order to prevent this from happening. In March 1973, *Lesbian Tide* published a short news item about *Roe* and a transcript of a speech delivered by Jeanne Cordova at an "abortion victory rally" in Los Angeles. After telling the story of a lesbian with an unwanted pregnancy and reminding her audience that lesbians had worked alongside straight women in the struggle for abortion rights, Cordova declared, "There is another connection between lesbianism and abortion. . . . That connection is that the demand for 'Freedom of Sexual Expression,' the freedom to choose and live out our own sexuality, like the demands for 'abortion on demand' and community controlled health care, speaks directly to our movement's fundamental demand, 'A woman's right to control her own body.'" According to Cordova, "The realization of abortion law repeal gives us more control over our reproduction, but we still have no control over a yet more fundamental right—our own sexuality. Right now, women have no right to choose a sexuality that does not include men. . . . If the Women's Movement is serious about human liberation it will have to take up the issue of sexuality." On the one hand, Cordova declared to potential gay male allies, "We refuse to be sold out by a movement which limits itself to the 'Police Beat, the defense of washroom sex and pornographic movies' and the right to marry." On the other hand, she insisted, "We also refuse to be co-opted by a movement which limits, yes limits, itself to demanding legal abortion, when we cannot even have legal sex." Cordova highlighted some of the limitations of *Roe*, but more generally the gay and lesbian press portrayed the Supreme Court as a supporter of sexual rights.[46]

Judges and Justices

Among the most influential readers of Supreme Court rulings were federal and state judges, who were expected to align their decisions with high court precedents. This was not always easy to do, as Supreme Court opinions often contained ambiguous language, contradictory elements, and reasoning that did not cover every factual situation. In the late 1960s and early 1970s, judges sometimes presented *Griswold*, *Fanny Hill*, *Loving*, *Eisenstadt*, and *Roe* as rulings that affirmed the special rights and privileges associated with heteronormative sex, marriage, and reproduction, but sometimes presented these decisions as more sexually libertarian and egalitarian. It would be difficult to quantify which types of judicial interpretations were more common, but the number and influence of those that presented the rulings as sexually libertarian and egalitarian were great enough to influence media representations and popular consciousness.[47]

In many cases, federal courts highlighted *Griswold*'s, *Loving*'s, *Eisenstadt*'s, and *Roe*'s emphasis on marital and reproductive rights without commenting on sexual rights. For example, in a 1965 ruling against a woman seeking Social Security benefits based on a common-law marriage, a federal judge in South Carolina cited *Griswold* after declaring, "Marriage is a sacred and noble institution, and is recognized as such." In 1969, the Fifth Circuit invoked *Griswold* in an inheritance case in which the mother of a man who died claimed that a daughter born to his wife was not his. The court ruled that under Louisiana law the deceased had failed to disavow his paternity in a timely manner and the daughter was thus his legitimate heir. Citing *Griswold*, the court declared, "Society—American society, indeed American constitutional society—is committed to the existence of some institutions, the stability of which is deemed essential for a healthy existence as a nation. The home-family is such an institution." Multiple birth control and abortion rulings likewise emphasized that *Griswold*, *Loving*, *Eisenstadt*, and *Roe* affirmed marital and reproductive rights.[48]

Consistent with these interpretations, several courts cited *Griswold* and *Eisenstadt* when upholding zoning laws that privileged marital and reproductive households. In 1970, a federal district court in California upheld a law that barred groups of four or more "unrelated" individuals from living together in a "single family residential" neighborhood. According to the court, "there is a long recognized value in the traditional family relationship which does not attach to the 'voluntary family'" and the state has a "clear interest in preserving the integrity of the biological and/or legal family." Insofar as *Griswold* recognized "marital privacy" and "family privacy," the district court viewed it as irrelevant. In 1972, a federal district court in New York ruled against the landlords and tenants of a one-family home occupied by six students. Upholding a local law that banned groups of more than two unrelated individuals from living together in a single-family residence, the judge observed that "such zoning is simply another of countless statutes of bounty and protection with which the states . . . and the Federal government alike aggressively surround the traditional family of parents and their children." According to the judge, "such cases as *Eisenstadt* ... may imply for the future that such a zoning ordinance could not be so applied as to exclude a family group that differed only in that husband and wife, while living together with their children, had not married ceremoniously," but "that is not the present case." On appeal, the Supreme Court upheld the zoning law. In a majority opinion by Douglas, the author of the majority opinion in *Griswold* argued that *Griswold* and *Eisenstadt* were not relevant because the local law did not interfere with the right of privacy.[49]

As this case suggests, in many instances the justices themselves referred to *Griswold*, *Loving*, *Eisenstadt*, and *Roe* as marital and reproductive rights decisions. In *Warden, Maryland Penitentiary* (1967), the majority upheld an armed robbery conviction based on evidence seized from the man's home, but Douglas argued in dissent that "the Framers ... knew what police surveillance meant and how the practice of rummaging through one's personal effects could destroy freedom." According to Douglas, "it was in that tradition that we held in *Griswold* ... that lawmakers could not, as respects husband and wife at least, make the use of contraceptives a crime." In 1971, *Boddie* overturned a law that prevented the indigent from obtaining divorces because of court fees they could not afford. According to the majority, "given the basic position of the marriage relationship in this society's hierarchy of values and the concomitant state monopolization of the means for legally dissolving this relationship," the state could not deny the indigent access to the courts for obtaining divorces. In a passage that referenced *Loving*, the opinion observed that "marriage involves interests of basic importance in our society." Two years later, the Court observed in *Kras* that *Boddie* concerned "the marital relationship" and "the associational interests that surround the establishment and dissolution of that relationship." Citing *Griswold*, *Loving*, and *Eisenstadt*, the majority noted that "on many occasions we have recognized the fundamental importance of these interests." Also in 1973, the Court in *San Antonio School District* cited *Roe* when declaring that "the right of procreation is among the rights of personal privacy protected under the Constitution."[50]

Some courts indicated more explicitly that the *Griswold* to *Roe* precedents did not apply to nonmarital sex. In *Smayda* (1965), the Ninth Circuit upheld oral copulation convictions for two men caught having sex in Yosemite National Park. Acknowledging that *Griswold* affirmed a right to privacy, the court declared, "When, as here, the police have reasonable cause to believe that public toilet stalls are being used in the commission of a crime, and when, as here, they confine their activities to the times when such crimes are most likely to occur, they are entitled to institute clandestine surveillance. . . . The public interest in its privacy, we think, must, to that extent, be subordinated to the public interest in law enforcement." A concurring opinion noted, with respect to *Griswold*, that "nothing in the present case resembles a 'right of privacy in marriage.'" In 1967, a California court rejected the use of *Griswold* in a decision concerning consensual sodomy in prison because *Griswold* focused on "the right of privacy in the marriage relation." According to the court, "Appellant wholly fails to bring himself within the ambit of *Griswold*. His relationship with his fellow prisoner can hardly . . . be deemed 'noble' or 'basic.'" Four years later, when a New Jersey court upheld a fornication conviction, it cited the passages in *Griswold* that referred to the legitimacy of fornication laws. Also in 1971, an Oklahoma decision upholding sodomy convictions for married partners who had forced a woman to engage in oral sex with them declared that *Griswold* "does not prohibit the state's regulation of sexual promiscuity or misconduct between non-married persons."[51]

Various courts also distinguished between marital, reproductive, and sexual rights in cases concerning sex with minors and incest. In 1970, a California court rejected the use of *Griswold* in an incest, oral sex, and sodomy case involving a man and his sixteen-year-old daughter. In fact, the court cited *Griswold* to support its conclusion that "penal statutes proscribing illicit sexual contacts constitute a legitimate and proper exercise" of state power. Two years later, an Oklahoma court upheld a sodomy conviction for a man who forced his stepson to have anal sex. Citing *Griswold*, the court emphasized the state's "right . . . to regulate sexual promiscuity and sexual misconduct between non-married persons."[52]

Several birth control and abortion rulings also distinguished more explicitly between marital, reproductive, and sexual rights. In *Sturgis* (1970), a Massachusetts court upheld a state law prohibiting doctors and pharmacists from supplying unmarried individuals with contraceptives. According to the court, *Griswold* "affirmed 'beyond doubt' the right of the State of Connecticut to enact statutes regulating the private sexual lives of single persons." Also in 1970, a federal court referenced *Griswold* when upholding Louisiana's anti-abortion law. According to this court, *Griswold* struck down Connecticut's law because it interfered with "the intimate relation of husband and wife," whereas the Louisiana statute concerned "embryonic and fetal organisms." Underscoring the limited nature of the privacy rights affirmed by the Supreme Court, the court quoted Harlan's dissent in *Poe* (1961), which stated, "The laws regarding marriage which provide both when the sexual powers may be used and the legal and societal context in which children are born and brought up, as well as the laws forbidding adultery, fornication and homosexual practices which express the negative of the proposition, confining sexuality to lawful marriage, form a pattern so deeply pressed into the substance of our social life that any Constitutional doctrine in this area must build upon that basis." A dissenting opinion cited *Griswold* after noting that "courts often affirm — almost most always in dictum — the propriety of statutes against fornication." Two years later, a federal court in New Jersey referenced *Griswold* and *Loving* in striking down that state's anti-abortion statute. According to the court, "the constitutional right or zone of privacy has been held to include and protect at least certain activities relating to marriage, sex, contraception, procreation, child-rearing and education." The court held that a "compelling state interest" could override this right and "control of sexual behavior" might be a compelling state interest, but the abortion law was not "compellingly related" to this interest and "the state has already implemented its power to regulate sexual behavior by . . . providing criminal sanctions for . . . fornication and adultery."[53]

As some of these examples suggest, some courts presented *Griswold* and *Loving* as upholding a right of sexual privacy within, but not outside of, marriage. In a 1966 ruling, a federal judge in Connecticut wrote that *Griswold* declared that the Constitution protects "the sanctity of sexual aspects of the marital relationship" and noted that the *Griswold* opinions "emphasize and re-emphasize that it is the special nature of the marriage bond that makes so patently offensive state intrusion into the area." In 1968, a federal judge in Ohio wrote, "The Court in *Griswold* regarded the marital sexual relationship as a somewhat special situation. This relationship is private by nature. And it is so basic and important to our society that it would be inconceivable that it is not protected from unwarranted interference." Also in 1968, the Seventh Circuit in *Cotner* cited *Griswold* in overturning a marital sodomy conviction in Indiana. This case concerned a man sentenced to two to fourteen years in prison based on his wife's claim that he had committed a crime against nature with her. According to the court, "the import of the *Griswold* decision is that private, consensual, marital relations are protected from regulation by the state." A footnote observed, "It is essential to the preservation of the right of privacy that a husband have standing to protect the marital bedroom against unlawful intrusion." After noting that the statute could be used to regulate consensual sex between unmarried partners and nonconsensual marital relations, the court concluded that, because there was no evidence that Cotner had used force, his conviction was inappropriate. Along similar lines, in a 1969 case involving a theatrical performance that led to arrests for obscenity, sodomy, lewdness, and indecency, a federal judge in New York rejected the notion that *Loving* could be used to strike down the sodomy statute. *Loving* was irrelevant because, the judge wrote, the statute did not discriminate on the basis of race and "a rational foundation exists for the state's discrimination between acts of consensual sodomy committed by married and unmarried persons."[54]

Two Texas rulings also interpreted the Court's decisions as though they protected sexual rights within, but not outside of, marriage. In *Buchanan* (1970), a federal court struck down the state's sodomy law as unconstitutionally overbroad because "it reaches the private, consensual acts of married couples." While the main complainant was a "homosexual" arrested for same-sex sodomy in a public restroom, he was joined by a married couple and a homosexual man who feared prosecution based on private acts. According to the court, the statute "operates directly on an intimate relation of husband and wife," which *Griswold* said was not constitutionally permissible. Making it clear that "the State has regulated sexual relations by the passage of laws prohibiting what it considers immoral acts, such as adultery and fornication and we believe that it has that right with reference to sodomy," the court quoted a passage from *Griswold* emphasizing that the ruling "'in no way interferes with a State's proper regulation of sexual promiscuity or misconduct.'" Disapproval of sodomy, however, was "not sufficient reason for the State to encroach upon the liberty of married persons." After the U.S. Supreme Court vacated the judgment in 1971 (without discussing the merits), a Texas court affirmed the constitutionality of the sodomy statute as applied to Buchanan. In *Pruett* (1970), another same-sex sodomy case, the same Texas court ruled that *Griswold* could not be used to strike down the state law. According to the court, "There are cases which say that it is *conceivable* that a husband and wife could be convicted of sodomy even though the proof established consent." The court contended, however, that "the question of whether the sodomy statute may be invoked against married couples for private consensual acts has never been presented to this court." After quoting *Griswold* passages that emphasized marital privacy, the court concluded, "To extend the protection of this right of privacy to destroy the sodomy statute, when successful prosecution of private consensual acts of sodomy are at most only 'conceivable' is not, in our view, consistent with the description of the marriage relationship and right of privacy" in *Griswold*.[55]

In *Paris* (1973), the Supreme Court read *Griswold, Loving, Eisenstadt,* and *Roe* as recognizing marital and reproductive rights and as having implications for marital sex, but only in private space. Emphasizing that *Griswold, Loving,*

Eisenstadt, and *Roe* recognized a constitutional right to privacy that "protects the personal intimacies of the home, the family, marriage, motherhood, procreation, and child rearing," the Court observed that these decisions were "not just concerned with a particular place, but with a protected intimate relationship." Nevertheless, the Court made it clear that "obviously, there is no necessary or legitimate expectation of privacy which would extend to marital intercourse on a street corner or a theater stage." In addition, "conduct involving consenting adults" remained subject to "state regulation" in the form of laws against adultery, bigamy, fornication, and prostitution.[56]

In short, many courts presented *Griswold*, *Loving*, *Eisenstadt*, and *Roe* as marital and reproductive rights decisions. Some read these precedents as affirming a right of sexual privacy within marriage, but as far as these courts were concerned the Court had not recognized sexual rights outside of marriage. In fact, some of these courts used the justices' comments about the constitutionality of sex laws to clarify what the Court had meant when it ruled in favor of marital and reproductive rights. Consistent with these interpretations, many sodomy, lewdness, and crimes-against-nature cases were decided without mention of *Griswold*, *Loving*, *Eisenstadt*, or *Roe*, presumably because these decisions were not seen as relevant in rulings about nonmarital sex.[57]

In many other cases, however, federal and state judges interpreted *Griswold*, *Loving*, *Eisenstadt*, and *Roe* as decisions that could be used to protect nonmarital sexual expression, despite the contrary indications by the Court. In 1966, for example, a federal judge in Tennessee cited *Griswold* in a concurring opinion on the rights of nudists. While the majority overturned the state's nudism law because it was vague, this opinion argued that the law violated the right of privacy affirmed in *Griswold*. In 1969, a federal court in Indiana observed in an obscenity case that "while only the right to *marital* privacy is covered by *Cotner* and *Griswold*, it is clear that this right stems from the greater right to individual privacy." One year later, the First Circuit in *Baird* criticized the claim by the Massachusetts Supreme Judicial Court in *Sturgis* that *Griswold* "affirmed 'beyond doubt' the right of the state 'to enact statutes regulating the private sexual lives of single persons.'" According to the First Circuit, "*Griswold* . . . in no way establishes 'beyond doubt' that the present statute is constitutional."[58]

Two 1973 Second Circuit decisions read *Griswold*, *Eisenstadt*, and *Roe* as having implications for sexual rights. In one, the court cited all three cases in announcing that "the most intimate phases of personal life have been held to be thus constitutionally protected." A few weeks later, the same court stated that *Griswold* and *Eisenstadt* "can be viewed as forecasting recognition of a constitutional right of men and women to decide, free of governmental interference, whether to minimize the risks of conception from sexual intercourse." According to the court, "Although ... the right to privacy which thus far has been granted constitutional protection relates only to 'the most intimate phases of personal life,' having to do with sexual intercourse and its possible consequences, it is not 'obvious' that the right will be thus confined."[59]

Some state courts likewise read *Griswold, Loving, Eisenstadt,* and *Roe* as sexual rights decisions. In a 1969 California case concerning a man whose teaching license had been suspended based on homosexual conduct, a state court cited *Griswold* after observing, "An unqualified proscription against immoral conduct would raise serious constitutional problems. Conscientious school officials concerned with enforcing such a broad provision might be inclined to probe into the private life of each and every teacher.... Such prying might all too readily lead school officials to search for 'telltale signs' of immorality in violation of the teacher's constitutional rights." In 1970, a California decision about the rights of a psychiatrist to refuse to provide evidence about a patient acknowledged that *Griswold* "involved only the marital relationship," but added that the "open-ended quality of that decision's rationale evidences its far-reaching dimension." The court continued, "The retention of a degree of intimacy in interpersonal relations and communications lies at the heart of the broad rationale of *Griswold*." In 1972, a New Mexico court upheld an attempted-sodomy conviction for a man who used force with a minor, but a dissenting opinion, citing *Griswold*, argued that the sodomy law was unconstitutional "because it regulates private sexual relations between two consenting adults, including husband and wife."[60]

Beginning in the late 1960s, multiple lower court rulings on abortion began claiming that the Supreme Court had already recognized rights of sexual privacy and liberty. In fact, these were the decisions that may have been most influential in leading the media and the public to believe that the Court had already recognized sexual privacy rights. In *Belous* (1969), the Supreme Court of California overturned the conviction of a doctor on abortion charges. Citing *Griswold* and *Loving*, the court referred to "the Supreme Court's and this court's repeated acknowledgment of a 'right of privacy' or 'liberty' in matters related to marriage, family, and sex." In *Vuitch* (1969), a federal judge ruled that Washington, D.C.'s anti-abortion statute was unconstitutionally vague. Citing *Griswold* and *Loving*, the judge asserted that there had been "an increasing indication in decisions of the Supreme Court of the United States that as a secular matter a woman's liberty and right of privacy extends to family, marriage and sex matters." Similar references to *Griswold* and *Loving* can be found in many other abortion rulings in 1970, 1971, and 1972, despite the fact that the Court never added "sex" to its inventory of protected private activities.[61]

Several decisions concerning nonmarital cohabitation also suggested that the Court had developed a doctrine of sexual privacy. In *Mindel* (1970), a federal judge in California ruled that a U.S. Post Office employee had been wrongfully terminated on the basis of "immoral conduct" because he had lived "with a young lady without the benefit of marriage." According to the judge, "Mindel's termination because of his private sex life violates the right to privacy." In support of this position, the judge noted that *Griswold* held that, absent a "compelling reason," the government "may not invade 'the sanctity of a man's home and the privacies of life.'" Two years later, a federal court in Washington, D.C., ruled that the food stamp program unconstitutionally discriminated against households of unrelated individuals. Responding to the notion that such discrimination was permissible because of the state's interest in "the fostering of morality," the court cited *Griswold* and *Eisenstadt* after stating that "the states . . . cannot in the name of morality infringe the rights to privacy and freedom of association *in the home*."[62]

Griswold was also cited as a sexual privacy precedent in several gay rights cases. In *One Eleven Wines* (1967), the New Jersey Supreme Court used *Griswold* to support "the rights of well behaved apparent homosexuals to patronize and meet in licensed premises." In 1969, the D.C. Circuit's ruling in *Norton* declared that a NASA budget analyst had been unlawfully discharged based on allegations about homosexual conduct. In a passage that cited *Griswold*, the court referred to "that ill-defined area of privacy which is increasingly if indistinctly recognized as a foundation of several specific constitutional protections." The opinion went on to note that "we are not prepared to say that the Commission could not reasonably find appellant's homosexual advance to be 'immoral,' 'indecent,' or 'notoriously disgraceful' under dominant conventional norms," but "the notion that it could be an appropriate function of the federal bureaucracy to enforce the majority's conventional codes of conduct in the private lives of its employees is at war with elementary concepts of liberty, privacy, and diversity." The commission had to show that the "immoral or indecent acts" had an "ascertainable deleterious effect on the efficiency of the service." In *Labady* (1971), a federal judge in New York granted the naturalization petition of a Cuban-born homosexual, citing *Griswold* to support the claim that "it is now established that official inquiry into a person's private sexual habits does violence to his constitutionally protected zone of privacy." Emphasizing the consensual and private nature of Labady's sexual conduct, the judge argued that "laws that seek to prohibit and punish private homosexual behavior between consenting adults . . . are probably unconstitutional in light of *Griswold*."[63]

The Supreme Court justices generally presented *Griswold, Loving, Eisenstadt*, and *Roe* as marital and reproductive rights decisions, rather than sexual rights decisions, but there were exceptions. In the pre-*Roe* era, two justices, Douglas and Marshall, presented these rulings as sexual rights precedents. In *Osborn*, a 1966 case involving an attempted bribery conviction based on a tape-recorded conversation, Douglas's lone dissent cited *Griswold* in a discussion of "the constitutional right of privacy." Noting that "we are rapidly entering the age of no privacy, where everyone is open to surveillance," Douglas offered as an example a fact revealed in *Smayda*: that "peepholes in men's rooms are there to catch homosexuals." After referring to "an alarming trend whereby the privacy and dignity of our citizens is being whittled away," Douglas mentioned that "we have here in the District of Columbia squads of officers who work the men's rooms in public buildings trying to get homosexuals to solicit them." Douglas did not specifically indicate that *Griswold* was a sexual privacy precedent, but this was implied by his comments. In *Vuitch* (1971), the Supreme Court reversed the 1969 district court decision, finding that the Washington, D.C., abortion statute was not unconstitutionally vague. In a dissenting opinion, Douglas wrote that "abortion touches intimate affairs of the family, of marriage, of sex, which in *Griswold* . . . we held to involve rights associated with several express constitutional rights and which are summed up in 'the right of privacy.'" The only other justice in the pre-*Roe* era who presented *Griswold, Loving, Eisenstadt*, or *Roe* as sexual rights precedents was Marshall. In a dissenting opinion in *California v. LaRue* (1972), Marshall disagreed with the majority's decision to uphold a prohibition on sexually explicit live entertainment in licensed bars and clubs. Citing *Griswold*, Marshall declared, "I have serious doubts whether the State may constitutionally assert an interest in regulating any sexual act between consenting adults." In this period, the other justices did not present *Griswold, Loving, Eisenstadt*, and *Roe* as sexual freedom decisions.[64]

As for obscenity decisions, the number of instances and the manner in which the Court reversed lower court rulings in the late 1960s and early 1970s are signs that the justices did not think their precedents were being interpreted correctly. Indeed, in obscenity cases the justices routinely disagreed with one another about how to read the precedents. In *Fanny Hill*, Clark, Harlan, and White criticized Brennan's plurality opinion for what they regarded as its revisionist interpretation of *Roth*. Lower courts tried to work with the obscenity tests outlined in *Fanny Hill*, but many found them difficult to interpret and disagreed with their logic. In addition, the number and diversity of conflicting Supreme Court opinions, the lack of a stable majority, and the modifications that were introduced created situations in which federal and state judges felt more free than usual to take liberties in their interpretations of precedents.

This does not necessarily mean that federal and state court readings of the Court's obscenity decisions followed the pattern described for their readings of *Griswold*, *Loving*, *Eisenstadt*, and *Roe*. Lower courts tended to be more sexually censorious than the Supreme Court was, and in many instances this led the Court to reverse anti-obscenity rulings by lower courts. To the extent that the lower courts based their rulings on Supreme Court precedents, this suggests that lower court judges tended to read the precedents as permitting more censorship than the justices did. But a new conservative majority coalesced in a set of obscenity cases decided in 1973, and these justices interpreted *Fanny Hill* not only as too liberal but as more liberal than the dissenters claimed it was. This was another instance in which readers of the Court's decisions portrayed them as more sexually liberal than the texts of the decisions stated or implied.

IN THE 1960S AND 1970S, many legal scholars joined their counterparts in the media and the courts in interpreting the *Griswold* to *Roe* rulings as decisions that supported sexual freedom and equality. In 1980, Stanford University law professor Thomas Grey surveyed forty-one law review articles published from 1965 to 1979 that "addressed the relationship between constitutional privacy . . . and legal prohibitions of consensual adult sex." According to Grey, the Court's rulings emphasized marital privacy and reproductive rights, yet "*Griswold* and its progeny were . . . read as leading toward a constitutional right of sexual freedom." Grey argued that "the *Griswold* opinions contained no hint of any endorsement of the sexual freedom of consenting adults" and "the Court has given no support to the notion that the right of privacy protects sexual freedom." In his view, "the Court meant what it said in *Griswold*: that the right of privacy protects only the historically sanctified institutions of marriage and the family, and has no implication for laws regulating sexual expression outside of traditional marriage." Grey stressed that in the 1973 *Paris* case the Court "decisively rejected the claim" that "the Constitution protects the right of consenting adults to engage in any sexual practices that cannot be shown to cause concrete harm." Nevertheless, of the articles identified by Grey, "almost all . . . found support in the privacy cases for the libertarian position on sexual morals legislation" and "only three could be read as negative or seriously equivocal on the question whether the *Griswold-Eisenstadt* doctrine, read fairly, supported adult sexual freedom." The vast majority "took the view that the better, natural, principled reading of the privacy cases would bring the sexual relations of consenting adults within the protection of the constitutional right of privacy." Grey did not discuss *Boutilier* and he only considered obscenity rulings insofar as they dealt with sexual privacy, but his conclusions are supported by a broader survey of the work of legal scholars in this period. Like the mainstream media, the gay and lesbian media, and federal and state courts, legal studies scholarship frequently obscured the extent to which the Court had adopted a heteronormative doctrine that granted special rights and privileges to marital, heterosexual, and reproductive forms of sexual expression.[65]

Grey was unusual in challenging these interpretations, but he joined the scholars he criticized in expressing optimism about the future of sexual freedom. Grey's conclusion declared, "I expect that within a few years fornication and sodomy laws will be found unconstitutional, on something like the very dogma of the right of consenting adults to control their own sex lives that the Court has until now so rigorously avoided." The reason, Grey claimed, "will have little to do with any notion in the justices' minds that sexual freedom is essential to the pursuit of happiness," but "will respond to the same demands of order and social stability that have produced the contraception and abortion decisions." He explained, "Thousands of couples are living together today outside of marriage. The fornication laws, otherwise empty formalities as they are, stand in the way of providing a stable legal framework for handling child rearing and property questions within these unions." Meanwhile he noted that "the homosexual community is becoming an increasingly public sector of our society" and "for that community to be governed effectively, it must be recognized as legitimate." Grey continued, "Perhaps something like marriage will have to be recognized for homosexual couples, not because *they* need it for their happiness (though they may), but because *society* needs it to avoid the insecurity and instability generated by the existence in its midst of a permanent and influential subculture outside the law." Grey predicted that because some "conservatives" will not see "this conservative necessity" and will block legislative change, the Court "will then step in and play its traditional role as enlightened conservator of the social interest in ordered stability, and will strike down those laws." As the next chapter demonstrates, these types of optimistic predictions were easier to make when *Boutilier* was forgotten and ignored.[66]

As a profoundly and transparently conservative ruling, *Boutilier* presented problems for those committed to the notion that the Court's doctrine was expansively liberal and liberalizing. Much of the mainstream and legal press resolved this problem by ignoring *Boutilier*, downplaying its significance, or emphasizing that the ruling concerned the limited rights of aliens rather than the full rights of citizens. As for judges, some acknowledged the central holdings of *Boutilier*, but others found ways to limit and qualify the decision's conservative meanings. Gay and lesbian periodicals initially denounced the ruling in *Boutilier*, but soon began to ignore and forget the case, partly because it concerned aliens, partly because it was not viewed as a useful precedent, and partly because of the historical amnesia that developed after New York City's Stonewall riots of 1969, when many gay liberationists and lesbian feminists began to dismiss the homophile struggles of the past. Clive Boutilier was ignored and forgotten as well. Deported from U.S. territorial space, he was also deported from U.S. collective memory.

Mainstream Media

In November 1967, the *New York Times Magazine* published "Civil Rights and the Homosexual," a lengthy article asserting that "attitudes toward homosexuality seem to be changing," but "laws are not." Accompanying the text by journalist Webster Schott was a photograph of a homophile movement demonstration in Philadelphia with a caption that declared, "Our sex attitudes have been updated—in some ways, drastically—but our sex laws are still those a Mayflower Pilgrim would approve." According to Schott, "To make private sexual acts between consenting adults an issue of morality, not law, is the first goal of those who care about the phenomenon of homosexuality in the United States." He observed, however, that "the United States homosexual wants more than freedom from prosecution as a sodomite." Activist Drew Shafer was quoted as saying that the "average homosexual . . . would really like to feel like a citizen." Summarizing Shafer's point, Schott wrote that the homosexual "wants to be free to pursue homosexual love, free to serve in the armed forces, free to hold a job or advance in his profession, free to champion the cause of homosexuality." Several of those interviewed "spoke seriously of the homosexual's desire for binding, legal homosexual marriage."

According to Schott, achieving these goals would require "dramatic changes in law," which could be accomplished in two ways. Following the lead of Illinois, legislatures or courts in the other forty-nine states could strike down all state sodomy laws, which Schott said was "about as likely as the sun's dropping from the sky." Alternatively, the Supreme Court could "render a decision declaring unconstitutional all state laws that attempt to regulate sexual behavior between consenting adults in private." This, observed the article, was "far more likely." "Eventually," Schott argued, "laws must change in response to new mores." With great confidence, he declared that the *Griswold* decision suggested that "if not next year or the next, then five years or ten years hence the United States Supreme Court will strike down existing state laws which make practicing homosexuals criminals." Schott predicted more broadly that "the right to have sex without state intrusion must inevitably be confirmed and codified by the Court." He explained this by asserting that the function of "sex in a modern industrialized society" had "changed from reproduction to pleasure" and "the effect of the Court's contraceptive decision was to note that reality."

In fact, Schott thought that change might occur quite soon. According to his article, "Curiously, the Supreme Court in modern times has not been confronted with a clear-cut case dealing with convictions in a state court of sodomy violations in private by mutual consent." ACLU chapters were looking for petitioners who could challenge sodomy laws, and Schott noted that "the Court appears destined to hear cases that may prepare the Justices for thinking through the place of law in the bedroom." For example, the Court "has been asked to hear a challenge to the New York vagrancy law that makes it a criminal offense for men to wear women's clothing in public." Moreover, the Second Circuit recently interpreted "the elusive euphemism 'psychopathic personality'" in U.S. immigration statutes "to mean the barring of homosexuals from this country," but the Ninth Circuit "twice ruled that section of the immigration law void for vagueness." According to Schott, "The Supreme Court will have to resolve the difference and may find opportunity to express itself on the constitutional rights of homosexuals."[1]

As we have seen, Schott was not alone in his confidence. Discussing sodomy law reform in 1965, homophile activist Clark Polak declared, "We see the solution within the Federal Court system, with the Supreme Court as the final voice. The Connecticut birth control decision points the way—invasion of privacy. Clear appreciation of the value of Church-State separation is another." In 1968, New York University law professor Gerhard Mueller told the *Wall Street Journal* that "until recently it would have been difficult" to get the Court to rule on a case challenging state laws against fornication, adultery, and sodomy, but "now . . . the court would declare them invalid as 'cruel and unusual punishment.'" In his 1972 book *Race, Marriage, and the Law*, Robert Sickels reached a similarly optimistic conclusion: "The taboo against homosexuality . . . is as strong as any in the culture and stronger even than the fear of miscegenation. For the Supreme Court to implant a homosexual bill of rights in the Fourteenth Amendment, though a logical extension of honored principles, is unlikely today. . . . But perhaps in 1975 and again in 1980 the Court will turn aside cases raising the issues, decide a secondary issue in 1985, and then, when the legal aspects of homosexuality are no longer controversial— let us say in 1990—it will hand down a ruling for homosexuals as comprehensive, and as quietly received, as *Loving*."[2]

From the perspective of the twenty-first century, it is easy to laugh at these predictions. State sodomy laws were struck down in 2003, not 1968, 1977, or 1990. Even after the Court took this step in *Lawrence*, it did not declare unconstitutional "all state laws that attempt to regulate sexual behavior between consenting adults in private." The "legal aspects of homosexuality" remain controversial. And *Lawrence* was not received "quietly." Perhaps even more open to criticism are Schott's comments about what, for him, was the present. Schott's article was published in November 1967, six months *after* the Court announced its ruling in *Boutilier*. By the time Schott's article appeared, Boutilier's lawyer Blanch Freedman was dead and Boutilier was in a New York hospital, having survived what may have been a suicide attempt. Around the time that Schott's article was published, the INS was trying to determine what to do about Boutilier given medical reports about his brain injuries, posttraumatic psychosis, and permanent disabilities.[3]

Several weeks after Schott's article was published, the *New York Times Magazine* published nine letters in response. Three were unsympathetic to sexual equality; six were sympathetic; none corrected Schott's mistake about the status of *Boutilier*. Schott's error and the absence of a letter calling attention to it are particularly noteworthy because the *New York Times* had covered the case as it proceeded through the courts. In July 1966, the newspaper published a seventeen-paragraph article after the Second Circuit ruled against Boutilier. In November, the *Times* presented nine paragraphs on the Supreme Court's decision to hear the case. Then in May 1967, the *Times* mentioned the final ruling briefly in two inventories of recent decisions and more expansively in a twelve-paragraph article headlined "High Court Denies Homosexual Plea." After summarizing the majority ruling and before turning to the "spirited" dissent, the *Times* noted, "The decision has limited effect, since it applies only to those who were homosexuals before they entered the country, and only to persons who entered between 1952 . . . and October 1965," when the INS began using the new "sexual deviation" amendment. This ignored the use of post-entry evidence in *Boutilier* and downplayed the clear indication that the Court would uphold the new statutory language. The article also did not consider the potential effects of the Court's comments about the power of Congress to define homosexuals as psychopaths and exclude aliens based on national, racial, and sexual "characteristics." Nevertheless, the story made it clear that the Court had issued a final ruling in *Boutilier*, which Schott and his editors apparently missed.[4]

The *New York Times* was not the only major periodical that made the mistake of placing the *Boutilier* ruling in the future, when it already had been announced. In the 1960s, perhaps no mass-circulation magazine in the United States devoted more space over a longer period of time to discussions about homosexuality than *Playboy*. The magazine created what may have been the country's most influential forum for public discussion about homosexuality during this period, and the Playboy Foundation, established in 1965, "aided individuals and their attorneys in challenging laws and policies that discriminate against people solely on the basis of their sexual orientation." This may seem surprising for a publication that aggressively promoted heterosexuality. But in several installments of Hugh Hefner's "Playboy Philosophy," which emphasized the rights of consenting adults to do as they wished in private, in dozens of letters published in the "Playboy Forum," and in interviews and roundtables with prominent public figures such as Allen Ginsberg and Gore Vidal, *Playboy* featured a wide range of comments on homosexuality.[5]

Playboy's letters to the editor began to address homosexuality and immigration in 1967. In July, an anonymous Chicago "homosexual" wrote that he had come to the United States in August 1965, just before "the statutes governing immigrants were changed to bar sexual deviates." The man recalled, "I . . . was a little perturbed at the rumors I had heard of the absurd American prejudice against homosexuality, but knew that in Illinois (my destination) homosexual acts in private between consenting adults were not illegal." Recently, however, he had learned about *Boutilier*. The man concluded, "Congress undoubtedly has the right to exclude whomever it pleases from the United States, but by labeling homosexuals psychopathic, it reflects also on the millions of American homosexuals born and bred in this 'land of the free.'" *Playboy*'s editorial response noted that the Second Circuit had ruled against Boutilier and the case was before the Supreme Court. "Hopefully," *Playboy* declared, "the high court will pay heed to Judge Leonard Moore's enlightened dissent." This was in an issue dated two months after the Court ruled against Boutilier.[6]

Two months later, *Playboy* published a letter from Joseph Murray of Hawaii, who praised Moore's "acute" observation that a broad definition of homosexuality would include "more than a few members of legislative bodies." Murray noted, however, that "the Supreme Court majority ignored it, ruling that homosexuals are, indeed, 'psychopathic' and, as such, can be deported." He concluded, "It is a dismaying example of hypocrisy that no Congressman has arisen to denounce the injustice in this deportation case and to propose legislation that would end this medieval governmental supervision of people's private sex lives."[7]

In December 1967, *Playboy* readers were reminded about the psychopathic personality statute when an anonymous man from Norway shared his story of migrating to the United States in 1959, obtaining a job as a hotel executive, and encountering trouble when he subscribed to two gay magazines. In Europe, similar publications were "sold openly," but in the United States his mail was "tampered with," he was "shadowed, both by car and on foot," and his "apartment was broken into and . . . a camera and a number of private papers and letters were taken." Then the INS ordered him to "come in for a 'hearing.'" There he was "confronted with evidence that could have been obtained only as a result of this burglary," as well as copies of letters to a friend in the U.S. Army. The writer continued, "I was questioned by psychiatrists in a military hospital, who concluded unanimously that I was a psychopath because I was homosexual. My own psychiatrist testified that, although I might have other problems, I was not a psychopath. He was overruled by Immigration authorities and I was deported within the month. The entire situation was handled in the same way that the Gestapo handled things in my country during the War."[8]

Playboy provided extensive information and commentary on U.S. sex laws, and those of its readers who looked at more than the photographs were likely among the U.S. Americans best informed in this area. So were the readers of *Sexology* magazine, which initially made the same mistake about *Boutilier*. The August 1967 issue of *Sexology*, published three months after the decision was announced, included an editorial that observed that the Court "now has before it" the case of Boutilier, "an admitted homosexual." Critical of the "psychopathic personality" law, the editorial mentioned the ACLU and HLRS briefs and noted proudly that the latter presented the views of "a long list of outstanding experts in the field—including four persons associated with *Sexology.*" The expert statements showed that "any attempt to classify a person solely on the basis of his sexual orientation was highly unscientific" and "grossly unjust." *Sexology* concluded, "This case is of importance not just to homosexuals, but to all persons who are concerned with the protection of constitutional guarantees and freedoms." Five months later, *Sexology* published a letter from Polak that highlighted the involvement of the HLRS in *Boutilier* and informed readers about the outcome: "Incredible or not, Boutilier was ordered to leave America."[9]

The fact that the *New York Times Magazine*, *Playboy*, and *Sexology* all published articles indicating that the *Boutilier* ruling was forthcoming when it had already been announced may reflect the limited media coverage the case received more generally. The *Wall Street Journal* published one sentence about *Boutilier* in its news highlights. The *Washington Post* and *Los Angeles Times* addressed the ruling briefly in their coverage of recent Supreme Court decisions. *Time* magazine covered the Second Circuit ruling in 1966, but not the final Supreme Court decision. In April 1967, the ACLU reported on the case in its weekly and monthly publications, but neither reported on the Court's May decision. Of the mainstream periodicals discussed in the last chapter, the vast majority did not report on the final *Boutilier* ruling.[10]

It may be tempting to assume that the lack of public attention reflected the invisibility of homosexuality in mainstream culture, but in 1967 the media provided extensive coverage of a national gay blackmailing ring, allegations about gay links to the assassination of President Kennedy, stories about homosexuals who worked for California governor Ronald Reagan, and a British gay spy scandal. There was coverage of electroshock treatments for homosexuality, religious perspectives on homosexuality, and police raids on gay bars, along with stories about homophile activism, homosexual law reform, and other gay-related court rulings. *America*, *Christian Century*, *Harper's*, *Look*, the *Nation*, the *New York Times*, *Newsweek*, *Philadelphia Magazine*, and *Time* all published significant stories on homosexuality in 1967. A press-clipping service used by *Drum* identified 1,964 newspaper and magazine articles on homosexuality in the twelve months preceding 30 November 1967.[11]

In the next few years, various mainstream media articles on homosexuality discussed legal reform, but these focused on issues other than immigration and highlighted legislative action and lower court rulings, not Supreme Court decisions. In one instance, *Philadelphia Daily News* columnist Tom Fox asserted that "the U.S. Supreme Court has never agreed to hear a homosexual case." This was in 1970, three years after *Boutilier* and more than a decade after *ONE*'s successful obscenity appeal. According to Fox, gay activist Frank Kameny had declared at a recent lecture, "We must fight for the recognition of the homosexual as a first-class citizen." Similar references to homosexuals as citizens, which ignored the problems confronting aliens, were made in "A Minority's Plea: U.S. Homosexuals Gain in Trying to Persuade Society to Accept Them," a front-page story in the *Wall Street Journal* in 1968. This article described federal agencies as "among the biggest targets" of legal reformers and highlighted the activities of the HLRS, but mentioned neither the INS nor *Boutilier*. Another article that mentioned the HLRS but not *Boutilier* was *Psychology Today*'s "Homosexual" by Martin Hoffman. According to Hoffman's 1969 essay, "The Homosexual Law Reform Society . . . wrote to a number of distinguished behavioral scientists, asking their opinions on the relation of homosexuality to psychopathology. The responses . . . supported the position that Dr. [Evelyn] Hooker and I hold: that homosexuals are not necessarily mentally ill." Hoffman mentioned neither the reason that HLRS collected the statements nor the Court's rejection of the argument.[12]

Why did the mainstream media not devote more attention to *Boutilier*? Homophile activists may have been reluctant to promote coverage of a decision that, from their perspective, was not a useful precedent. As for mainstream journalists, there are revealing hints in the stories discussed above. For instance, when Schott mentioned that Drew Shafer stated that the "average homosexual" wanted to feel "like a citizen," the assumption was that the "average homosexual" *was* a U.S. citizen. This was the position of the U.S. homophile movement in general, which privileged the concerns of citizens. *Boutilier* may have not seemed significant to the mainstream media because it concerned aliens rather than citizens. Schott's article also indicated that, while there were many issues on the homophile legal agenda, sodomy law reform was the critical one. To the extent that journalists regarded sodomy laws as the critical element in the legal treatment of homosexuality, they may have regarded immigration laws as marginal.

Perhaps the most revealing hint about why journalists ignored *Boutilier* is suggested by the fact that Schott misrepresented not only the status of the case but also the decision in *Griswold*, the birth control ruling that he said would lead inevitably to the end of sodomy laws. The justices had made it clear in *Griswold* that their constitutional vision did not extend to the "right to have sex without state intrusion" or the right of "consenting adults" to have sex "in private." Like the mainstream media articles discussed in the last chapter, Schott's feature presented the Court as developing an expansive and expanding vision of sexual freedom. In this context, *Boutilier* did not fit readily into the stories the mainstream media were telling about the Supreme Court's sexual revolution.

Legal Media

As the last chapter noted, legal journals joined the mainstream press in transforming the meanings of the Court's decisions on sex, marriage, and reproduction. In this context, legal journals paid little attention to *Boutilier*, a ruling that was difficult to reconcile with the image of the Court as sexually liberal.

In the 1950s, legal periodicals occasionally mentioned the provisions of the Immigration and Nationality Act challenged in *Boutilier*, and in the mid-1960s several discussed the 1965 sexual deviation amendment.[13] Four journals published articles on the Second Circuit's ruling in *Boutilier*. A short note in the *Catholic University Law Review* criticized the decision for ignoring the Ninth Circuit's holding in *Fleuti* that the "psychopathic personality" language did not provide adequate notice that post-entry conduct might be used to prove the existence of a pre-entry condition. A longer article by John Brock in the *San Diego Law Review* reviewed several key issues in the case, observed that "the behavior against which Congress attempted to legislate repels the ordinary person," and then added that "in reality, homosexuals as a group are neither particularly dangerous nor are they easily definable." He asked, "Is behavior which is contrary to the norm, even disgusting to most of the populace, justifiable grounds for exclusion?" After acknowledging that the country should not become "a haven for persons afflicted with various kinds of sexual deviations," Brock pointed out that epilepsy had been deleted as a basis for exclusion in light of "advanced medical knowledge." Along similar lines, "as the knowledge of psychosexual behavior develops . . . , Congress may see that the general classification of sexual deviates may include a number of persons who can be an asset to this country." Brock concluded that the INS should have "the latitude of making individual determinations as to whether an applicant for citizenship has a record of past behavior or a particular trait which will prevent him from becoming a useful member of a democratic society."[14]

The *NYU Law Review* also published a critical analysis of the Second Circuit ruling. According to the article, "It is not clear whether the congressional intent to exclude homosexuals extends to any person who has undergone at least one homosexual experience or is limited to those evidencing a long-standing condition with frequent activity." The article also stated that the term psychopathic personality was "seriously deficient" and that even among medical experts there was "no consensus" regarding its "appropriate use." Conceding that the dissenting opinion "extends the fiction of the vagueness doctrine to an unreasonable limit by imputing knowledge of the content of our laws . . . to persons throughout the world," the author contended that the argument was valid in *Boutilier* because the INS had relied on post-entry evidence. The article then pointed out that "the problems involved in the *Boutilier* case could have been alleviated to some extent had Congress more carefully chosen its terms." After observing that the 1965 sexual deviation amendment was "an improvement," the author noted that "if Congress desired to exclude all homosexuals, it should have done so explicitly."[15]

The fourth article on the Second Circuit ruling, authored by Marc Kaplin and published in the *Villanova Law Review*, criticized the court's interpretation of the relationship between exclusion and deportation. According to Kaplin, "If an entering alien must be given a medical examination in order to be certified a psychopathic personality and therefore excludable at the time of entry, and excludability at the time of entry is the crucial prerequisite to his present deportability, does it not follow that he must now be given a medical examination to establish excludability?" Kaplin also discussed the vagueness argument, raising questions about the meaning of the terms "sexual deviate" and "homosexual" and asking, "Is the evidence of Boutilier's pre-entry behavior persuasive enough to justify a determination that he is a homosexual or sexual deviate?" He concluded that "Congress has the right to exclude whomever it pleases," but "in this case classification is based on open-ended medical terms, the nature and extent of which are not agreed upon by competent medical authority." Noting that the Supreme Court had accepted *Boutilier* for review, Kaplin expressed the hope that the justices would resolve the vagueness issue and determine whether medical examinations were required.[16]

With this level of interest in the Second Circuit's ruling, it might be expected that the Supreme Court decision would have been the subject of significant discussion in law journals. But in the years immediately following the ruling, only one law review article examined *Boutilier*. Authored by Thomas Byrne Jr. and Francis Mulligan, the article appeared in a special 1967 issue of *Temple Law Quarterly* that focused on psychiatry and law. Its overall conclusions were critical, declaring that "an aberration in the development of constitutional due process is likely to result from the tyranny of the labels 'psychopathic personality' and 'sexual deviation.'" Byrne and Mulligan's main point was that if the labels were medical then deportation required a medical examination; if the labels were legal then the statute was unconstitutionally vague.[17]

First, the article developed the argument for medical examinations. Citing a variety of scientific authorities, Byrne and Mulligan defined a psychopath as a person with an incurable mental illness characterized by antisocial outbreaks and recidivism. Using this as a guide, they argued that, medically speaking, homosexuals were not necessarily psychopaths. Some homosexual behavior was the product of single-sex "institutional settings" or periods in life when the libido might be "channeled in a homosexual direction." Moreover, the authors noted that many homosexuals felt "guilt or shame" about their condition, whereas psychopaths lacked guilt or remorse. As for antisocial behavior, the article asserted that homosexuals generally avoided disclosing their tendencies to family members and coworkers and tried to contain their sexual urges, while the psychopath acted "with manifest indifference to his social environment." In terms of recidivism, many homosexuals did not have "repeated brushes with the law." Finally, the authors claimed that "homosexuality can often be 'cured.'" For these reasons, the article concluded that medical examinations were necessary to prove that a homosexual was a psychopath.[18]

Byrne and Mulligan then offered an argument that had not been emphasized by Boutilier's lawyers: that there was a divergence between the official INS position, which was that medical examinations were not required, and several unreported decisions of the Board of Immigration Appeals (BIA) and a federal district court, which treated psychopathic personality as "a medical term requiring expert medical diagnosis." Among these were decisions holding that admissions of homosexual conduct and convictions for sexual crimes were insufficient in the absence of medical examinations. In a footnote, Byrne and Mulligan suggested that the BIA did not report these cases because it wanted to preserve "precedential consistency in its reported cases, and still allow itself to do justice in individual cases."[19]

Byrne and Mulligan next turned to the alternative position, which was based on the notion that the term "psychopathic personality" was legal rather than medical. From this perspective, they argued that the law presented problems of vagueness. Responding to the notion that vagueness did not apply since Boutilier was being deported for pre-entry characteristics rather than post-entry conduct, Byrne and Mulligan pointed out that this position was "operationally unsound" since post-entry conduct is what generally led to these types of proceedings. In light of this, the authors argued that "due process should require that the alien be forewarned that homosexual behavior in the United States may lead to subsequent deportation."[20]

Byrne and Mulligan proceeded to argue that similar problems were now presented by the 1965 sexual deviation amendment: because "sexual deviation" had not been defined by Congress, "the wide variety of sexual conduct considered deviant within various regions of the United States" meant that "uniform application of the law is scarcely possible." Would officials regard as deviant "any pattern of sexual behavior which differs from normal coitus"? How much "homosexual experience" was necessary to define a person as a "sexual deviant"? What about "fornication, adultery and masturbation"? Byrne and Mulligan also raised the issue of cultural and national differences: "Suppose an alien before entering the United States engaged in what we would consider deviant sexual behavior, but which conformed to the prevailing practices of his former peer group without violating the laws of his native land. The important question would seem to be not whether his conduct was deviant by our standards, but whether he was capable of understanding and likely to conform to the standards of his new environment." In a footnote, they observed that "many homosexuals from Belgium, Denmark, Greece, Italy, Spain, or Sweden would be in such a situation."[21]

Byrne and Mulligan saved a final criticism for their conclusion, where they pointed out that the Supreme Court "has held that individuals cannot be punished for manifestations of an illness; they must be treated." Referring to recent rulings on drug addiction and alcoholism, they argued that the criminalization of disease had been classified as "cruel and unusual punishment." If homosexuality was an illness, deportation of aliens on the basis of homosexuality constituted punishment based on illness.[22]

Byrne and Mulligan's article was marked by some of the same ambivalence about homosexuality found in the arguments of Boutilier's advocates, but it is also the exception that proves the rule that law reviews, like mainstream periodicals, expressed minimal interest in Boutilier. The lack of attention is particularly striking given the interest shown by law journals in homosexuality during this period. The regulation of same-sex sexual conduct was discussed in more than two dozen law review articles in the 1960s and early 1970s, and court rulings on antihomosexual employment discrimination, homosexuality in the military, and sodomy convictions received significant attention. Boutilier was almost never cited or discussed in these articles.[23] In an exceptional instance, Robert Evans mentioned Boutilier in a footnote in "The Crimes Against Nature," which was published in the Journal of Public Law in 1967. Referring to a 1963 article by Louis B. Schwartz, Evans wrote, "As to the Supreme Court's attitude toward the existing laws concerning homosexuality, Schwartz considers indicative One . . . , in which the Court reversed an obscenity conviction of a magazine which was avowedly published for, by, and about homosexuals and which championed elimination of the sodomy laws. See also Boutilier." Evans neglected to mention that Boutilier cast considerable doubt on Schwartz's optimistic assessment. More generally, law journals in this period ignored *Boutilier*, which was consistent with their presentation of the Supreme Court as affirming rights of sexual freedom and equality.[24]

Judges and Justices

While the mainstream and legal press paid little attention to *Boutilier*, the ruling was invoked by U.S. courts and administrative tribunals in several different contexts. Some interpreted *Boutilier* in ways that limited its application, but others invoked it in ways that recognized, affirmed, and extended the heteronormative doctrine.

Two gay immigration decisions were appealed to the Supreme Court around the same time that the Second Circuit ruling in *Boutilier* was appealed. In *Lavoie*, the INS challenged the Ninth Circuit's 1966 decision, which used the vagueness doctrine to overturn the deportation of a permanent resident who had been classified as a "psychopathic personality." Two weeks after *Boutilier* was announced, the Court reversed the Ninth Circuit's decision, but several months later the justices amended the decision. Citing *Boutilier*, the Court remanded the case to deal with a new question: whether Lavoie was a homosexual when he entered the United States in 1960. In 1968, the BIA reconsidered the case. Acknowledging Lavoie's claim that he "had intercourse with females about two dozen times during the time he was in the Navy (up to 1945) and approximately seven or eight times after he left the Navy," the BIA nonetheless concluded that "the evidence that the respondent engaged in repeated homosexual acts 12 to 24 times a year over a period of 11 years which preceded his entry into the United States . . . establishes that he was a homosexual at the time of entry." Moreover, Lavoie "admitted that he was a homosexual" in 1961. Asserting that *Boutilier* was "remarkably similar on the facts," the BIA explained that "in that case the alien had a long-continued but somewhat less active history of homosexual relations prior to his entry into the United States and had also engaged in heterosexual relations on several occasions." When the Ninth Circuit reconsidered *Lavoie* in 1969, it reviewed Lavoie's sexual history and his 1961 guilty plea on a charge of committing a lewd, obscene, and indecent act. The court concluded, "The Boutilier case is controlling in the case before us. In both, the person ordered to be deported had frequently, over a period of years before entry engaged in homosexual acts. Each was a person who, in common opinion, would be regarded as a homosexual." Psychiatric evaluations were "irrelevant" in light of *Boutilier*. Over the objections of Douglas, the Supreme Court denied Lavoie's final appeal in 1970.[25]

The Court did not invoke *Boutilier* when it denied *cert* in *Tovar*, but *Boutilier* likely influenced the decision. In this case, the Ninth Circuit upheld the deportation of an alien convicted three times of lewd vagrancy in public bathrooms, which made him ineligible for suspension of deportation because he was not a "person of good moral character." *Boutilier* was probably not cited because the deportation was not based on affliction with psychopathic personality at time of entry; it was based on failure to demonstrate good moral character after entry. Nevertheless, the timing of the ruling, which occurred three weeks after *Boutilier* was announced, suggests the influence of the decision.[26]

In the next several years, several courts invoked *Boutilier* in cases not directly related to gay immigration, most commonly in rulings that addressed the vagueness doctrine and the powers of Congress to exclude aliens with specified characteristics.[27] There were also several courts and tribunals that referenced *Boutilier* in cases dealing with immigration, naturalization, and sexuality. In 1967, the BIA's decision in *Steele* upheld the deportation of a Canadian citizen as a "person of constitutional psychopathic inferiority" based on evidence of homosexuality before entry in 1952. According to the BIA, *Boutilier*'s logic suggested that "proof an alien was a homosexual at the time of entry would be sufficient to find he was deportable." Rejecting the argument that Steele was being excluded on the basis of post-entry evidence, the BIA concluded that the deportation was based on post-entry admissions concerning pre-entry "homosexual tendencies" and "homosexual relations."[28]

In *Campos* (1968), the Ninth Circuit referenced *Boutilier* in a case that also concerned immigration and homosexuality. Crisologo Redondo Campos, a citizen of the Philippines, had lived in the United States since 1954, first as a non-immigrant visitor and then as a student. After Campos applied for permanent residency in 1965, the INS learned that he had twice been convicted of public indecency and lewd conduct, classified him as a sexual deviate, and began deportation proceedings. Rejecting Campos's claim that the psychopathic personality provision did not apply because his "problem developed several years after he was inspected and admitted to the United States," the Ninth Circuit concluded that whereas *Boutilier* concerned an alien who was deportable because he was "a homosexual *upon entry*," this case concerned a request for permanent resident status, which "requires him to be currently admissible."[29]

Boutilier was less useful as a precedent for courts more sympathetic to the appeals of gay and lesbian aliens; in such situations *Boutilier* was best ignored or its facts distinguished from the case at hand. *Boutilier* was not invoked by the Supreme Court of New York in *Schmidt*. Olga Schmidt, a citizen of Denmark who immigrated to the United States in 1948, filed a petition for naturalization in 1961. At a hearing in 1962, Schmidt acknowledged having sex with a girlfriend over a six-year period in Denmark and with two women in the United States over a twelve-year period. After the INS initiated deportation proceedings on the grounds that Schmidt was a sexual deviate at time of entry, the BIA terminated the proceedings because the INS failed to prove its case. When her naturalization hearings resumed, however, the INS held that "the nature and extent of petitioner's homosexual activities were more clearly established." These included sexual relations with six women with whom she had lived successively. Based on the evidence of these relationships, the INS denied the naturalization petition in 1967 because Schmidt had not met the requirement of "good moral character" for five years. In 1968, the Supreme Court of New York dismissed Schmidt's appeal, concluding that "her admitted practices of these sexual deviations continually during the five years preceding the filing of her petition, are not . . . consistent with good moral character as the 'ordinary man or woman' sees it." It is likely that *Boutilier* was not invoked because *Schmidt* concerned an application for citizenship and the requirement of "good moral character," not a deportation based on psychopathic personality. Perhaps more importantly, *Boutilier* would not have been a good case to cite given what appears to have been the court's interest in finding a path to citizenship for Schmidt. In the final lines of its decision, the court noted that its "dismissal is without prejudice to the filing of a new petition" and sent a message about its meaning by observing that, now that more time had passed, "there is no evidence in the record before the court of homosexual practices within the past five years."[30]

For similar reasons, *Boutilier* was not mentioned in *Matter of Belle*, a 1969 federal district court decision that found that a "bisexual with homosexual tendencies" could meet the "good moral character" requirement for naturalization because he had not broken New York's law against "deviate sexual intercourse." While the judge noted that *Belle* did not present "a generic issue, the resolution of which will serve as a decisional rubric for others," he concluded that Belle was "no more than an ailing person whose compulsive behavior, private, unobtrusive and noncriminal, does not offend community standards unless brought to its notice by official inquisition." His "secret actions are unpleasantly peculiar," but "he would not be fairly dealt with were there added to the burden of his involuntary sickness the characterization that he lacks the good moral character the statute demands."[31]

While courts limited the application of *Boutilier* by not invoking it in *Schmidt* and *Belle*, in *Labady* a federal district court limited *Boutilier's* application by distinguishing the facts. According to the 1971 ruling, Manuel Labady was a citizen of Cuba who had entered the United States at age fourteen in 1960. Despite making it known to INS officials when he entered the country that he had been a homosexual in Cuba, he was not certified as a psychopathic personality, possibly because U.S.-Cuban tensions after the Cuban Revolution led to exceptional treatment of Cuban immigrants. The court explained, "Since petitioner validly entered the country without deceit, the Service concedes that he is not now deportable." In 1969, however, Labady filed a naturalization petition, which the INS rejected because, insofar as "he has been a homosexual," he had not established that "within the five years immediately preceding the date of filing his petition he 'has been and still is a person of good moral character.'" In a footnote, the court explained that "*Boutilier* does not control the present case . . . because petitioner in this case was lawfully admitted" and *Boutilier* involved at least one "episode" of "public homosexuality."[32]

Turning to the issue of "good moral character," the court noted that "if the criterion were our own personal moral principles, we would deny the petition, subscribing as we personally do to the general 'revulsion' or 'moral conviction or instinctive feeling' against homosexuality." The court argued, however, that this should not be the criterion, noting instead that "the most important factor to be considered is whether the challenged conduct is public or private." Public conduct could "pose a threat to the community," whereas with private conduct "the likelihood of harm to others is minimal and any effort to regulate or penalize the conduct may lead to an unjustified invasion of the individual's constitutional rights." Describing what rights it had in mind, the court referenced *Griswold*, which "established that official inquiry into a person's private sexual habits does violence to his constitutionally protected zone of privacy," and *Stanley*, which upheld the "'right to be free . . . from unwarranted governmental intrusion into one's privacy.'" The court concluded that "to hold otherwise would be to encourage governmental inquisition into an applicant's purely personal private temperament and habits," including "masturbation, autoeroticism, fornication, or the like." Responding to the INS contention that Labady had broken New York's sodomy law, the court asserted that "the statute does not specifically extend to consensual sodomy performed *in private*" and a violation of sodomy law, like a violation of fornication law, "would not necessarily preclude a finding of good moral character." Again citing *Griswold* and *Stanley*, the court also argued that "to the extent that these laws seek to prohibit and punish private homosexual behavior between consenting adults, they are probably unconstitutional." According to the court, Labady had "led a quiet, peaceful, law-abiding life," he was "gainfully employed"; "he has submitted to therapy that was unsuccessful"; and "he has not corrupted the morals of others, such as minors, or engaged in any publicly offensive activities." In these circumstances, the court ruled in favor of Labady.[33]

Labady's interpretation of *Griswold* and *Stanley*, which invoked a notion of sexual privacy that the Supreme Court had never endorsed, was consistent with many of the interpretations discussed in chapter 6. But here the interpretation took an additional step as the court claimed that aliens, along with citizens, could claim a right of sexual privacy. As for its interpretation of *Boutilier*, *Labady* suggested that the critical issues were public homosexual conduct and deception at the border. In relation to the former, it is worth noting that the evidence of public sex in *Boutilier* was limited. As for the latter, *Labady* suggested that aliens at the border had a difficult choice: admit one's homosexuality and be vulnerable to immediate exclusion or withhold such information and be vulnerable to deportation based on deception.

While *Labady* limited the application of *Boutilier* in a very specific and unusual set of circumstances, the Second Circuit's 1973 ruling in *Kovacs* clarified the limitation. The case concerned a Hungarian citizen who had entered the United States as a permanent resident in 1959 and applied for naturalization in 1968. In his application, Kovacs disclosed that he had been convicted on three occasions in the United States, once for engaging in homosexual conduct in a subway men's toilet, once for loitering, and once for engaging in homosexual activities in the men's room of a public theater. Questioned by a naturalization examiner, Kovacs claimed that "he was not now a homosexual, had never been one, and had never engaged in homosexual acts other than . . . in the two men's room incidents." According to the court, however, in a 1962 affidavit, Kovacs admitted to "a large number of homosexual acts, including about fifty acts of fellatio per year since 1959." Following this admission, Kovacs was certified as a psychopathic personality by a PHS psychiatrist, but INS deportation proceedings were discontinued after the Ninth Circuit's 1962 ruling in *Rosenberg*. Six years later, Kovacs told the naturalization examiner that the contents of the affidavit he signed in 1962 were untrue. The examiner concluded that the "petitioner's denials in the face of the evidence are incredible," but recommended naturalization, citing *Labady* and noting that there was no evidence that Kovacs had engaged in any homosexual acts in the five years preceding his petition. The INS, however, continued to pursue the case, and in 1971 a judge denied Kovacs's petition, arguing that "petitioner's lack of candor . . . is in itself incompatible with any reasonable standard of good behavior." Two years later, the Second Circuit upheld the judge's determination. Emphasizing that "petitioner is not being denied naturalization for his sexual activities—but rather for his lack of candor under oath," the court explicitly distinguished his case from that of Labady. "Had Kovacs testified truthfully about his past," the court asserted, "the petition might well have been granted." In a footnote, the court noted with "sympathy" Kovacs's claim that his record since his 1962 arrest was "unblemished." The court concluded that "if his apparently exemplary public behavior continues, a greater exhibition of candor at a later date might well lead to a different result in his efforts to become a citizen." Now aliens applying for naturalization faced a similar choice to the one facing aliens at the border: tell the truth about one's homosexuality and risk exclusion or withhold information and be vulnerable to deportation based on deception.[34]

In one final ruling in 1973, the D.C. Circuit invoked *Boutilier* to buttress its contention that homosexuality should be understood as a form of sexual perversion. The ruling covered three linked cases, *Gayer*, *Ulrich*, and *Wentworth*, all of which involved Defense Department denials of security clearance on grounds of sexual perversion. In the latter, Benning Wentworth's clearance was denied when in 1966 the Department learned that he "may have engaged in certain homosexual activity with a high school senior in 1964." After Wentworth appealed, an examiner concluded that, "on the basis of appellee's past homosexual activity and his intention to continue such activity," he was "engaging in both criminal conduct and sexual perversion," each of which were grounds for denying security clearance. The examiner also found Wentworth vulnerable to "coercion and influence," another ground for denying clearance. The D.C. Circuit subsequently issued a mixed ruling, declaring that security clearances could be denied if there was a rational basis for the conclusion that an employee's homosexuality was inconsistent with the national interest and if the employee was questioned about his sexual life in a reasonable and limited way. One section of the opinion considered Wentworth's claim that homosexual conduct was not a form of sexual perversion. Excerpting a passage from *Boutilier* that referred to the congressional intent to exclude "all homosexuals and other sex perverts," the D.C. Circuit stated that "we think it clear that 'sexual perversion' . . . must be construed as intended to include homosexual activity."[35] *Boutilier* was rarely cited or invoked by judges in the late 1960s and early 1970s, but when it was, the results tended to support the doctrine of heteronormative supremacy.

Gay and Lesbian Media

Boutilier was a topic of significant interest for a short period of time in the gay and lesbian press, which interpreted the decision in distinct ways. To begin with, the coverage was more extensive than it was in the mainstream press. Beginning in August 1966, homophile periodicals published stories covering each stage in the legal process. *Drum* and the *Janus Society Newsletter* published the largest number of stories and the most detailed ones, which is not surprising given their organizational links to the HLRS. *Drum*, for instance, devoted much of its March 1967 issue to excerpts of the HLRS brief, which appeared alongside photographs of nearly nude young men. Some readers objected to *Drum*'s focus on legal matters. A letter from Pennsylvania to the editor stated, "Perhaps some Drum readers appreciated the long article on the Boutilier deportation case, but I would have preferred just that many more pictures." One from Washington complained, "I don't want to join a 'movement.' I just want to subscribe to a groovy magazine. That's why I think you should spend more time making Drum bigger and better and much less on legal matters." A reader from Ohio wrote, "What's this nonsense about printing Supreme Court briefs in Drum? What's the matter, you running out of ideas?" For *Drum*, *Boutilier* was significant not only as a newsworthy legal case but also as a tool for politicizing and mobilizing the gay community.[36]

Homophile press coverage of *Boutilier* also differed from mainstream media coverage in situating the case within a longer history of Supreme Court decisions concerning homosexuality. This is not to say that every gay and lesbian press article avoided the mistake made by the *Philadelphia Daily News* columnist who declared in 1970 that the Court had never heard a gay rights case. Discussing *Boutilier* in its March 1967 newsletter, the New York chapter of the Daughters of Bilitis reported that the Court "has accepted a case involving the rights of a homosexual for review" and "it is believed to be the first such case to be considered by the high court." This claim may have been based on an HLRS press release, which asserted that "this case is the first involving the rights of a homosexual that the Supreme Court is known to have accepted for review." Most homophile periodicals did not identify *Boutilier* as the Court's first gay rights case, but the list of relevant prior cases was not self-evident. In December 1966, *Drum* reported in a "late news flash" that "for the first time since 1964" the Court had "agreed to hear a case involving homosexuality." In March 1967, *Drum* asserted that the Court had previously agreed to hear "three cases involving homosexuality": *ONE* (1958), *Manual* (1962), and *Dew*

(1964). The 1963 immigration ruling in *Rosenberg* and the 1966 obscenity rulings were not mentioned.[37]

As *Boutilier* made its way to the Supreme Court, the homophile press did not present many biographical details about the man at the center of the case. When Boutilier was described, some articles adopted the objective pose favored by the mainstream media, but some presented Boutilier more sympathetically. Many mentioned Boutilier's nationality, occupation, age, and sexual history. They did not highlight many of the respectable characteristics emphasized by Boutilier's lawyers, including his farming roots, family ties, work habits, or leisure activities, but they also did not mention his sodomy arrest. In fact, after noting that the government attempted to deport Boutilier "upon learning of his homosexuality," *Drum* asserted that "there are no other allegations against him." Mattachine New York's newsletter mentioned that there was "no question of being a dangerous character here" and reported that "two independent psychiatrists have examined him and found no pathology." Meanwhile, headlines such as "May They Stay in U.S.A.?" in *Homosexual Citizen*, a joint publication of two Mattachine groups, presented Boutilier as an immigrant who wanted to remain in the United States. The homophile press also highlighted the troubles Boutilier experienced as a result of his legal situation. In late 1966, *Drum* reported that "Boutilier was fired from his job as maintenance man shortly after the Court's acceptance was publicized," and Mattachine New York noted that Boutilier "lost his job because of the publicity."[38]

In the months leading up to the ruling, homophile periodicals were invested in the notion that Boutilier did not have a psychopathic personality, but they had greater interest in the more general claim that homosexuality was not psychopathological. In December 1966, Mattachine New York emphasized that the Court "will now be placed in the unusual position of deciding whether or not homosexuality is a 'sickness'!" In January 1967, *Drum* noted that the HLRS was in the process of collecting "more statements from psychiatrists and psychologists that, in their professional opinions, homosexuality is not psychopathology than were ever brought together before in history." Around the same time, the Janus newsletter reported that HLRS had contacted "a large number of psychiatrists, psychologists, sociologists, and anthropologists throughout the world and solicited their opinion." Then in March 1967, *Drum* declared that the central questions of the case were "whether or not it is moral to exclude homosexuals from U.S. citizenship under the ruse that we are—in the law's term—'psychopathic personalities'" and "whether the morality that condemns us is inferior or superior to the morality of truth." *Drum* then referred to the experts whose views had been solicited by the HLRS, noting that "twenty-eight replied that, in their professional opinions, homosexuality was not an illness," while "one replied saying he thought it was pathology." Shortly thereafter, DOB–New York's newsletter reported on the HLRS brief, with an editor's note that described "psychopathic personality" as "a psychiatric concept . . . defined as a person who has little or no superego (conscience)," a deficiency that "permits the person to lie, steal, cheat, etc., without guilt feelings." According to the newsletter, "Many years ago most schools of psychiatric thought included homosexuals in this class," but "about 20 years ago psychiatrists and psychologists began to change this viewpoint because they had homosexual patients *with* guilt feelings." The note concluded by emphasizing that "most leading schools of psychiatric thought no longer consider homosexuals as psychopaths." These formulations depicted the more pro-gay position as modern, scientific, and progressive.[39]

Homophile press coverage of *Boutilier* was distinctive not only because the gay and lesbian press did not typically pretend to be neutral observers of the news but also because it presented itself as part of a movement making news. *Drum*'s "news flash" announced that the HLRS, which was funded by *Drum*, would submit a brief and support the case financially. The Janus newsletter reported in December 1966 that it had "agreed to finance as much of the Boutilier Supreme Court case as is practical," provided an inventory of expenses totaling $1769.40, and noted that this did not include "even a small legal fee to the lawyer." Around the same time, Mattachine New York's newsletter mentioned that "all of these cases involve money, more money than MSNY has to give." In early 1967, *Drum* underscored its commitment by reporting that HLRS lawyers were "working through the Christmas holiday" on their brief. In January, the HLRS distributed a press release that announced the submission of its brief, described the HLRS as having "the international support of 15 thousand homosexuals and heterosexuals who are concerned with securing equal treatment for homosexuals," and depicted itself as "the largest such organization in America." Shortly thereafter, Polak announced in the Janus newsletter that the brief had been filed and declared, "Since I had little to do with its writing, I feel free to say that it is both masterful and complete. There is a frequent and unfortunate temptation to dramatize and/or over-state pleas for acceptance. Our attorney's brief . . . is a model of soft-spoken, quiet, concise, logical, perceptive reasoning."[40]

Nor did the homophile press view its readers as passive spectators. *Drum*'s initial article supplied information about how readers could obtain copies of the Second Circuit's opinion. *Drum* also informed readers that "contributions for Boutilier's subsistence or legal fees" could be sent to the HLRS or Blanch Freedman. After providing its inventory of *Boutilier* expenses, the Janus newsletter encouraged contributions to Janus. Mattachine New York's newsletter, after discussing its various cases, noted that "this isn't really the right place for a donation pitch," but declared that "you *can* help" and emphasized that "even if you think you're doing all right as is and don't need any new laws, think of the other guy." In an early 1967 update, *Drum* encouraged readers to send contributions to Janus and noted that "a minimum of $3,000 is needed." After the HLRS brief was filed, the Janus newsletter announced that it was selling copies for $1.00. Shortly thereafter, New York's Daughters of Bilitis chapter encouraged its newsletter readers to send contributions to Freedman. Then in May, the newsletter of Personal Rights in Defense and Education (PRIDE), which was the forerunner of the *Advocate*, published a letter from Polak thanking the Los Angeles homophile group for contributing money to Boutilier's defense.[41]

Another distinctive feature of homophile press coverage in the months leading up to the ruling was the emphasis on *Boutilier*'s importance. In March 1967, Mattachine New York's newsletter noted that the INS "is again victimizing homosexuals—in this case a thirty-nine-year-old lesbian who has been in the country for twenty years." This was Olga Schmidt, and the report about her case implicitly underscored the significance of the outcome in *Boutilier*. More explicitly, *Drum* declared, "Homophile leaders indicate that, regardless of the Court's decision [in *Boutilier*], the case will have ramifications affecting a significant percentage of America's homosexuals." Noting that "the specific issue is quite narrow," *Drum* pointed out that "the Court might make a pronouncement that will weaken—or strengthen—the Federal government's stand that homosexuals are unacceptable as Federal employees." Like the mainstream press, *Drum* downplayed the implications of *Boutilier* for aliens, but unlike the mainstream media the homophile press emphasized the case's significance.[42]

After the HLRS brief was filed, the homophile press simultaneously began to celebrate its accomplishments and dampen expectations. *Drum* noted that Boutilier had appealed to the Supreme Court, which "surprisingly" accepted the case for argument. Then *Drum* mentioned three earlier gay victories in Supreme Court cases, which seemed to convey optimism about *Boutilier*, but the magazine cautioned that "movement officials are not hopeful in this case" and the likelihood of success was "dim." Three reasons for pessimism were offered: "For one thing, an immigrant has very few rights until he becomes a citizen; for another, Congress has the legal right to decree what classes of

people will be either permitted or denied citizenship; and, possibly most damaging, it appears as if Congress intended to exclude homosexuals—even if we
are not 'psychopaths.'" These were striking public admissions to be making
as the Court was in the process of deciding *Boutilier*. *Drum* appears to have
been trying to lower expectations, perhaps because it was already looking forward to new struggles. Hedging its bets, *Drum* declared, "Whatever the eventual outcome, however, the Homosexual Law Reform Society has presented
a masterful plea for Boutilier and, through him, the 15 million or so other
homosexuals in America today." In short, *Drum* believed that the litigation
could have positive effects even if it was unsuccessful in its immediate goals.
After describing the central message of the HLRS brief, that homosexuality
was not psychopathological, the magazine reported that Polak gave the case
"only a 30% chance of succeeding," but noted that "such an appraisal is not as
pessimistic as it first appears" because "if some of the Justices issue dissenting
opinions—like Judge Moore's in the court below—the dissent could presage
events to come." *Drum* concluded, "Only time will reveal the outcome and the
movement for homosexual civil liberties and rights is just beginning to flourish. Time and ultimate morality are on our side."[43]

In March, the *Janus Society Newsletter* provided its readers with a short
but detailed report about the oral arguments. According to the newsletter,
"It is impossible, and a bit foolhardy, to attempt to predict what the final outcome will be from the questions the Justices asked, but it is apparent that the
amicus brief filed by the H.L.R.S. . . . made a positive impression on at least
three of the members of the Court." Stewart "told the Government attorney
that it appeared to him that the term 'psychopathic personality' was a code
word of some sort that no one but those on the in could understand to mean
homosexuality." The justice "asked if it had been applied to other persons or
groups" and when the lawyer said he did not know, Stewart "asked him to find
out." On 17 March, HLRS lawyer Gilbert Cantor "received a carbon of a letter
sent to Stewart which explained that though they could not point to specific
examples the Immigration and Naturalization Service was sure that it had
been applied elsewhere." The newsletter reported that Warren "said nothing
. . . but listened with rapt attention"; Douglas "spent the whole time 'writing
notes furiously'"; and Fortas was "among those who questioned the Government on their position that all homosexuals were 'psychopaths.'" If Janus was
predicting favorable votes from these four, it was prescient about Douglas and
Fortas but wrong about Stewart and Warren.[44]

The Court's May 1967 announcement of the *Boutilier* decision received significant coverage in homophile periodicals. Reactions were critical, though

some expressed more surprise than others. In July, the *Pride Newsletter* reported that Polak "deplored" the decision. In August, *Drum* described the ruling as "predicted." Mattachine New York's newsletter declared, "We were downright shocked to learn that the Supreme Court had handed down . . . the decision to uphold the deportation order."[45]

Much of the homophile press coverage criticized the ruling for ignoring the views of scientific experts. The *Pride Newsletter* cited Polak's comment that "the decision 'flew in the face of psychiatric opinion and logic.'" In August 1967, *Drum* published a letter from Kinsey associate Clyde Martin, who wrote that the HLRS brief "seems to be an excellent argument and one which goes to the heart of the matter." In the next issue, a letter from Nebraska stated, "I considered Lawyer Cantor's discussion of the homosexual sickness question one of the best I have ever seen, though I do take issue with his reference to Dr. Szasz. Szasz, according to Cantor, has pointed out that homosexuality is a rejection of heterosexuality. I would not consider this to be any more true than saying that heterosexuality is a rejection of homosexuality." *Drum* also published a response from a Wisconsin reader who asked, "If homosexuality is not a sickness, then what makes so many homosexuals sick?" A sarcastic response from Toronto, Ontario, declared, "I'm not sick, I just happen to prefer second class status. It gives one so much to strive for."[46]

One potential response to the ruling was to turn Boutilier into an icon, hero, or martyr, and though this did not occur in the long-term, some early homophile comments highlighted Boutilier's positive qualities. In *Sexology*, Polak referred to Boutilier's "refusal to lie to the INS about his homosexuality," which suggested honesty, strength, and courage, but Polak also mentioned Boutilier's "foolish" admission, which implied that he had been innocent and naive. *Pride Newsletter* referenced Boutilier's sodomy arrest, but noted that the charges had been dismissed, reported that "Boutilier lived a useful and productive life," and asserted that "it was his honesty" that led to his troubles. The newsletter of the New York Daughters of Bilitis cited Polak's assertions that "Boutilier's case was 'not complicated by any wrong-doing on his part,'" that he "'had a stable employment record and no criminal record,'" and that he "naively refused to lie . . . about his homosexuality." The DOB newsletter also emphasized that two psychiatrists "testified that they could find no symptoms of 'psychopathology.'" What others represented as foolish courage, honest transparency, or naive resistance, Mattachine New York portrayed as active protest, observing that "the Canadian had made no secret of his homosexuality, contesting the *law* rather than maintaining his innocence of any crime *under* the law." In fact, Boutilier had initially denied engaging in homosexual acts before entry and after his arrest; he was not appealing a criminal conviction; and his lawyers had questioned whether he could be classified as a homosexual. Mattachine New York apparently wanted to turn Boutilier into an out-and-proud gay activist.[47]

The homophile press also highlighted the Second Circuit and Supreme Court dissents. Mattachine New York concluded, "We are very grateful for Justice Douglas' voice among some rather harsh ones." According to *Drum*, "Those supporting the homosexual case were accorded a victory of sorts: Justice William O. Douglas issued an impassioned dissent that was accorded heavy publicity." This exaggerated the extent of the publicity, but *Drum* also made a more critical observation, reporting that "it is not clear why Justice Douglas noted that homosexuals had risen high in both the Congress and the executive branches of government while failing to include his own judiciary branch."[48]

While much of the homophile press coverage emphasized Boutilier's positive qualities and highlighted the dissents, there was less agreement about who or what should receive credit or blame for the outcome. Except for *Cases in Review*, the newsletter of the National Legal Defense Fund (NLDF), none of the post-ruling coverage mentioned Freedman. Mattachine New York mentioned neither the ACLU nor the HLRS, perhaps because of the conflicts over which organization would take the lead in supporting the litigation and perhaps because of Mattachine's longstanding conflicts with Polak and Janus. *Cases in Review*, which supported NLDF's efforts to become the national coordinator of gay rights litigation, did not mention the ACLU or the HLRS, reporting instead that the national DOB (which like the NLDF was based in San Francisco) had donated $1500 to the Fund and "requested that, if we found the case to be meritorious, a portion of the contribution be spent for the Boutilier case." After providing a brief report on the "adverse" outcome, along with status reports on three other cases, *Cases in Review* concluded that "our experience has made one thing clear: the Fund needs the right test case." "The test case must be carefully selected," the newsletter explained, "so that the facts will directly raise the issues of law we most want to challenge." The "'ideal' test case" would "confront prohibitive sexual laws at their most vulnerable points." These comments were implicitly critical of the actions HLRS had taken in relation to *Boutilier*. In contrast, the DOB–New York newsletter highlighted the roles of Polak and the HLRS, *Mattachine Midwest* emphasized the roles of Janus and the ACLU, and the *Pride Newsletter* mentioned the ACLU and HLRS, along with its own contributions. As for *Drum*, its August 1967 report explained that the Court rejected the HLRS's argument that "Congress was in error in classing homosexuals as 'psychopaths'" and the ACLU's argument that "the term 'psychopathic personality' was too vague to be meaningful."[49]

After the ruling was announced, the gay and lesbian press confronted a set of choices: Should it downplay the significance of *Boutilier* in order to promote optimism and hope about the future? Should it emphasize the case's importance as a way to mobilize and politicize readers? Homophile activists had viewed the Supreme Court as the branch of the federal government most likely to aid their cause, in part because the justices were appointed for life and were therefore insulated from unfavorable popular opinion, in part because of activists' assessment of the Court's role in recent civil rights struggles, and also because of their faith in the Constitution. In the context of a federal system, homophile activists also looked to the Court as a powerful institution capable of effecting national, rather than state or local, change. In this respect, too, the gay and lesbian press faced choices about how to cover law reform. Should it focus on the Supreme Court? Should it highlight legislative, executive, state, or local branches of government? Or should it emphasize changing minds rather than laws?

In the aftermath of *Boutilier*, some homophile commentators began to express doubts about strategies that depended on the Court. In a September 1967 discussion of parliamentary reform in Great Britain, which had decriminalized private homosexual acts by consenting adults, *Drum* observed, "Even this limited reform of the laws affecting homosexuals could not come about in America as it has in England. In the United States the courts have held that morals legislation, in most cases, is a matter for each state to decide independently." In 1968, the HLRS announced that it was pursuing sodomy law reform in Delaware through a legislative strategy and declared, "We hope that it will point to a practical road to sodomy law reform in the other states." Three years later, Walter Barnett, a lawyer involved in the Texas sodomy law challenge in *Buchanan*, wrote in the *Advocate* that future constitutional challenges to sodomy laws were not "worthless," but "the prospects for a successful challenge are now less promising." As an alternative, Barnett recommended legislative reform, arguing that "the chances of law reform by means of the legislatures are better now than they have ever been." Several weeks later, Barnett wrote that his earlier "forecast," which emphasized that "the prospects for law reform via the courts have been dimmed by very recent decisions," had been "confirmed" by the Court's ruling against Buchanan.[50]

Notwithstanding these comments, there is evidence that gay and lesbian hopes for legal reform still rested with the courts in general and the Supreme

Court in particular. Legislative and executive reform were also seen as key avenues for social change, but homophile activists had a difficult time imagining that elected officials, especially at the federal level and in more conservative parts of the country, would ever champion their cause. Summarizing the previous year's developments in an article published in early 1968, *Drum* observed, "It has been a great year for sex. If things continue in their current direction, it might even be legal some day soon." *Drum* continued, "The Supreme Court, probably unwillingly and through the default of lower courts and society as a whole, seems to have become the chief source of moral legislation, albeit legislation by court decree, in America today. That's an unhappy state of affairs, but a state that those who believe in a measure less of official restraint of matters sexual can profit from." Ignoring *Ginzburg, Mishkin,* and *Landau, Drum* noted that the justices continued to deny constitutional protection to obscenity, but they "just haven't seen any real obscenity in a long time." Ignoring the marital and reproductive focus of *Griswold,* the magazine continued, "They also found, in the famous Connecticut birth control decision, that sex, the hetero kind at least, can be had for pleasure alone." Turning to the legal record of Janus/H LRS, *Drum* noted, "The Society's legal batting average stands one won (Val's Bar), one lost (Boutilier's deportation case) and one still up for grabs (the test of Miami's antihomosexual bar ordinance)." The article concluded that "like the weather, change is inevitable and we're going to have plenty of it." Several months later, the *Ladder* reprinted a *Wall Street Journal* story that highlighted "a growing list of court cases" supported by the HLRS, NLDF, and Mattachine. Polak was quoted as saying that the HLRS formerly took cases "we couldn't avoid," but "now we are very much concerned with initiating litigation."[51]

The pages of the *Advocate,* first published in 1967 and for the next few decades the most widely circulating gay and lesbian periodical, bear witness to the movement's ongoing optimism about achieving legal reform through the courts. In its first several years of publication, the *Advocate* published articles on dozens of employment discrimination, gay bar, same-sex marriage, national security, obscenity, sex crime, and sodomy cases. In one of the first, which concerned a California gay bar case, attorney Herbert Selwyn promised to appeal to the Supreme Court if necessary and asserted that the Court had "already stated that homosexuals cannot be expected to have a higher standard of conduct than heterosexuals." When the Court declined to consider the appeal in 1968, Selwyn denied that this was a "great defeat" and reasoned, "It took over 100 years for many of the unjust race laws to be overruled by the courts. These other laws will fall in time." In 1969, the *Advocate* used the language of Thurgood Marshall's majority opinion in the *Stanley* obscenity case to ask, "Does an American have 'the right to satisfy his intellectual and emotional needs in the privacy of his home?'" After noting that the Court had answered this question affirmatively, the *Advocate* declared, "Thus an important precedent has been established for possible future challenges of laws which make crimes of voluntary sexual practices of adults in their homes." Before *Buchanan* was decided, Walter Barnett told the *Advocate*, "If, hopefully, the Supreme Court upholds the lower court (and it will be difficult, I think, for it to reverse a unanimous opinion of three lower federal judges), then all of the sodomy statutes of the 48 states that still have them will have been swept away in one fell swoop. Years and maybe decades of laborious effort to get each of the 48 legislatures to repeal these laws, or each of the 48 state Supreme Courts to declare them unconstitutional, will have been avoided."[52]

The election of Richard Nixon as U.S. president in 1968 and his four Supreme Court appointments were perceived as serious causes for concern, but did not lead the movement to turn away from court-based strategies. In August 1969, the Philadelphia-based *Homophile Action League Newsletter* declared, "Homosexuals join others committed to civil liberties in concern over the rightward drift of our society and its institutions. The Warren Court, with its many landmark decisions extending the application of the Bill of Rights, is no more. A new breed—the Burger Court—takes its place, and we must look realistically at what new challenges this fact will present to the homosexual." The newsletter pointed specifically to Burger's dissent at the appeals court level in *Scott*, in which the future chief justice "took the position that it *is* relevant for the [U.S. Civil Service] Commission to take into consideration private, consensual, adult homosexual acts when determining suitability for Federal employment." The article pointed out, however, that "one justice does not make a court" and then reproduced a statement by the North American Conference of Homophile Organizations: "Cases will have to be brought upon narrower and more formalistic Constitutional bases, and those will have to be crafted with greater care than they might have needed to be in the past.... We do not see the situation as necessarily dark or bleak—we feel that, in the long run, we have too much working for us—but we do not see it as being quite as bright as it would probably have been over the next decade had events led to a Court different from the one which seems likely to take form now."[53]

Undeterred, an *Advocate* editorial in 1970 proposed the creation of a Homosexual Civil Liberties Foundation or Homosexual Law Institute, whose "battery of lawyers" would "see the legal attack as the one most likely to yield the best results." By October 1971, an *Advocate* editorial was warning that "prospects at the highest level—the U.S. Supreme Court—are becoming more dismal." Still, the editorial noted that "no one . . . can ever say for sure what philosophy of law or government a Supreme Court justice will eventually take" and "other court members have wound up fooling the presidents who appointed them." "If we are lucky," the *Advocate* concluded, "perhaps the remaining justices on the High Court can hold up just long enough to outlast Nixon." Six months later, after the Court refused to review the *McConnell* employment discrimination case, an *Advocate* editorial claimed that the "shocking" decision "surprised nearly everyone," since "it seemed certain that victory would result." "We are incredulous at the court's refusal to grant to Gays the protections of the U.S. Constitution," the *Advocate* declared, and "the court's action drives home with the force of a sledgehammer how much the Nixon appointments to the Supreme Court have already destroyed the formerly liberal bent of that body." While the language used here was pessimistic about the future, there would have been no surprise and shock if the movement had not expected greater success. Several weeks later, a letter by Walter Barnett tried to revive gay and lesbian optimism by insisting that "you make too much of the court's action." Acknowledging the "bitter disappointment" in the *McConnell* decision, Barnett argued that a *cert* denial does not indicate "agreement or disagreement with the decision of the lower court" and "has no legal significance." Two years later, Barnett's *Sexual Freedom and the Constitution* presented a book-length argument about how to achieve homosexual law reform through constitutional litigation based on *Griswold*, *Eisenstadt*, and other precedents.[54]

In the short term, the homophile press presented *Boutilier* as a setback, and a few articles highlighted the negative implications for immigrants and aliens in particular. The *Pride Newsletter* reported that the decision "puts countless thousands of aliens in jeopardy." There were also occasional signs that, in the aftermath of *Boutilier*, the homophile movement would recognize the specific concerns of noncitizens. In 1968, when the North American Conference of Homophile Organizations adopted a "homosexual bill of rights," it included a statement that "a person's sexual orientation or practice shall not be a factor in the granting of Federal security clearance, visas and citizenship." In 1969, there was a brief revival of interest in *Boutilier* when another immigration case came to public attention. According to the *Ladder*, "We all remember the infamous deportation of a Canadian national from the United States recently, simply on the grounds of homosexuality." In February 1969, a federal judge in New York ruled that "the petition of one Mario Belle for citizenship could not be denied simply because the man describes himself as a bisexual with homosexual tendencies." The magazine explained that the judge had ruled that "as long as the man's sex life was with consenting adults he was still 'of good moral character.'" The INS, however, had appealed the ruling. "Undoubtedly 'big brother' will win, in a higher court," the *Ladder* concluded, "but in any case, there are some men in white hats sitting on the court bench." Along similar lines, Ada Bello, a Cuban immigrant, published an article on Belle's case in the *Homophile Action League Newsletter*. Titled "Give Me Your Tired, Your Poor ..., etc.," the article invoked the well-known lines from the poem at the base of the Statue of Liberty. Bello explained that "a foreign-born homosexual who wishes to become a naturalized United States citizen runs the risk of deportation if his or her homosexuality is discovered during the proceedings." After reviewing what happened in *Boutilier*, Bello noted that "to our knowledge no further challenge of this unfair restriction had occurred until this year," when a federal judge ruled in the case of Belle (a Yugoslavian national applying for U.S. citizenship) that "'private deviate sexual practices with consenting adults' did not prevent him from being 'of good moral character.'" Bello cautioned, however, that the INS had appealed, and in any event there were "two factors" that would "limit the future usefulness of this case." First, "bisexuality might be more palatable than exclusive homosexuality to the deciding authorities." Second, the judge warned that "his decision should not be regarded as a precedent-setting ruling." Bello concluded, "Traditionally this country has held its doors open to oppressed minorities. In the case of homosexuals, it has chosen the role of oppressor. How long will this inconsistency remain?"[55]

More generally, and over the long term, the gay and lesbian movement lost interest in *Boutilier*. The 1968 *Wall Street Journal* article on homosexual law reform, for instance, highlighted the work of the HLRS and NLDF, but did not mention *Boutilier*. HLRS lawyer Gilbert Cantor was quoted as saying "I admire their willingness to assert their rights as citizens," a formulation that is noteworthy for a lawyer who had just defended an alien. In the same year, four San Francisco–based groups published a sixty-seven-page booklet titled *The Challenge and Progress of Homosexual Law Reform*. Presenting itself as a comprehensive national overview, the booklet argued for decriminalizing "homosexual acts committed in private between consenting adults." An endnote explained that employment and military policy would be dealt with in a future publication, and the booklet contained brief sections dealing with sexual psychopath laws, police practices, harassment of bars, postal surveillance, violence, blackmail and extortion, and solicitation. There was no mention of the two issues, obscenity and immigration, that had been the subject of Supreme Court gay rights rulings. *Boutilier* was referenced only once, in the context of a discussion of state sexual psychopath laws, which allowed authorities to incarcerate or hospitalize homosexuals for indeterminate sentences. According to the booklet, "Recently in one of its less enlightened decisions, the Supreme Court, despite the presentation of extensive medical evidence that all homosexuals can by no means be classified as psychopaths, ruled that the term 'psychopathic personality,' as used by Congress, was meant to include homosexuals." Only the accompanying endnote explained that the case concerned an immigrant subject to deportation. Concluding that "homosexual law reform will come," in part because of "today's sexual revolution," the booklet presented an optimistic vision of homosexual citizenship while setting aside the interests of aliens.

In an early 1970 set of predictions about the new decade, the *Homophile Action League Newsletter* looked forward to "a Supreme Court decision striking down the multitudinous state laws which define as criminal most homosexual, and many heterosexual, acts between consenting adults." Describing the basis for this prediction, the newsletter observed, "During the past sixteen years, the Supreme Court and other bodies have consistently addressed themselves to the task of defining more fully and working out plans to implement the civil liberties guaranteed by the Constitution. The tide cannot be turned. And it is the duty of the homophile movement to see that it is not stopped short of completion." Insofar as *Boutilier* presented problems for such optimistic predictions, it was best forgotten.[56]

Freedman and Boutilier

In the course of losing interest in the *Boutilier* case, the press and public lost interest in Boutilier. None of the mainstream, legal, or homophile press coverage of the ruling mentioned that Boutilier's lawyer, Blanch Freedman, died before the Court announced its decision. According to Freedman's brother Paul Laven, "Blanch was deathly sick from scleroderma [an auto-immune disease] when she argued the case . . . and suffered greatly during the proceedings. When she finished, she checked into a hospital to die." Laven later recalled, "She had a very tough time during those proceedings. She said she had a horrible thirst and couldn't swallow her saliva—all from her scleroderma." Freedman died on 16 April 1967, a little more than a month after she appeared for the last time before the Court and several weeks before the *Boutilier* decision was announced. Asked decades later about the *Boutilier* case, Laven noted, "When Blanch was dying in the hospital, I know for a fact she learned she lost the Supreme Court's decision. We were all thinking how pathetic the timing was." Laven added, "My sister Jeanette . . . remembers meeting Boutilier when he visited Blanch in the hospital. It was in 1967 and both knew they lost the Supreme Court decision. While he came to console her, Jeanette says Blanch ended up consoling Boutilier." It is possible, though unlikely, that Freedman received advance word of the decision. She may have anticipated the negative outcome or wanted to prepare Boutilier for the worst. And Freedman's siblings may have wanted to remember their sister as having followed one final fight through to its bitter end. Whether or not Freedman knew the outcome, readers of her *New York Times* obituary did not learn about her recent participation in *Boutilier*. Over the next several decades, as *Boutilier* was largely forgotten, Freedman's role in his case was forgotten too. On the rare occasion that her work as Boutilier's lawyer was mentioned in published work on gay and lesbian legal history, her long career as a defender of immigrants, leftists, women, and workers was not discussed.[57]

As for Boutilier, he was deported to Canada on 10 November 1968, almost eighteen months after the Court ruled against him. There is conflicting information about what happened to him around the time of the Court's 1967 decision. In December 1968, Mattachine New York's newsletter announced that "Boutilier is in the news again." After summarizing the Court's ruling, the newsletter reported, "According to a reliable source, he walked in front of a bus (whether attempted suicide or accident we don't know) and was hospitalized for three months. He's out now, collected a large settlement from an insurance company and is living back in Canada with his mother in a brand new house." Who the source was remains a mystery, though the published information suggests that someone with a connection to the homophile movement maintained a connection to Boutilier after he moved to Canada.[58]

In 2001, Boutilier's niece, whom I located through a genealogical website, provided the following account of what happened to Boutilier:

> Well it seems that my grandmother and mother do not want to open old wounds. I discussed this with my mother who was not very informative and my grandmother who didn't want the subject brought up at all. I informed them that I was going to relay all the information that I have to you as I see no harm in doing so. . . . Clive was hit by a car while crossing a street in New York in 1967. He was in a coma for 30 days and was left brain damaged. I truly believe this was an attempt at suicide because of the Court's decision and my siblings concur. Unfortunately we may never know for sure but it sure was coincidental and ironically the car that hit him was driven by a Customs Officer. My grandmother, grandfather, and Clive returned

to Canada after his release from the hospital and took up residence in Niagara Falls, Ontario. My grandmother cared for Clive at home for several years until she could not do it anymore. He has always been mobile and can dress and feed himself but walks as if in a drunken stupor. He has resided in group homes for the disabled since the early 90's. I do believe that he remembers his lifestyle because I have a nephew who is gay and Clive once said to me, "He has the problem too, doesn't he?" I am sure that my grandmother drummed it into his head that what happened was to never be brought into the light of day ever again.

In subsequent correspondence, Boutilier's niece wrote, "They moved to Niagara Falls to be close to the border as my grandmother's husband was an American. The rest of the children were married or in the Army so there was nothing stopping them from moving back to Canada." Niagara Falls was likely appealing as the region of Canada closest to the New York metropolitan area, where some of Boutilier's married siblings and their children were living.[59]

After hearing from Boutilier's niece, I requested contact information for Boutilier. The niece replied, "I am sure that Clive may remember that event in his life but my family is very adamant about keeping all of this away from him. If you forward your questions to me I will personally review them with him. My sister . . . believes as I do that we have a right to know our family history." Later in 2001, she wrote, "I have not been able to talk to Clive yet and I know that there is no way that they will let you talk to him as my grandmother has left strict orders that no one be allowed to confront him after the last incidents. I am going to discuss with my sister . . . the possibility of her and I, and possibly you, taking him out for a couple of hours to visit. Then you may get answers to your questions if he is willing to talk about it. I can't promise anything but will try. I know that my grandmother will be very upset after the fact because Clive tells her everything but she will get over it."

The "incidents" mentioned by Boutilier's niece likely relate to the efforts made by journalists Joyce Murdoch and Deb Price to interview Boutilier for their 2001 book *Courting Justice: Gay Men and Lesbians v. the Supreme Court*. According to *Courting Justice*, Boutilier was living in a "rest home in Willand, Ontario." (The correct spelling is Welland.) Murdoch and Price continue, "Speaking haltingly, he confirmed that he moved back to Canada immediately after losing his legal fight. His seven-year relationship with Eugene O'Rouke [*sic*], the American he lived with before the INS turned his life upside down, was his only long-term relationship. O'Rouke [*sic*] has 'passed away,' Boutilier said. Twenty-one years after being deported, Boutilier contended that he'd made a mistake in telling the U.S. military that he was homosexual—though the records indicate his INS troubles were triggered by his citizenship application. How did he feel when he heard the court's decision? 'No comment!'"[60]

Shortly after their book was published, I e-mailed Murdoch and Price to ask about how they found Boutilier. Murdoch, who said she knew nothing about Boutilier's accident and injuries, before or after talking with him, responded, "It took us years to track down Clive Boutilier. His mother was quite hostile—even threatening. . . . Eventually I located Clive at what must be essentially a nursing home. He is clearly in no condition to give a real interview. I spoke with him very, very briefly and decided that pressing him to say more would have been taking unfair advantage of what apparently is a very severe mental handicap." Subsequently Murdoch wrote, "I expect that at least until his mother's death the chances of doing a real interview with him are slim to none—plus, as I said, his mind is not at all sharp." Later she wrote, "He told me that he didn't want to say anything else. Perhaps that's just because talking is difficult for him. But perhaps he just doesn't want to dig up the past." In another letter, she added, "After a gazillion long-distance calls, I finally tracked down the rest home where Clive was living. I very briefly talked to him on the phone. He clearly did not want to talk at all but answered a few questions anyway. He seemed a bit addled—well, more than a bit, frankly—so I didn't press him the way I would have felt free to press, say, a Harvard-educated Supreme Court clerk. I let him know how he could contact me if he changed his mind and wanted to talk more. I never heard from him." I asked Murdoch several times for Boutilier's telephone number and address, but she wrote that she was not able to access her research files.[61]

In 2003, Boutilier's niece informed me that Boutilier had died on 12 April 2003 of complications related to a heart condition, several months shy of his seventieth birthday. He had lived in Canada for nearly thirty-five years following his deportation. His niece wrote, "I know that he is now at peace because his life as you know was not a very comfortable one. I never did get a chance to talk with him about the past and will never know his side of the story but I am grateful that he no longer has to suffer with any prejudices of society, and I know that he can now live in the hereafter the way he truly wanted to live his life." No obituaries were published, in the mainstream or the alternative press, in the United States or Canada.[62]

Three years after Boutilier's death, I received the results of a Freedom of Information Act (FOIA) request I filed with the U.S. government. Some of the information I obtained is consistent with what Boutilier's niece told me; other information is not. According to these documents, on 3 July 1967 the INS informed the Royal Canadian Mounted Police that the United States would soon deport Boutilier to Canada. By way of explanation, the INS provided a brief summary of Boutilier's sexual history, the INS's actions, and the unsuccessful appeals. Several days later, the INS wrote to Boutilier, informing him that he would be deported shortly. On 10 July, Boutilier's lawyer, Robert Brown, informed the INS that Boutilier had been hit by a car on 10 May and continued to be hospitalized in critical condition. Four days later, Dr. Edward McGovern informed the INS that Boutilier had been admitted to Methodist Hospital in Brooklyn on 10 May after being hit by a car. According to McGovern, Boutilier "sustained a severe head injury which resulted in his being in a coma for about three (3) weeks after which period the patient was barely able to speak and was not oriented as to time and space." Assuming the date is correct, Boutilier's accident took place several weeks after Freedman's death but twelve days before the Court's decision was announced. This does not necessarily mean that Boutilier's family members were wrong in thinking that Boutilier had attempted suicide; his psychological health could have been affected by many factors, including sadness about Freedman's death, pessimism about the forthcoming decision, anxieties about media publicity, worries about finances and unemployment, and tensions with his family. It is also possible, though unlikely, that Freedman and Boutilier knew what the Court had decided before the ruling was announced. It also may be that Boutilier was not attempting suicide and just happened to be hit by a car days before the Court ruled against him.[63]

In any case, on 14 August Brown wrote to the INS, noting that Boutilier remained in the hospital and promising to keep the INS informed about his condition. About two months later, Brown informed the INS that Boutilier had been transferred to Brooklyn State Hospital in early September. In early November, the INS asked for an update. According to a report filed by Dr. Alan Joseph, Boutilier was suffering from "post-traumatic psychosis" and was "confused and paranoid." The car accident and coma had resulted in "diffuse encephalopathy characterized by diffuse neurological signs, difficulty in calculation, memory loss with lack of insight." Joseph also stated, "On psychiatric examination on November 21, 1967, he was inclined to be explosive, suddenly showing a hostile attitude without apparent provocation. He exhibited paranoid ideation concerning his parents." In February and May 1968, Brooklyn State Hospital director Nathan Beckenstein responded to further INS queries by reporting that Boutilier was still a patient there. The FOIA materials do not reveal when Boutilier was discharged, but INS documents indicate that he was deported on 10 November.[64]

We may never know the precise nature of Boutilier's accident and injuries, but if Boutilier was explosive and confused, who could say he did not have cause? If he was hostile, who could claim that he had not been provoked? If he lacked insight about his situation and could not remember the past, who could blame him? If he was paranoid about those responsible for taking care of him, who could deny that he had reasons to think the system was out to get him? If Boutilier was now psychotic, who could discount the possibility that the INS and the Supreme Court had produced the very condition they used to justify his deportation?

Many questions about Boutilier and his encounters with the U.S. legal system remain unanswered. With Boutilier's death, for example, it became impossible to ask him directly whether he thought of himself as homosexual in 1955 when he migrated to the United States, in 1957 when he was classified 4F by the U.S. military, in 1959 when he was arrested for sodomy, in 1963 when he applied for citizenship, in 1964 when he was interrogated by a naturalization examiner, in 1967 when the Supreme Court ruled against him, or over the course of the rest of his life. When in 1967 the *Pride Newsletter* reported that "there was never any argument over whether Boutilier is a homosexual or was one at the time of entry," it reproduced one of the assertions made by the Court, but this was based on limited evidence. There is significant evidence that Boutilier acknowledged having engaged in same-sex sexual acts before he entered the United States and over the next several years, but little about whether he thought of himself as homosexual. Today, many scholars argue that most people who engage in same-sex sexual activities do not view themselves as homosexual or gay. Presuming to label someone homosexual or gay who might not have labeled themselves as such typically reveals more about the presumer than the presumed.[65]

According to *Courting Justice*, decades later Boutilier referred to the "mistake" he made in telling the U.S. military that he was homosexual. Murdoch and Price find this response puzzling since his troubles began with his citizenship application. They miss the possibility that Boutilier focused on his admission to the military because in the absence of that admission he might have served in the military, avoided his sodomy arrest, and become a U.S. citizen. They also miss the possibility that Boutilier believed that, had he not told the military he was homosexual, he could have avoided telling immigration officials about his sodomy arrest. It is also possible that Boutilier meant that he was *not* homosexual, and the mistake was in saying he was. I asked Murdoch about this, and she replied, "My memory of my brief phone conversation with Clive Boutilier isn't crystal clear, but I do know that I had no doubt that he still thought of himself as homosexual." Murdoch may have had no doubt, but that could have been a product of her assumptions rather than a reflection of anything Boutilier confirmed or denied.[66]

The recent accounts by Boutilier's niece and Murdoch suggest that, whether or not he thought of himself as homosexual, he may have lived out his life in Canada as a severely disabled man under the control of a profoundly antigay mother. But she also may have been a fiercely protective parent who wanted to shield her son from harm, a conservative Christian who was troubled by her son's sexual history, an angry mother who blamed the U.S. government for disrupting her family, a cautious guardian who had little reason to aid the efforts of U.S. "experts," or a savvy political observer who disdained the hypocrisy of liberals and conservatives who valorized "family values." According to Boutilier's niece, he told his mother "everything," but we do not know whether this reflected the existence of a close mother-son bond, a relationship in which mother controlled son, both, or neither. Regardless, Boutilier's circumstances may have made it difficult for him to develop a positive relationship to his or to anyone else's sexuality. It is unclear whether it was Boutilier or his niece who thought of homosexuality as a "lifestyle," a term that has been criticized for diminishing the significance of gay "life." If his niece reported his comments accurately, Boutilier apparently regarded homosexuality as a "problem" he shared with his grandnephew. One of his psychiatrists wrote in 1965 that Boutilier "has abandoned all sexual practices within the past several months because of his annoyance and disgust with the problems these activities have brought about." We do not know whether Boutilier ever resumed sexual activities after 1965 and, if he did, whether his partners were male, female, both, or neither.

All of that said, for reasons that may say more about me than about him, I believe there is evidence that Boutilier retained a meaningful level of autonomy in relation to his family, and that autonomy may have allowed him to have connections to wider worlds, including gay ones. The bond that Boutilier seems to have felt toward his grandnephew is suggestive. So is Murdoch and Price's indication that Boutilier was aware that his former partner Eugene O'Rourke had died. It is possible that O'Rourke died before Boutilier moved to Canada, but it is more likely that the two men remained in touch, directly or indirectly, after Boutilier's deportation. In any event, the complicated connections and disconnections between Boutilier's world and ours have motivated the writing of this book, and hopefully your reading of it as well.

Epilogue

In eight momentous years from 1965 to 1973, the Supreme Court developed a doctrine of heteronormative supremacy. The justices legitimized laws that protected and promoted favored forms of sexual expression, condoned discrimination against other types of sex, and permitted punishment for those who violated sexual norms. In decisions concerning birth control, obscenity, homosexuality, interracial marriage, and abortion, the Court created a constitutional framework for the regulation of sex and the production of sexuality. Notwithstanding minor modifications, that framework survived for the next thirty years. Only one justice from the *Griswold* to *Roe* era was still serving three decades later, but the doctrine remained firmly in place until the Court overturned state sodomy laws in *Lawrence* (2003). A court of six Democratic and three Republican appointees in 1965 became a court of either seven or eight Republican and one or two Democratic appointees for decades after 1975, but partisan shifts did not yield significant changes in the doctrine. When the legal regulation of sex changed between 1973 and 2003, the Court played a limited role. More often than not, legal change occurred at subnational levels as states and municipalities repealed, modified, and invalidated laws against adultery, cohabitation, fornication, sodomy, and other sexual offenses. Subnational jurisdictions were also the primary arenas for the enactment of laws against sexual discrimination. The legal regulation of sex changed in many parts of the country, but the Court's doctrine meant that federal, state, and local governments could continue to deny sexual freedom and equality, which they did.

When the Court revised the doctrine in *Lawrence*, it rewrote the history of the rulings of the late 1960s and early 1970s. Instead of acknowledging the sexually conservative aspects of *Griswold, Fanny Hill, Boutilier, Loving, Eisenstadt,* and *Roe* and presenting *Lawrence* as a bold new departure, the justices portrayed *Lawrence* as fully consistent with the precedents. This was certainly not the first time the Court shifted direction without acknowledging that it was doing so. In this case, the activists, advocates, journalists, judges, and scholars who began representing the Court's rulings as sexually libertarian and egalitarian in the 1960s helped persuade the justices serving decades later to revise the heteronormative doctrine.

From *Roe* (1973) to *Bowers* (1986)

What did the Court do when the legal regulation of sex was challenged in the years between *Roe* and *Lawrence*? It made its most forceful statement on the subject in *Bowers* (1986), but in the years between *Roe* and *Bowers* the justices continued to accept, condone, and promote sexual discrimination. In abortion and birth control cases, for instance, the Court continued to offer limited recognition of reproductive rights without extending protection to sexual rights. In *Carey* (1977), the Court struck down a state law criminalizing the sale or distribution of contraceptives to minors under the age of sixteen, the distribution of contraceptives by anyone other than licensed pharmacists, and the advertising or display of contraceptives. In a section of his opinion endorsed by a majority of the justices, Brennan observed that "while the outer limits of this aspect of privacy have not been marked by the Court," several rulings had affirmed that "the decision whether or not to beget or bear a child is at the very heart of this cluster of constitutionally protected choices." As for sexual rights, Brennan wrote that "the Court has not definitively answered the difficult question whether and to what extent the Constitution prohibits state statutes regulating [private consensual sexual] behavior among adults . . . and we do not purport to answer that question now" (brackets in original). This seemingly neutral comment proved too much for several of Brennan's colleagues, who did not want to be outmaneuvered by the Court's leading liberal tactician. Two justices clarified their positions in concurrences. White wrote, "I do not regard the opinion . . . as declaring unconstitutional any state law forbidding extramarital sexual relations" and "the legality of state laws forbidding premarital intercourse is not at issue here." Stevens added, "I would not leave open the question of whether there is a significant state interest in discouraging sexual activity among unmarried persons under 16 years of age." Rehnquist's dissent declared that "while we have not ruled on every conceivable regulation affecting such conduct the facial constitutional validity of criminal statutes prohibiting certain consensual acts has been 'definitively' established."[1]

As the federal government and states passed restrictive abortion regulations in the post-*Roe* period, the Court debated the scope and limits of constitutionally protected reproductive rights without addressing sexual rights. In a series of cases, the justices upheld denials of public funding for abortions and addressed the constitutionality of informed consent, parental consent, spousal consent, waiting period, and other abortion restrictions. In this period, the Court split into three factions in abortion cases. Some of the justices continued to embrace the trimester-based reasoning of *Roe*; some endorsed the notion of reproductive rights but argued that restrictive laws were acceptable if they did not impose an undue burden; some rejected *Roe* entirely. None of the factions used abortion cases to argue that the Constitution protected sexual rights.[2]

In another set of cases, the Court addressed the regulation of heterosexual cohabitation and sex more directly. In *Matlock* (1974), the Court considered the question of whether a woman's statement that she cohabited with a man, which the police used to gain her permission to search their home without a warrant, was admissible in court. One part of White's majority opinion, which ruled admissible the woman's statement, pointed out that "cohabitation out of wedlock would not seem to be a relationship that one would falsely confess" since it is "a crime in . . . Wisconsin." Also in 1974, *Village of Belle Terre* upheld a zoning law prohibiting more than two unrelated individuals from living together, with an exception for servants. Responding to the claim that "if two unmarried people can constitute a 'family,' there is no reason why three or four may not," Douglas's majority opinion noted that in this situation the "exercise of discretion" was "a legislative, not a judicial, function." Only two justices, Brennan and Marshall, dissented, with Marshall writing that "the choice of household companions . . . involves deeply personal considerations as to the kind and quality of intimate relationships within the home" and "that decision surely falls within the ambit of the right to privacy protected by the Constitution." Three years later, *Moore* overturned a zoning law that prevented a grandmother, her son, and two grandsons from living together because they did not constitute a nuclear family. Zoning laws could not interfere with the cohabitation rights of extended family members, these rulings suggested, but they could discriminate against nonfamilial cohabitants.[3]

As for heterosexual sex, in *Rose* (1975) the Court upheld the constitutionality of Tennessee's crime-against-nature law in a case involving a man who had forced a woman to submit to cunnilingus. According to the *per curiam* opinion, the phrase "crimes against nature" was not unconstitutionally vague, it had been used among "English-speaking people" for centuries, and a "substantial number of jurisdictions in this country continue to utilize it." Rejecting the claim that the law did not make clear whether it encompassed just "sodomy" or "additional forms of sexual aberration," the Court declared, "We have twice before upheld statutes against similar charges." This clarified the meaning of two instances in which the Court had declined to hear same-sex sodomy appeals. As the Court now explained in *Rose*, in *Crawford* (1972) the justices had dismissed an appeal of a decision holding that Missouri's crime-against-nature law "embraced sodomy, bestiality, buggery, fellatio, and cunnilingus," and in *Wainwright* (1973) the Court had upheld Florida's law against "the abominable and detestable crime against nature."[4]

In subsequent years, the Court continued to defer or decline opportunities to overturn laws and practices that discriminated against non-normative heterosexual sex. In *Lovisi* (1976), the Court declined to consider a challenge to Virginia's sodomy law by a husband and wife convicted of having illegal sex with one another after the wife was photographed performing oral sex on her husband and another man. According to the lower court, whose opinion was sustained, "the married couple has welcomed a stranger to the marital bedchamber, and what they do is no longer in the privacy of their marriage." Two years later, *Zablocki* overturned a Wisconsin law preventing men who owed child-support from getting married. Insisting that the law violated the fundamental right to marry, the majority opinion by Marshall observed that "if appellee's right to procreate means anything at all, it must imply some right to enter the only relationship in which . . . Wisconsin allows sexual relations legally to take place." In the same year, *Hollenbaugh* dismissed an appeal of a decision upholding the firing of two public library employees for living together in "open adultery." The Court also denied *cert* in *Jarrett* (1980), which was an appeal of a decision granting custody of three children to their father after their mother began cohabiting with another man in violation of the state's law against cohabitation and fornication.[5]

The Court also dismissed appeals in cases challenging other types of laws against non-normative heterosexual sex. In *Michael M* (1981), the Court rejected an appeal by a seventeen-year-old male convicted of having illegal sex with a female under the age of eighteen (she was sixteen). Responding to the claim that the statutory rape law violated the equal protection clause because it discriminated on the basis of sex (the law only criminalized actions by males), the Court ruled that the law served legitimate state interests in preventing "illegitimate" pregnancies. In *Whisenhunt* (1983), the Court denied *cert* in an appeal by two police officers, one male and one female, who had been suspended from their jobs for nonmarital cohabitation. In a dissenting opinion joined by Marshall and Blackmun, Brennan cited a long line of cases to support his contention that "the intimate, consensual, and private relationship" was entitled to constitutional protection. Two years later, in *North Muskegon* the Court denied *cert* in the other direction, refusing to consider an appeal by a Michigan city that had suspended a male police officer who was separated from his wife and living with another married woman. According to the city, the policeman was violating state laws against adultery and co-habitation, but a federal appellate court ruled that the city's actions violated the man's sexual privacy rights. This time White, Burger, and Rehnquist dissented from the *cert* denial, arguing that the Court should resolve the conflict between *Whisenhunt* and *North Muskegon*, which was "evidence of a broader disagreement over whether extramarital sexual activity . . . is constitutionally protected." Because these justices believed that "this case presents an important issue of constitutional law regarding the contours of the right of privacy afforded individuals for sexual matters," they wanted to hear the appeal. The outcome was a minor victory for sexual freedom, but as long as the Court continued to deny *cert* in cases like *Whisenhunt*, most state laws against adultery, cohabitation, fornication, and sodomy remained in force.[6]

Meanwhile, in case after case dealing with antihomosexual discrimination, the Court declined to consider appeals of conservative lower court rulings. For example, in 1977 the Court turned away an appeal of a decision permitting a public university student newspaper to refuse to publish an advertisement for a gay rights organization. In three mid-1970s cases and one in 1985, the justices refused to consider appeals of rulings that upheld antihomosexual employment discrimination. In two 1981 decisions, the Court declined to consider appeals by servicemen discharged on the basis of antihomosexual military policies and practices. Then in 1986, the justices denied *cert* in *Kowalski*, which let stand a lower court decision granting guardianship of a disabled woman to her father rather than her female partner.[7]

The Court directly addressed bans on same-sex sex in several cases in the 1970s and early 1980s. In *Wainwright* (1973), the Court offered its clearest statement thus far on the subject. In an unsigned *per curiam* opinion (authored by White), the justices affirmed several crimes-against-nature convictions based on same-sex sex. According to the Court, the state statutes were not unconstitutionally vague because "these very acts had long been held to constitute 'the abominable and detestable crime against nature.'" The Court dismissed several appeals of state sodomy convictions for same-sex sex based on the notion that the cases did not present a "substantial federal question." Then in *Doe* (1976), the Court affirmed, without comment, a district court ruling upholding Virginia's sodomy law. Emphasizing that *Griswold* was based on privacy rights related to marriage, home, and family, the district court highlighted passages in *Griswold* and other rulings that referred to the constitutionality of laws against nonmarital sex in general and same-sex sex in particular. Insofar as homosexuality was "obviously no portion of marriage, home or family life," the privacy rights affirmed in *Griswold* and other cases did not apply. By the end of the 1970s, twenty-one states had repealed their sodomy laws, but the Court's rulings made clear that such laws remained constitutional.[8]

The Court's reluctance to consider appeals of gay and lesbian rights rulings meant that many conservative lower court decisions were sustained, but occasionally the results were different. In 1978, the Court denied *cert* in an appeal of a decision favoring the right of a gay student group to be recognized by a Missouri public university. Three years later, the Court denied *cert* when New York appealed a ruling that invalidated the state's criminalization of non-marital consensual sodomy (homosexual and heterosexual). The Court also declined, in 1981 and 1982, to consider an appeal by a Texas county treasurer who fired an employee after the latter expressed his intention to speak publicly about gay rights, which the Fifth Circuit ruled was a violation of the First Amendment. Another ambiguous victory occurred in 1985, when an equally divided Court (with Powell not participating because of illness) affirmed a Tenth Circuit decision overturning an Oklahoma statute allowing school boards to fire teachers who engaged in public homosexual "conduct," which was defined to include "advocating, soliciting, encouraging or promoting public or private homosexual activity." According to the Tenth Circuit, it was constitutional to fire teachers for engaging in public homosexual "activity," but the law's broad definition of "conduct" violated the First Amendment.[9]

In 1984, gay rights advocates grew concerned when the Court initially granted *cert* in New York's appeal of a lower court ruling striking down a state statute prohibiting public loitering for the purpose of soliciting deviate sex. Apart from obscenity cases, *Uplinger* was the first time since *Boutilier* that the Court heard oral arguments in a gay rights case. This move seems to have reflected a new confidence on the part of the more sexually conservative justices. In the end, however, the Court took the unusual step of ruling that *cert* had been "improvidently granted" because the case "provides an inappropriate vehicle for resolving the important constitutional issues raised." Four of the more sexually conservative justices dissented, but in *Bowers* they would soon gain the fifth vote they needed for a majority in these types of cases. In the meantime, the Court's tendency to deny *cert* in gay and lesbian rights cases meant that more conservative lower courts could continue to uphold anti-homosexual laws and practices.[10]

Two significant gay immigration cases were appealed to the Supreme Court in the early 1980s. In *Adams* (1982), the Court denied *cert* after the Ninth Circuit affirmed a decision by the Board of Immigration Appeals to deny a petition to classify a male alien as an immediate relative of a U.S. citizen on the basis of his marriage to a male U.S. citizen. The men had obtained a marriage license from a Colorado county clerk and were married by a minister, but according to the Ninth Circuit the family-preference provisions of federal immigration statutes were not meant to apply to same-sex couples. In support of its conclusion, the court cited *Boutilier*, partly to emphasize that the intent of federal immigration legislation was to "exclude homosexuals" and partly to underscore the power of Congress to "'exclude those who possess those characteristics which Congress has forbidden.'"[11]

The Court also denied *cert* in *Longstaff* (1984), which challenged a Fifth Circuit ruling allowing the INS to deny naturalization to a resident alien because he was a homosexual at time of entry. Longstaff had been admitted to the United States as a permanent resident in 1965 and applied for naturalization ten years later, but the INS denied his application after he admitted that he was a homosexual and had engaged in homosexual acts before entering the United States. In many respects, the outcome in *Longstaff* followed directly from *Boutilier*, but *Longstaff* was significant because the legal situation had changed. In 1979, Surgeon General Julius Richmond (appointed by President Carter) announced that the Public Health Service (PHS) no longer regarded homosexuality as a type of mental illness or defect and therefore would not conduct the examinations or provide the certifications required to exclude homosexuals as psychopathic personalities or sexual deviates. According to the Justice Department's Office of Legal Counsel, Richmond lacked the authority to do this, but he refused to change his position. The INS then adopted new guidelines stipulating that arriving aliens would not be asked questions about sexual preference and would only be excluded as homosexual psychopathic personalities or sexual deviates if they made "unambiguous oral or written admission of homosexuality" or if a third party arriving at the same time "voluntarily states" that the alien is "a homosexual." Aliens could also be denied citizenship or be deported if they admitted their homosexuality later. As for Longstaff, the Fifth Circuit ruled that because he had admitted that he was a homosexual and had been one at time of entry, medical certification was unnecessary and naturalization could be denied. Six years later in 1990, Congress repealed the psychopathic personality and sexual deviation provisions of federal immigration law.[12]

Meanwhile, in obscenity and obscenity-related cases the justices routinely declined to consider appeals of lower court decisions as long as those decisions relied on the obscenity tests adopted in 1973. If there were reasons to think they did not rely on the 1973 tests, the justices typically vacated the judgment and remanded the case to the lower court for further consideration. These rulings permitted some restrictions on depictions of conventional heterosexual sex, but the Court's discriminatory standards were evident when the justices encountered other types of sexual representations. In a 1974 case, for example, White's majority opinion condemned "an unremitting series of explicit photographs of a wide spectrum of sexual conduct, including homosexual acts, anal intercourse, fellatio, cunnilingus, and group orgies." In another 1974 case, Rehnquist's majority opinion affirmed an obscenity conviction based on the mailing of an advertising brochure for *The Illustrated Presidential Report of the Commission on Obscenity and Pornography*. Referencing *Mishkin*, Rehnquist emphasized that "consideration may be given to the prurient appeal of the material to clearly defined deviant sexual groups."[13]

In several cases decided in this period, the Court developed new tests for sexual representations of children and sexual expression by minors. In a 1982 decision, the Court ruled that in such cases three aspects of the 1973 *Miller* tests were not required: the material need not appeal to "the prurient interest of the average person," the sexual conduct need not be portrayed "in a patently offensive manner," and the material "need not be considered as a whole."[14] The Court also developed new rules to guide decisions about zoning and other regulations for sexually oriented businesses. Stevens declared for the majority in a 1976 adult-theater case that "reasonable regulations of the time, place, and manner of protected speech, where those regulations are necessary to further significant governmental interests, are permitted."[15]

Perhaps the clearest indication of the heteronormative features of the Court's obscenity tests in this period came in 1985, when the justices addressed "material that aroused only a normal, healthy interest in sex." In *Brockett*, the Ninth Circuit overturned a Washington state obscenity law on the grounds that it permitted suppression of such material. The Supreme Court reversed the decision, but only because the section of the law that was unconstitutional was severable from the rest of the law. According to a significant passage in White's majority opinion, the Ninth Circuit "did not believe that *Roth* had intended to characterize as obscene material that provoked only normal, healthy sexual desires" or "'good, old fashioned, healthy' interest in sex." White declared for the majority, "We do not differ with that view."[16]

Bowers (1986)

Having developed a doctrine of heteronormative supremacy in the *Griswold* to *Roe* era and having applied and affirmed that doctrine after *Roe*, the Court proceeded to uphold state sodomy laws in *Bowers* (1986). Rather than representing a conservative departure and a rightwing reversal, which is what many liberal critics of the decision claim, *Bowers* was the logical culmination of the comments about sex that the Court had been making since 1965. *Bowers* was an appeal by Georgia of an Eleventh Circuit ruling that overturned the state's sodomy law, which criminalized oral and anal sex (homosexual and heterosexual). The case involved Michael Hardwick, who had been arrested for engaging in consensual same-sex sex in his home, which police discovered while attempting to serve an arrest warrant for public drinking. According to White's majority opinion, the Eleventh Circuit read *Griswold*, *Eisenstadt*, *Stanley*, and *Roe* to mean that "homosexual activity is a private and intimate association that is beyond the reach of state regulation." White and four other justices rejected this interpretation. Framing the question as "whether the Federal Constitution confers a fundamental right upon homosexuals to engage in sodomy," White denied that the precedents, which concerned "family, marriage, or procreation," had "any resemblance" or "connection" to "homosexual activity." Citing *Carey*, he argued that "any claim that these cases nevertheless stand for the proposition that any kind of private sexual conduct between consenting adults is constitutionally insulated from state proscription is unsupportable." Turning from the precedents to the Constitution, White insisted that there was no "fundamental right to engage in homosexual sodomy." Such a right was neither "implicit in the concept of ordered liberty" nor "deeply rooted in this Nation's history and tradition." As for privacy in the home, White argued that "it would be difficult . . . to limit the claimed right to homosexual conduct while leaving exposed to prosecution adultery, incest, and other sexual crimes . . . committed in the home." Having rejected the "fundamental rights" argument, which would have placed a substantial burden on the state to justify its law, the majority then applied its more deferential "rational basis" test. According to the Court, the rational basis for the Georgia law was morality. Observing that "the law . . . is constantly based on notions of morality," the majority upheld the statute because it was based on "the presumed belief of a majority of the electorate in Georgia that homosexual sodomy is immoral."[17]

White's opinion has been subjected to justifiable criticism for its failure to address the criminalization of heterosexual sodomy, its weak comprehension of the history of sexuality and sodomy, its conflation of sexual acts and identities, its constricted view of constitutional liberty and privacy rights, and its antigay rhetoric and reasoning. But its depiction of *Griswold*, *Eisenstadt*, *Stanley*, and *Roe* as heteronormative precedents was reasonable. Conversely, the dissents by Blackmun, Brennan, Marshall, and Stevens offered compelling criticisms of White's opinion, but transformed the meanings of the heteronormative precedents. On behalf of the dissenters, Blackmun began by denying that the main issue presented by the case was whether there was a "fundamental right to engage in homosexual sodomy." The central issue was what Justice Louis Brandeis once described as "the right to be let alone." More specifically, the dissenters argued that the case concerned the rights of individuals to "decide for themselves whether to engage in particular forms of private, consensual sexual activity" and make choices about "the most intimate aspects of their lives." According to Blackmun, while the majority opinion exhibited an "almost obsessive focus on homosexual activity," the statute criminalized both heterosexual and homosexual sodomy. The state may have enforced the law differentially, but Blackmun contended that Hardwick's claim that the statute "involves an unconstitutional intrusion into his privacy and his right of intimate association does not depend in any way on his sexual orientation." Blackmun proceeded to discuss "the decisional and the spatial aspects" of privacy. According to the dissenters, the *Griswold* to *Roe* precedents and other decisions that protected familial, marital, and reproductive rights were based on the rights of the individual and "the fact that individuals define themselves in a significant way through their intimate sexual relationships." Emphasizing that the majority failed to recognize "the fundamental interest all individuals have in controlling the nature of their intimate associations," the dissenters also argued that the majority failed to recognize the Constitution's special protection for conduct in the home. According to Blackmun, "The right of an individual to conduct intimate relationships in the intimacy of his or her own home seems to me to be the heart of the Constitution's protection of privacy."[18]

Having established that the law violated fundamental rights, Blackmun proceeded to criticize the state's main justifications for the law. First, there was no evidence to support the claim that the law promoted public health and welfare by preventing the spread of communicable diseases, discouraging criminal activity, or protecting individuals from danger. As for the morality argument, Blackmun insisted (citing *Loving*) that neither the length of time one set of moral values has been dominant nor the strength of religious convictions about those values could shield statutes from judicial scrutiny. Nor could the state invoke its interest in protecting the public environment, since "the mere fact that intimate behavior may be punished when it takes place in public cannot dictate how States can regulate intimate behavior that occurs in intimate places." In a footnote, Blackmun distinguished between laws against sodomy, adultery, and incest. In his analysis, adultery laws punished violations of the marital contract and injuries to third parties. Incest laws could be justified because "the nature of familial relationships renders true consent to incestuous activity sufficiently problematical." The footnote concluded by noting that the majority made "no effort to explain why it has chosen to group private, consensual homosexual activity with adultery and incest rather than with private, consensual activity by unmarried persons or, indeed, with oral or anal sex within marriage."[19]

By 1986, then, the four dissenters were prepared to extend constitutional protection to certain types of sexual rights, as distinct from marital, familial, and reproductive rights. For these four justices, laws that criminalized consensual, private, nondangerous sexual conduct by adults violated the Constitution (as long as the conduct did not violate marriage contracts or cause injuries to third parties). But rather than acknowledge that this represented a departure from the reasoning of the *Griswold* to *Roe* rulings, the dissenters presented their position as fully consistent with the precedents and accused the majority of misreading the earlier decisions. This required Brennan to ignore the fact that he had joined a *Griswold* opinion that referred to the constitutionality of laws against nonmarital sex, and it required all of the dissenters to avoid acknowledging that they had used language in the 1960s and 1970s that the majority could readily appropriate in the 1980s. It was the dissenters who ignored the fact that a majority of the justices in the *Griswold* to *Roe* era had suggested that laws against nonmarital sex were constitutionally permissible. The dissenters were more supportive of sexual freedom and equality, but their interpretations of the rulings from *Griswold* to *Roe* were at odds with the interpretations of the justices who decided these cases in the 1960s and 1970s.

From *Bowers* (1986) to *Lawrence* (2003)

After *Bowers*, the Court continued to affirm the doctrine of heteronormative supremacy, though the justices in the majority did not always agree on how to interpret the relevant precedents. In *Michael H.* (1989), the Court ruled against a man seeking to establish paternity and gain the right to visit his daughter, whom he had fathered in an adulterous relationship with a married woman. According to the plurality opinion by Scalia, California law presumed that a child born to a married woman who lived with her husband was the husband's child. Noting that the only liberties protected by the Constitution were those that were "fundamental" and "traditionally protected by our society," Scalia emphasized "the historic respect — indeed, sanctity would not be too strong a term — traditionally accorded to the relationships that develop within the unitary family." A footnote explained that the "unitary family" was "typified, of course, by the marital family, but also includes the household of unmarried parents and their children." Scalia did not offer evidence to support his claim that the households of unmarried parents and their children had been "accorded traditional respect in our society," but presumably he believed that such families were close enough to the heteronormative ideal to merit protection. Four justices endorsed these conclusions, while a fifth, Stevens, concurred with the judgment because the appellant had been given a fair opportunity to argue in court for his parental rights.[20]

Michael H. continued a discussion that began in Bowers about how the Court should identify which liberty or privacy interests were protected by the Constitution. All of the justices seemed to agree that it was important to consider which interests were historically protected and recognized in the United States, but they disagreed on whether those interests should be defined in specific, narrow, and concrete terms or in general, broad, and abstract ones. Discussing Bowers and Michael H., Scalia claimed in a footnote that "we refer to the most specific level at which a relevant tradition protecting, or denying protection to, the asserted right can be identified." Just as the Court had asked in Bowers whether "homosexual sodomy" was traditionally protected, in Michael H. the Court asked whether "the rights of an adulterous natural father" were traditionally protected. Significantly, only Rehnquist endorsed Scalia's footnote; O'Connor and Kennedy agreed with all aspects of Scalia's opinion except this footnote. Citing Griswold, Eisenstadt, and Loving, their concurring opinion argued that "on occasion the Court has characterized relevant traditions protecting asserted rights at levels of generality that might not be 'the most specific level' available." O'Connor and Kennedy were apparently concerned that Scalia's reasoning could have led to different outcomes in cases such as Loving, since the Court might have asked whether the specific right to marry across racial lines, as opposed to the general right to marry, was traditionally protected. Writing in dissent for himself, Marshall, and Blackmun, Brennan criticized Scalia for identifying traditional rights in such narrow terms. Just as Blackmun had emphasized that Bowers concerned not the narrow issue of homosexual sodomy but the general issue of sexual privacy, Brennan argued that the core issue in Michael H. was not adulterous parenthood but parenthood more generally. Brennan also echoed the concerns expressed by O'Connor and Kennedy about what Scalia's reasoning would have meant for Griswold, Loving, and Eisenstadt. In the end, Michael H. left in place the heteronormative doctrine, though Scalia's effort to achieve doctrinal consistency may have had unintended consequences as Kennedy and O'Connor began distancing themselves from his reasoning.[21]

Meanwhile, various states continued to enact more restrictive abortion laws and the Court continued to uphold them as long as they did not violate the central holdings of *Roe*.[22] The most significant abortion rights ruling in this period was *Casey* (1992), in which a centrist plurality of three justices (Kennedy, O'Connor, and Souter) affirmed what it regarded as the main holdings of *Roe*: the right of a woman to have an abortion before fetal viability without undue state interference, the power of the state to restrict post-viability abortions with exceptions for pregnancies that threaten the pregnant woman's life or health, and the legitimate interests of the state in protecting the health of the pregnant woman and the life of the fetus after viability. These justices rejected *Roe*'s trimester framework and adopted the alternative "undue burden" test. Using this test, the Court upheld Pennsylvania's informed consent, twenty-four-hour waiting period, and parental consent laws, but overturned its spousal notification requirement. Four dissenting justices wanted to overturn *Roe*, but a narrow majority—the three centrists plus abortion rights liberals Blackmun and Stevens—continued to support abortion rights.

As for sexual rights, the plurality opinion in *Casey* referred to precedents that afford "constitutional protection to personal decisions relating to marriage, procreation, contraception, family relationships, child rearing, and education." This list did not include sex, but the opinion more abstractly declared, "These matters, involving the most intimate and personal choices a person may make in a lifetime, choices central to personal dignity and autonomy, are central to the liberty protected by the Fourteenth Amendment. At the heart of liberty is the right to define one's own concept of existence, of meaning, of the universe, and of the mystery of human life." The plurality opinion also characterized *Roe* as a decision about "personal autonomy and bodily integrity." These were broad formulations that gestured in the direction of sexual rights. In dissent, Scalia (joined by White, Rehnquist, and Thomas) objected that the plurality's language contradicted *Bowers*, which had affirmed that "forms of conduct that have long been criminalized" are "not entitled to constitutional protection." According to Scalia, "homosexual sodomy, polygamy, adult incest, and suicide" involved "'intimate' and 'deeply personal' decisions involving 'personal autonomy and bodily integrity,'" but all could be proscribed. Once again, Scalia's effort to achieve doctrinal consistency may have had unintended consequences, as his logic suggested to Kennedy and O'Connor that *Bowers* should be reconsidered.[23]

After *Bowers*, gay and lesbian rights advocates continued to appeal cases to the Supreme Court, though they were rarely successful. In case after case, the Court denied *cert* in such appeals. Just after *Bowers*, the Court denied *cert* in a challenge to a Fifth Circuit ruling that upheld the constitutionality of a Texas law prohibiting deviate sexual intercourse with a person of the same sex. Ten years later, in a case involving a man who propositioned an undercover policeman, the Court also denied *cert*, rejecting challenges to a ruling that upheld Oklahoma's law against public solicitation for nonmarital lewdness. Laws against same-sex and nonmarital sex remained constitutional through the end of the twentieth century.[24]

Gay and lesbian rights advocates were also generally unsuccessful in cases concerning employment discrimination. In 1988, the Court upheld the procedures used by the National Security Agency to fire an employee based on his homosexual relationships with foreign nationals. In the same year, the Court ruled that the Central Intelligence Agency's firing of an employee based on his disclosure that he was a homosexual was subject to judicial review, but several years later the Court denied *cert* after lower courts reviewed and rejected his claims. The Court was not willing to let the federal government fire homosexual employees at will, but to satisfy the justices the government had to do little more than explain the basis for its actions. In the 1990s, the Court denied *cert* in a set of appeals of decisions permitting private businesses to discriminate against employees based on homosexual conduct, character, or speech. One of the only gay-related employment discrimination cases accepted for argument in this period was *Oncale* (1998). In this case the justices unanimously held that under certain circumstances same-sex sexual harassment was prohibited under federal legislation banning workplace sex discrimination. According to Scalia's opinion, three male employees (two in supervisory positions) had subjected Oncale to "sex-related, humiliating actions," two had "physically assaulted Oncale in a sexual manner," and one had "threatened him with rape." As Scalia explained, the critical issue was that Oncale had experienced discrimination on the basis of sex, not antigay discrimination. In other words, he had been treated more negatively than women had been treated in comparable circumstances. Except in special circumstances, federal law prohibited employment discrimination favoring men over women or women over men, but employment discrimination favoring heterosexuals over homosexuals was permissible.[25]

In another series of cases, the Court denied *cert* in challenges to antihomosexual military policies and practices. One important exception was *Watkins* (1990), in which the Court denied *cert* after the Ninth Circuit ruled that the army could not use homosexuality as the basis for denying Watkins' reenlistment. The reason for this unusual outcome was that Watkins had informed the military about his homosexuality at various points in his career and the army had allowed him to reenlist. Two years later, in another exceptional gay and lesbian rights victory, the Court denied *cert* after the Ninth Circuit ruled that the Army Reserve had to supply the rational basis for its policy before it could discharge a member for acknowledging her homosexuality. After the Court denied *cert*, the army settled the case with the reservist, who was allowed to retire with a promotion and full benefits. While this served notice that the military would have to offer justifications for its antihomosexual policies, the policies remained constitutional.[26]

After *Bowers*, the Court considered several appeals concerning the rights of gay and lesbian activists in the context of public demonstrations, marches, and events. In *Ward* (1987), the Court denied *cert* after the Second Circuit ruled that the New York City police could not deny a Catholic gay and lesbian group the right to demonstrate in front of St. Patrick's Cathedral during a gay pride parade. The Second Circuit also indicated, however, that restrictions on the demonstrators were permissible and fashioned an order allowing only twenty-five protesters to demonstrate for thirty minutes in a location behind police barricades; the order also granted equal time and space to antihomosexual protesters. In *San Francisco Arts and Athletics* (1987), the Court ruled that federal legislation allowed the U.S. Olympic Committee to prohibit the organizers of the "Gay Olympic Games" from using the word "olympic" in their promotional materials. Eight years later, the Court unanimously ruled in *Hurley* that the organizers of the St. Patrick's Day parade in Boston had the right to exclude an Irish-American gay, lesbian, and bisexual group from participating in the parade. Two years later, the Court denied *cert* in an appeal of a New York ruling that upheld disorderly conduct convictions for activists who disrupted traffic during a St. Patrick's Day gay and lesbian march.[27]

By the end of the 1990s, eleven states and more than one hundred municipalities in the United States had banned discrimination on the basis of sexual orientation, with most of the laws covering employment, housing, and public accommodations. In *Boy Scouts* (2000), the Court addressed the question of whether New Jersey's law banning sexual orientation discrimination in public accommodations could be used to challenge a Boy Scouts decision to revoke the membership of an assistant scoutmaster on the basis of his public acknowledgment that he was gay. According to the majority opinion by Rehnquist, the law could not be so used since this would violate the First Amendment rights of the Scouts to express themselves by excluding individuals whose conduct was inconsistent with Scout values. Because the Boy Scouts was a private membership organization, it had the right to exclude homosexuals.[28]

As was the case in the *Boutilier* to *Bowers* era, the Court's tendency to deny *cert* in lesbian and gay rights cases meant that after *Bowers* there were occasional lesbian and gay victories in circumstances where lower courts reached favorable decisions. In *Rent Stabilization Association of New York City* (1994), the Court denied *cert* after a lower court upheld municipal rent control regulations that included same-sex partners within the category of family members entitled to succession rights. This was a victory, but it did not challenge the power of other jurisdictions to practice sexual discrimination. Along similar lines, in *Knott* (1995) the Court denied *cert* in a biological mother's appeal of a Wisconsin court decision granting her female ex-partner the right to petition for visitation rights. This was a positive outcome for the nonbiological parent, but did nothing to challenge the power of other jurisdictions to restrict the rights of lesbian and gay parents. Another *cert* denial with positive implications for gay and lesbian rights on a subnational level occurred in 1997, when *Hacklander-Ready* effectively upheld a lower court ruling against two Wisconsin women who refused to rent a room to a third woman because she was a lesbian, which violated a local ordinance prohibiting housing discrimination based on sexual orientation.[29]

After *Bowers*, the Court continued to use the 1973 *Miller* tests in obscenity and obscenity-related cases, modified by its new child-protection rules and its new approach to municipal zoning regulations targeting sex businesses. Changing communication technologies, which led to new legislation and litigation concerning the telephone, cable television, and the Internet, did not lead to significant changes in the Court's treatment of these types of cases.[30] In the late 1980s, the Court added prisoners to the list of groups for whom special anti-obscenity restrictions would be upheld. In 1989, the majority upheld regulations authorizing federal prison officials to reject incoming publications based on legitimate penological interests. According to Blackmun's majority opinion, federal regulations did not allow officials to reject a publication "solely because its content is religious, philosophical, political, social or sexual," but permitted rejection if "the publication is detrimental to security." Blackmun reasoned that because "homosexually explicit material may identify the possessor as homosexual and target him for assault," such materials could be restricted.[31]

While the justices continued to argue that the Constitution was more protective of sexual expression than sexual conduct, they also emphasized that rights of sexual expression did not include rights of equal treatment in government programs that funded artistic expression. In *National Endowment for the Arts* (1998), the Court ruled that the NEA could deny funding to four performance artists whose work was recommended for funding by an advisory panel of experts but subsequently rejected on grounds of "indecency." According to O'Connor's majority opinion, the federal law did not violate the First Amendment because it did not categorically prohibit the funding of "indecent" projects but simply required that the agency take decency "into consideration." Moreover, the government had the right to set "spending priorities" and the legislation was not unconstitutionally vague. According to the Court's reasoning, the federal government could use its power of the purse to promote heteronormative sexual expression.[32]

Romer (1996) and *Lawrence* (2003)

By 1996, a majority of the states had repealed or invalidated their laws against fornication, cohabitation, sodomy, and several other criminalized forms of sex, but elsewhere these and other sex laws remained in force, as they did in specific federal jurisdictions such as the U.S. military. Nothing the Court had said or done suggested that these laws were unconstitutional and in several decisions the Court had affirmed their validity. Nine states had passed laws prohibiting discrimination on the basis of sexual orientation in areas such as housing, employment, and public accommodations, but sexual discrimination in other states, at the federal level, and in other arenas of public and private life remained constitutional.

For decades, the Court had applied "strict scrutiny" to laws that interfered with "fundamental" rights and laws that used "suspect" classifications, but until *Romer* (1996) and *Lawrence* (2003) these standards were of limited use in sexual rights cases. Which rights were fundamental and which classifications were suspect were not spelled out in the U.S. Constitution or in federal legislation; these were matters of debate and discussion by judges. By 1996, the Court had recognized marital and reproductive rights as fundamental, and race was the paradigmatic example of a suspect classification. In strict scrutiny cases, the burden was on the government to prove that its laws served legitimate, compelling, and substantial state interests and that they were narrowly tailored and necessary to serve those interests. In *Griswold*, *Fanny Hill*, *Loving*, and *Roe*, the Court had decided that there were fundamental marital, reproductive, and speech rights at stake, and in *Loving* the Court had indicated that racial classifications in marriage laws were suspect. This meant that the government's burden had been heavy, and in each of these cases the Court ruled that the government failed to meet its burden.

Beginning in the 1970s, the Court had applied "intermediate scrutiny" to laws that used "quasi-suspect" classifications. Sex classifications that distinguished between males and females were the paradigmatic example of a quasi-suspect classification. In these instances, the burden was still on the government, but it was lighter; it could be met if the government showed that the law served an important state interest and that there was a substantial relationship between the law and its objectives. The Court offered two reasons for treating race and sex differently. First, the Constitution and federal law treated the two differently, regarding racial discrimination with greater suspicion. Second, according to the justices, race and sex *were* different, and these differences (and especially the biological significance of sex differences) justified more judicial deference toward laws that distinguished between males and females.

Activists and advocates interested in challenging sexual (as distinct from sex) discrimination confronted two major problems. First, the Court did not regard sexual privacy or intimacy outside of marriage as a fundamental right. Second, the Court did not regard classifications that distinguished between homosexuality and heterosexuality as suspect or quasi-suspect. In cases involving neither fundamental rights nor suspect or quasi-suspect classifications, the burden on the government was relatively light. All the government had to do was show that the law's classifications served a reasonable government interest and that there was a rational relationship between the law and the interest it served. Occasionally, as in *Eisenstadt*, the Court struck down laws using the minimum scrutiny–rational basis test, but generally the justices were reluctant to do so. The Court regarded national security, military strength, public health and safety, morality, and child protection as reasonable government interests and the justices generally accepted arguments asserting a rational relationship between sexually discriminatory laws and these interests. In most cases involving sexual discrimination in the post-*Roe* era, the Court thus ruled that the government had met its burden, but in two major cases in 1996 and 2003 the Court ruled that the government had not.

In *Romer* (1996), the Court overturned a Colorado state constitutional amendment, adopted in a referendum, that prohibited the state, its municipalities, and all government agencies in the state from enacting, adopting, or enforcing any statute, regulation, or policy permitting any person or group to use homosexuality or bisexuality as the basis of a discrimination claim or a claim of minority status, quota preference, or protected status. The amendment invalidated antidiscrimination laws enacted in various Colorado municipalities, but according to the majority opinion by Kennedy, it did much more than this. As the six justices in the majority observed, "It prohibits all legislative, executive or judicial action at any level of state or local government designed to protect . . . homosexual persons." In this respect, the law "deprives gays and lesbians even of the protection of general laws and policies that prohibit arbitrary discrimination." Kennedy's opinion continued, "Even if, as we doubt, homosexuals could find some safe harbor in laws of general application, we cannot accept the view that Amendment 2's prohibition on specific legal protections does no more than deprive homosexuals of special rights. To the contrary, the amendment imposes a special disability upon those persons alone. Homosexuals are forbidden the safeguards that others enjoy. . . . These are protections against exclusion from an almost limitless number of transactions and endeavors that constitute ordinary civic life in a free society." In these respects, Amendment 2 violated the fundamental rights of homosexuals to participate in society and politics.[33]

Kennedy then proceeded to argue that, even if the law did not interfere with fundamental rights, the state had failed to meet its burden of showing that its classifications had a rational relationship to a legitimate government interest. According to the majority, the amendment's "sheer breadth is so discontinuous with the reasons offered for it that the amendment seems inexplicable by anything but animus toward the class that it affects." Describing the amendment as "unprecedented in our jurisprudence," Kennedy wrote that "a law declaring that in general it shall be more difficult for one group of citizens than for all others to seek aid from the government is itself a denial of equal protection of the laws in the most literal sense." Against the state's argument that the law served its interest in protecting "the liberties of landlords or employers who have personal or religious objections to homosexuality" and "conserving resources to fight discrimination against other groups," the Court argued that "the breadth of the Amendment is so far removed from these particular justifications that we find it impossible to credit them." Kennedy concluded, "Amendment 2 classifies homosexuals not to further a proper legislative end but to make them unequal to everyone else. This Colorado cannot do. A State cannot so deem a class of persons a stranger to its laws."[34]

Romer marked a significant departure in the way the Court discussed homosexuals and treated homosexuality, but its historical significance lies as much in what it signaled about the future alignment of the justices as in what it meant in the short term for the doctrine of heteronormative supremacy. After all, sexually discriminatory laws, including sodomy laws, remained constitutional after *Romer*. Moreover, two years after *Romer* the Court denied *cert* in *Equality Foundation of Greater Cincinnati*, which sustained a lower court decision upholding a Cincinnati city charter amendment that resembled Colorado's Amendment 2. This was a local, as opposed to a state, law, but the different outcomes in *Romer* and *Equality Foundation* may have reflected the Court's conclusion that in the Cincinnati case there was no reason to discount the claim that the amendment did nothing more than remove "sexual orientation" from the city's antidiscrimination ordinance. Meanwhile, in most of the country discrimination on the basis of sexual orientation remained constitutional after *Romer*, as did laws against same-sex sex. Nevertheless, it was significant that Kennedy and O'Connor joined Stevens, Souter, Ginsburg, and Breyer in *Romer* rather than siding with Scalia, Rehnquist, and Thomas, whose vituperative dissent attacked the majority for (among other things) contradicting the reasoning in *Bowers*. According to Scalia, if it was constitutional to criminalize homosexual conduct, why was it not constitutional "to deny special favor and protection to those with a self-avowed tendency or desire to engage in the conduct"? Scalia's dissent asked a good question, but it seems to have prompted Kennedy and O'Connor to reverse the terms: if it was unconstitutional to deny protection against discrimination to homosexuals, why was it constitutional to criminalize homosexual conduct? When the Court addressed this question in *Lawrence* (2003), its answers confronted the doctrine of heteronormative supremacy.[35]

Lawrence challenged a Texas law that criminalized same-sex oral and anal sex. By the Court's reckoning, three other states had similar laws, while nine states criminalized homosexual and heterosexual oral and anal sex performed in private by consenting adults. Five justices voted to strike down the Texas law as unconstitutional because it violated fundamental rights of private sexual expression. O'Connor concurred in the judgment on the grounds that the Texas law violated the equal protection clause because it treated homosexual and heterosexual conduct differently. While O'Connor's reasoning would have struck down state laws that treated homosexual and heterosexual sex differently, the majority ruling had implications for all thirteen states with these types of laws. According to the opening lines of Kennedy's majority opinion, "Liberty protects the person from unwarranted intrusions into a dwelling or other private places. In our tradition the State is not omnipresent in the home. And there are other spheres of our lives and existence, outside the home, where the State should not be a dominant presence. Freedom extends beyond spatial bounds. Liberty presumes an autonomy of self that includes freedom of thought, belief, expression, and certain intimate conduct. The instant case involves liberty of the person both in its spatial and in its more transcendent dimensions."[36]

In applying these principles to the Texas sodomy law, the Court not only overruled *Bowers* but also revised, without acknowledging that it was doing so, the reasoning of *Griswold, Loving, Eisenstadt*, and *Roe*. After describing the basic facts of the case, Kennedy's opinion noted that the decision turned on "whether the petitioners were free as adults to engage in the private conduct in the exercise of their liberty under the Due Process Clause." To answer this question in the affirmative, the majority adopted the position of the dissenters in *Bowers*. According to the *Lawrence* majority, *Griswold* was "the most pertinent beginning point" for considering the "substantive reach of liberty" under the due process clause. Acknowledging that *Griswold* "placed emphasis on the marriage relation and the protected space of the marital bedroom," Kennedy did not address what seven justices had said in the various *Griswold* opinions about the constitutionality of laws against nonmarital sex. Kennedy then observed, "After *Griswold* it was established that the right to make certain decisions regarding sexual conduct extends beyond the marital relationship." Referencing *Eisenstadt*, he noted that the Court had decided that a law prohibiting the distribution of contraceptives to unmarried people "impaired the exercise of their personal rights" and was "in conflict with fundamental human rights." The majority opinion in *Eisenstadt* had emphasized the rights of the unmarried to make decisions about reproduction, but the *Lawrence* majority presented *Eisenstadt* as a ruling about sex. This required ignoring *Eisenstadt*'s comments about sex laws and its conclusion that the case could be decided without addressing "fundamental freedoms." Kennedy then turned to *Roe* and *Carey*, which "confirmed that the reasoning of *Griswold* could not be confined to the protection of rights of married adults." This may have been true, but these decisions had not made it clear that the reasoning of *Griswold* extended beyond reproductive rights. For decades, dissenting justices, lower court judges, legal advocates, and media commentators had been claiming that the Court of the late 1960s and early 1970s had recognized constitutional rights of sexual privacy. Now, for the first time, the Court endorsed this interpretation.[37]

Having laid this foundation, Kennedy proceeded to overturn *Bowers*. According to his opinion, when the *Bowers* Court presented the issue as whether the Constitution "confers a fundamental right upon homosexuals to engage in sodomy," it failed to "appreciate the extent of the liberty at stake." Kennedy claimed that the *Bowers* Court had "demean[ed] the claim the individual put forward, just as it would demean a married couple were it to be said marriage is simply about the right to have sexual intercourse." Insofar as the laws challenged in *Bowers* and *Lawrence* touched upon "the most private human conduct, sexual behavior, and in the most private of places, the home," they attempted "to control a personal relationship that, whether or not entitled to formal recognition in the law, is within the liberty of persons to choose." Kennedy continued, "Adults may choose to enter upon this relationship in the confines of their homes and their own private lives and still retain their dignity as free persons. When sexuality finds overt expression in intimate conduct with another person, the conduct can be but one element in a personal bond that is more enduring. The liberty protected by the Constitution allows homosexual persons the right to make this choice." After challenging the claims made by the *Bowers* majority about the long history of proscriptions against homosexuals, homosexuality, and sodomy, Kennedy turned to the "laws and traditions in the past half century," which revealed "an emerging awareness that liberty gives substantial protection to adult persons in deciding how to conduct their private lives in matters pertaining to sex." According to Kennedy, *Casey* and *Romer* supported this conclusion, and it was now clear that "when homosexual conduct is made criminal by the law of the State, that declaration in and of itself is an invitation to subject homosexual persons to discrimination." *Bowers*, declared Kennedy, "demeans the lives of homosexual persons."[38]

As he moved toward his conclusion, Kennedy formally endorsed a passage in the *Bowers* dissent by Stevens that had declared, "First, the fact that the governing majority in a State has traditionally viewed a particular practice as immoral is not a sufficient reason for upholding a law prohibiting the practice; neither history nor tradition could save a law prohibiting miscegenation. . . . Second, individual decisions by married persons, concerning the intimacies of their physical relationship, even when not intended to produce offspring, are a form of 'liberty' protected by the Due Process Clause. . . . Moreover, this protection extends to intimate choices by unmarried as well as married persons." As for the Texas litigants, "The petitioners are entitled to respect for their private lives. The State cannot demean their existence or control their destiny by making their private sexual conduct a crime." Depicting his ruling as fully consistent and compatible with the words and values of the Constitution's framers, Kennedy concluded, "Had those who drew and ratified the Due Process Clauses . . . known the components of liberty in its manifold possibilities, they might have been more specific. They did not presume to have this insight. They knew times can blind us to certain truths and later generations can see that laws once thought necessary and proper in fact serve only to oppress. As the Constitution endures, persons in every generation can invoke its principles in their own search for greater freedom."[39]

The majority opinion in *Lawrence* positioned itself as the logical culmination of the rulings in *Griswold*, *Loving*, *Eisenstadt*, and *Roe*, and it did so by ignoring the heteronormative aspects of the Court's rulings of the late 1960s and early 1970s. Paradoxically, *Lawrence* is also a heteronormative ruling, though it is based on a different articulation of heteronormative values. As queer studies critics of *Lawrence* have noted, Kennedy's rhetoric depicted sex as deserving of constitutional protection because of its links to the autonomy of the self, the private space of the home, and the transcendent aspects of liberty. For Kennedy, sex itself was not the issue, and he indicated that it was demeaning to suggest otherwise. Rather, sex was important because it fostered intimate relationships and enduring bonds. Sex in this sense was imagined as an activity engaged in by human couples, not by solitary individuals or larger groups; it was intimate, not anonymous; and it was respectable in relationships with a past and future, not encounters in the present. Kennedy's opinion portrayed the individual who engaged in sex with another person as aspiring to respect and dignity, not as engaging in physical exercise, enjoying libido and lust, exploring shame and debasement, experiencing power and powerlessness, or experimenting with transgression and subversion. The *Lawrence* majority had very particular ideas about the significance of sex and sexuality, and from a variety of queer perspectives these ideas are heteronormative, even if they have also become homonormative.[40]

Kennedy's opinion was also quite explicit about the ruling's limits. One of his concluding paragraphs explained, "The present case does not involve minors. It does not involve persons who might be injured or coerced or who are situated in relationships where consent might not easily be refused. It does not involve public conduct or prostitution. It does not involve whether the government must give formal recognition to any relationship that homosexual persons seek to enter. The case does involve two adults who, with full and mutual consent from each other, engaged in sexual practices common to a homosexual lifestyle." Kennedy's clarifications were based on a set of heteronormative ideas about adulthood and childhood, coercion and consent, and privacy and publicity. Moreover, these clarifying comments and other passages in the majority opinion made it clear that *Lawrence* does not mean that governments now have to treat heterosexuality and homosexuality equally.[41]

It is too early to know what the Supreme Court will do with sex and sexuality after *Lawrence*, but the history of the Court's "sexual revolution" in the late 1960s and the early 1970s suggests that we should be cautious about declaring victory and celebrating our liberation. In the twenty-first century it seems particularly important to recognize that marital and reproductive rights are related to, but also distinguishable from, sexual rights. We should be careful, cautious, and critical when progressive advocates and activists claim to be working toward sexual freedom and equality but use strategies and tactics that undermine these goals. And we should be mindful of the ways in which we invent sexual rights and wrongs as we remember and forget the decisions of the Supreme Court.

Notes

HALN	*Homophile Action League Newsletter*
HLBP	Hugo L. Black Papers, Manuscript Division, Library of Congress, Washington, D.C.
HLRS	Homosexual Law Reform Society
HPP	Harriet F. Pilpel Papers, Sophia Smith Collection, Smith College, Northampton, Massachusetts
HRW	Human Rights for Women
HRWC	Human Rights for Women Collection, Schlesinger Library, Radcliffe College, Cambridge, Massachusetts
INS	Immigration and Naturalization Service
JHP	John Harlan Papers, Seeley G. Mudd Manuscript Library, Princeton University, Princeton, New Jersey
JSN	*Janus Society Newsletter*
LAT	*Los Angeles Times*
MR	*Mattachine Review*
MMN	*Mattachine Midwest Newsletter*
MSNYN	*Mattachine Society of New York Newsletter*
MSNYR	Mattachine Society, Inc. of New York Records, Manuscripts and Archives Division, The New York Public Library, New York, New York
NAACP	National Association for the Advancement of Colored People
NARAL	National Association for Repeal of Abortion Laws
NASR	National Association for Sexual Research
NCCIJ	National Catholic Conference for Interracial Justice
NLDF	National Legal Defense Fund
NOP	Norman Oshtry Papers, Philadelphia, Pennsylvania
NOW	National Organization for Women
NYCLU	New York Civil Liberties Union
NYT	*New York Times*
NYTM	*New York Times Magazine*
ONENGLA	ONE National Gay and Lesbian Archives, University of Southern California, Los Angeles, California
PHS	Public Health Service
PLDMP	Phyllis Lyon and Del Martin Papers, Gay, Lesbian, Bisexual, Transgender Historical Society, San Francisco, California
PPFA	Planned Parenthood Federation of America
PPFAP	Planned Parenthood Federation of America Papers, Sophia Smith Collection, Smith College, Northampton, Massachusetts
PPLC	Planned Parenthood League of Connecticut
PPLM	Planned Parenthood League of Massachusetts
PRIDE	Personal Rights in Defense and Education
PW	*Publishers Weekly*
RSP	Richard Schlegel Papers, Rare and Manuscript Collections, Carl A. Kroch Library, Cornell University Library, Ithaca, New York
SLA	State Liquor Authority (New York)
TCP	Tom Clark Papers, Jamal Center for Legal Research, Tarlton Law Library, University of Texas School of Law, Austin, Texas

TEP	Thomas Emerson Papers, Manuscripts and Archives, Yale University Library, New Haven, Connecticut
TMP	Thurgood Marshall Papers, Manuscript Division, Library of Congress, Washington, D.C.
USNWR	*U.S. News and World Report*
WBP	William Brennan Papers, Manuscript Division, Library of Congress, Washington, D.C.
WODP	William O. Douglas Papers, Manuscript Division, Library of Congress, Washington, D.C.
WP	*Washington Post*
WSJ	*Wall Street Journal*

Preface

1. See Peter Novick, *That Noble Dream: The "Objectivity Question" and the American Historical Profession* (New York: Cambridge University Press, 1988).

2. I use "U.S. Americans" to make it clear that I am referring to a subgroup of North, Central, and South Americans and to resist the ways in which conventional U.S. use of the term "American" implies that the United States has a claim on all of the lands of the Americas.

3. See John Brigham, *The Cult of the Court* (Philadelphia: Temple University Press, 1987); Barbara A. Perry, *The Priestly Tribe: The Supreme Court's Image in the American Mind* (Westport, Conn.: Praeger, 1999); John E. Semonche, *Keeping the Faith: A Cultural History of the U.S. Supreme Court* (Lanham, Md.: Rowman and Littlefield, 1998).

4. *Griswold v. Connecticut*, 381 U.S. 479 (1965); *A Book Named "John Cleland's Memoirs of a Woman of Pleasure" v. Attorney General of Massachusetts* (commonly referred to as *Fanny Hill*), 383 U.S. 413 (1966); *Loving v. Virginia*, 388 U.S. 1 (1967); *Eisenstadt v. Baird*, 405 U.S. 438 (1972); *Roe v. Wade*, 410 U.S. 113 (1973).

5. *Bowers v. Hardwick*, 478 U.S. 186 (1986).

6. Marc Stein, *City of Sisterly and Brotherly Loves: Lesbian and Gay Philadelphia, 1945–1972* (Chicago: University of Chicago Press, 2000); *Boutilier v. Immigration and Naturalization Service*, 387 U.S. 118 (1967).

7. Boutilier was born on 3 Sept. 1933; he was deported on 10 Nov. 1968. Marian Smith, Historian, U.S. Citizenship and Immigration Services, supplied me with the deportation date (see INS File A10082545), which I confirmed with materials obtained through FOIA.

8. See Robert McRuer and Abby Wilkerson, eds., *Desiring Disability: Queer Theory Meets Disability Studies*, a special issue of *GLQ: A Journal of Lesbian and Gay Studies* 9 (2003): 1–255; Robert McRuer, *Crip Theory: Cultural Signs of Queerness and Disability* (New York: New York University Press, 2006).

9. Marc Stein, "Forgetting and Remembering a Deported Alien," History News Network, 3 Nov. 2003, http://hnn.us/articles/1769.html (accessed 4 Nov. 2003).

10. See Marc Stein, "Crossing Borders: Memories, Dreams, Fantasies, and Nightmares of the History Job Market," *Left History* 9 (Spring/Summer 2004): 119–39.

11. See Eithne Luibhéid, *Entry Denied: Controlling Sexuality at the Border* (Minneapolis: University of Minnesota Press, 2002), 25–27; *NYT*, 31 Oct. 2009, A9; Philip Girard, "From Subversion to Liberation: Homosexuals and the Immigration Act, 1952–1977," *Canadian Journal of Law and Society* 2 (1987): 1–27; Richard Green, "'Give Me Your Tired, Your Poor, Your Huddled Masses' (of Heterosexuals): An Analysis of American and Canadian Immigration Policy," *Anglo-*

American Law Review 16 (1987): 139–59; Ralf Jürgens, *HIV Testing and Confidentiality: Final Report* (Toronto: Canadian HIV/AIDS Legal Network and Canadian AIDS Society, 1998); David Garmaise, *Questions and Answers: Canada's Immigration Policies as They Affect People Living with HIV/AIDS* (Toronto: Canadian HIV/AIDS Legal Network, 2003, updated 2009).

12. See "Roundtable: Self and Subject," *Journal of American History* 89 (2002): 17–53; Ruth Behar, *The Vulnerable Observer: Anthropology That Breaks Your Heart* (Boston: Beacon, 1996).

Introduction

1. *Lawrence v. Texas*, 539 U.S. 558 (2003).

2. See Richard A. Posner and Katharine B. Silbaugh, *A Guide to America's Sex Laws* (Chicago: University of Chicago Press, 1996); William N. Eskridge Jr., *Dishonorable Passions: Sodomy Laws in America, 1861–2003* (New York: Viking, 2008). On sexual citizenship, see Lauren Berlant, *The Queen of America Goes to Washington City: Essays on Sex and Citizenship* (Durham, N.C.: Duke University Press, 1997); Margot Canaday, "'Who Is A Homosexual?': The Consolidation of Sexual Identities in Mid-Twentieth-Century American Immigration Law," *Law and Social Inquiry* 28 (2003): 351–86; Margot Canaday, "Building a Straight State: Sexuality and Social Citizenship under the 1944 G.I. Bill," *Journal of American History* 90 (2003): 935–57; Eithne Luibhéid, *Entry Denied: Controlling Sexuality at the Border* (Minneapolis: University of Minnesota Press, 2002); Jeffrey Weeks, "The Sexual Citizen," *Theory, Culture, and Society* 15 (1998): 35–52.

3. Jim Yardley, "Unmarried and Living Together, Till the Sheriff Do Us Part," *NYT*, 25 Mar. 2000, A9; *Williams v. Pryor*, 240 F.3d 944 (2001), 947, 949; Eric Frazier and Gary L. Wright, "Halt Cohabiting or No Bail, Judge Tells Defendants," *Charlotte Observer*, 4 Apr. 2001; "Cohabitation Illegal," *NYT*, 4 Apr. 2003, A12. On repeal of the North Dakota law, see *NYT*, 2 Mar. 2007, A13.

4. Mireya Navarro, "Arrest Startles Saleswomen of Sex Toys," *NYT*, 20 Jan. 2004, A12; *Williams v. Morgan*, 378 F.3d 1232 (2004); *Reliable Consultants v. Earle*, 517 F.3d 738 (2008); *Williams v. Morgan*, 478 F.3d 1316 (2007); *1568 Montgomery Highway v. Hoover*, Alabama Supreme Court, 1191, No. 1070531 (2009); *Kansas v. Limon*, 32 Kan. App. 2d 369 (2004); *Kansas v. Limon*, 280 Kan. 275 (2005); "Virginia Sodomy Law Challenged," Associated Press, 13 July 2004; *U.S. v. Marcum*, 60 M.J. 198 (2004); "No to Cohabitation," *NYT*, 30 Mar. 2005, A13; Patrick Jonsson, "Some 1.6 Million Americans in Seven States Are Breaking Old Anticohabitation Rules," *Christian Science Monitor*, 9 Feb. 2004; Nancy Larson, "Gay Families, Keep Out!" *Advocate*, 18 July 2006, 34–35; Brenda Goodman, "Day of Split Outcomes in Teenage Sex Case," *NYT*, 12 June 2007, A12; Brenda Goodman, "Georgia Supreme Court Hears Two Appeals in Teen Sex Case," *NYT*, 21 July 2007, A9; Brenda Goodman, "Man Convicted as Teenager in Sex Case Is Ordered Freed by Georgia Court," *NYT*, 27 Oct. 2007, A9.

5. Rick Santorum, cited by the Associated Press, 21 Apr. 2003; Mr. Allen, "Did Gays Get All They Want from the Supreme Court? (Really?)," History News Network, 7 July 2003, http://hnn.us/articles/1542.html (accessed 17 July 2003).

6. See *Lawrence*, 564–65.

7. See Michael Warner, ed., *Fear of a Queer Planet: Queer Politics and Social Theory* (Minneapolis: University of Minnesota Press, 1993).

8. See David Allyn, *Make Love, Not War: The Sexual Revolution* (Boston: Little, Brown, 2000); Beth L. Bailey, *From Front Porch to Back Seat: Courtship in Twentieth-Century America* (Baltimore: Johns Hopkins University Press, 1988); Beth Bailey, *Sex in the Heartland* (Cambridge, Mass.: Harvard University Press, 1999); Nancy F. Cott, *Public Vows: A History of Marriage and the Nation* (Cambridge, Mass.: Harvard University Press, 2000), 180–227; John D'Emilio and Estelle Freedman, *Intimate Matters: A History of Sexuality in America* (New York: Harper and Row, 1988),

239–343; Barbara Ehrenreich, Elizabeth Hess, and Gloria Jacobs, *Re-Making Love: The Feminization of Sex* (Garden City, N.Y.: Anchor, 1986); Jane Gerhard, *Desiring Revolution: Second-Wave Feminism and the Rewriting of American Sexual Thought, 1920 to 1982* (New York: Columbia University Press, 2001); John Heidenry, *What Wild Ecstasy: The Rise and Fall of the Sexual Revolution* (New York: Simon and Schuster, 1997); Jonathan Ned Katz, *The Invention of Heterosexuality* (New York: Dutton, 1995), 83–166; Robert O. Self, "Sex in the City: The Politics of Sexual Liberalism in Los Angeles, 1963–79," *Gender and History* 20 (2008): 288–311; Kevin White, *Sexual Liberation or Sexual License?: The American Revolt Against Victorianism* (Chicago: Ivan R. Dee, 2000), 134–82.

9. See, in addition to note 8, Christina Simmons, "Modern Sexuality and the Myth of Victorian Repression," in *Passion and Power: Sexuality in History*, eds. Kathy Peiss and Christina Simmons (Philadelphia: Temple University Press, 1989), 157–77; Kevin White, *The First Sexual Revolution: The Emergence of Male Heterosexuality in Modern America* (New York: New York University Press, 1993).

10. On the Warren and Burger Courts, see Vincent Blasi, ed., *The Burger Court: The Counter-Revolution That Wasn't* (New Haven, Conn.: Yale University Press, 1983); Morton Horwitz, *The Warren Court and the Pursuit of Justice* (New York: Hill and Wang, 1998); Earl Maltz, *The Chief Justiceship of Warren Burger, 1969–1986* (Columbia: University of South Carolina Press, 2000); Lucas Powe Jr., *The Warren Court and American Politics* (Cambridge, Mass.: Harvard University Press, 2000); Bernard Schwartz, *The Ascent of Pragmatism: The Burger Court in Action* (Reading, Pa.: Addison-Wesley, 1990); Bernard Schwartz, *Super Chief: Earl Warren and His Supreme Court* (New York: New York University Press, 1983); Bernard Schwartz, ed., *The Warren Court: A Retrospective* (New York: Oxford University Press, 1996); Bernard Schwartz with Stephan Lesher, *Inside the Warren Court* (Garden City, N.Y.: Doubleday, 1983); Herman Schwartz, ed., *The Burger Years: Rights and Wrongs in the Supreme Court, 1969–1986* (New York: Viking, 1987); Mark V. Tushnet, ed., *The Warren Court in Historical and Political Perspective* (Charlottesville: University of Virginia Press, 1993); Bob Woodward and Scott Armstrong, *The Brethren: Inside the Supreme Court* (New York: Simon and Schuster, 1979); Tinsley Yarbrough, *The Burger Court: Justices, Rulings, and Legacy* (Santa Barbara, Calif.: ABC-CLIO, 2000).

11. See Howard Ball, *A Defiant Life: Thurgood Marshall and the Persistence of Racism in America* (New York: Crown, 1998); Howard Ball, *Hugo L. Black: Cold Steel Warrior* (New York: Oxford University Press, 1996); Howard Ball and Phillip J. Cooper, *Of Power and Right: Hugo Black, William O. Douglas, and America's Constitutional Revolution* (New York: Oxford University Press, 1992); Hugo L. Black and Elizabeth Black, *Mr. Justice and Mrs. Black: The Memoirs of Hugo L. Black and Elizabeth Black* (New York: Random House, 1986); Hugo Black Jr., *My Father: A Remembrance* (New York: Random House, 1975); Sally Blackmun, introduction to *The War on Choice*, by Gloria Feldt (New York: Bantam, 2004), xv–xxiii; Donald E. Boles, *Mr. Justice Rehnquist, Judicial Activist: The Early Years* (Ames: Iowa State University Press, 1987); Hunter Clark, *Justice Brennan: The Great Conciliator* (New York: Birch Lane, 1995); Ed Cray, *Chief Justice: A Biography of Earl Warren* (New York: Simon and Schuster, 1997); Michael D. Davis and Hunter R. Clark, *Thurgood Marshall: Warrior at the Bar, Rebel on the Bench* (New York: Birch Lane, 1992); Sue Davis, *Justice Rehnquist and the Constitution* (Princeton, N.J.: Princeton University Press, 1989); John W. Dean, *The Rehnquist Choice* (New York: Free Press, 2001); William O. Douglas, *The Court Years, 1939–1975: The Autobiography of William O. Douglas* (New York: Random House, 1980); William O. Douglas, *The Douglas Letters: Selections from the Private Papers of Justice William O. Douglas*, ed. Melvin J. Urofsky (Bethesda, Md.: Adler and Adler, 1987); William O. Douglas, *Go East, Young Man: The Early Years* (New York: Random House, 1974);

Gerald Dunne, *Hugo Black and the Judicial Revolution* (New York: Simon and Schuster, 1977); James C. Duram, *Justice William O. Douglas* (Boston: Twayne, 1981); Kim Isaac Eisler, *A Justice for All: William J. Brennan, Jr., and the Decisions That Transformed America* (New York: Simon and Schuster, 1993); Tony A. Freyer, *Hugo L. Black and the Dilemma of American Liberalism* (Glenview, Ill.: Scott, Foresman, 1990); Dorothy Kurgans Goldberg, *A Private View of a Public Life* (New York: Charterhouse, 1975); Roger Goldman with David Gallen, *Justice William J. Brennan, Jr.: Freedom First* (New York: Carroll and Graf, 1994); Linda Greenhouse, *Becoming Justice Blackmun: Harry Blackmun's Supreme Court Journey* (New York: Times, 2005); Dennis J. Hutchinson, *The Man Who Once Was Whizzer White: A Portrait of Justice Byron R. White* (New York: Free Press, 1998); John C. Jeffries Jr., *Justice Lewis F. Powell, Jr.* (New York: Scribner's, 1994); Laura Kalman, *Abe Fortas: A Biography* (New Haven, Conn.: Yale University Press, 1990); Joyce Murdoch and Deb Price, *Courting Justice: Gay Men and Lesbians v. the Supreme Court* (New York: Basic, 2001); Bruce Allen Murphy, *Fortas: The Rise and Ruin of a Supreme Court Justice* (New York: Morrow, 1988); Bruce Allen Murphy, *Wild Bill: The Legend and Life of William O. Douglas* (New York: Random House, 2003); Roger K. Newman, *Hugo Black: A Biography* (New York: Pantheon, 1994); Jim Newton, *Justice for All: Earl Warren and the Nation He Made* (New York: Riverhead, 2006); Jack Harrison Pollack, *Earl Warren: The Judge Who Changed America* (Englewood Cliffs, N.J.: Prentice-Hall, 1979); E. Joshua Rosenkranz and Bernard Schwartz, eds., *Reason and Passion: Justice Brennan's Enduring Influence* (New York: Norton, 1997); Carl T. Rowan, *Dream Makers, Dream Breakers: The World of Justice Thurgood Marshall* (Boston: Little, Brown, 1993); Robert Shogan, *A Question of Judgment: The Fortas Case and the Struggle for the Supreme Court* (New York: Bobbs-Merrill, 1972); James F. Simon, *Independent Journey: The Life of William O. Douglas* (New York: Harper and Row, 1980); David Stebenne, *Arthur J. Goldberg: New Deal Liberal* (New York: Oxford University Press, 1996); Virginia van der Veer Hamilton, *Hugo Black: The Alabama Years* (Baton Rouge: Louisiana State University Press, 1972); Earl Warren, *The Memoirs of Earl Warren* (Garden City, N.Y.: Doubleday, 1977); G. Edward White, *Earl Warren: A Public Life* (New York: Oxford University Press, 1982); Stephen L. Wasby, ed., *"He Shall Not Pass This Way Again": The Legacy of Justice William O. Douglas* (Pittsburgh, Pa.: University of Pittsburgh Press, 1990); J. Harvie Wilkinson III, *Serving Justice: A Supreme Court Clerk's View* (New York: Charterhouse, 1974); Juan Williams, *Thurgood Marshall: American Revolutionary* (New York: Times, 1998); Woodward and Armstrong, *The Brethren*; Tinsley E. Yarbrough, *Mr. Justice Black and His Critics* (Durham, N.C.: Duke University Press, 1988); Tinsley E. Yarbrough, *John Marshall Harlan: Great Dissenter of the Warren Court* (New York: Oxford University Press, 1992); Tinsley E. Yarbrough, *Harry A. Blackmun: The Outsider Justice* (New York: Oxford University Press, 2008).

12. Harry Datcher, cited in Murphy, *Wild Bill*, 368; handwritten notes, 16 Nov. 1971 and 15 Oct. 1973, Box 116, HABP.

13. Davis and Clark, *Thurgood Marshall*, 281; Murdoch and Price, *Courting Justice*, 78; Brennan, cited in Edward de Grazia, *Girls Lean Back Everywhere: The Law of Obscenity and the Assault on Genius* (New York: Random House, 1992), 274; Hugh Hefner to Brennan, c. 1966, Box 135, WBP; "U.S. Supreme Court Reexamines Precedents in Hearings on Three Book Censorship Cases," *PW*, 27 Dec. 1965, 62; Fortas to Brennan, 10 Feb. 1966, Box 139, WBP; Fortas to Douglas, 10 Apr. 1967, Box 1379, WODP; handwritten notes, Box I-88, AFP; Rehnquist to Blackmun, 26 Mar. 1975, Box 116, HABP; Douglas, cited in Harry Ashmore, "Doubling the Standard," *Virginia Quarterly Review* 62 (1986), 71; W. V. Gullickson to the Law Clerks, 9 Feb. 1972, and to Burger, 14 Feb. 1972, Box 78, TMP; "Amicae Curiae," *National Lampoon*, Feb. 1974.

14. Murdoch and Price, *Courting Justice*, 18–26, 117, 187; Robert Mnookin, cited in Yar-

brough, *John Marshall Harlan*, 343; Cathy Douglas Stone, cited in Murdoch and Price, *Courting Justice*, 108, 129; Douglas, *Go East*, 104–5; Murdoch and Price, *Courting Justice*, 129; Black, *My Father*, 128; Eskridge, *Dishonorable Passions*, 89.

15. Kalman, *Abe Fortas*, 196; FBI documents, 20 and 24 July 1967, reproduced in J. J. Maloney, "Was Abe Fortas Gay?" *Crime Magazine*, http://www.crimemagazine.com/Corruption/abe.htm (accessed 14 July 2000). I thank Douglas Charles for confirming that the FBI documents are included in the materials deposited by Athan Theoharis at Marquette University. I thank Tuan Samahon for sharing his work-in-progress on Fortas. See also Boxes I-92–99, AFP; Susan Braudy, *Family Circle: The Boudins and the Aristocracy of the Left* (New York: Knopf, 2003), 331, 431; Alexander Charns and Paul M. Green, "Playing the Information Game," in *A Culture of Secrecy: The Government Versus the People's Right to Know*, ed. Athan G. Theoharis (Lawrence: University Press of Kansas, 1998), 103–8; Murphy, *Fortas*; Shogan, *A Question of Judgment*; Marc Stein, "Did the FBI Try to Blackmail Supreme Court Justice Abe Fortas?" History News Network, 19 July 2005, http://hnn.us/articles/13170.html (accessed 20 July 2005); Whitney Strub, "Perversion for Profit: Citizens for Decent Literature and the Arousal of an Antiporn Public in the 1960s," *Journal of the History of Sexuality* 15 (2006): 282–84. According to journalist Fred Graham's notes on a 29 Aug. 1969 conversation with journalist Bill Lambert, "Lambert also knows about the report that the FBI had a morals file on Fortas. One of his contacts telephoned him shortly after the life [magazine] story broke, informing him that the Washington field office of the FBI had a file that showed that Fortas had been identified as a man who had been accused of homosexual relations with a 16-year-old boy." See Box 8, FGP.

16. See Barbara A. Perry, *The Priestly Tribe: The Supreme Court's Image in the American Mind* (Westport, Conn.: Praeger, 1999).

17. Eva R. Rubin, *The Supreme Court and the American Family: Ideology and Issues* (New York: Greenwood, 1986), 190; Christopher Lasch, *Haven in a Heartless World: The Family Besieged* (New York: Basic, 1977).

18. See preface notes 3 and 5.

19. Allyn, *Make Love*, 38, 56, 266. See also Bailey, *Sex in the Heartland*, 7, 15, 129–30, 182; Cott, *Public Vows*, 198–201, 210–16; D'Emilio and Freedman, *Intimate Matters*, 250, 277, 287–88, 315, 327, 350; Heidenry, *What Wild Ecstasy*, 79–84, 117–18; Self, "Sex in the City," 288, 291–93, 298, 301; White, *Sexual Liberation*, 137–38, 141, 161, 176.

20. *Boutilier* and related cases have attracted minimal attention by historians, but more by legal studies scholars (see chapters 2 and 7). Important exceptions in history and related fields include William B. Turner, "Lesbian/Gay Rights and Immigration Policy: Lobbying to End the Medical Model," *Journal of Policy History* 7 (1995): 208–25; Luibhéid, *Entry Denied*, 77–101; Canaday, "'Who Is A Homosexual?'"; Susana Peña, "'Obvious Gays' and the State Gaze: Cuban Gay Visibility and U.S. Immigration Policy during the 1980 Mariel Boatlift," *Journal of the History of Sexuality* 16 (2007): 482–514; Siobhan B. Somerville, "Queer *Loving*," *GLQ: A Journal of Gay and Lesbian Studies* 11 (2005): 335–70.

21. For early examples, see Thomas C. Grey, "Eros, Civilization and the Burger Court," *Law and Contemporary Problems* 43 (1980): 83–100; Bruce C. Hafen, "The Constitutional Status of Marriage, Kinship, and Sexual Privacy," *Michigan Law Review* 81 (1983): 463–574. See also David B. Cruz, "'The Sexual Freedom Cases'? Contraception, Abortion, Abstinence, and the Constitution," *Harvard Civil Rights–Civil Liberties Law Review* 35 (2000): 299–383.

22. A recent exception is Suzanne U. Samuels, *First Among Friends: Interest Groups, the U.S. Supreme Court, and the Right to Privacy* (Westport, Conn.: Praeger, 2004).

23. In an entry on *Boutilier* in *Sexuality and the Law: An Encyclopedia of Major Legal Cases*

(New York: Garland, 1993), Arthur Leonard, one of the few scholars to mention the HLRS, claims incorrectly that it "may have been formed primarily to file a brief in this case" (644). For scholarship on later litigation, see Ellen Ann Andersen, *Out of the Closets and into the Courts: Legal Opportunity Structure and Gay Rights Litigation* (Ann Arbor: University of Michigan Press, 2005); Patricia A. Cain, *Rainbow Rights: The Role of Lawyers and Courts in the Lesbian and Gay Civil Rights Movement* (Boulder, Colo.: Westview, 2000); David Rayside, *Queer Inclusions, Continental Divisions: Public Recognition of Sexual Diversity in Canada and the United States* (Toronto: University of Toronto Press, 2008); Miriam Smith, *Political Institutions and Lesbian and Gay Rights in the United States and Canada* (New York: Routledge, 2008). When discussing lesbian and gay activism before the 1970s, many legal studies scholars and political scientists rely on John D'Emilio, *Sexual Politics, Sexual Communities: The Making of a Homosexual Minority in the United States, 1940–1970* (Chicago: University of Chicago Press, 1983), but ignore more recent work, including Nan Alamilla Boyd, *Wide Open Town: A History of Queer San Francisco to 1965* (Berkeley: University of California Press, 2003); Marcia M. Gallo, *Different Daughters: A History of the Daughters of Bilitis and the Rise of the Lesbian Rights Movement* (New York: Carroll and Graf, 2006); Daniel Hurewitz, *Bohemian Los Angeles and the Making of Modern Politics* (Berkeley: University of California Press, 2007); David K. Johnson, *The Lavender Scare: The Cold War Persecution of Gays and Lesbians in the Federal Government* (Chicago: University of Chicago Press, 2004); Martin Meeker, *Contacts Desired: Gay and Lesbian Communications and Community, 1940s–1970s* (Chicago: University of Chicago Press, 2006); Marc Stein, *City of Sisterly and Brotherly Loves: Lesbian and Gay Philadelphia* (Chicago: University of Chicago Press, 2000). For legal studies scholarship that addresses litigation before the 1970s, see, for example, William N. Eskridge Jr., *Gaylaw: Challenging the Apartheid of the Closet* (Cambridge, Mass.: Harvard University Press, 1999); Eskridge, *Dishonorable Passions*; Murdoch and Price, *Courting Justice*.

24. Helpful works include Gregory A. Caldeira, "Courts and Public Opinion," in *The American Courts: A Critical Assessment*, ed. John B. Gates and Charles A. Johnson (Washington, D.C.: Congressional Quarterly Press, 1991), 303–34; Bradley C. Canon and Charles A. Johnson, *Judicial Policies: Implementation and Impact*, 2nd ed. (Washington, D.C.: Congressional Quarterly Press, 1999); Valerie J. Hoekstra, *Public Reactions to Supreme Court Decisions* (New York: Cambridge University Press, 2003); William Haltom, *Reporting on the Courts: How the Mass Media Cover Judicial Actions* (Chicago: Nelson-Hall, 1998); William Haltom and Michael McCann, *Distorting the Law: Politics, Media, and the Litigation Crisis* (Chicago: University of Chicago Press, 2004). For relevant historical scholarship, see David J. Garrow, *Liberty and Sexuality: The Right to Privacy and the Making of* Roe v. Wade (Berkeley: University of California Press, 1994), 263–69, 600–617; Marian Faux, Roe v. Wade: *The Untold Story of the Landmark Supreme Court Decision That Made Abortion Legal* (New York: Macmillan, 1988), 303–26; John W. Johnson, Griswold v. Connecticut: *Birth Control and the Constitutional Right of Privacy* (Lawrence: University Press of Kansas, 2005), 184–97; Peggy Pascoe, *What Comes Naturally: Miscegenation Law and the Making of Race in America* (New York: Oxford University Press, 2009), 287–314.

25. For recent discussions of popular constitutionalism, see Reva B. Siegel, "Constitutional Culture, Social Movement Conflict and Constitutional Change: The Case of the De Facto ERA," *California Law Review* 92 (2006): 1323–1419; Jack M. Balkin and Reva B. Siegel, "Principles, Practices, and Social Movements," *University of Pennsylvania Law Review* 154 (2006): 927–50; Eskridge, *Dishonorable Passions*, 369–71.

26. See Deborah Nelson, *Pursuing Privacy in Cold War America* (New York: Columbia University Press, 2002).

27. See Michael C. Dorf, "Dicta and Article III," *University of Pennsylvania Law Review* 142

(1994): 1997–2069; Richard A. Posner, *The Federal Courts: Challenge and Reform* (Cambridge, Mass.: Harvard University Press, 1996), 371–82; Michael Abramowicz and Maxwell Stearns, "Defining Dicta," *Stanford Law Review* 57 (2004): 953–1094.

28. *ONE v. Olesen*, 355 U.S. 371 (1958); *Manual Enterprises v. Day*, 370 U.S. 478 (1962); *Rosenberg v. Fleuti*, 374 U.S. 449 (1963).

29. For transnational comparisons, see David Rayside, *On the Fringe: Gays and Lesbians in Politics* (Ithaca, N.Y.: Cornell University Press, 1998); Rayside, *Queer Inclusions*; Smith, *Political Institutions*.

30. See Angela Y. Davis, *Women, Race, and Class* (New York: Random House, 1981), 202–21; Rhonda Copelon, "From Privacy to Autonomy: The Conditions for Sexual and Reproductive Freedom," in *From Abortion to Reproductive Freedom: Transforming a Movement*, ed. Marlene Gerber Fried (Boston: South End, 1990), 27–43; Linda Gordon, *Woman's Body, Woman's Right: Birth Control in America*, rev. ed. (1974; repr., New York: Penguin, 1990), 391–412; Jennifer Nelson, *Women of Color and the Reproductive Rights Movement* (New York: New York University Press, 2003); Linda Przybyszewski, "The Right to Privacy: A Historical Perspective," in *Abortion, Medicine, and the Law*, 4th ed., eds. J. Douglas Butler and David F. Walbert (New York: Facts on File, 1992), 667–92; Dorothy Roberts, *Killing the Black Body: Race, Reproduction, and the Meaning of Liberty* (New York: Random House, 1997), 56–103; Rickie Solinger, *Wake Up Little Susie: Single Pregnancy and Race Before* Roe v. Wade (New York: Routledge, 1992); Rickie Solinger, *Pregnancy and Power: A Short History of Reproductive Politics in America* (New York: New York University Press, 2005), 79–102, 128–208; Rickie Solinger, ed., *Abortion Wars: A Half Century of Struggle, 1950–2000* (Berkeley: University of California Press, 1998), 95–110, 161–207; Kendall Thomas, "Beyond the Privacy Principle," *Columbia Law Review* 92 (1992): 1431–1516.

31. See George L. Mosse, *Nationalism and Sexuality: Respectability and Abnormal Sexuality in Modern Europe* (New York: Howard Fertig, 1985); Evelyn Brooks Higginbotham, *Righteous Discontent: The Women's Movement in the Black Baptist Church, 1880–1920* (Cambridge, Mass.: Harvard University Press, 1993), 185–229.

32. "What Justice Powell Says Is Wrong with America," *USNWR*, 28 Aug. 1972, 41–42; *Miller v. California*, 413 U.S. 15 (1973), 36.

33. *Lawrence*, 562, 567.

Chapter 1

1. See Hugh M. Hefner, "The Playboy Philosophy," *Playboy*, Apr. 1964, 63–68, 176–84; Harriet F. Pilpel, "Sex vs. the Law: A Study in Hypocrisy," *Harper's*, Jan. 1965, 35–40; Gore Vidal, "Variety: But Is It Legal?" *Partisan Review*, Winter 1965, 79–87; Hugh M. Hefner, "The Legal Enforcement of Morality," *University of Colorado Law Review* 40 (1968): 199–221; Richard Rhodes, "Sex and Sin in Sheboygan," *Playboy*, Aug. 1972, 129–30, 186–90; Richard A. Posner and Katharine B. Silbaugh, *A Guide to America's Sex Laws* (Chicago: University of Chicago Press, 1996).

2. For historical accounts of *Griswold*, see David J. Garrow, *Liberty and Sexuality: The Right to Privacy and the Making of* Roe v. Wade (Berkeley: University of California Press, 1994), 196–269; John W. Johnson, Griswold v. Connecticut: *Birth Control and the Constitutional Right of Privacy* (Lawrence: University Press of Kansas, 2005).

3. *Griswold v. Connecticut*, 381 U.S. 479 (1965), 480–81.

4. The Court did not address whether other states had laws similar to Connecticut's, but in oral arguments Thomas Emerson claimed that no other state "makes it a criminal offense to use contraceptive devices" and Massachusetts was the only other state with a birth control law "in-

terpreted to apply without exception" to "married persons" and "doctors." Thomas Emerson, oral arguments, *Griswold*, 29 Mar. 1965.

5. *Griswold*, 484. The case cited was *Boyd v. United States*, 116 U.S. 616 (1886).

6. *Griswold*, 480–82, 485–86.

7. Ibid., 488, 495–96. See also *Poe v. Ullman*, 367 U.S. 497 (1961). The other cases cited were *Meyer v. Nebraska*, 262 U.S. 390 (1923); *Pierce v. Society of Sisters*, 268 U.S. 510 (1925); *Prince v. Massachusetts*, 321 U.S. 158 (1944).

8. *Griswold*, 485.

9. Ibid., 496–99.

10. Ibid., 502, 505.

11. For internal Court discussions about *Griswold*, see Box 383, HLBP; Boxes I-113–14, I-126, II-6, WBP; Boxes A178, A211, B202, C81, TCP; Box 1347, WODP; Box 235, JHP; Boxes 126–27, 267, 379, 520, EWP. These materials show that Brennan persuaded Douglas to revise his draft, which emphasized First Amendment rights of association; Warren had doubts about signing the Douglas opinion, which helped prompt Goldberg to write his concurring opinion; and Warren initially indicated he would join White's concurrence but later joined Goldberg's.

12. *Griswold*, 481. See also *Barrows v. Jackson*, 346 U.S. 249 (1953).

13. *Griswold*, 503. See also Nancy F. Cott, *Public Vows: A History of Marriage and the Nation* (Cambridge, Mass: Harvard University Press, 2000); John D'Emilio and Estelle Freedman, *Intimate Matters: A History of Sexuality in America* (New York: Harper and Row, 1988); Jacqueline Jones, *Labor of Love, Labor of Sorrow: Black Women, Work, and the Family from Slavery to the Present* (New York: Basic, 1985); Jennifer Nelson, *Women of Color and the Reproductive Rights Movement* (New York: New York University Press, 2003).

14. *Griswold*, 494, 496; *Olmstead v. United States*, 277 U.S. 438 (1928); Brennan to Douglas, 24 Apr. 1965, Box 1347, WODP; Gail Bederman, *Manliness and Civilization: A Cultural History of Gender and Race in the United States, 1880–1917* (Chicago: University of Chicago Press, 1995).

15. See *Griswold*, 491, 493, 496, 501; Matthew Connelly, *Fatal Misconception: The Struggle to Control World Population* (Cambridge, Mass.: Harvard University Press, 2008).

16. See Lee Rainwater and William L. Yancey, *The Moynihan Report and the Politics of Controversy* (Cambridge, Mass.: MIT Press, 1967); Ruth Feldstein, *Motherhood in Black and White: Race and Sex in American Liberalism, 1930–1965* (Ithaca, N.Y.: Cornell University Press, 2000), 139–64. For pre-*Griswold* media examples, see *Good Housekeeping*, Aug. 1964, 59, 152–58; *Life*, 10 May 1963, 37–40; *NYTM*, 31 Jan. 1965, 12–13, 52–55.

17. For historical accounts of *Fanny Hill*, see Edward de Grazia, *Girls Lean Back Everywhere: The Law of Obscenity and the Assault on Genius* (New York: Random House, 1992); Richard F. Hixson, *Pornography and the Justices: The Supreme Court and the Intractable Obscenity Problem* (Carbondale: Southern Illinois University Press, 1996); Charles Rembar, *The End of Obscenity: The Trials of Lady Chatterley, Tropic of Cancer, and Fanny Hill* (New York: Random House, 1968). See also *Ginzburg v. U.S.*, 383 U.S. 463 (1966); *Mishkin v. New York*, 383 U.S. 502 (1966).

18. *A Book Named "John Cleland's Memoirs of a Woman of Pleasure" v. Attorney General of the Commonwealth of Massachusetts* (commonly referred to as *Fanny Hill*), 383 U.S. 413 (1966), 421–22.

19. *A Book Named*, 418–21. See also *Roth v. United States*, 354 U.S. 476 (1957). Brennan cited *Jacobellis v. Ohio*, 378 U.S. 184 (1964), but presumably also referred to *Manual Enterprises v. Day*, 370 U.S. 478 (1962).

20. Stewart wrote in *Jacobellis*: "Criminal laws in this area are constitutionally limited to hard-core pornography. I shall not today attempt further to define the kinds of material I

understand to be embraced within that shorthand description and perhaps I could never succeed in intelligibly doing so. But I know it when I see it" (197). Harlan agreed with Stewart's position on hardcore pornography, but only in federal cases. Harlan developed this position in *Roth* and applied it in *Manual*, *Jacobellis*, and the three 1966 cases.

21. *A Book Named*, 428.

22. Ibid., 427; *Ginzburg*, 479–81, 489–90.

23. *A Book Named*, 420; *Ginzburg*, 466–67, 475. According to *Girls Lean Back*, Brennan came to believe that the pandering decision was his "worst mistake" (503). Several weeks after the rulings were announced, Fortas wrote to Douglas, "I think I was wrong in Ginzburg. I was alarmed by Brennan's vote at Conference to affirm the ban on *Fanny Hill*. So contrary to my principles, I went to work, suggested the 'pandering' formula to Bill (which I still think is as good as any for this cess-pool problem) and came out against Ginzburg. I guess that subconsciously I was affected by G's slimy qualities—but if I had it to do over again, I'd vote to reverse at least as to all except his publication of 'Liaison.' Well, live and learn." See Fortas to Douglas, 15 Apr. 1966, Box 1364, WODP.

24. *Mishkin*, 508.

25. *A Book Named*, 419, 424–25, 446.

26. *Ginzburg*, 466–68, 472, 487, 489, 499–500.

27. *Mishkin*, 503, 505, 508. In unpublished notes, Brennan wrote, "It was necessary . . . to adjust the prurient appeal criterion to cover the so-called deviant material, and this innovation caused some concern on the part of Justice Fortas." Fortas wanted to rely on the pandering argument to uphold Mishkin's conviction. Brennan "rejected the suggestions, adding only a sentence that used *Ginzburg* as a supporting or alternative basis for finding the requisite prurient appeal. Apparently this met Justice Fortas' approval." See Brennan's notes on the Oct. 1965 term, Box II-6, WBP.

28. *ONE v. Olesen*, 355 U.S. 371 (1958); *Womack v. U.S.*, 365 U.S. 859 (1961); *Manual*; *Darnell v. U.S.*, 375 U.S. 916 (1963); *U.S. v. Darnell*, 316 F.2d 813 (1963), 814, 816; *Jacobellis*, 195–96. For examples of antigay discrimination in obscenity prosecutions, see Whitney Strub, "The Clearly Obscene and the Queerly Obscene: Heteronormativity and Obscenity in Cold War Los Angeles," *American Quarterly* 60 (2008): 373–98.

29. *Landau v. Fording*, 245 Cal. App. 2d 820 (1966), 388 U.S. 456 (1967); *G.I. Distributors v. New York*, 389 U.S. 905 (1967); *Ginsberg v. New York*, 390 U.S. 629 (1968), 631; *Redrup v. New York*, 386 U.S. 767 (1967); *Stanley v. Georgia*, 394 U.S. 557 (1969), 559, 565. This paragraph is also based on a survey of obscenity decisions from 1966 to 1973.

30. *Miller v. California*, 413 U.S. 15 (1973), 24, 30, 33. See also *Paris Adult Theatre I v. Slaton*, 413 U.S. 49 (1973); *U.S. v. Orito*, 413 U.S. 139 (1973); *Kaplan v. California*, 413 U.S. 115 (1973); *U.S. v. 12 200-Ft. Reels Of Super 8MM Film*, 413 U.S. 123 (1973).

31. *Paris*, 65–68. For internal Court discussions about these cases, see Boxes 388–89, HLBP; Boxes I-129–39, II-3, II-6, WBP; Boxes A185–86, A190, A211, B208–209, C82, TCP; Box 1364, 1368, WODP; Boxes I-1–3, 13, 17, AFP; Boxes 248, 250, 258, 538, 583, JHP; Boxes 53, 78, 99, 105, 119, TMP; Boxes 126–27, 136, 277–80, 380–81, 529–32, EWP. These materials show that Brennan and Warren initially voted against *Fanny Hill* (for a 5–4 vote against the novel); Fortas helped persuade Brennan and Warren to change their votes; the three-part test in Brennan's *Fanny Hill* opinion was originally part of his *Ginzburg* draft but was moved, in part to win White's and Clark's concurrences in *Ginzburg*; Stewart initially supported the test, but later withdrew his endorsement; Fortas initially found two of the three *Ginzburg* publications obscene but was persuaded by Warren to uphold all of the convictions; Fortas initially voted in favor of Mishkin but in the

end joined Brennan's opinion; and Powell initially sided with Brennan in *Miller*, which would have given Brennan a majority.

32. *A Book Named*, 415–16; *A Book Named*, Suffolk County Superior Court, 3 Sept. 1964; Charles Rembar, "Reply Brief for Appellant," *A Book Named*, Supreme Court, Oct. 1965, 4–5.

33. *Ginzburg*, 466; Jason Epstein, "The Obscenity Business," *Atlantic*, Aug. 1966, 59; *Mishkin*, 505.

34. *Ginzburg*, 473; *Stanley*, 564; *Paris*, 61, 63; de Grazia, *Girls Lean Back*, 510–11; Nesson memo to Harlan, 15 Mar. 1965, Box 583, JHP; MWM memo to Clark, 13 Mar. 1965, Box B208, TCP; *Ginzburg*, 487–88. On race and obscenity, see Whitney Strub, "Black and White and Banned All Over: Race, Censorship and Obscenity in Postwar Memphis," *Journal of Social History* 40 (2007): 685–715.

35. Ward Caille to Harlan, 24 Mar. 1966, Box 248, JHP; Ginzburg, cited in Merle Miller, "Ralph Ginzburg, Middlesex, N.J., and the First Amendment," *NYTM*, 30 Apr. 1972; "Playboy Interview: Ralph Ginzburg," *Playboy*, July 1966, 120.

36. *Mishkin*, 505; *Ginzburg*, 467, 484, 488; *Stanley*, 565; Paul Bender and William Brennan, oral arguments, *Ginzburg*, 7 Dec. 1965.

37. Bob Woodward and Scott Armstrong, *The Brethren: Inside the Supreme Court* (New York: Simon and Schuster, 1979), 192–94.

38. For historical accounts of *Loving*, see Rachel F. Moran, *Interracial Intimacy: The Regulation of Race and Romance* (Chicago: University of Chicago Press, 2001), 76–100; Phyl Newbeck, *Virginia Hasn't Always Been for Lovers* (Carbondale: Southern Illinois University Press, 2004); Peggy Pascoe, *What Comes Naturally: Miscegenation Law and the Making of Race in America* (New York: Oxford University Press, 2009); Renee C. Romano, *Race Mixing: Black-White Marriage in Postwar America* (Cambridge, Mass.: Harvard University Press, 2003), 175–215; Robert J. Sickels, *Race, Marriage and the Law* (Albuquerque: University of New Mexico Press, 1972); Walter Wadlington, "The *Loving* Case: Virginia's Anti-miscegenation Statute in Historical Perspective," *Virginia Law Review* 52 (1966): 1189–1223; Peter Wallenstein, *Tell the Court I Love My Wife: Race, Marriage, and Law—An American History* (New York: Palgrave, 2002).

39. *Loving v. Virginia*, 388 U.S. 1 (1967), 2, 4. Virginia defined a "white person" as a person with "no trace whatever of any blood other than Caucasian," plus those who have "one-sixteenth or less of the blood of the American Indian and have no other non-Caucasic blood." A "colored person" was defined as a person "in whom there is ascertainable any Negro blood." An American Indian was defined as a person who was "not a colored person having one fourth or more of American Indian blood . . . ; except that members of Indian tribes existing in this Commonwealth having one fourth or more of Indian blood and less than one sixteenth of Negro blood shall be deemed tribal Indians." *Loving*, 5.

40. *Loving*, 7–13.

41. *McLaughlin v. Florida*, 379 U.S. 184 (1964). In an exchange with Virginia's lawyer R. D. McIlwaine during oral arguments in *Loving*, one justice asked whether a black/white couple that married in New York and moved to Virginia could be punished under Virginia's adultery, fornication, or cohabitation laws. McIlwaine answered in the affirmative. See also Ariela R. Dubler, "From *McLaughlin v. Florida* to *Lawrence v. Texas*: Sexual Freedom and the Road to Marriage," *Columbia Law Review* 106 (2006): 1165–87.

42. *Loving*, 12; *Skinner v. Oklahoma*, 316 U.S. 535 (1942), 541.

43. For internal Court discussions about *Loving*, see Box 392, HLBP; Boxes I-145, I-156, WBP; Boxes A207, A211, B218, C84, TCP; Boxes 1373, 1379, WODP; Boxes I-21, I-23, I-42, I-88, AFP; Box 285, JHP; Boxes 126–27, 149, 297, 382, 620, EWP. These materials show that Black and White ex-

pressed reservations about Warren's first draft, which placed greater emphasis on due process and the right to marry; in response, Warren deleted a long excerpt of *Meyer*.

44. *Loving*, 11–12; *Hirabayashi v. United States*, 320 U.S. 81 (1943).

45. *Skinner*, 536, 541.

46. For historical accounts of *Eisenstadt*, see Garrow, *Liberty and Sexuality*, 517–20, 536, 541–44.

47. *Eisenstadt v. Baird*, 405 U.S. 438 (1972), 440–41.

48. *Eisenstadt*, 440, 462, 465, 472. According to Harriet F. Pilpel and Nancy F. Wechsler, "Brief of the Planned Parenthood Federation of America," *Eisenstadt*, 5, "Massachusetts and Wisconsin are unique in proscribing contraceptive services for the unmarried."

49. *Eisenstadt*, 453.

50. *Eisenstadt*, 447, 453.

51. Ibid., 443, 448–51.

52. For internal Court discussions about *Eisenstadt*, see Boxes 116, 136, HABP; Boxes I-258, I-280, WBP; Box 1544, WODP; Box 81, TMP. These materials discuss Brennan's effort to include language that would encompass abortion and affect the outcome of *Roe*; Stewart's effort to have Brennan remove a paragraph citing *Griswold* and dealing with discrimination against the poor; Brennan's efforts to win the votes of Blackmun, Douglas, and Stewart; Burger's efforts to influence Blackmun; and Burger's and White's shifting arguments and votes.

53. See David B. Cruz, "'The Sexual Freedom Cases'? Contraception, Abortion, Abstinence, and the Constitution," *Harvard Civil Rights–Civil Liberties Law Review* 35 (2000): 299–383.

54. *Eisenstadt*, 445, 453–54.

55. Joseph Tydings, oral arguments in *Eisenstadt*, 17 Nov. 1965; *Eisenstadt*, 452–53, 456.

56. *Roe v. Wade*, 410 U.S. 113 (1973), 163. For historical accounts of *Roe* and its companion case, *Doe v. Bolton*, 410 U.S. 179 (1973), see Marian Faux, Roe v. Wade: *The Untold Story of the Landmark Supreme Court Decision That Made Abortion Legal* (New York: Macmillan, 1988); Garrow, *Liberty and Sexuality*, 389–599; Linda Greenhouse, *Becoming Justice Blackmun: Harry Blackmun's Supreme Court Journey* (New York: Holt, 2005), 72–101; N. E. H. Hull and Peter Charles Hoffer, Roe v. Wade: *The Abortion Rights Controversy in American History* (Lawrence: University Press of Kansas, 2001), 89–179; Leslie J. Reagan, *When Abortion Was A Crime: Women, Medicine, and Law in the United States, 1867–1973* (Berkeley: University of California Press, 1997); Woodward and Armstrong, *The Brethren*, 165–89, 229–40.

57. *Roe*, 120.

58. Ibid., 128.

59. Ibid., 152–54, 164–65. Stewart's concurring opinion explained, "The *Griswold* decision can be rationally understood only as a holding that the Connecticut statute substantively invaded the 'liberty' that is protected by the Due Process Clause of the Fourteenth Amendment. As so understood, *Griswold* stands as one in a long line of pre-*Skrupa* cases decided under the doctrine of substantive due process, and I now accept it as such" (168).

60. *Roe*, 152–54. See *Jacobson v. Massachusetts*, 197 U.S. 11 (1905); *Buck v. Bell*, 274 U.S. 200 (1927).

61. *Roe*, 129, 148, 128. In oral arguments in *Roe*, when Jay Floyd, representing Texas, declared, "As far as the freedom over one's body is concerned, this is not absolute — the use of illicit drugs; the indecent exposure legislation; and, as Mr. Goldberg stated in the *Griswold* case, that adultery and fornication are constitutional beyond doubt," one of the justices interrupted to clarify: "Do you mean laws against them are constitutional?" Floyd replied, "The laws against them are constitutional."

62. *United States v. Vuitch*, 402 U.S. 62 (1971), 78; *California v. LaRue*, 409 U.S. 109 (1972), 132.

63. For internal Court discussions about *Roe* and *Doe*, see Boxes 420, 437, HLBP; Boxes 151–53, HABP; Boxes I-278, I-280, I-285–86, WBP; Boxes 1589–90, WODP; Boxes 78, 95, 98, 99, TMP. These materials discuss major procedural conflicts. According to a Dec. 1971 memorandum from Douglas to Burger, copied to the other justices, the initial vote in *Doe* was 4–3 in favor of Doe. Douglas complained that with Burger and Blackmun in the minority, Burger should not have selected which justice would write the majority opinion and Blackmun should not have received the assignment. Burger responded that the votes in *Roe* and *Doe* had been unclear and that he had made the assignments in that context. Soon it became apparent that Blackmun was voting with Brennan, Douglas, Marshall, and Stewart in *Doe* and *Roe*, but Blackmun was taking a long time to circulate his opinions. Douglas then strongly objected to Burger's proposal to have *Roe* and *Doe* held over for re-argument, which he accused Burger of suggesting so the two new justices could participate. In June 1972, Douglas drafted a scathing public dissent from the re-argument order, which he distributed to the other justices but later withdrew. In late 1972 and early 1973, additional conflicts erupted after the *Washington Post*, the *New York Times*, and *Time* published articles that reported on the Court's discussions, conflicts, and votes in the abortion cases, before the Court announced its rulings. In early 1973, Burger called a meeting of the justices to discuss the "gross breach of security," which has subsequently been attributed to Stewart and a Powell clerk. See Burger to the Conference, 24 Jan. 1973, Box 95, TMP; Garrow, *Liberty and Sexuality*, 558, 588; Woodward and Armstrong, *The Brethren*, 237–38. Also of interest are materials that document Brennan's efforts to include language in *Eisenstadt* that would influence the outcome in *Roe*; Blackmun's revision process; Marshall's and Brennan's efforts to convince Blackmun to set fetal viability as the moment when the state's interest in preserving potential life could override the interests of the pregnant woman, an effort opposed by Douglas; and Burger's efforts to have Blackmun address the rights of fathers and the rights of parents of minors.

64. Roy Lucas, Sarah Weddington, James R. Weddington, Linda N. Coffee, Fred Burner, Roy L. Merrill Jr., Norman Dorsen, "Brief for Appellants," *Roe*, 9, 44; *Roe*, 116, 153.

65. *Doe*, 185.

66. *Roe*, 129, 138. See also 129–52; 160–62.

67. *Roe*, 117, 159, 163–64.

Chapter 2

1. *Boutilier v. the Immigration and Naturalization Service*, 387 U.S. 118 (1967). On the rights of the mentally ill, see Bruce Ennis, "The Rights of Mental Patients," in *The Rights of Americans*, ed. Norman Dorsen (New York: Pantheon, 1970), 484–98; Bruce Ennis, *Prisoners of Psychiatry: Mental Patients, Psychiatrists, and the Law* (New York: Harcourt, 1972); Judith Lynn Failer, *Who Qualifies for Rights?: Homelessness, Mental Illness, and Civil Commitment* (Ithaca, N.Y.: Cornell University Press, 2002).

2. *ONE v. Olesen*, 355 U.S. 371 (1958); *Manual Enterprises v. Day*, 370 U.S. 478 (1962); *Rosenberg v. Fleuti*, 374 U.S. 449 (1963); *Mishkin v. New York*, 383 U.S. 502 (1966). For discussion of the cases in this and the next paragraph, see Joyce Murdoch and Deb Price, *Courting Justice: Gay Men and Lesbians v. the Supreme Court* (New York: Basic, 2001), 27–141. On *Manual*, see Rodger Streitmatter and John C. Watson, "Herman Lyn Womack: Pornographer As First Amendment Pioneer," *Journalism History* 28 (2002): 56–65. See also Boxes I-76, I-91, WBP; Boxes A145, A211, B188, C78, TCP; Boxes 1184, 1280–81, WODP; Box 176, JHP.

3. *Babouris v. Esperdy*, 362 U.S. 913 (1960); *Ganduxe y Marino v. Esperdy*, 364 U.S. 824 (1960);

Hudson et al. v. Esperdy, 368 U.S. 918 (1961); *Wyngaard v. Kennedy*, 368 U.S. 926 (1961); *Kameny v. Brucker*, 365 U.S. 843 (1961); *Shields v. Sharp*, 366 U.S. 917 (1961); *Williams v. Zuckert*, 371 U.S. 531 (1963); *Caplan v. Korth*, 373 U.S. 915 (1963); *Womack v. U.S.*, 365 U.S. 859 (1961); *Darnell v. U.S.*, 375 U.S. 916 (1963); *Poore v. Mayer*, 379 U.S. 928 (1964); *Chamberlain v. Ohio*, 385 U.S. 844 (1966); *Robillard v. New York*, 385 U.S. 928 (1966). See also *Dew v. Halaby*, 379 U.S. 951 (1964). On *Kameny*, see David K. Johnson, *The Lavender Scare: The Cold War Persecution of Gays and Lesbians in the Federal Government* (Chicago: University of Chicago Press, 2004), 179–82.

4. See Eithne Luibhéid, *Entry Denied: Controlling Sexuality at the Border* (Minneapolis: University of Minnesota Press, 2002); David Carliner et al., *The Rights of Aliens and Refugees: The Basic ACLU Guide to Alien and Refugee Rights*, 2nd ed. (Carbondale: Southern Illinois University Press, 1990); Mae M. Ngai, *Impossible Subjects: Illegal Aliens and the Making of Modern America* (Princeton, N.J.: Princeton University Press, 2004).

5. Immigration Act of 3 Mar. 1891, §1, 26 Stat. 1084; Immigration Act of 5 Feb. 1917, §3, 39 Stat. 874–75. See also Margot Canaday, "'Who Is A Homosexual?': The Consolidation of Sexual Identities in Mid-Twentieth-Century American Immigration Law," *Law and Social Inquiry* 28 (2003): 351–86; Ariela Dubler, "Immoral Purposes: Marriage and the Genus of Illicit Sex," *Yale Law Journal* 115 (2006): 756–812; William N. Eskridge Jr., *Gaylaw: Challenging the Apartheid of the Closet* (Cambridge, Mass.: Harvard University Press, 1999), 35–36, 69–70, 132–34, 383–84; Luibhéid, *Entry Denied*; Shannon Minter, "Sodomy and Public Morality Offenses Under U.S. Immigration Law: Penalizing Lesbian and Gay Identity," *Cornell International Law Journal* 26 (1993): 771–818; Ngai, *Impossible Subjects*; William T. Reynolds, "The Immigration and Nationality Act and the Rights of Homosexual Aliens," *Journal of Homosexuality* 5 (1979–80): 79–87; Maurice A. Roberts, "Sex and the Immigration Laws," *San Diego Law Review* 14 (1976): 9–41; Siobhan B. Somerville, "Queer *Loving*," *GLQ: A Journal of Lesbian and Gay Studies* 11 (2005): 335–70; Steven L. Strange, "Private Consensual Sexual Conduct and the 'Good Moral Character' Requirement of the Immigration and Nationality Act," *Columbia Journal of Transnational Law* 14 (1975): 357–81.

6. Immigration and Nationality Act of 1952, §212(a)(4), 66 Stat. 163, 182; Eskridge, *Gaylaw*, 383–84; Canaday, "'Who Is A Homosexual?'"; Luibhéid, *Entry Denied*. See also note 5; Estelle Freedman, "'Uncontrolled Desires': The Response to the Sexual Psychopath, 1920–1960," *Journal of American History* 74 (1987): 83–106.

7. Immigration and Nationality Act of Oct. 3, 1965, §15(b), 79 Stat. 911, 919.

8. On *Boutilier*, see, in addition to note 5 and the law review articles cited in chapter seven, Marc Bogatin, "The Immigration and Nationality Act and the Exclusion of Homosexuals: *Boutilier v. INS* Revisited," *Cardozo Law Review* 2 (1981): 359–96; William N. Eskridge Jr., "Gadamer/Statutory Interpretation," *Columbia Law Review* 90 (1990): 609–81; Eskridge, *Dynamic Statutory Interpretation* (Cambridge, Mass.: Harvard University Press, 1994), 48–80; Murdoch and Price, *Courting Justice*, 103–34.

9. See note 3; *Babouris v. Esperdy*, 269 F.2d 621 (1959); *Ganduxe y Marino v. Murff*, 183 F. Supp. 565 (1959), *Ganduxe y Marino v. Esperdy*, 278 F.2d 330 (1960); *Hudson et al. v. Esperdy*, 290 F.2d 879 (1961); *Wyngaard v. Kennedy*, 295 F.2d 184 (1961); *Quiroz v. Neely*, 291 F.2d 906 (1961). See also *U.S. v. Flores-Rodriguez*, 237 F.2d 405 (1956). For discussions of these cases and the cases discussed in the next paragraph, see Canaday, "Who Is A Homosexual?"; Luibhéid, *Entry Denied*, 77–101; Minter, "Sodomy"; Murdoch and Price, *Courting Justice*, 89–101, 106–7, 132–34.

10. *Fleuti v. Rosenberg*, 302 F.2d 652 (1962); *Rosenberg*; *Tovar v. INS*, 368 U.S. 1006 (1966), 388 U.S. 915 (1967); *Lavoie v. INS*, 360 F.2d 27 (1966), *INS v. Lavoie* 387 U.S. 572 (1967); *Boutilier v. Immigration and Naturalization Service*, 363 F.2d 488 (1966). After *Rosenberg* was decided, the INS

attempted to deport Fleuti as a constitutional psychopathic inferior, but in 1965 the BIA ruled that "while the record reveals respondent had an inclination toward homosexuality, it appears to be one respondent can control and that he had it under control before he entered." See *Matter of Fleuti*, BIA Interim Decision 1754, 27 Dec. 1965. After losing at the Supreme Court, Lavoie requested a rehearing on several grounds, one of which was that he was not a homosexual at time of entry. In *INS v. Lavoie*, 389 U.S. 908 (1967), the Court remanded the case for reconsideration. In *Lavoie v. INS*, 418 F.2d 732 (1969), the Ninth Circuit determined that he was deportable. Lavoie lost his final appeal in 1970; see 400 U.S. 854.

11. See Ronald Radosh and Joyce Milton, *The Rosenberg File: A Search for the Truth* (New York: Holt, Rinehart and Winston, 1983); Robert and Michael Meeropol, *We Are Your Sons: The Legacy of Ethel and Julius Rosenberg*, rev. ed.(Urbana: University of Illinois Press, 1986), 370–83.

12. One brief was signed by Marshall, Fred M. Vinson Jr., Beatrice Rosenberg, and Paul C. Summitt; another was signed by Marshall, Vinson, and Philip R. Monahan. Nathan Lewin presented the oral arguments.

13. *Boutilier*, 496–98.

14. Ibid., 489–90, 495. On homosexuality as conduct and character, see Janet E. Halley, "The Politics of the Closet: Towards Equal Protection for Gay, Lesbian, and Bisexual Identity," *UCLA Law Review* 36 (1989): 915–76; Eve Kosofsky Sedgwick, *Epistemology of the Closet* (Berkeley: University of California Press, 1990); Daniel Hurewitz, *Bohemian Los Angeles and the Making of Modern Politics* (Berkeley: University of California Press, 2007); Regina Kunzel, *Criminal Intimacy: Prison and the Uneven History of Modern American Sexuality* (Chicago: University of Chicago Press, 2008).

15. *Boutilier*, 118–19. According to *Courting Justice* (115), Clark's clerk Stuart Ross wrote the first draft of the opinion and Clark drew on this work when he produced his drafts, which were modified in minor ways by other justices. See Box A207, TCP.

16. *Boutilier*, 120.

17. Ibid., 119.

18. Ibid. The draft by Clark's clerk stated that "petitioner freely admitted that the circumstances leading to his arrest involved acts of sodomy and fellatio with a 17 year old male." See Box A207, TCP. In his 13 Jan. 1964 affidavit, included in the Supreme Court case file, Boutilier stated, "I inserted my penis in his rectum and had an orgasm. . . . Later I put my penis in his mouth and had a blowjob." The papers of Boutilier's lawyer Blanch Freedman indicate that in 1963 Boutilier filed a naturalization application, had a hearing, and was advised that he needed another year "for 5 years good moral conduct." See BF. Ngai's *Impossible Subjects* (75–89) explains that the INS had the power to waive deportation after five years of good moral conduct.

19. *Boutilier*, 119–20. Boutilier's psychiatrist Montague Ullman wrote in a letter included in the Supreme Court case file (dated 30 Mar. 1965) that Boutilier's first sexual experience took place when he was sixteen years old; all other sources indicate he was fourteen when this incident took place.

20. *Boutilier*, 490. The draft by Clark's clerk described Boutilier's role in his first homosexual experience as "involuntary" and "passive" and stated that he subsequently engaged in such experiences "voluntarily" and was "generally the active participant." See Box A207, TCP.

21. I obtained the 1963 documents through an FOIA request. The 1964 and 1965 documents are included in the Supreme Court case file. See Boutilier affidavit, 6 Sept. 1963; Naturalization Examiner memo to file, 6 Sept. 1963; Boutilier and James B. Sarsfield, Record of Sworn Statement, 13 Jan. 1964; Montague Ullman, Clinical Abstract for Boutilier, 30 Mar. 1965.

22. The draft by Clark's clerk did not include the reference to sex in a Halifax public park;

this was added by Clark. Clark's first and second drafts stated that Boutilier was currently living with his mother and stepfather, but this was not included in the published opinion. See Box A207, TCP; Boutilier and Sarsfield, Record of Sworn Statement; Ullman, Clinical Abstract. Freedman's Boutilier file indicates that O'Rourke was a U.S. citizen.

23. *Boutilier*, 120.

24. *Boutilier*, 120; Fieldsteel and Freedman, Transcript of Hearing, 26 July 1965; Edward F. Falsey to Robert Brown, 2 Mar. 1964; Ullman, Clinical Abstract. See Alfred C. Kinsey, Wardell B. Pomeroy, and Clyde E. Martin, *Sexual Behavior in the Human Male* (Philadelphia: Saunders, 1948).

25. *Boutilier*, 120.

26. See Allan Bérubé, *Coming Out Under Fire: The History of Gay Men and Women in World War Two* (New York: Free Press, 1990); Margot Canaday, "Building a Straight State: Sexuality and Social Citizenship under the 1944 G.I. Bill," *Journal of American History* 90 (2003): 935–57.

27. *Boutilier*, 120–21. For discussion of the multiple and changing meanings of these terms, see Elise Chenier, *Strangers in Our Midst: Sexual Deviancy in Postwar Ontario* (Toronto: University of Toronto Press, 2008).

28. *Boutilier*, 122.

29. *Report of the Public Health Service on the Medical Aspects of H.R. 2379*, 15 May 1951, House Report No. 1365, 82nd Congress, 2nd Sess. (14 Feb. 1952), *U.S. Code, Congressional and Administrative News*, 82nd Congress, 2nd Session (1952), vol. 2, p. 1700; *Boutilier*, 494. The other case was *Matter of Anne-Lise Coppo*, File A-6845593, 1965.

30. Report of the Public Health Service, 1701.

31. *Boutilier*, 122–23.

32. Blanch Freedman and David M. Freedman, "Reply Brief," *Boutilier*, 2–3.

33. Boutilier and Sarsfield, Record of Sworn Statement; *Boutilier* oral arguments. In the earlier passage about the period between Boutilier's Halifax park encounter and his U.S. entry, Clark's first draft referred to six years, but his later and final versions said five. The fact that Clark did not similarly correct the figure in this passage (or a later one that referred to six and one-half years) supports the notion that he regarded Boutilier's "involuntary" experience as part of his "continued course of homosexual conduct." See Box A207, TCP.

34. Boutilier and Sarsfield, Record of Sworn Statement. Boutilier was beyond draft age, but he may not have known this, and the draft age was subject to change. In the 1963 affidavit, which was not included in the Supreme Court case file, Boutilier wrote, "I had admitted to the selective service board that I was a homosexual."

35. *Boutilier*, 123; Thurgood Marshall, Fred M. Vinson, and Philip R. Monahan, "Brief for Respondent," 36–37.

36. *Boutilier*, 124.

37. Ibid., 125. Clark's opinion stopped just short of declaring that medical examinations were necessary for excluding, but not deporting, aliens as psychopaths. This would have been inconsistent with the practice of granting more rights to resident aliens than to nonresident aliens.

38. *Boutilier*, 124. For the drafts, see Box A207, TCP.

39. Canaday, "'Who Is A Homosexual?'" 355, 381, 383; *Manual*, 481–82, 526–27; *Mishkin*, 508.

40. *Boutilier*, 123–24. The brief by Marshall, Vinson, and Monahan, citing the Chinese Exclusion cases, argued, "Congress has plenary authority to make rules and regulations for the admission of aliens and to establish categories of aliens who shall be excluded or deported." They continued, "This authority includes the power to exclude aliens applying for admission whom Congress deems undesirable because of some mental or physical condition, and to direct their

deportation if their inadmissibility is discovered only after entry." See Marshall et al., "Brief for Respondent," 39–40; *Chae Chan Ping v. U.S.*, 130 U.S. 581 (1889).

41. *Report of the Public Health Service on the Medical Aspects of H.R. 2379*, 1701; *Boutilier*, 492; Marshall et al., "Brief for Respondent," 16. On the link between privacy and secrecy, see Deborah Nelson, *Pursuing Privacy in Cold War America* (New York: Columbia University Press, 2002).

42. See Boxes I-144–45, I-157, WBP; Boxes A207, A211, B219, C84, TCP; Boxes 1373, 1391, WODP; Box I-21, AFP; Box 286, JHP; Boxes 126–27, 149, 297, 382, 539, EWP; Murdoch and Price, *Courting Justice*, 112–17.

43. According to Douglas's notes, Clark was convinced that "sex perversion was included in psychopathic personality." Box 1391, WODP.

44. *Boutilier* oral arguments.

45. Thurgood Marshall to John F. Davis, 15 Mar. 1967, Charles Gordon to Thurgood Marshall, 15 Mar. 1967, BF; Box 1391, WODP.

46. Box 1281, WODP.

47. Box 1391, WODP; Box I-21, AFP. One significant deletion in the drafts Clark circulated, which was prompted by a note from Black (see Box A207, TCP), was a footnote that stated, "This Court has sustained the power of the Congress to enact grounds for deportation retroactively. *Harisiades v. Shaughnessy*, 342 U.S. 580 (1952). While that is not the situation in the instant case, it most certainly meets the argument of the petitioner that upon entry he was entitled to notice of what conduct *could* result in his deportation. In fact no such right exists. . . . Congress, in the exercise of its plenary power over the admission and expulsion of aliens, can make conduct or characteristics which were not grounds for exclusion at the time of entry, grounds for deportation after entry."

48. Murdoch and Price, *Courting Justice*, 114.

49. CDK Memoranda to Warren, 15 Oct. 1966 and 16 Feb. 1967, Box 297, EWP; Box 145, WBP; Box 1391, WODP. See also Box A211, TCP; Box 127, EWP.

50. Boxes 1280–81, WODP; Goldberg, draft *Rosenberg* opinion; Brennan to Goldberg, 6 June 1963; Box I-91, WBP. See also Box 176, JHP.

51. Box 1391, WODP; *Boutilier*, 125; *Boutilier*, 496–98.

52. *Boutilier*, 496, 499.

53. Ibid., 498–99.

54. Ibid., 497–98. See Henry Abelove, "Freud, Male Homosexuality, and the Americans," *Dissent* 33 (1986): 59–69; Ronald Bayer, *Homosexuality and American Psychiatry: The Politics of Diagnosis* (New York: Basic, 1981).

55. *Boutilier* oral argument. See also *Matter of P*, 7 I&N Dec. 258 (1956), 264: "A heterosexual individual can perform homosexual acts."

56. Box 1391, WODP; Fortas, handwritten comment on Douglas, draft *Boutilier* dissent, Box I-42, AFP.

57. *Boutilier*, 125, 127, 130, 132. According to his own notes, Douglas voted to reverse the Second Circuit's decision because the "act now adds 'sexual deviates'"; presumably this meant that insofar as the 1965 legislation added an explicit reference to deviates, the 1952 statute should not be read as covering them. Box 1391, WODP.

58. *Boutilier*, 129–30, 134–35.

59. Ibid., 131–32.

60. Ibid., 135, 133.

61. Ibid., 127–30. An earlier draft of the dissent included this additional excerpt by Hender-

son: "We should not condemn them; we have no right to do so, they are as much the victim of their constitutions as we are of ours, and we can only step in when their conduct becomes subversive of society, or when they request help so as to enable them to reach a more mature level. Because of this anomaly only in their sexual development we are not entitled to describe them as psychopaths; in all other respects they may be perfectly decent, law-abiding citizens." This draft also stated, "The homosexual is one, who but for the grace of God, might be almost anyone," which was revised in the final version to read, "The homosexual is one, who by some freak, is the product of an arrested development." The earlier draft included a sentence from the 1944 text by Abrahamsen that was not used in the final version: "One may within certain limits say that the homosexual is an individual who really belongs to the opposite sex." One clerk (LBM) recommended that Douglas delete a large section containing the Kinsey excerpt, the passages from the 1949 and 1944 texts, and the sentence referring to homosexuals in Congress and the Executive Branch; the clerk suggested replacing all of this with the following: "According to some, the incidence of homosexual actions is high (Kinsey, Sexual Behavior in the Human Male 259–260 [1948]), there is indication 'that a trace of homosexuality, no matter how weak it may be, exists in every human being' (Abrahamsen, Crime and the Human Mind 117 [1944]) and the causes of homosexual activity are many (Henderson, Mental Abnormality and Crime 114 [1949]). The homosexual is not necessarily suffering from psychoses or neuroses (Kinsey, supra, at 201–202) nor do all homosexuals become involved in violations of law." This would have removed much of the antigay language discussed here, but Douglas rejected the advice. See Box 1391, WODP.

62. *Boutilier*, 132–34.

63. Ibid., 135.

64. See Box 1391, WODP; Murray Schumach, "On the Third Sex," *NYT*, 7 May 1967.

65. See Box 1391, WODP; Edmund Bergler, *Homosexuality: Disease or Way of Life?* (New York: Hill and Wang, 1956).

66. *Tovar v. INS*, 388 U.S. 915 (1967); *INS v. Lavoie* 387 U.S. 572 (1967), 389 U.S. 908 (1967), 400 U.S. 854 (1970); *Inman v. Miami*, 389 U.S. 1048 (1968); *Talley v. California*, 390 U.S. 1031 (1968); *Adams v. Laird*, 397 U.S. 1039 (1970); *Schlegel v. U.S.*, 397 U.S. 1039 (1970); *McConnell v. Anderson*, 405 U.S. 1046 (1972); *Baker v. Nelson*, 409 U.S. 810 (1972); *Buchanan v. Texas*, 405 U.S. 930 (1972); *Crawford v. Missouri*, 409 U.S. 811 (1972); *Connor v. Arkansas*, 414 U.S. 991 (1973); *Canfield v. Oklahoma*, 414 U.S. 991 (1973); *Wainwright v. Stone*, 414 U.S. 21 (1973), 22. See also *U.S. v Nardello*, 393 U.S. 286 (1969).

Chapter 3

1. See Linda Gordon, *Woman's Body, Woman's Right: Birth Control in America*, rev. ed. (1974; repr., New York: Penguin, 1990); David J. Garrow, *Liberty and Sexuality: The Right to Privacy and the Making of* Roe v. Wade (Berkeley: University of California Press, 1994). See also James W. Reed, *From Private Vice to Public Virtue* (New York: Basic, 1978); Carole R. McCann, *Birth Control Politics in the United States, 1916–1945* (Ithaca, N.Y.: Cornell University Press, 1994); Donald T. Critchlow, ed., *The Politics of Abortion and Birth Control in Historical Perspective* (University Park: Pennsylvania State University Press, 1996); Donald T. Critchlow, *Intended Consequences: Birth Control, Abortion, and the Federal Government in Modern America* (New York: Oxford University Press, 1999); Rickie Solinger, *Pregnancy and Power: A Short History of Reproductive Politics in America* (New York: New York University Press, 2005); Suzanne U. Samuels, *First Among Friends: Interest Groups, the U.S. Supreme Court, and the Right to Privacy* (Westport, Conn.: Praeger, 2004); John W. Johnson, Griswold v. Connecticut: *Birth Control and the Consti-*

tutional Right of Privacy (Lawrence: University Press of Kansas, 2005). For discussions of *Griswold* strategy, see Box 7:8, HPP; Boxes II-184–85, PPFAP; Boxes 12:176, 27:410–16, 63: 876–77, TEP; Box 1412, ACLUP; C. Lee Buxton, "Birth Control Problems in Connecticut," *Connecticut Medicine* 28 (Aug. 1964): 581–84; Harriet F. Pilpel, "A Right Is Born: Privacy As A Civil Liberty," *CL*, Nov. 1965, 2; Harriet F. Pilpel, "Birth Control and a New Birth of Freedom," *Ohio State Law Journal* 27 (1966): 679–90; Harriet F. Pilpel, "Sex vs. the Law: A Study in Hypocrisy," *Harper's*, Jan. 1965, 35–40; Catherine G. Roraback, "*Griswold v. Connecticut*: A Brief Case History," *Ohio Northern University Law Review* 16 (1989): 395–401; Melvin L. Wulf, "On the Origins of Privacy," *Nation*, 27 May 1991, 700–704.

2. Garrow, *Liberty and Sexuality*, 201; Gordon, *Woman's Body*, 406; Harper, cited in Garrow, *Liberty and Sexuality*, 201; Harold Berg, cited in Andi Rierden, "Griswold v. Connecticut, Landmark Case Recalled," *NYT*, 28 May 1989, 6. See also Jeanette B. Cheek interview with Estelle Griswold, 17 Mar. 1976, 27–38, FPOHP; Mary L. Dudziak, "Just Say No: Birth Control in the Connecticut Supreme Court before *Griswold v. Connecticut*," *Iowa Law Review* 75 (1990): 915–39.

3. Garrow, *Liberty and Sexuality*, 206.

4. Ibid., 210, 214.

5. John de J. Pemberton Jr. to John E. Coons, 31 Jan. 1963; Coons to Pemberton, 13 Feb. 1963, Box 1412, ACLUP. See also Russell W. Gibbons to Pemberton, 12 Feb. 1963, Box 1412, ACLUP.

6. Fowler V. Harper, "Jurisdictional Statement," *Griswold v. Connecticut* 381 U.S. 479 (1965); Morris Ernst and Harriet Pilpel, "Brief for Planned Parenthood Federation of America," *Griswold*; Thomas I. Emerson and Catherine G. Roraback, "Brief for Appellants," *Griswold*, 4–5.

7. Harper, "Jurisdictional Statement," 13; Emerson and Roraback, "Brief for Appellants," 12, 83, 86.

8. Rhoda H. Karpatkin, Melvin L. Wulf, and Jerome E. Caplan, "Brief for the American Civil Liberties Union and the Connecticut Civil Liberties Union," *Griswold*, 7, 11; Robert B. Fleming, "Brief for the Catholic Council on Civil Liberties," *Griswold*, 7; Ernst and Pilpel, "Brief for Planned Parenthood," 10, 13.

9. Harper, "Jurisdictional Statement," 7–8; Emerson and Roraback, "Brief for Appellants," 7–8, 45–46, 62, 64.

10. Lawrence Livingston to Wulf, 19 May 1964, Box 1412, ACLUP; Pilpel to Fred Jaffe and Nancy F. Wechsler, 22 Jan. 1965, Box II-184:23, PPFAP; ACLU Office to ACLU Board of Directors, 24 Nov. 1965, Box III-7, GPACLUP. On the ACLU policy, see ACLU Board of Directors Minutes, 14 Sept. 1964, Reel 17; ACLU Annual Report, 1964–65, pp. 46–47, Box 1880:17; ACLU News Release, 9 Mar. 1965, Reel 17; ACLU Weekly Bulletin 2224, 12 Apr. 1965, Reel 17, ACLUP; *CL*, May 1965, 3; *CL*, Sept. 1965, 2; Samuel Walker, *In Defense of American Liberties: A History of the ACLU* (New York: Oxford University Press, 1990), 300–301.

11. Harper, "Jurisdictional Statement," 18; Emerson and Roraback, "Brief for Appellants," 12.

12. *Griswold* oral arguments, 2, 5–6.

13. Emerson and Roraback, "Brief for Appellants," 36–39, 61; Ernst and Pilpel, "Brief for Planned Parenthood," 6.

14. Harper, "Jurisdictional Statement," 6; Emerson and Roraback, "Brief for Appellants," 76–77, 89.

15. See Charles Rembar, *The End of Obscenity: The Trials of Lady Chatterley, Tropic of Cancer and Fanny Hill* (New York: Random House, 1968), 417–20.

16. See Edward de Grazia, *Girls Lean Back Everywhere: The Law of Obscenity and the Assault on Genius* (New York: Vintage, 1992), 295–326. On the ACLU, see Boxes 1880:17–18, 1922:1–3,

1923:2, ACLUP; *CL*, Mar. 1964, 3; *CL*, June 1964, 5; *CL*, Mar. 1965, 4; *CL*, Dec. 1965, 2, 4; *CL*, May 1966, 1; *CL*, Oct. 1966, 3–4; ACLU News Releases, 15 Jan. 1964, 12 May 1964, 1 Feb. 1965, 18 Oct. 1965, 6 Dec. 1965, 14 Feb. 1966, 18 Apr. 1966, 28 Apr. 1966, Reel 17, ACLUP; Walker, *In Defense*, 227–36, 350–55; William A. Donohue, *The Politics of the American Civil Liberties Union* (New Brunswick, N.J.: Transaction, 1985), 244–46, 286–98, 341–45; Charles Lam Markmann, *The Noblest Cry: A History of the American Civil Liberties Union* (New York: St. Martin's, 1965), 298–321.

17. See Rembar, *The End of Obscenity*; de Grazia, *Girls Lean Back*. See also Edward de Grazia and Roger K. Newman, *Banned Films: Movies, Censors and the First Amendment* (New York: Bowker, 1982), 100–145; Edward de Grazia, introduction to *Censorship Landmarks* (New York: Bowker, 1969), xvii–xxxii; Charles Rembar, introduction to *Obscenity: The Complete Oral Arguments before the Supreme Court in the Major Obscenity Cases*, ed. Leon Friedman (New York: Chelsea House, 1970), ix–xxii.

18. Rembar, *The End of Obscenity*, 4, 82, 157. See also de Grazia, *Girls Lean Back*, 369.

19. Rembar, *The End of Obscenity*, 87, 119, 192–93.

20. Ibid., 407–8. See also Richard H. Kuh, *Foolish Figleaves?: Pornography in — and out of — Court* (New York: Macmillan, 1967), 136.

21. Charles Rembar, "Jurisdictional Statement," *A Book Named "John Cleland's Memoirs of a Woman of Pleasure" v. Attorney General of the Commonwealth of Massachusetts* (commonly referred to as *Fanny Hill*), *383 U.S. 413 (1966)*, 15, 25; Charles Rembar, "Brief for Appellant," *A Book Named*, 7; Charles Rembar, "Reply Brief," *A Book Named*, 27; *A Book Named* oral arguments, 37, 41.

22. Transcript of Record, *A Book Named*, 21, 25, 31, 55.

23. Ibid., 46, 52–53, 73, 93. See also Rembar, *The End of Obscenity*, 251, 270, 278–79.

24. Rembar, "Jurisdictional Statement," 8, 21; Rembar, "Brief for Appellant," 6; Rembar, "Reply Brief," 19; Charles Rembar, "Supplemental Brief," *A Book Named*, 3.

25. Charles Rembar, *The End of Obscenity: The Trials of Lady Chatterley, Tropic of Cancer and Fanny Hill* (1968; New York: Harper & Row, 1986), xiv, xvii, 488–89.

26. See Martha Hodes, ed., *Sex, Love, Race: Crossing Boundaries in North American History* (New York: New York University Press, 1999); Alex Lubin, *Romance and Rights: The Politics of Interracial Intimacy, 1945–1954* (Jackson: University Press of Mississippi, 2005); Rachel F. Moran, *Interracial Intimacy: The Regulation of Race and Romance* (Chicago: University of Chicago Press, 2001); Phyl Newbeck, *Virginia Hasn't Always Been for Lovers* (Carbondale: Southern Illinois University Press, 2004); Peggy Pascoe, *What Comes Naturally: Miscegenation Law and the Making of Race in America* (New York: Oxford University Press, 2009); Renee C. Romano, *Race Mixing: Black-White Marriage in Postwar America* (Cambridge, Mass.: Harvard University Press, 2003); Robert J. Sickels, *Race, Marriage, and the Law* (Albuquerque: University of New Mexico Press, 1972); Peter Wallenstein, *Tell the Court I Love My Wife: Race, Marriage, and Law — An American History* (New York: Palgrave, 2002).

27. Pascoe, *What Comes Naturally*, 178, 186. See also Newbeck, *Virginia*, 47–54.

28. Wallenstein, *Tell the Court*, 179, 184; Romano, *Race Mixing*, 23–26, 155, 179; Lubin, *Romance*, 66–122. See also *Jackson v. Alabama*, 348 U.S. 888 (1954); *Naim v. Naim*, 350 U.S. 891 (1955), 350 U.S. 985 (1956); Gregory Michael Dorr, "Principled Expediency: Eugenics, *Naim v. Naim*, and the Supreme Court," *American Journal of Legal History* 42 (1998): 119–59; Philip Elman, interview by Norman Silber, "The Solicitor General's Office, Justice Frankfurter, and Civil Rights Litigation, 1946–1960: An Oral History," *Harvard Law Review* 100 (1987): 845–47; Moran, *Interracial Intimacy*, 88–90; Newbeck, *Virginia*, 55–102; Pascoe, *What Comes Naturally*,

163–245; Romano, *Race Mixing*, 96–101, 156, 186; Sickels, *Race, Marriage, and the Law*, 3–6, 87–88; Chang Moon Sohn, "Principle and Expediency in Judicial Review: Miscegenation Cases in the Supreme Court," (Ph.D. diss., Columbia University, 1970).

29. *Perez v. Sharp*, 32 Cal. 2d 711 (1948); Carliner, "Reply Brief," cited in Dorr, "Principled Expediency," 139. See also Moran, *Interracial Intimacy*, 84–90, 216; Newbeck, *Virginia*, 75–116; Pascoe, *What Comes Naturally*, 205–50; Sickels, *Race, Marriage, and the Law*, 103–4; Sohn, "Principle and Expediency," 43–48, 73–94, 122–58; Wallenstein, *Tell the Court*, 180–214.

30. Sohn, "Principle and Expediency," 132–33.

31. See Ariela R. Dubler, "From *McLaughlin v. Florida* to *Lawrence v. Texas*: Sexual Freedom and the Road to Marriage," *Columbia Law Review* 106 (2006): 1165–87; Newbeck, *Virginia*, 117–31; Moran, *Interracial Intimacy*, 92–94, 218; Pascoe, *What Comes Naturally*, 246–70; Romano, *Race Mixing*, 185–91; Sickels, *Race, Marriage, and the Law*, 86–87, 100–103; Sohn, "Principle and Expediency," 48–49, 94–139; Wallenstein, *Tell the Court*, 203–213.

32. See Newbeck, *Virginia*, 9–22, 135–90; Pascoe, *What Comes Naturally*, 270–84; Robert A. Pratt, "Crossing the Color Line: A Historical Assessment and Personal Narrative of *Loving v. Virginia*," *Howard Law Journal* 41 (1998): 229–44; Wallenstein, *Tell the Court*, 1–2, 215–29; *NYT*, 6 May 2008, C13. On the ACLU, see also Sickels, *Race, Marriage, and the Law*, 2–3, 76–110; Moran, *Interracial Intimacy*, 95–99, 219; Sohn, "Principle and Expediency," 107–20; *CL*, Apr. 1965, 3; *CL*, Sept. 1966, 7; *CL*, Sept. 1967, 5; ACLU Weekly Bulletin 2227, 15 Mar. 1965; ACLU Weekly Bulletin 2269, 13 June 1966; ACLU Weekly Bulletin 2303, 26 June 1967; ACLU News Release, 28 July 1966; ACLU News Release 18 Feb. 1967, Reel 17, ACLUP.

33. Bernard S. Cohen, Philip J. Hirschkop, Melvin L. Wulf, and David Carliner, "Jurisdictional Statement," *Loving v. Virginia*, 388 U.S. 1 (1967), 15, 17; Cohen, Hirschkop, William D. Zabel, Arthur L. Berney, Marvin M. Karpatkin, Wulf, and Carliner, "Brief for Appellants," *Loving*, 32; William M. Marutani and Donald W. Kramer, "Brief for the Japanese American Citizens League," *Loving*, 3; Robert L. Carter and Andrew D. Weinberger, "Brief of the NAACP," *Loving*, 5; Jack Greenberg, James M. Nabrit, Michael Meltsner, and Melvyn Zaar, "Brief of the NAACP Legal Defense and Educational Fund," *Loving*, 9; William M. Lewers and William B. Ball, "Brief of the National Catholic Conference for Interracial Justice, the National Catholic Social Action Conference et al.," *Loving*, 5–6.

34. Cohen et al., "Jurisdictional Statement," 18.

35. Cohen et al., "Brief for Appellants," 39; Carter and Weinberger, "Brief of the NAACP," 6; Lewers and Ball, "Brief of the NCCIJ et al.," 12–15.

36. *Loving* oral arguments, 9–10, 17.

37. Cohen et al., "Jurisdictional Statement," 18; Cohen et al., "Brief for Appellants," 14, 26; Marutani and Kramer, "Brief for the JACL," 9–10.

38. Cohen et al., "Jurisdictional Statement," 16, 18; Marutani and Kramer, "Brief for the JACL," 3, 9; Lewers and Ball, "Brief of the NCCIJ et al.," 20.

39. "War on Poverty's Birth Control Rules Unlawful, Charges ACLU," *CL*, May 1966, 1. See also ACLU Annual Report, 1965–67, 27–28, Box 1880:18; ACLU News Release, 1 Aug. 1966; ACLU Bulletin 2259, 14 Feb. 1966; ACLU Bulletin 2301, 5 June 1967, Reel 17, ACLUP; Harriet Pilpel, Memorandum to Planned Parenthood Board of Directors et al., 15 June 1965, Box II-184:23, PPFAP; Boxes 3:2, 5:4, HPP.

40. Garrow, *Liberty and Sexuality*, 314–15. See also C. Thomas Dienes, *Law, Politics, and Birth Control* (Urbana: University of Illinois Press, 1972), 210–52.

41. Garrow, *Liberty and Sexuality*, 321; Gayle Pollard, "Baird on Baird: 15 Years of Crusading,"

Boston Globe, 4 Apr. 1982, B2. See also Ray Mungo, *Beyond the Revolution* (Chicago: Contemporary Books, 1990).

42. Elliot Blinder, "Bill Baird: Man with a Mission," *Boston University News*, 3 May 1967, 7; Pollard, "Baird on Baird," B2; "Baird and Betrayal," *Boston University News*, 13 Sept. 1967, 10; Blinder, "Bill Baird," 7; James Reed interview with Loraine Campbell, Dec. 1973–Mar. 1974, 68–69, FPOHP. See also Garrow, *Liberty and Sexuality*, 320–23, 343, 372–74, 410, 457, 487, 517–20. On the ACLU's involvement in *Eisenstadt* and related cases, see Boxes 1364, 1881, ACLUP; *CL*, Feb. 1969, 28; *CL*, Mar. 1970, 6; *CL*, Nov. 1971, 3, 6; *CL*, Dec. 1971, 16. For the supplemental brief, see Box 2, HRWC.

43. HRW press release, 15 July 1969, Box 1, HRWC; Bill Baird, Playboy Forum, *Playboy*, July 1972, 57. See also *Playboy*, Jan. 1973, 57; Karen O'Connor, *Women's Organizations' Use of the Courts* (Lexington, Mass.: Heath, 1980), 7–9, 93–94, 101–2, 115.

44. Gregory McDonald, "Baird to Test Birth Law in Court Monday," *Boston Globe*, 7 May 1967, 22.

45. Joseph J. Balliro, "Brief for the Appellee," *Eisenstadt v. Baird*, 405 U.S. 438 (1972), 6; Harriet F. Pilpel and Nancy F. Wechsler, "Brief for PPFA," *Eisenstadt*, 6; Sylvia S. Ellison, "Brief for HRW," *Eisenstadt*, 8; Melvin L. Wulf, Lawrence G. Sager, and John A. Robertson, "Brief for the ACLU and CLUM," *Eisenstadt*, 6, 16.

46. The development of the intermediate scrutiny standard began with *Reed v. Reed*, 404 U.S. 71 (1971) and achieved majority support in *Craig v. Boren*, 429 U.S. 190 (1976).

47. Roger P. Stokey and Stephen M. Weiner, "Brief for PPLM," *Eisenstadt*, 5; Ellison, "Brief for HRW," 7; Pilpel and Wechsler, "Brief for PPFA," 36, 38.

48. Pilpel and Wechsler, "Brief for PPFA," 20–22; Balliro, "Brief for the Appellee," 8–12; Ellison, "Brief for HRW," 8–9.

49. Balliro, "Brief for the Appellee," 7, 13, 21–22.

50. Ibid., 24–25, 31.

51. Stokey and Weiner, "Brief for PPLM," 8–9.

52. Ellison, "Brief for HRW," 2–3, 5–6, 8.

53. Robertson to Wulf, 3 June 1971; Wulf to Robertson, 1 July 1971; Robertson to Wulf, 7 July 1971, Box 1364, ACLUP. See also John A. Robertson, "Procreative Liberty and the Control of Conception, Pregnancy, and Childbirth," *Virginia Law Review* 69 (1983): 405–64.

54. Wulf, Sager, and Robertson, "Brief for ACLU/CLUM," 7–8, 11, 21–22.

55. Ibid., 16, 22.

56. Pilpel and Wechsler, "Brief for PPFA," 7, 12, 16–17, 26–28, 31–32.

57. See Critchlow, *Intended Consequences*; Critchlow, ed., *The Politics of Abortion*; Garrow, *Liberty and Sexuality*; Gordon, *Woman's Body*; N. E. H. Hull and Peter Charles Hoffer, Roe v. Wade: *The Abortion Rights Controversy in American History* (Lawrence: University Press of Kansas, 2001); Laura Kaplan, *The Story of Jane: The Legendary Underground Feminist Abortion Service* (New York: Pantheon, 1995); Peter Irons, *The Courage of Their Convictions* (New York: Free Press, 1988), 253–79; Carole Joffe, *Doctors of Conscience: The Struggle to Provide Abortion Before and After* Roe v. Wade (Boston: Beacon, 1995); Jennifer Nelson, *Women of Color and the Reproductive Rights Movement* (New York: New York University Press, 2003); Leslie J. Reagan, *When Abortion Was A Crime: Women, Medicine, and Law in the United States, 1867–1973* (Berkeley: University of California Press, 1997); Dorothy Roberts, *Killing the Black Body: Race, Reproduction, and the Meaning of Liberty* (New York: Vintage, 1997); Rickie Solinger, ed., *Abortion Wars: A Half Century of Struggle, 1950–2000* (Berkeley: University of California Press, 1998); Rickie Solinger, *The*

Abortionist: A Woman Against the Law (New York: Free Press, 1994); Suzanne Staggenborg, *The Pro-Choice Movement: Organization and Activism in the Abortion Conflict* (New York: Oxford University Press, 1991); Raymond Tatalovich and Byron W. Daynes, *The Politics of Abortion: A Study of Community Conflict in Public Policy Making* (New York: Praeger, 1981).

58. Garrow, *Liberty and Sexuality*, 277.

59. Reagan, *When Abortion*, 221; "Policy Statement of the ACLU on State Laws Prohibiting Abortion," 10 Sept. 1969, Box 1921:5, ACLUP. See also Garrow, *Liberty and Sexuality*, 270–472; Gordon, *Woman's Body*, 402–53; Hull and Hoffer, Roe v. Wade, 89–134; Harriet Pilpel, "The Right of Abortion," *Atlantic*, June 1969, 69–71; Alan F. Guttmacher and Harriet F. Pilpel, "Abortion and the Unwanted Child," *Family Planning Perspectives* 2, no. 2 (1970): 16–24; Harriet Pilpel, "The Voluntary Approach: Population Control," *CL*, Nov. 1971, 3, 6; O'Connor, *Women's Organizations' Use of the Courts*, 98–112; Staggenborg, *The Pro-Choice Movement*, 13–54; Tatalovich and Daynes, *The Politics of Abortion*, 33–75, 82–100, 150–54. On the ACLU, see *CL*, Jan. 1968, 3; *CL*, Mar.–Apr. 1968, 9; ACLU News Release, 25 Mar. 1968, Reel 17, ACLUP; Donohue, *The Politics of the American Civil Liberties Union*, 95–103; Aryeh Neier, *Only Judgment: The Limits of Litigation in Social Change* (Middletown, Conn.: Wesleyan University Press, 1982), 110–26; Walker, *In Defense*, 267–68, 301–2, 318.

60. See *People v. Belous*, 71 Cal. 2d 954 (1969); *Hall v. Lefkowitz*, 305 F. Supp. 1030 (1969); *U.S. v. Vuitch*, 305 F. Supp. 1032 (1969); *U.S. v. Vuitch*, 402 U.S. 62 (1971); *Babbitz v. McCann*, 306 F. Supp. 400 (1969); *State v. Hodgson*, 295 Minn. 294 (1973); *Doe v. Bolton*, 319 F. Supp. 1048 (1970); *Doe v. Bolton*, 410 U.S. 179 (1973); Garrow, *Liberty and Sexuality*, 307–599; Hull and Hoffer, Roe v. Wade, 97–113; Roy Lucas and Richard D. Lamm, "Abortion: Litigative and Legislative Processes," *Human Rights* 1, no. 2 (1971): 23–53; Nancy Stearns, "Roe v. Wade: Our Struggle Continues," *Berkeley Women's Law Journal* 4 (1988–89): 1–11. On the ACLU, see Boxes 1146:4, Box 1881:2–4, ACLUP; *CL*, Apr. 1969, 5; *CL*, Dec. 1969, 6; *CL*, Feb. 1970, 3; *CL*, May 1970, 1, 4; *CL*, Dec. 1970, 2; *CL*, Mar. 1971, 8; *CL*, Dec. 1971, 16; *CL*, Feb. 1972, 2; *CL*, Apr. 1972, 8; *CL*, Mar. 1973, 1; ACLU News Release, 30 Sept. 1969, Reel 17, ACLUP; Walker, *In Defense*, 302–4.

61. Sarah Weddington, *A Question of Choice* (New York: Penguin, 1992), 12, 51; Norma McCorvey with Andy Meisler, *I Am Roe: My Life, Roe v. Wade, and Freedom of Choice* (New York: HarperCollins, 1994), 112. See also Garrow, *Liberty and Sexuality*, 386–407, 433–44, 461–65, 485–599; Hull and Hoffer, Roe v. Wade, 1–3, 113–34; Samuels, *First Among Friends*, 53–64, 94–96. On McCluskey and *Bachelor*, see Garrow, *Liberty and Sexuality*, 398–404, 485. For strategy discussions about *Roe* and *Doe*, see, in addition, Box 1146:4, ACLUP. For more by and about Weddington, see Jeanette Cheek interview with Weddington, Mar. 1976, FPOHP; Vicki Quade, "Our Bodies, Our Law: *Barrister* Interview with Sarah Weddington," *Barrister* 13 (Summer 1986): 12–16, 54, 56; Sarah Weddington, "*Roe v. Wade*: Past and Future," *Suffolk University Law Review* 24 (1990): 601–20; Sarah Weddington, "*Roe v. Wade*: Memories of Its Beginnings," in *A Documentary History of the Legal Aspects of Abortion in the United States: Roe v. Wade*, vol. 1, comp., Roy M. Mersky and Gary R. Hartman, (Littleton, Colo.: Rothman, 1993), xi–xvii; Weddington, "Reflections on the Twenty-Fifth Anniversary of *Roe v. Wade*," *Albany Law Review* 62 (1999): 811–32.

62. McCorvey, *I Am Roe*, 11, 109, 123; Weddington, *A Question of Choice*, 52–53; Cheek interview with Weddington, 24–25. See also Garrow, *Liberty and Sexuality*, 402–5, 439–40, 461; Norma McCorvey in *The Choices We Made*, ed., Angela Bonavoglia (New York: Random House, 1991), 137–43; Norma McCorvey with Gary Thomas, *Won By Love* (Nashville, Tenn.: Nelson, 1997); Weddington, "*Roe v. Wade*: Past and Future," 603–4; Hull and Hoffer, Roe v. Wade, 2–3; Weddington, *A Question of Choice*, 51–57, 256–60.

63. McCorvey, *I Am Roe*, 2. See also *NYT*, 28 July 1994, C1, C9; McCorvey, *Won By Love*.

64. Roy Lucas, Norman Dorsen, Linda N. Coffee, Sarah Weddington, Roy L. Merrill Jr., "Jurisdictional Statement," *Roe v. Wade*, 410 U.S. 113 (1973), 15–16, 19–20, 30.

65. Roy Lucas, Sarah Weddington, James R. Weddington, Linda N. Coffee, Fred Bruner, Roy L. Merrill Jr., and Norman Dorsen, "Brief for Appellants," *Roe*, 50, 109.

66. Harriet F. Pilpel and Nancy F. Wechsler, "Brief for PPFA and American Association of Planned Parenthood Physicians," *Roe* and *Doe*, 10–11; Carol Ryan, "Brief of the American College of Obstetricians and Gynecologists, the American Psychiatric Association, the American Medical Women's Association, the New York Academy of Medicine, and A Group of 178 Physicians," *Roe*, 16.

67. Nancy Stearns, "Brief of New Women Lawyers, Women's Health and Abortion Project, and National Abortion Action Coalition," *Roe* and *Doe*, 6–7; Joan K. Bradford, "Brief for the California Committee to Legalize Abortion, South Bay Chapter of the National Organization for Women, Zero Population Growth, Cheriel Moench Jensen, and Lynette Perkes," *Roe* and *Doe*, 3.

68. Lucas et al., "Jurisdictional Statement," 15–16, 30; Lucas et al., "Brief for Appellants," 99, 101, 103, 107. See also Tom C. Clark, "Religion, Morality, and Abortion: A Constitutional Appraisal," *Loyola University of Los Angeles Law Review* 2 (Apr. 1969): 1–11.

69. Lucas et al., "Brief for Appellants," 9; Lucas et al., "Jurisdictional Statement," 16; Stearns, "Brief of New Women Lawyers et al.," 22; Pilpel and Wechsler, "Brief of PPFA et al.," 27.

70. Lucas et al., "Brief for Appellants," 108–9; Pilpel and Wechsler, "Brief for PPFA et al.," 10; Stearns, "Brief for New Women Lawyers et al.," 26, 34–35, 40.

71. Lucas et al., "Jurisdictional Statement," 30; Lucas et al., "Brief for Appellants," 10–11, 74.

72. Lucas et al., "Brief for Appellants," 114, 117–18.

73. Pilpel and Wechsler, "Brief for PPFA et al.," 40.

74. Stearns, "Brief for New Women Lawyers et al.," *Roe*, 46; Bradford, "Brief for California Committee to Legalize Abortion et al.," *Roe*, 27–30.

Chapter 4

1. See Robert C. Cottrell, *Roger Nash Baldwin and the American Civil Liberties Union* (New York: Columbia University Press, 2000); William A. Donohue, *The Politics of the American Civil Liberties Union* (New Brunswick: Transaction, 1985); Norman Dorsen, ed., *The Rights of Americans* (New York: Pantheon, 1970); Diane Garey, *Defending Everybody: A History of the American Civil Liberties Union* (New York: TV, 1998); Judy Kutulas, *The American Civil Liberties Union and the Making of Modern Liberalism, 1930–1960* (Chapel Hill: University of North Carolina Press, 2006); Charles Lam Markmann, *The Noblest Cry: A History of the American Civil Liberties Union* (New York: St. Martin's, 1965); Samuel Walker, *In Defense of American Liberties: A History of the ACLU* (New York: Oxford University Press, 1990).

2. See Vern L. Bullough, "Lesbianism, Homosexuality, and the American Civil Liberties Union," *Journal of Homosexuality* 13 (Fall 1986): 23–33; John D'Emilio, *Sexual Politics, Sexual Communities: The Making of a Homosexual Minority in the United States, 1940–1970* (Chicago: University of Chicago Press, 1983); Harry Hay, *Radically Gay*, ed. Will Roscoe (Boston: Beacon, 1996); Daniel Hurewitz, *Bohemian Los Angeles and the Making of Modern Politics* (Berkeley: University of California Press, 2007); David K. Johnson, *The Lavender Scare: The Cold War Persecution of Gays and Lesbians in the Federal Government* (Chicago: University of Chicago Press, 2004); Terence Kissack, *Free Comrades: Anarchism and Homosexuality in the United States, 1895–*

1917 (Oakland, Calif.: AK, 2008); Marc Stein, *City of Sisterly and Brotherly Loves: Lesbian and Gay Philadelphia, 1945–1972* (Chicago: University of Chicago Press, 2000); Stuart Timmons, *The Trouble with Harry Hay* (Boston: Alyson, 1990).

3. See the *Boutilier v. Immigration and Naturalization Service*, 387 U.S. 118 (1967), case file and BF.

4. Freedman to Ullman, 24 Mar. 1965, BF. Ullman, an emeritus professor of psychiatry at the Albert Einstein College of Medicine, recalled his connection to the Laven/Freedman family in a telephone conversation with the author on 5 Nov. 2004.

5. Paul Laven to Marc Stein, 29 Mar. 2001. This paragraph is also based on my correspondence with members of Freedman's family (including Allen Young, Michael Freedman, Paul Laven, and Anne Laven), and Michael Meeropol, 22 Mar.–18 Apr. 2001; "Mrs. Blanch Freedman," *NYT*, 17 Apr. 1967, 37.

6. Agrin, cited in Ronald Radosh and Joyce Milton, *The Rosenberg File: A Search for the Truth* (New York: Holt, Rinehart and Winston, 1983), 535; Paul Laven to Marc Stein, 2 Apr. 2001. See also note 5; "Mrs. Carol King, 56, Noted Lawyer, Dies," *NYT*, 23 Jan. 1952, 27.

7. See, in addition to notes 5–6, *NYT*, 27 Jan. 1938, 23; *NYT*, 8 Oct. 1943, 16; *NYT*, 24 Apr. 1945, 20; *NYT*, 21 Oct. 1947, 2; *NYT*, 24 Aug. 1949, 15.

8. See *Dennis*, 339 U.S. 162 (1950); *Freedom of the Press*, 198 Misc. 1084 (1950); *Kern*, 133 N.Y.S.2d 718 (1953); *Unger*, 18 F.R.D. 27 (1955); *Davis*, 178 N.Y.S.2d 465 (1958); 179 N.Y.S.2d 572 (1958); *McManus*, 179 N.Y.S.2d 866 (1958); 182 N.Y.S.2d 516 (1958); *Fabian*, 198 N.Y.S.2d 751 (1960); *Powell*, 387 U.S. 933 (1967).

9. "Mrs. Carol King," *NYT*, 23 Jan. 1952, 27; *U.S. ex. rel. Jankowski v. Shaughnessy*, 186 F.2d 580 (1951); *U.S. ex. rel. Harisiades v. Shaughnessy*, 187 F.2d 137 (1951); *U.S. ex rel. Heikkinen v. Gordon*, 190 F.2d 16 (1951); *Gordon v. Heikkinen*, 343 U.S. 903 (1952); 344 U.S. 870 (1952).

10. See Radosh and Milton, *The Rosenberg File*, 191, 319, 343, 385, 402, 414–15, 535–36; Robert and Michael Meeropol, *We Are Your Sons: The Legacy of Ethel and Julius Rosenberg*, rev. ed. (Urbana: University of Illinois Press, 1986), 265, 270, 286; Michael Meeropol, ed., *The Rosenberg Letters* (New York: Garland, 1994), 66, 113, 440, 600.

11. *U.S. v. Radzie*, 14 F.R.D. 151 (1953); 16 F.R.D. 137 (1954); 16 F.R.D. 378 (1954); *Barber v. Gonzales*, 347 U.S. 637 (1954); *Nukk et al. v. Shaughnessy*, 125 F. Supp. 498 (1954); *Nukk et al. v. Shaughnessy*, 348 U.S. 925 (1955); *Nukk et al. v. Shaughnessy*, 350 U.S. 869 (1955).

12. *Dickhoff v. Shaughnessy*, 142 F. Supp. 535 (1956), 537, 542.

13. "Dr. Du Bois Lacking Passport to Ghana," *NYT*, 2 Mar. 1957, 22; David Levering Lewis, *W. E. B. Du Bois* (New York: Holt, 2000), 547–66; *Siminoff v. Murff*, 164 F. Supp. 34 (1958); *Siminoff v. Esperdy*, 267 F.2d 705 (1959); *Niukkanen v. McAlexander*, 362 U.S. 901 (1960); 362 U.S. 390 (1960).

14. See Robert J. Corber, *Homosexuality in Cold War America: Resistance and the Crisis of Masculinity* (Durham, N.C.: Duke University Press, 1997); D'Emilio, *Sexual Politics*, 40–87; Hurewitz, *Bohemian Los Angeles*; Johnson, *Lavender Scare*.

15. Leonard to Freedman, 9 Dec. 1966, BF.

16. See Freedman correspondence, 4 Feb. 1965–30 Jan. 1967, BF; *Drum*, Dec. 1966, 36.

17. See introduction, note 23. This section is based on a comprehensive survey of *ONE*, *MR*, *Ladder*, and *Drum*.

18. *ONE*, Oct.–Nov. 1956, 18. See also *ONE*, Nov. 1955, 30; *ONE*, Jan. 1956, 4; *ONE*, Jan. 1966, 7; David S. Churchill, "Transnationalism and Homophile Political Culture in the Postwar Decades," *GLQ: A Journal of Lesbian and Gay Studies* 15 (2009): 31–66.

19. For exceptional references to immigration cases in the homophile press, see *ONE*, Sept.

1962, 13; Sept. 1963, 14. On Kwan, see Joyce Murdoch and Deb Price, *Courting Justice: Gay Men and Lesbians v. the Supreme Court* (New York: Basic, 2001), 91–101.

20. *MR*, Jan.–Feb. 1955, 12; May–June 1955, 48. See also Churchill, "Transnationalism."

21. *Ladder*, Dec. 1959, 11; *ONE*, Apr. 1961, 9. For discussions about a Homosexual Bill of Rights, see *ONE* and *Ladder*, Nov. 1960–Aug. 1961. For exceptional references to constitutional reform, see *Ladder*, July 1961, 20; *Ladder*, Aug. 1961, 17; *Drum*, June 1965, 31.

22. See, for examples, *Ladder*, Mar. 1959, 4–5; Dec. 1959, 4–13, 24–25; Feb. 1960, 5–9, 19–20. See *MR*, Mar. 1959, 2, 11–14, 19–21; Sept. 1960, 2, 9; Mar. 1961, 4–6; Oct. 1961, 30. See also *ONE*, Feb. 1957, 26–27; May 1957, 11–12; Dec. 1957, 22; Mar. 1958, 15–17; July 1958, 21–22; Mar. 1959, 4–9; June 1959, 13; Aug. 1959, 17–18; May 1960, 18–19; Oct. 1960, 19–20; Nov. 1960, 16–17; May 1961, 15. See also Nan Alamilla Boyd, *Wide Open Town: A History of Queer San Francisco to 1965* (Berkeley: University of California Press, 2003), 121–47, 206–7; Hurewitz, *Bohemian Los Angeles*, 261–63; Johnson, *Lavender Scare*, 176–78.

23. *ONE*, Oct. 1963, 31; *Janus*, Mar. 1964, 3; *Ladder*, Feb.–Mar. 1965, 14–16. For earlier examples, see *ONE*, Dec. 1957, 30–31; Aug. 1958, 30–31; May 1960, 18; Oct. 1960, 19–20.

24. *Ladder*, Jan. 1965, 10, 16–17.

25. See Johnson, *Lavender Scare*, 179–208.

26. *MR*, Apr.–Sept. 1964, 16, 18–20. See also *MR*, Jan.–Feb. 1965, 8–9; *Ladder*, Feb.–Mar. 1965, 4–5; June 1966, 14; *Drum*, Nov. 1966, 5; *Smayda v. U.S.*, 382 U.S. 981 (1966); Eric Marcus, *Making History: The Struggle for Gay and Lesbian Equal Rights, 1945–1990* (New York: HarperCollins, 1992), 54–58, 147–65; Boyd, *Wide Open Town*, 221–26, 231–36.

27. *ONE*, Dec. 1965, 8; *Ladder*, Mar. 1966, 12; *Ladder*, June 1966, 10; *MMN*, Oct. 1966.

28. Freedman to Leitsch, 22 July 1966, BF.

29. Leitsch to Henry, 23 Mar. 1967, Box 1:14, MSNYR. See also Mattachine Society of New York to all homophile organizations, c. Nov. 1966, Box 19:32, PLDMP; *Drum*, Dec. 1964, 25; *Drum*, Sept. 1966, 5, 40; *Drum*, Aug. 1967, 24; *Drum*, Mar. 1968, 21; *MSNYN*, Dec. 1966, 1–2; *MSNYN*, Mar. 1967, 4; *In the Matter of Anne-Lise Coppo*, File A-6845593, 1965; *In the Matter of Olga Schmidt*, 56 Misc. 2d 456 (1968).

30. Leitsch to Freedman, 28 July 1966, BF; Jeanette Laven, cited by Paul Laven in correspondence with the author, 2 Apr. 2001; "Boutilier Fund" flier, c. Aug. 1966, BF.

31. Freedman to Leitsch, 19 Jan. 1967, Box 1:15, MSNYR; *MSNYN*, June 1967, 1; Bert Ford to Mattachine Society, 19 Dec. 1967; Leitsch to Ford, 21 Dec. 1967, Box 1:15, MSNYR.

32. East Coast Homophile Organizations 1964 Conference Program, 14, ECHOP; *JSN*, Feb. 1965, 2. See also Stein, *City*, 226–302.

33. Joan Frazer (for ECHO) to Polak, c. Feb. 1965, ECHOP; Leitsch to Barbara Horowitz, 7 Apr. 1965, Box 7:18, MSNYR; *EMM*, Nov.–Dec. 1965, 19; Frank Kameny, typescript of presentation to the Second National Planning Conference of Homophile Organizations, Aug. 1966, DOBP.

34. *Drum*, Dec. 1965, 14–15; *JSN*, Sept. 1966, 1–2; *JSN*, Jan. 1965, 2; Report of the Philadelphia Postal Inspector, 24 Feb. 1970, NOP.

35. *JSN*, Oct. 1963, 3; Polak to Janus Society Board, 28 Oct. 1964, Janus Society file, ONENGLA.

36. ECHO Minutes, 5 Dec. 1964, ECHOP; *Janus*, Apr. 1964, 12; *Janus*, May 1964, 14.

37. *JSN*, Feb. 1965, 2; *Drum*, Apr. 1965, 2, 4.

38. *Drum*, May 1965, 6; *JSN*, July 1965, 1; *Drum*, Sept. 1965, 4; Polak to Leitsch, 29 Nov. 1965, Box 5:2, MSNYR; *JSN*, Dec. 1965, 3.

39. *Drum*, Jan. 1966, 12, 23, 26; Feb. 1966, 21; Sept. 1966, 31; Polak, typescript of presentation

to the Second National Planning Conference of Homophile Organizations, Aug. 1966, DOBP; *JSN*, Sept. 1966, 2; *Drum*, Sept. 1966, 52.

40. *Drum*, Mar. 1968, 21–22. See also *Ladder*, June 1966, 14. See also *Drum*, Sept. 1966, 5, 29; Jan. 1967, 5; Sept. 1967, 6; Oct. 1967, 27; Jan. 1968, 4, 9; Dec. 1968, 40. See also *JSN*, Feb. 1968, 1–2; *HALN*, Jan. 1973, 1, 4; *Inman*, 197 So. 2d 50 (1967), 389 U.S. 1048 (1968).

41. Charles Alverson, "U.S. Homosexuals Gain in Trying to Persuade Society to Accept Them," *WSJ*, 17 July 1968, 1, 22.

42. *EMM*, Jan. 1966, 2.

43. *Drum*, Feb. 1966, 4; Mar. 1967, 6.

44. *Val's Bar v. Division of Alcoholic Beverage Control*, 50 N.J. 329 (1967), 342; *Drum*, Jan. 1968, 23. See also Bryant Simon, "New York Avenue: The Life and Death of Gay Spaces in Atlantic City, New Jersey, 1920–1990," *Journal of Urban History* 28 (2002): 300–27.

45. Polak to Freedman, 15 Nov. 1966, Freedman to Polak, 18 Nov. 1966, BF.

46. Polak to Freedman, 17 Nov. 1966, Freedman to Polak, 18 Nov. 1966, BF.

47. Mattachine Society of New York to all homophile organizations, c. Nov. 1966; Polak to Leitsch, 25 Nov. 1966, Leitsch to Polak, 28 Nov. 1966, Box 1:12, MSNYR.

48. *Drum*, Dec. 1966, 36; Gilbert M. Cantor, "Brief of the Homosexual Law Reform Society," *Boutilier*, 28.

49. *Ladder*, June 1967, 25; Freedman to NLDF, 2 Mar. 1967, BF. See also *Ladder*, Apr. 1966, 4; *Ladder*, Jan. 1968, 21–27; *Ladder*, Oct.–Nov. 1968, 38–40; *Ladder*, June–July 1969, 39–40; *DOBNYN*, Mar. 1967, 2; *Pride Newsletter*, May 1967, 10; *JSN*, Aug. 1967, 1–2; Alverson, "U.S. Homosexuals," *WSJ*, 17 July 1968, 1, 22; *HALN*, Mar. 1969, 3–4; Aug.–Sept. 1969, 7; NLDF file and NACHO file, ONENGLA; NLDF materials, c. 1966–67, Boxes 18:17 and 20:7, PLDMP.

50. See Gilbert M. Cantor, *The Barnes Foundation: Reality vs. Myth* (Philadelphia: Chilton, 1963); *Commonwealth v. Robin*, 421 Pa. 70 (1966); Gilbert M. Cantor, "The Need for Homosexual Law Reform," in *The Same Sex: An Appraisal of Homosexuality*, ed. Ralph W. Weltge (Philadelphia: Pilgrim, 1969), 83–94; Seymour Kurland, "Gilbert M. Cantor: Profile of Retiring Shingle Editor," *The Shingle* 37 (1974): 107–109; Gilbert M. Cantor and Robert L. Franklin, *The Ten Best Ways to Save Estate Taxes* (Englewood Cliffs, N.J.: Institute for Business Planning, 1978); Gilbert M. Cantor, *How to Totally Avoid Estate Taxes* (Wilmington, Del.: Enterprise, 1980); Gilbert M. Cantor, *The Lawyer's Complete Guide to the Perfect Will* (Philadelphia: Cato, 1984); *Philadelphia Inquirer*, 2 Apr. 1987, D16; Stein, *City*, 251, 256, 300. I thank Anthony Cantor for providing me with information and materials about his father.

51. Alverson, "U.S. Homosexuals," *WSJ*, 17 July 1968, 22; *JSN*, Apr. 1965, 2. See also *JSN*, Jan. 1966, 2; *Drum*, Mar. 1966, 5.

52. Gilbert M. Cantor, typescript, "Anticipations—Legal and Philosophical," 5 Sept. 1965, Box III-7, GPACLUP. See also *Ladder*, Jan. 1966, 9, 11, 15–17; *Ladder*, May 1966, 16; *JSN*, Oct. 1965, 3; *Drum*, Dec. 1965, 15; *EMM*, Jan. 1966, 3.

53. Gil Cantor, "How Black Is Black?" *Legal Intelligencer*, 21 July 1966, 1, 5.

54. Ronald Bayer, *Homosexuality and American Psychiatry: The Politics of Diagnosis* (New York: Basic, 1981).

55. *MR*, July 1966, 28; Kameny to Freedman, 9 Feb. 1967, BF.

56. See Freedman correspondence with Alan Levine and Clark Polak, 26 Aug. 1966–30 Jan. 1967, BF.

57. "Homosexuality and Civil Liberties," *CL*, Mar. 1957, 3. This paragraph is also based on a survey of lesbian and gay publications; the works cited in note 2; Box III-7, GPACLUP; ACLU and Janus Society folders, ONENGLA; Boxes 790–95, 842, 1127, ACLUP; ACLU Bulletin 1993,

20 Apr. 1959; ACLU Bulletin 2015, 26 Oct. 1959; ACLU Bulletin 2251, 13 Dec. 1965; ACLU News Release, 17 Nov. 1965, 27 Feb. 1970. On the ACLU and *ONE*, see Murdoch and Price, *Courting Justice*, 31.

58. "Homosexuality and Civil Liberties," 3.

59. *Ladder*, Mar. 1957, 8; *MR*, Mar. 1957, 7; *ONE*, Apr. 1957, 13; *Ladder*, July 1960, 12–13. See also *Civil Liberties Record*, Apr. 1964, 2–3; *Janus*, May 1964, 10–11; *Drum*, Oct. 1964, 15–16; *Drum*, Sept. 1966, 30, 39–40; *Ladder*, Nov. 1964, 21; *ONE*, Jan. 1966, 4–8.

60. ACLU Annual Report, 1960–61, Box 1880:13; Kameny to ACLU, 15 May 1962; Reitman to Kameny, 28 May 1962; Kameny to Reitman, 18 June 1962; Reitman to Kameny, 3 Jul. 1962; Reitman to E. A. Dioguardi, 10 May 1962, Box 1127:16, ACLUP; Reitman to Coxe, 28 Aug. 1963, Box III-7, GPACLUP.

61. ACLU Office to ACLU Board of Directors, 24 Nov. 1965, Box III-7, GPACLUP. See also Harriet F. Pilpel, "Sex vs. the Law: A Study in Hypocrisy," *Harper's*, Jan. 1965, 35–40; *ONE*, Jan. 1963, 20–21.

62. Reitman to Thomas Maddux, 31 Mar. 1966, Box 1127:22, ACLUP.

63. ACLU Office to ACLU Board of Directors, 24 Nov. 1965. See also Boxes 1127:18 and 1143:21, ACLUP.

64. ACLU Office to ACLU Board of Directors, 10 Nov. 1966, Box 19:5; ACLU Board of Directors Minutes, 16 Nov. 1966, Box 19:6, ACLUP. See also Boxes 1143:21 and 1127:22, ACLUP.

65. ACLU Statement on Homosexuality, 31 Aug. 1967, Box 1921:1. See also ACLU News Release, 31 Aug. 1967; ACLU Bulletin 2308, 9 Oct. 1967; *CL*, Dec. 1967, 8.

66. Kameny to Lynn Rosner, 17 Sept. 1967; Reitman to Kameny, 25 Sept. 1967, Box 1127:25, ACLUP.

67. Polak to Reitman, 31 Aug. 1967, Box 1127:25, ACLUP. See also Boxes 794:10 and 1127:25, ACLUP; Box III-7, GPACLUP; *CL*, Mar.–Apr. 1968, 4.

68. Donohue, *The Politics of the ACLU*, 171; typescript, "Statement by David Carliner on Behalf of the American Civil Liberties Union before the Immigration Subcommittee of the Senate Judiciary Committee," 12 Mar. 1965, Box 842:1, ACLUP. See also ACLU Bulletin 2214, 26 Oct. 1964; Markmann, *The Noblest Cry*, 105–31; Walker, *In Defense*, 43–45, 59, 96–97, 123–24; ACLU Annual Report, 1964–65, 60–61, ACLU Annual Report 1965–67, 35, Box 1880:17, ACLUP.

69. Thomas S. Szasz, "The ACLU's 'Mental Illness' Cop-Out," *Reason*, Jan. 1974, 4, 8. See also ACLU Annual Report, 1964–65, 61–62; ACLU Annual Report 1965–67, 35–36; Bruce J. Ennis, "The Rights of Mental Patients," in Dorsen, *The Rights of Americans*, 484–98; Bruce J. Ennis, *Prisoners of Psychiatry: Mental Patients, Psychiatrists, and the Law* (New York: Harcourt, 1972), x, xv–xvii, 4, 214–15; Aryeh Neier, *Only Judgment: The Limits of Litigation in Social Change* (Middletown, Conn.: Wesleyan University Press, 1982), 170–93; Donohue, *The Politics of the ACLU*, 88–89; Markmann, *The Noblest Cry*, 399–406; Walker, *In Defense*, 277, 309–10, 338, 376.

70. Burt Neuborne correspondence with the author, 2 and 4 May 2005. See also author correspondence with Neuborne and Alan Levine, 1–14 Mar. 2005, and references to the lawyers in Donohue, *The Politics of the ACLU*; Garey, *Defending Everybody*; Walker, *In Defense*.

71. See *NYT*, 22 June 1972, 46; 16 Oct. 1972, 82; 12 Nov. 1976, 41; 31 Oct. 1982, 78; 5 Apr. 1989, B10.

72. *Marcello v. Bonds*, 349 U.S. 302 (1955), 314; *Brownell v. Shung*, 352 U.S. 180 (1956); *Lehmann v. Carson*, 353 U.S. 685 (1957); *Klig v. Brownell*, 355 U.S. 809 (1957); David Carliner, *The Rights of Aliens: The Basic ACLU Guide to An Alien's Rights* (New York: Avon, 1977). On Carliner's background, see Gregory Michael Dorr, "Principled Expediency: Eugenics, *Naim v. Naim*, and the Supreme Court," *American Journal of Legal History* 42 (1998): 130–31; *NYT*, 22 Sept. 2007, B10; *WP*, 27 Sept. 2007, A24; Phyl Newbeck, "David Carliner," *Guardian*, 8 Oct. 2007.

73. *Wyngaard v. Rogers*, 187 F. Supp. 527 (1960), 527; *Wyngaard v. Kennedy*, 295 F.2d 184 (1961), 185; *Wyngaard v. Kennedy*, 368 U.S. 926 (1961).

74. *Scott v. Macy*, 349 F.2d 182 (1965), 184–85. See also *Scott v. Macy*, 402 F.2d 644 (1968); *Ladder*, Aug. 1963, 19; *Ladder*, Oct. 1964, 12; *Ladder*, Jan. 1965, 10, 16–17; *Ladder*, Jan. 1966, 22–24; *ONE*, Aug. 1963, 13; *ONE*, Jan. 1966, 29; *Drum*, Nov. 1964, 14; *Drum*, Apr. 1965, 6; *Drum*, May 1965, 5–6; *Drum*, Dec. 1966, 25. The government declined to appeal the ruling in *Scott*, but later declined to consider Scott for employment. See also Box 1127:18, 22, ACLUP.

75. Polak to Freedman, 11 Jan. 1967; Freedman to Polak, 18 Jan. 1967, BF.

76. Jeffrey Toobin, "Sex and the Supremes," *New Yorker*, 1 Aug. 2005, 33. See also introduction, note 23.

Chapter 5

1. Blanch Freedman and Robert Brown, "Petition for a Writ of Certiorari," *Boutilier v. Immigration and Naturalization Service*, 387 U.S. 118 (1967), 10; Blanch Freedman and David M. Freedman, "Brief for Petitioner," *Boutilier*, 15. The brief for petitioner and reply brief were attributed to Freedman and Brown, but the title pages indicated that David and Blanch Freedman were "on the brief."

2. Freedman and Freedman, "Brief for Petitioner," 12; Gilbert M. Cantor, "Brief of the Homosexual Law Reform Society of America," *Boutilier*, 44, 53; David Carliner, Burt Neuborne, Nanette Dembitz, and Alan H. Levine, "Brief of American Civil Liberties Union and New York Civil Liberties Union," *Boutilier*, 7–8.

3. Freedman and Freedman, "Brief for Petitioner," 13, 48; Carliner et al., "Brief of ACLU/NYCLU," 4; Cantor, "Brief of HLRS," 2, 29, 44, 52.

4. Blanch Freedman and David Freedman, "Reply Brief," *Boutilier*, 5–6; *Boutilier* oral arguments, 14 Mar. 1967, National Archives, Washington, D.C.

5. Freedman and Brown, "Petition," 9.

6. Carliner et al., "Brief of ACLU/NYCLU," 8.

7. Freedman and Freedman, "Brief for Petitioner," 8; *Boutilier* oral arguments; Carliner et al., "Brief of ACLU/NYCLU," 14.

8. Freedman and Brown, "Petition," 6, Freedman and Freedman, "Brief for Petitioner," 18, 27–28.

9. Freedman and Freedman, "Brief for Petitioner," 14–15, 19, 44; *Boutilier*, 363 F.2d 488 (1966), 494.

10. Cantor, "Brief of HLRS," 2, 12.

11. Ibid., 11.

12. *Boutilier* oral arguments.

13. Freedman and Freedman, "Brief for Petitioner," 15; Cantor, "Brief of HLRS," 26, 33–34, 45.

14. Cantor, "Brief of HLRS," 33, 40; Freedman and Freedman, "Brief for Petitioner," 46–47.

15. Cantor, "Brief of HLRS," 10, 61.

16. Ibid., 26, 30, 70, 74. See also Michael S. Sherry, *Gay Artists in Modern American Culture: An Imagined Conspiracy* (Chapel Hill: University of North Carolina Press, 2007).

17. Cantor, "Brief of HLRS," 33, 43, 51–52; *Boutilier* oral arguments.

18. Freedman and Freedman, "Brief for Petitioner," 17.

19. Ibid., 22, 24, 26–27.

20. Ibid., 11; Freedman and Freedman, "Reply Brief," 12.

21. Freedman and Brown, "Petition," 5; Freedman and Freedman, "Brief for Petitioner," 28–30.

22. Freedman and Freedman, "Brief for Petitioner," 30.

23. Ibid.

24. Exhibit 6, Report of Dr. Falsey, 2 Mar. 1964, *Boutilier* case file, 13; Exhibit 7, Report of Dr. Ullman, 30 Mar. 1965, *Boutilier* case file, 15–16.

25. Freedman and Freedman, "Brief for Petitioner," 9–10, 32.

26. Freedman and Brown, "Petition," 6, 10; Freedman and Freedman, "Brief for Petitioner," 16; Carliner et al., "Brief of ACLU/NYCLU," 12–13.

27. Freedman and Freedman, "Brief for Petitioner," 35; Carliner et al., "Brief of ACLU/NYCLU," 12.

28. Freedman and Freedman, "Brief for Petitioner," 17, 32.

29. Ibid., 10; Freedman and Freedman, "Reply Brief," 2–3, 11.

30. Freedman and Freedman, "Brief for Petitioner," 10, 45, 50; Freedman and Freedman, "Reply Brief," 4.

31. Cantor, "Brief of HLRS," 21–26, 29–30, 33–41, 48–52, 54, 56–59, 61, 69–70, 72–76, 78, 81; Carliner et al., "Brief of ACLU/NYCLU," 14, 19.

32. Thurgood Marshall, Fred M. Vinson Jr., and Philip R. Monahan, "Brief for Respondent," *Boutilier*, 36–37.

33. Freedman and Brown, "Petition," 4; Freedman and Freedman, "Brief for Petitioner," 5; Carliner et al., "Brief of ACLU/NYCLU," 16–17.

34. Marshall et al., "Brief for Respondent," 5.

35. Carliner et al., "Brief of ACLU/NYCLU," 2; Freedman and Freedman, "Reply Brief," 17.

36. Cantor, "Brief of HLRS," 3–4.

37. Report of Dr. Falsey, 12; Report of Dr. Ullman, 14; Freedman and Freedman, "Brief for Petitioner," 4; *Boutilier* oral arguments.

38. Report of Dr. Ullman, 14–15.

39. Report of Dr. Falsey, 12–13; Report of Dr. Ullman, 14, 16; Freedman and Freedman, "Brief for Petitioner," 4–5, 12; Carliner et al., "Brief of ACLU/NYCLU," 14.

40. Report of Dr. Falsey, 13; Report of Dr. Ullman, 15; Freedman and Freedman, "Brief for Petitioner," 4.

41. Report of Dr. Ullman, 14; Freedman and Freedman, "Brief for Petitioner," 4, 34; *Boutilier* oral arguments. Boutilier's family name may have seemed French, but his first name, Clive, was likely viewed as English, and Boutilier's niece told me that Boutilier's immediate family did not speak French and pronounced the name "Boot'leer."

42. Report of Dr. Ullman, 15; Freedman and Freedman, "Brief for Petitioner," 5, 31, 34, 46; Carliner et al., "Brief of ACLU/NYCLU," 2, 5–6.

43. Report of Dr. Ullman, 15–16; Freedman and Freedman, "Brief for Petitioner," 5, 8, 16–17; *Boutilier* oral arguments.

44. Freedman and Freedman, "Brief for Petitioner," 4. The hint is a handwritten line that reads, "Gibson—told truth—Gibson came to apartment." The line appears in notes about the Sarsfield interrogation. On Boutilier's syphilis diagnosis and treatment, see handwritten notes, undated; Jacob Abramson to Whom It May Concern, 28 Jan. 1965, BF.

45. Transcript of Hearing on July 26, 1965 before Special Inquiry Officer, *Boutilier* case file, 19–20. See also Marshall et al., "Brief for Respondent," 11–12, 17.

46. Clive Boutilier, INS Affidavit, 6 Sept. 1963 (obtained through an FOIA request); INS Record of Sworn Statement, January 13, 1964, *Boutilier* case file, 9; Report of Dr. Falsey, 12; Report of Dr. Ullman, 15; Freedman and Freedman, "Brief for Petitioner," 34; Cantor, "Brief of HLRS," 27.

47. *Boutilier* oral arguments.

48. Report of Dr. Ullman, 14–15; Freedman and Freedman, "Brief for Petitioner," 9; Carliner et al., "Brief of ACLU/NYCLU," 15; Freedman and Freedman, "Reply Brief," 11.

49. Freedman and Brown, "Petition," 10; Freedman and Freedman, "Brief for Petitioner," 5; Freedman and Freedman, "Reply Brief," 13.

50. On the use of analogies in post-Stonewall lesbian and gay rights cases, see Evan Gerstmann, *The Constitutional Underclass: Gays, Lesbians, and the Failure of Class-Based Equal Protection* (Chicago: University of Chicago Press, 1999); Janet E. Halley, "'Like Race' Arguments," in *What's Left of Theory? New Work on the Politics of Literary Theory*, eds. Judith Butler, John Guillory, and Kendall Thomas (New York: Routledge, 2000), 40–74; Andrew Koppelman, *The Gay Rights Question in Contemporary American Law* (Chicago: University of Chicago Press, 2002); David A. J. Richards, *Identity and the Case for Gay Rights: Race, Gender, Religion as Analogies* (Chicago: University of Chicago Press, 1999). For related pre-Stonewall examples, see Siobhan B. Somerville, "Queer *Loving*," *GLQ: A Journal of Lesbian and Gay Studies* 11 (2005): 335–70; Siobhan B. Somerville, "Sexual Aliens and the Racialized State: A Queer Reading of the 1952 U.S. Immigration and Nationality Act," in *Queer Migrations: Sexuality, U.S. Citizenship, and Border Crossings*, eds. Eithne Luibhéid and Lionel Cantú Jr. (Minneapolis: University of Minnesota Press, 2005), 75–91.

51. Cantor, "Brief of HLRS," 16, 79, 94.

52. Freedman and Freedman, "Brief for Petitioner," 10; Cantor, "Brief of HLRS," 36, 89.

53. Freedman and Freedman, "Brief for Petitioner," 47.

54. Ibid., 50; Cantor, "Brief of HLRS," 48.

55. Cantor, "Brief of HLRS," 57.

56. Freedman and Freedman, "Brief for Petitioner," 11.

57. Ibid., 47; Cantor, "Brief of HLRS," 36, 71–72.

58. Freedman and Freedman, "Repy Brief," 17; Cantor, "Brief of HLRS," 5; Carliner et al., "Brief of ACLU/NYCLU," 10–11.

59. Freedman and Freedman, "Brief for Petitioner," 51; Cantor, "Brief of HLRS," 3, 18.

60. Cantor, "Brief of HLRS," 42, 46, 52, 74.

61. Freedman and Freedman, "Brief for Petitioner," 12; Freedman and Freedman, "Reply Brief," 11, 15, 17.

62. Cantor, "Brief of HLRS," 61, 73; Freedman and Freedman, "Reply Brief," 17.

63. Cantor, "Brief of HLRS," 2, 17, 45.

64. Ibid., 4–5.

Chapter 6

1. Bob Woodward and Scott Armstrong, *The Brethren: Inside the Supreme Court* (New York: Simon and Schuster, 1979), 253; "Burger Suggests Some Judges Err in Closing Trials," *NYT*, 9 Aug. 1979, A17; "Powell Says Court Has No Hostility Toward Press," *NYT*, 14 Aug. 1979, A13; Nat Hentoff, "The Justice Breaks His Silence," *Playboy*, July 1991, 122; Sarah Weddington, *A Question of Choice* (New York: Penguin, 1992), 129.

2. See introduction, note 19.

3. This section is based on a survey of more than thirty major periodicals, including liberal and conservative publications and several that targeted Christian, black, or female readers.

4. Fred P. Graham, "High Court Bars Curbs on Birth Control," *NYT*, 8 June 1965, 1, 35; "News Summary and Index," *NYT*, 8 June 1965, 43; Fred P. Graham, "Court Bans Birth Control Curbs," *NYT*, 13 June 1965, 6E; Richard Wilson, "How Many People Is Too Many?" *LAT*, 17 June 1965,

A6; "Margaret Sanger Is Dead at 83," *WP*, 7 Sept. 1966, B3. See also *LAT*, 8 June 1965, 1, 14; *LAT*, 13 June 1965, F3, F4; *LAT*, 6 July 1965, 1, 8; *LAT*, 18 July 1965, F7; *LAT*, 22 July 1965, A5; *NYT*, 8 June 1965, 34, 58; *NYT*, 9 June 1965, 46; *NYT*, 10 June 1965, 30; *NYT*, 13 June 1965, E13; *NYT*, 14 June 1965, 38; *NYT*, 15 June 1965, 25; *NYT*, 17 June 1965, 1, 22; *NYT*, 10 July 1965, 1, 14; *NYT*, 8 Aug. 1965, 53; *NYT*, 26 Aug. 1965, 42; *WP*, 8 June 1965, A1, A5, A18; *WP*, 13 June 1965, A34; *WP*, 6 Aug. 1965, A6.

5. Webster Schott, "Civil Rights and the Homosexual," *NYTM*, 12 Nov. 1967, 59; Fred P. Graham, "Smut and Sex on Trial Again in Supreme Court," *NYT*, 25 Oct. 1970, E8.

6. "Birth Control Decision," *America*, 19 June 1965, 875–76; "Supreme Court Reverses Birth Control Law," *Christian Century*, 23 June 1965, 796–97; "Now, Legal Family Planning," *Christian Century*, 4 Aug. 1965, 970–72; "End of Term Decisions," *New Republic*, 19 June 1965, 8; "Population Control Takes a Forward Step," *Business Week*, 19 June 1965, 108–10; "Consensus Grows on Birth Control," *Business Week*, 9 Oct. 1965, 36; Kenneth Crawford, "Birth Control," *Newsweek*, 12 July 1965, 32; "Supreme Court: Which Way Now?" *USNWR*, 2 Aug. 1965, 56; Steven M. Spencer, "The Birth Control Revolution," *Saturday Evening Post*, Jan. 1966, 22; "The Connecticut Decision," *Commonweal*, 25 June 1965, 427. See also *America*, 9 Dec. 1967, 712; *Atlantic*, June 1969, 70–71; *Harper's Bazaar*, Apr. 1966, 169; *Newsweek*, 21 June 1965, 26–27, 60; *PW*, 26 July 1965, 29; *USNWR*, 21 June 1965, 16; 5 July 1965, 14.

7. William B. Ball, "The Court and Birth Control," *Commonweal*, 9 July 1965, 491–93; "Priceless Privacy," *Christian Science Monitor*, 21 July 1965, 14; James D. Carroll, "The Forgotten Amendment," *Nation*, 6 Sept. 1965, 122; "Emanations from a Penumbra," *Time*, 18 June 1965, 48; "Life, Liberty and 'Privacy,'" *Life*, 2 July 1965, 4.

8. For examples, see *Playboy*, Dec. 1965, 79, 83–87, 220–25; Jan. 1966, 64–66, 208; Feb. 1966, 45–46; Mar. 1966, 37–38; Apr. 1966, 66–68, 158–59; July 1966, 142–44; Aug. 1966, 39–44, 144–45; Sept. 1966, 90, 197–99; Nov. 1966, 63–68; Dec. 1966, 89–93.

9. Editorial Reply, Playboy Forum, *Playboy*, Aug. 1965, 135; Donald MacChesney, Mrs. Derrick W. Brown, Editorial Reply, Playboy Forum, *Playboy*, Sept. 1965, 79–81.

10. Hugh M. Hefner, "The Playboy Philosophy," *Playboy*, Nov. 1965, 70; R. Lucas, Playboy Forum, *Playboy*, May 1966, 58; "The Playboy Panel: Religion and the New Morality," *Playboy*, June 1966, 148; Nat Hentoff, "The Supreme Court," *Playboy*, Nov. 1966, 253; R. Michael Gross, Playboy Forum, *Playboy*, Mar. 1968, 140; Peter Andrews, "A.C.L.U.—Let There Be Law," *Playboy*, Oct. 1971, 226.

11. See *America*, 2 Apr. 1966, 430; *America*, 30 Apr. 1966, 614; *Commonweal*, 15 Apr. 1966, 94–95; *LAT*, 23 Mar. 1966, 25, A4; *LAT*, 27 Mar. 1966, J1, J2, J4, J6; *LAT*, 29 Mar. 1966, A5; *LAT*, 7 Apr. 1966, A5; *LAT*, 30 Apr. 1966, 21; *LAT*, 31 May 1966, A5; *Life*, 1 Apr. 1966, 4; *Life*, 22 Apr. 1966, 26; *Nation*, 4 Apr. 1966, 379–80; *National Review*, 19 Apr. 1966, 346; *NYT*, 22 Mar. 1966, 24–26, 43, 64; *NYT*, 24 Mar. 1966, 31, 38; *NYT*, 27 Mar. 1966, Sec. 2, p. 1; *NYT*, 3 Apr. 1966, E14; *NYTM*, 25 Sept. 1966, 131; *New Yorker*, 9 Apr. 1966, 31; *Playboy*, July 1966, 41–44, 140–42; *Playboy*, Sept. 1966, 197; *Playboy*, Oct. 1966, 7, 10; *Playboy*, Nov. 1966, 247–48; *Progressive*, June 1967, 32; *PW*, 25 Apr. 1966, 82, 91; *PW*, 26 Sept. 1966, 108; *PW*, 26 Dec. 1966, 55; *USNWR*, 4 Apr. 1966, 69; *WP*, 23 Mar. 1966, A20; 29 Mar. 1966, A3, A12; *WP*, 30 Mar. 1966, C28; *WP*, 7 Apr. 1966, A25; *WP*, 10 Apr. 1966, E3.

12. "Court Stirs a Hornet's Nest," *Christian Century*, 13 Apr. 1966, 451; "Obscenity Test—A Legal Poser," *Newsweek*, 4 Apr. 1966, 19–22. See also *America*, 13 Aug. 1966, 156; *Harper's*, Dec. 1968, 30; *LAT*, 22 Mar. 1966, 1, 7; *New Republic*, 3 Apr. 1966, 5–6; *New Republic*, 27 May 1967, 15–17; *NYT*, 22 Mar. 1966, 1, 25; *NYT*, 23 Mar. 1966, 1; *NYT*, 27 Mar. 1966, E3, E8, E11; *NYT*, 2 May 1966, 30; *NYT*, 3 May 1966, 1, 23; *Newsweek*, 4 Apr. 1966, 19–22; *Playboy*, July 1966, 42, 47, 142; *PW*, 28 Mar. 1966, 43–44; *PW*, 11 Apr. 1966, 29–30; *PW*, 18 Apr. 1966, 79; *PW*, 9 May 1966, 49; *PW*,

30 May 1966, 59; *Ramparts*, Apr. 1966, 3–5; *Reader's Digest*, Feb. 1967, 147–52; *Time*, 1 Apr. 1966, 56, 58; *WP*, 22 Mar. 1966, A1, A6; *WP*, 23 Mar. 1966, A2.

13. James Conway, Playboy Forum, *Playboy*, July 1966, 41; "*Playboy* Interview: Ralph Ginzburg," *Playboy*, July 1966, 53; Ralph Ginzburg, Playboy Forum, *Playboy*, Jan. 1971, 12; Jason Epstein, "The Obscenity Business," *Atlantic*, Aug. 1966, 59; "Ginzburg and Pornography," *National Review*, 19 Apr. 1966, 346; "A Society's Lack of Confidence in Itself," *PW*, 4 Apr. 1966, 41.

14. Alexander M. Bickel, "Obscenity Cases," *New Republic*, 27 May 1967, 16; "Possession of Pornography," *Playboy*, July 1969, 44; "*Eros* Publisher Jailed," *Playboy*, May 1972, 64. See also *WP*, 9 May 1967, A1; *Time*, 23 June 1967, 45.

15. Fred P. Graham, "No Censorship in the Home," *NYT*, 13 Apr. 1969, E13; Graham, "Smut and Sex."

16. Fred P. Graham, "Nixon Appointees May Change Supreme Court," *NYT*, 2 Oct. 1972, 16; Paul Bender, "The Obscenity Muddle," *Harper's*, Feb. 1973, 46, 52; *Roe v. Wade*, 410 U.S. 113 (1973), 154; *Paris Adult Theatre I v. Slaton*, 413 U.S. 49 (1973), 68.

17. "The Right to Marry," *NYT*, 20 June 1967, 38; "Justices Upset All Bans on Interracial Marriage," *NYT*, 13 June 1967, 1, 28. See also *Christian Century*, 28 June 1967, 827; *Jet*, 29 June 1967, 15, 18, 24–25; *LAT*, 13 June 1967, 1, 7; *LAT*, 15 June 1967, B6; *LAT*, 18 June 1967, K4; *LAT*, 21 June 1967, A5; *NYT*, 13 June 1967, 29, 32, 49; *NYT*, 14 June 1967, 32; *NYT*, 18 June 1967, 6E; *NYT*, 11 July 1967, 23; *NYT*, 22 July 1967, 11; *NYT*, 13 Aug. 1967, 31; *Newsweek*, 26 June 1967, 36; *Time*, 23 June 1967, 38–39; *USNWR*, 26 June 1967, 25; *WP*, 13 June 1967, A1, A11; *WP*, 15 June 1967, A20, A21.

18. See *Christian Century*, 28 June 1967, 828; *Jet*, 29 June 1967, 24; *LAT*, 13 June 1967, 1; *NYT*, 30 Sept. 1967, 28; 7 Oct. 1967, 58; *Playboy*, Sept. 1967, 184.

19. David Margolick, "A Mixed Marriage's 25th Anniversary of Legality," *NYT*, 12 June 1992, B20. See also *NYT*, 30 Mar. 1996, 21; 31 Mar. 1996, TE3, 13; 6 May 2008, C13; Phyl Newbeck, *Virginia Hasn't Always Been for Lovers* (Carbondale: Southern Illinois University Press, 2004), 10.

20. Simeon Booker, "The Couple That Rocked Courts," *Ebony*, Sept. 1967, 78–84.

21. Richard Butler, Playboy Forum, *Playboy*, Sept. 1967, 184. See also *Playboy*, Nov. 1967, 160.

22. "Court Voids an Anti-Contraceptive Law," *NYT*, 23 Mar. 1972, 22; Arlie Schardt, "The Nixon Court: Just One More Vote," *Progressive*, Oct. 1972, 27–29; "The Controversial 'Miranda Ruling' Back Before Court," *USNWR*, 3 Apr. 1972, 35; Bender, "The Obscenity Muddle," 51. See also *NYT*, 25 Mar. 1972, 30; *Playboy*, June 1972, 66; Dec. 1972, 87.

23. "The Perils of the Pill," *Ramparts*, May 1969, 48; "Court Voids"; "Court Upsets Law on Contraceptives," *LAT*, 22 Mar. 1972, 2.

24. Bill Baird, Playboy Forum, *Playboy*, July 1972, 57; John P. MacKenzie, "Unwed Win Equality in Birth Control," *WP*, 23 May 1972, A14; Schardt, "The Nixon Court," 27–28; Bender, "The Obscenity Muddle," 51.

25. *People v. Belous*, 71 Cal. 2d 954 (1969), 963; *U.S. v. Vuitch*, 305 F. Supp. 1032 (1969), 1035. See also *LAT*, 31 Oct. 1969, B7; *LAT*, 11 Nov. 1969, 6; *NYT*, 14 Sept. 1969, 66; *NYT*, 12 Nov. 1969, 46; *NYT*, 16 Nov. 1969, E9; *NYT*, 23 Nov. 1969, 78; *NYT*, 8 Dec. 1969, 1, 53; *NYT*, 13 Dec. 1969, 37; *NYTM*, 25 Jan. 1970, 30, 90; *Playboy*, Dec. 1969, 72; *Time*, 21 Nov. 1969, 65; *WP*, 11 Nov. 1969, A1, A17.

26. See *America*, 3 Feb. 1973, 81; 2 June 1973, 506–7, 515–17; *Christian Century*, 28 Feb. 1973, 254–55; 4 Apr. 1973, 406; 25 Apr. 1973, 477–79; *Commonweal*, 16 Feb. 1973, 434–36; *Commonweal*, 23 Mar. 1973, 51–52; *Commonweal*, 30 Mar. 1973, 75, 94–95; *Commonweal*, 13 Apr. 1973, 133–35; *Good Housekeeping*, June 1973, 77–79, 148, 150–52; *LAT*, 22 Jan. 1973, 1, C6; *LAT*, 23 Jan. 1973, A1, 12; *LAT*, 25 Jan. 1973, 4; *LAT*, 26 Jan. 1973, 6, 8A; *Ms.*, Apr. 1973, 44–49, 116, 118; *Ms.*, June 1973, 8; *Nation*, 5 Feb. 1973, 165; *National Review*, 16 Feb. 1973, 193; *National Review*, 2 Mar. 1973, 249–50,

260–64; *New Republic*, 10 Feb. 1973, 9; *New Republic*, 24 Mar. 1973, 32; *NYT*, 23 Jan. 1973, 1, 20, 22; *NYT*, 24 Jan. 1973, 13, 14, 40; *NYT*, 27 Jan. 1973, 8; *NYT*, 28 Jan. 1973, 45, Sec. 4, p. 3; *NYT*, 29 Jan. 1973, 28; *NYT*, 30 Jan. 1973, 80; *NYT*, 2 Feb. 1973, 35; *NYT*, 3 Feb. 1973, 28; *NYT*, 4 Feb. 1973, 39; *NYT*, 8 Feb. 1973, 42; *NYT*, 14 Feb. 1973, 40; *NYT*, 18 Feb. 1973, Sec. 4, p.10; *NYT*, 19 Mar. 1973, 32; *NYT*, 20 Mar. 1973, 38; *NYT*, 27 Mar. 1973, 46; *Newsweek*, 5 Feb. 1973, 27–28, 66, 69; *Newsweek*, 19 Feb. 1973, 4; *Playboy*, Apr. 1973, 58; *Playboy*, May 1973, 71; *Playboy*, June 1973, 56; *Reader's Digest*, Mar. 1973, 69–71; *Saturday Review*, Apr. 1973, 30–35; *Scientific American*, Mar. 1973, 44–45; *Time*, 19 Feb. 1973, 6–7; *Time*, 26 Feb. 1973, 4, 6; *USNWR*, 5 Feb. 1973, 36; *WP*, 23 Jan. 1973, A1, A2; *WP*, 25 Jan. 1973, A15; *WP*, 26 Jan. 1973, A2, A12.

27. "Abortion on Demand," *Time*, 29 Jan. 1973, 46; "A Stunning Approval for Abortion," *Time*, 5 Feb. 1973, 48; Anthony Lewis, "Liberty, New and Old," *NYT*, 3 Feb. 1973, 29; J. Claude Evans, "The Abortion Decision," *Christian Century*, 14 Feb. 1973, 195; Richard J. Neuhaus, "Sense and Nonsense About Victimless Crimes," *Christian Century*, 7 Mar. 1973, 281–82.

28. Robert M. Byrn, "Goodbye to the Judeo-Christian Era in Law," *America*, 2 June 1973, 513; Robert F. Drinan, "The Abortion Decision," *Commonweal*, 16 Feb. 1973, 438; Susan Sontag, "The Third World of Women," *Partisan Review*, Spring 1973, 204.

29. This section is based on a survey of approximately 30 periodicals. See Edward Alwood, *Straight News: Gays, Lesbians, and the News Media* (New York: Columbia University Press, 1996); Rodger Streitmatter, *Unspeakable: The Rise of the Gay and Lesbian Press in America* (Boston: Faber and Faber, 1995); Martin Meeker, *Contacts Desired: Gay and Lesbian Communications and Community, 1940s–1970s* (Chicago: University of Chicago Press, 2006).

30. *Drum*, Nov. 1964, 24; *EMM*, Mar. 1965, 9. See also *ONE*, Oct. 1954, 4; Apr. 1955, 6; Apr.–May 1956, 20–22; Mar. 1958, 9; Jan. 1960, 18–19; Feb. 1960, 4; July 1960, 5; Sept. 1960, 15–16; Dec. 1961, 15; Feb. 1963, 4–5; Feb. 1964, 17; Jan. 1965, 18; Apr. 1965, 5–6; May 1965, 6–10; July 1965, 28–29. See also *MR*, Mar. 1958, 22–23; May 1959, 20; Oct. 1959, 23; Jan. 1960, 8, 30; June 1963, 2; Jan.–Feb. 1965, 2, 20–21. See also *Ladder*, Nov. 1958, 4–5; Jan. 1960, 20; Mar. 1961, 15–17; Oct. 1962, 7; Jan. 1963, 25; Sept. 1963, 7–23. See also *Drum*, Oct. 1964, 15; Mar. 1965, 22; Apr. 1965, 4; June 1965, 4, 20, 31; Aug. 1965, 19; Dec. 1965, 15, 17.

31. *Drum*, Sept. 1965, 4; *ONE*, Dec. 1965, 20; *ONE*, Jan. 1966, 7–8; *Drum*, Jan. 1968, 4.

32. *Advocate*, 14 Apr. 1971, 8. See also Walter Barnett, *Sexual Freedom and the Constitution* (Albuquerque: University of New Mexico Press, 1973).

33. See *Ladder*, Dec. 1963, 14–15; *MR*, Sept. 1956, 4; *MR*, Mar. 1957, 4–6; *MR*, July 1957, 8–14; *MR*, Feb. 1958, 2, 4–7, 28; *ONE*, July 1955, 6; *ONE*, Mar. 1957, 21; *ONE*, Feb. 1958, 16–17; *ONE*, Mar. 1958, 5–6, 15–17; *ONE*, Aug. 1958, 4–5; *ONE*, May 1963, 13. For the vote in *ONE*, see Box 1184, WODP.

34. *MR*, Aug. 1958, 16; *ONE*, Jan. 1960, 18; *MR*, Jan. 1962, 2. See also *ONE*, Nov. 1960, 18–19; Jan. 1961, 19; Aug. 1961, 18; Apr. 1962, 12. See also *Drum*, May 1965, 2; July 1965, 2, 22.

35. *ONE*, Feb. 1959, 15; *MR*, Nov. 1960, 21; *ONE*, Nov. 1960, 16; *ONE*, Dec. 1961, 10. See also *MR*, July 1957, 2.

36. *MR*, Aug. 1962, 2; *ONE*, Sept. 1962, 12; *Ladder*, Nov. 1962, 5; *Drum*, Oct. 1965, 11. See also *MR*, July 1962, 34; *ONE*, Oct. 1962, 19–20; *ONE*, Feb. 1963, 6–8.

37. *MSNYN*, Mar. 1966, 2–3.

38. *ONE*, Apr.–May 1966, 20; *Drum*, Sept. 1966, 30–31. See also *Ladder*, Sept. 1966, 5.

39. *Ladder*, Apr.–May 1969, 39; *Drum*, Jan. 1968, 4; *Drum*, Mar. 1968, 5. See also *Advocate*, Dec. 1967, 1, 4; *Potomac News*, 389 U.S. 47 (1967); *Central Magazine Sales*, 389 U.S. 50 (1967).

40. *ONE*, Nov. 1955, 8; *MSNYN*, June 1967, 2.

41. On same-sex marriage, see *Drum*, July 1965, 20; Sept. 1965, 32; Dec. 1965, 15; Sept. 1967, 7;

Mar. 1968, 27. See also *Ladder*, Mar. 1961, 13–14; Oct. 1962, 7–10; Oct.–Nov. 1968, 46–47; Aug.–Sept. 1969, 44; Feb.–Mar. 1971, 44. See also *MR*, Feb. 1956, 32–33. On interracial same-sex relationships, see *MR*, Apr. 1961, 4–6; *MR*, May 1961, 2; *ONE*, Oct. 1964, 17–21.

42. *Lesbian Tide*, Oct. 1972, 3.

43. *Advocate*, 11 Oct. 1972, 1; 25 Oct. 1972, 3; 8 Nov. 1972, 12; 31 Jan. 1973, 1, 16.

44. *Advocate*, 3 Jan. 1973, 36; 31 Jan. 1973, 3.

45. *Advocate*, 28 Feb. 1973, 23; 28 Mar. 1973, 1.

46. *Off Our Backs*, Feb.–Mar. 1973, 4; *Lesbian Tide*, Mar. 1973, 9, 26.

47. This section is based on a comprehensive survey of relevant Supreme Court and federal court cases, as well as selected state cases.

48. *Mincey v. Celebrezze*, 246 F. Supp. 447 (1965), 451; *Murphy v. Houma Well Service*, 413 F.2d 509 (1969), 512. For state court examples, see *Burton*, 99 N.J. Super. 516 (1967), 525; *Aguiar*, 257 Cal. App. 2d 597 (1968), 605; *Baker*, 291 Minn. 310 (1971), 314–15.

49. *Palo Alto Tenants Union v. Morgan*, 321 F. Supp. 908 (1970), 909–12; *Boraas v. Village of Belle Terre*, 367 F. Supp. 136 (1972), 146; 416 U.S. 1 (1974), 8.

50. *Warden, Maryland Penitentiary v. Hayden*, 387 U.S. 294 (1967), 324; *Boddie v. Connecticut*, 401 U.S. 371 (1971), 374, 376; *U.S. v. Kras*, 409 U.S. 434 (1973), 444; *San Antonio School District v. Rodriguez*, 411 U.S. 1 (1973), 34.

51. *Smayda v. U.S.*, 352 F.2d 251 (1965), 257–58; *People v. Frazier*, 256 Cal. App. 2d 630 (1967), 631; *New Jersey v. Lutz*, 57 N.J. 314 (1971), 315; *Warner v. State*, 489 P.2d 526 (1971), 528.

52. *People v. Hurd*, 5 Cal. App. 3d 865 (1970), 877; *Moore v. Oklahoma*, 501 P.2d 529 (1972), 532. See also *Jones*, 85 Nev. 411 (1969), 414.

53. *Sturgis v. Attorney General*, 358 Mass. 37 (1970), 41; *Rosen v. Louisiana State Board of Medical Examiners*, 318 F. Supp. 1217 (1970), 1229–30, 1232, 1240; *YWCA of Princeton v. Kugler*, 342 F. Supp. 1048 (1972), 1071–74.

54. *Travers v. Paton*, 261 F. Supp. 110 (1966), 113; *U.S. v. Laub Baking Co.*, 283 F. Supp. 217 (1968), 227; *Cotner v. Henry*, 394 F.2d 873 (1968), 875; *Raphael v. Hogan*, 305 F. Supp. 749 (1969), 756.

55. *Buchanan v. Batchelor*, 308 F. Supp. 729 (1970), 732–33, 735; *Pruett v. Texas*, 463 S.W.2d 191 (1970), 193–95. See also *Wade v. Buchanan*, 401 U.S. 989 (1971); *Buchanan v. Texas*, 471 S.W.2d 401 (1971), 405 U.S. 930 (1972).

56. *Paris Adult Theatre I v. Slaton*, 413 U.S. 49 (1973), 65, 67–68.

57. See *Hayes*, 346 F.2d 991 (1965); *Frost*, 249 F. Supp. 349 (1965); *Williams*, 357 F.2d 481 (1966); *Harding*, 251 F. Supp. 710 (1966); *Humphries*, 373 F.2d 200 (1967); *Thompson*, 275 F. Supp. 65 (1967); *Pacheco*, 295 F. Supp. 829 (1968); *Coltrane*, 418 F.2d 1131 (1969); *Raphael*, 305 F. Supp. 749 (1969); *Brown*, 447 F.2d 980 (1971); *Parker*, 329 F. Supp. 1400 (1971); *Harris*, 470 F.2d 190 (1972); *Miami Health Studios*, 353 F. Supp. 593 (1972); *Foy*, 481 F.2d 286 (1973); *Stone*, 478 F.2d 390 (1973); *Wainwright*, 414 U.S. 21 (1973); *Canfield*, 414 U.S. 991 (1973); *Connor*, 414 U.S. 991 (1973); *Jellum*, 475 F.2d 829 (1973).

58. *Roberts v. Clement*, 252 F. Supp. 835 (1966); *Henley v. Wise*, 303 F. Supp. 62 (1969), 67; *Baird v. Eisenstadt*, 429 F.2d 1398 (1970), 1400.

59. *Rosenberg v. Martin*, 478 F.2d 520 (1973), 524–25; *Roe v. Ingraham*, 480 F.2d 102 (1973), 107.

60. *Morrison v. State Board of Education*, 1 Cal. 3d 214 (1969), 233–34; *In re Lifschutz*, 2 Cal. 3d 415 (1970), 432; *New Mexico v. Trejo*, 83 N.M. 511 (1972), 513.

61. *People v. Belous*, 71 Cal. 2d 954 (1969), 963; *U.S. v. Vuitch*, 305 F. Supp. 1032 (1969), 1035. See also *Babbitz*, 310 F. Supp. 293 (1970), 299–300; *Roe*, 314 F. Supp. 1217 (1970), 1222; *Doe*, 321 F. Supp. 1385 (1971), 1389–90; *Wyman*, 66 Misc. 2d 402 (1971), 413, 417; *Crossen*, 344 F. Supp. 587 (1972), 590–91; *YWCA of Princeton*, 342 F. Supp. 1048 (1972), 1067, 1071–72; *Abele*, 342 F. Supp.

800 (1972), 805; *Byrn*, 38 A.D.2d 316 (1972), 327; *Schulman*, 70 Misc. 2d 1093 (1972), 1095; *Sasaki*, 485 S.W.2d 897 (1972), 901–2.

62. *Mindel v. U.S. Civil Service Commission*, 312 F. Supp. 485 (1970), 486, 488; *Moreno v. U.S. Department of Agriculture*, 345 F. Supp. 310 (1972), 314.

63. *One Eleven Wines & Liquors v. Division of Alcoholic Beverage Control*, 50 N.J. 329 (1967), 341; *Norton v. Macy*, 417 F.2d 1161 (1969), 1164–65; *In re Labady*, 326 F. Supp. 924 (1971), 927, 929.

64. *Osborn v. U.S.*, 385 U.S. 323 (1966), 341–43; *U.S. v. Vuitch*, 402 U.S. 62 (1971), 78; *California v. LaRue*, 409 U.S. 109 (1972), 133. See also Marshall's dissent in *Village of Belle Terre*, 416 U.S. 1 (1974).

65. Thomas C. Grey, "Eros, Civilization and the Burger Court," *Law and Contemporary Problems* 43 (Summer 1980): 85–87, 89, 98–99.

66. Ibid., 97.

Chapter 7

1. Webster Schott, "Civil Rights and the Homosexual: A 4-Million Minority Asks for Equal Rights," *NYTM*, 12 Nov. 1967, 44–45, 49–54, 59.

2. *Drum*, Sept. 1965, 4; Gerhard Mueller, cited in Stanford N. Sesser, "Sex and the Law," *WSJ*, 5 July 1968, 1; Robert J. Sickels, *Race, Marriage, and the Law* (Albuquerque: University of New Mexico Press, 1972), 8–9.

3. The evidence about what happened to Freedman and Boutilier is presented below.

4. Letters to the Editor, *NYTM*, 3 Dec. 1967, 12, 32–34, 42; Letters to the Editor, *NYTM*, 10 Dec. 1967, 40, 42; Sidney E. Zion, "U.S. Appeals Court Backs Order Deporting Alien as Homosexual," *NYT*, 9 July 1966, 12; "Court Will Rule on Homosexuals," *NYT*, 8 Nov. 1966, 24; "Supreme Court's Actions," *NYT*, 23 May 1967, 33; "Supreme Court Actions," *NYT*, 23 May 1967, 61; "High Court Denies Homosexual Plea," *NYT*, 23 May 1967, 49.

5. "Annual Report: The Playboy Foundation," *Playboy*, Jan. 1973, 57. For examples, see *Playboy*, Apr. 1964, 63–68, 176–84; Oct. 1964, 63–64; June 1965, 74; July 1965, 45; Nov. 1965, 12–14, 70, 159; Jan. 1966, 64–66, 208; Feb. 1966, 45–46; Mar. 1966, 38; June 1966, 148, 150; July 1966, 42; Aug. 1966, 144–45; Oct. 1966, 63–64; Jan. 1967, 55–56, 218; Feb. 1967, 38; Apr. 1967, 51–52; May 1967, 147–48; June 1967, 174; Aug. 1967, 38, 146; Sept. 1967, 81; Oct. 1967, 56; Nov. 1967, 74; Dec. 1967, 23, 83–86.

6. Anonymous, Editorial Reply, Playboy Forum, *Playboy*, July 1967, 135.

7. Joseph Murray, Playboy Forum, *Playboy*, Sept. 1967, 184.

8. Anonymous, Playboy Forum, *Playboy*, Dec. 1967, 86.

9. "Deportation of Homosexuals—An Important Case," *Sexology*, Aug. 1967, 71; Clark P. Polak, letter to the editor, *Sexology*, Jan. 1968, 388.

10. See *WSJ*, 23 May 1967, 1; *WP*, 23 May 1967, A2; *LAT*, 23 May 1967, 6; *LAT*, 28 May 1967, D4; *Time*, 22 July 1966, 45–46; ACLU Bulletin 2295, 3 Apr. 1967, 4; *CL*, Apr. 1967, 6. Using newspaperarchive.com, I have identified eight newspapers with more limited circulation that covered *Boutilier* in one or two sentences on 23–24 May 1967; nine that published short AP-based articles on *Boutilier* on the same dates; and five that published short UPI-based articles on 23–25 May 1967.

11. *Drum*, Jan. 1968, 4. This paragraph is based on a comprehensive survey of the *NYT*, along with *America*, 3 June 1967, 802–3; *Christian Century*, 13 Dec. 1967, 1587–88; *Harper's*, Mar. 1967, 107–20; *Look*, 10 Jan. 1967, 30–33; *Nation*, 9 Jan. 1967, 54–57; *Newsweek*, 2 Jan. 1967, 28, 30; 13 Feb. 1967, 63; 17 July 1967, 59; *Philadelphia Magazine*, Nov. 1967, 66–71, 84–93; *Time*, 14 July 1967, 30.

12. Tom Fox, "The Rights of Homosexuals," *Philadelphia Daily News*, 30 Apr. 1970, 4; Charles Alverson, "A Minority's Plea," *WSJ*, 17 July 1968, 1; Martin Hoffman, "Homosexual," *Psychology*

Today, July 1969, 43. See also *America*, 14 Nov. 1970, 406–7; *Christian Century*, 5 June 1968, 744–45; 1 Jan. 1969, 29–30; *Christianity Today*, 19 Jan. 1968, 24–25; 1 Mar. 1968, 23; *Esquire*, Dec. 1969, 178–79, 304–18; *Harper's*, Sept. 1970, 37–51; *Newsweek*, 14 Oct. 1968, 108; 5 Aug. 1968, 63; *Saturday Review*, 12 Feb. 1972, 23–28; *Time*, 31 Oct. 1969, 56–67.

13. "Developments in the Law: Immigration and Nationality," *Harvard Law Review* 66 (1953): 643–745; "Limitations on Congressional Power to Deport Resident Aliens Excludable as Psychopaths at Time of Entry," *Yale Law Journal* 68 (1959): 931–48; Irving Appleman, "That New Immigration Act," *American Bar Association Journal* 52 (1966): 717–20; Thomas J. Scully, "Is the Door Open Again? — A Survey of Our New Immigration Law," *UCLA Law Review* 13 (1966): 227–49.

14. "Alien's Deportation," *Catholic University Law Review* 16 (1967): 320–22; John F. Brock, "Aliens and Citizenship," *San Diego Law Review* 4 (1967): 153–54.

15. "Administrative Law — Deportation," *NYU Law Review* 42 (1967): 122–26.

16. Marc B. Kaplin, "Aliens — McCarran Act," *Villanova Law Review* 12 (1967): 338, 341–42.

17. Thomas R. Byrne Jr. and Francis M. Mulligan, "'Psychopathic Personality' and 'Sexual Deviation': Medical Terms or Legal Catch-Alls — Analysis of the Status of the Homosexual Alien," *Temple Law Quarterly* 40 (1967): 328.

18. Ibid., 333–34.

19. Ibid., 335–36. The cases cited were *Lionel Colin Roberts*, No. A12-463-838, BIA, 20 May 1964; *Matter of Beaton*, No. A2-486-963, BIA, 16 Jan. 1943; *Norman David Flight*, No. A12-944-125, BIA, 8 Sept. 1965; [Name not disclosed], No. A11-065-813, BIA, 6 June 1964; *Leblanc v. Bouchard*, no. 1308-58 (D.N.J., 15 June 1959).

20. Byrne and Mulligan, "'Psychopathic Personality,'" 342.

21. Ibid., 344–45.

22. Ibid., 346–47.

23. This is based on searches of several electronic databases of legal journals.

24. Robert J. Evans, "The Crimes Against Nature," *Journal of Public Law* 16 (1967): 178–79.

25. *Lavoie v. INS*, 360 F.2d 27 (1966); *INS v. Lavoie*, 387 U.S. 572 (1967); *INS v. Lavoie*, 389 U.S. 908 (1967); *Matter of Lavoie*, A-10767234, BIA Interim Decision #1890, 31 July 1968, 822–23; *Lavoie v. INS*, 418 F.2d 732 (1969), 736; *Lavoie v. INS*, 400 U.S. 854 (1970).

26. *Tovar v. INS*, 368 F.2d 1006 (1966); *Tovar v. INS*, 388 U.S. 915 (1967).

27. See *Banks*, 314 F. Supp. 285 (1970); *Hall*, 459 F.2d 831 (1971, amended 1972); *James J. Brown*, 478 F.2d 606 (1973); *Ramirez*, 413 F.2d 405 (1969); *Weitzman*, 426 F.2d 439 (1970); *Mandel*, 325 F. Supp. 620 (1971); *Kleindienst*, 408 U.S. 753 (1972).

28. *Matter of Steele*, A-8199592, BIA Interim Decision #1752, 11 July 1967.

29. *Campos v. INS*, 402 F.2d 758 (1968), 759–60.

30. *Matter of Olga Schmidt*, 289 N.Y.S.2d 89 (1968), 90, 92.

31. *Matter of Mario Belle*, E.D.N.Y., 19 Feb. 1969, #681121, excerpted in *Interpreter Releases* 46 (1969), 78.

32. *Labady v. U.S.*, 326 F. Supp. 924 (1971), 925–26.

33. Ibid., 927–30.

34. *Kovacs v. U.S.*, 476 F.2d 843 (1973), 844–45.

35. *Gayer v. Schlesinger*, *Ulrich v. Schlesinger*, and *Wentworth v. Schlesinger*, 490 F.2d 740 (1973), 744–45, 748.

36. *DOBNYN*, Aug. 1966, 4; *Drum*, Mar. 1967, 3, 10–19; *Drum*, Sept. 1967, 33; *Drum*, Dec. 1966, 34; *Drum*, Sept. 1967, 34. See also *MMN*, Sept. 1966, 11.

37. *DOBNYN*, Mar. 1967, 2; HLRS press release, 12 Jan. 1967, BF; *Drum*, Dec. 1966, 36; *Drum*, Mar. 1967, 3.

38. *Drum*, March 1967, 3; *MSNYN*, Dec. 1966, 2; *Homosexual Citizen*, Sept. 1966, 6; *Drum*, Dec. 1966, 36.

39. *MSNYN*, Dec. 1966, 1–2; *Drum*, Jan. 1967, 3; *JSN*, Feb. 1967, 2; *Drum*, Mar. 1967, 3, 10; *DOBNYN*, Mar. 1967, 2.

40. *Drum*, Dec. 1966, 36; *JSN*, Dec. 1966, 2; *MSNYN*, Dec. 1966, 2; *Drum*, Jan. 1967, 3; HLRS press release, 12 Jan. 1967, BF; *JSN*, Feb, 1967, 2.

41. *Drum*, Oct. 1966, 8; *Drum*, Dec. 1966, 36; *JSN*, Dec. 1966, 2; *MSNYN*, Dec. 1966, 2; *Drum*, Jan, 1967, 3; *JSN*, Feb. 1967, 2; *DOBNYN*, Mar. 1967, 2; *Pride Newsletter*, May 1967, 10.

42. *MSNYN*, Mar. 1967, 4; *Drum*, Dec. 1966, 36.

43. *Drum*, Mar. 1967, 3, 10.

44. *JSN*, Mar. 1967, 2.

45. *Pride Newsletter*, July 1967, 6; *Drum*, Aug. 1967, 25; *MSNYN*, June 1967, 2.

46. *Pride Newsletter*, July 1967, 6; *Drum*, Aug. 1967, 38; *Drum*, Sept. 1967, 33–34.

47. *Sexology*, Jan. 1968, 387; *Pride Newsletter*, July 1967, 6–7; *DOBNYN*, Jan. 1968, 4; *MSNYN*, June 1967, 3.

48. *MSNYN*, June 1967, 3; *Drum*, Aug. 1967, 25.

49. *Cases in Review*, no. 1, 1967, 3–4; *DOBNYN*, Jan. 1968, 4; *MMN*, June 1967, 4; *Pride Newsletter*, July 1967, 6; *Drum*, Aug. 1967, 25.

50. *Drum*, Sept. 1967, 6; *JSN*, Feb. 1968, 1–2; *Advocate*, 14 Apr. 1971, 8; *Advocate*, 12 May 1971, 12. See also *Drum*, Mar. 1968, 21–22; *Drum*, Dec. 1968, 40; *Advocate*, 26 May 1971, 22.

51. *Drum*, Jan. 1968, 4; *Ladder*, Oct.–Nov. 1968, 39. See also *Ladder*, June–July 1969, 40; *HALN*, Aug.–Sept. 1969, 7.

52. *Advocate*, Sept. 1967, 2; Nov. 1968, 3; May 1969, 2; 13 May 1970, 3. See also *Advocate*, Dec. 1967, 1, 2, 4; Jan. 1968, 1, 2, 4; Mar. 1968, 3; May 1968, 2; Oct. 1968, 4–5, 18–19; Jan. 1969, 1, 14; Feb. 1969, 6–7; Mar. 1969, 16; May 1969, 9; Sept. 1969, 1–2, 4–5, 15, 23; Oct. 1969, 29; Dec. 1969, 1, 4.

53. *HALN*, Aug.–Sept. 1969, 3–4.

54. *Advocate*, Jan. 1970, 22; *Advocate*, 13 Oct. 1971, 28; *Advocate*, 26 Apr. 1972, 28; *Advocate*, 24 May 1972, 30; Walter Barnett, *Sexual Freedom and the Constitution* (Albuquerque: University of New Mexico Press, 1973). See also *Advocate*, Aug. 1969, 1, 12; 24 Nov. 1971, 24; 29 Mar. 1972, 29; 25 Oct. 1972, 28.

55. *Pride Newsletter*, July 1967, 6; *Ladder*, Oct.–Nov. 1968, 37; *Ladder*, June–July 1969, 41; *HALN*, July 1969, 3–4. See also *Advocate*, Apr. 1969, 1; *Playboy*, June 1969, 65.

56. Alverson, "A Minority's Plea"; Council on Religion and the Homosexual, Daughters of Bilitis, Society for Individual Rights, and Tavern Guild, *The Challenge and Progress of Homosexual Law Reform*, 1968, 6, 8–9, 36–37, 43, 57. See also *Advocate*, 12 May 1971, 2, 15; *Advocate*, 26 May 1971, 2, 12; *Advocate*, 20 Dec. 1972, 33; *HALN*, Jan.–Feb. 1970, 1.

57. Author correspondence with Paul Laven, 26 Mar.–12 Apr. 2001. See also *NYT*, 17 April 1967, 37.

58. *MSNYN*, Dec. 1968, 17.

59. Boutilier's niece told me that she conferred with her family before supplying me with this account. I discuss my search for Boutilier in "Crossing the Border to Memory: In Search of Clive Michael Boutilier (1933–2003)," *torquere* 6 (2004): 91–115.

60. Joyce Murdoch and Deb Price, *Courting Justice: Gay Men and Lesbians v. the Supreme Court* (New York: Basic, 2001), 132.

61. Author's correspondence with Murdoch, 20 Aug. 2001–16 Sept. 2004.

62. See also Death Certificate D208544 for Clive Michael Boutilier, Ministry of Consumer and Business Services, Office of the Registrar General, Ontario. For a remembrance of Boutilier, see Marc Stein, "Forgetting and Remembering a Deported Alien," History News Network, 3 Nov. 2003, http://hnn.us/articles/1769.html (accessed 4 Nov. 2003).

63. Samuel L. Huttner to Commissioner, Royal Canadian Mounted Police, 3 July 1967; Robert P. Brown to INS, 10 July 1967; Edward R. McGovern to INS, 14 July 1967, FOIA File NYC 2005001860.

64. Robert P. Brown to INS, 14 Aug. 1967, 18 Oct. 1967; Ada Moyer to George Schwarz, 13 Oct. 1967; Samuel L. Huttner to Superintendent, Brooklyn State Hospital, 7 Nov. 1967; Alan E. Joseph, medical certificate for Clive Michael Boutilier, 27 Nov. 1967; Nathan Beckenstein—INS correspondence, 27 Nov. 1967, 13 Feb. 1968, 23 May 1968, FOIA File NYC 2005001860.

65. *Pride Newsletter*, July 1967, 7.

66. Author's correspondence with Murdoch, 15 Sept. 2004.

Epilogue

1. *Carey v. Population Services International*, 431 U.S. 678 (1977), 684–85, 688, 702, 713, 718. See also *Bolger*, 463 U.S. 60 (1983). On abortion and birth control cases after *Roe*, see David J. Garrow, *Liberty and Sexuality*, 2nd ed. (Berkeley: University of California Press, 1998), 600–739.

2. See *Singleton*, 428 U.S. 106 (1976); *Planned Parenthood of Central Missouri*, 428 U.S. 52 (1976); *Bellotti*, 428 U.S. 132 (1976); *Guste*, 429 U.S. 399 (1977); *Maher*, 432 U.S. 464 (1977); *Poelker*, 432 U.S. 519 (1977); *Beal*, 432 U.S. 438 (1977); *Colautti*, 439 U.S. 379 (1979); *Bellotti*, 443 U.S. 622 (1979); *Harris*, 448 U.S. 297 (1980); *Williams*, 448 U.S. 358 (1980); *H. L.*, 450 U.S. 398 (1981); *Simopoulos*, 462 U.S. 506 (1983); *Planned Parenthood Association of Kansas City*, 462 U.S. 476 (1983); *Akron*, 462 U.S. 416 (1983); *Diamond*, 476 U.S. 54 (1986); *Thornburgh*, 476 U.S. 747 (1986).

3. *U.S. v. Matlock*, 415 U.S. 164 (1974), 176; *Village of Belle Terre v. Boraas*, 416 U.S. 1 (1974), 8, 16; *Moore v. East Cleveland*, 431 U.S. 494 (1977).

4. *Rose v. Locke*, 423 U.S. 48 (1975), 50–51. See also *Crawford*, 409 U.S. 811 (1972); *Wainwright*, 414 U.S. 21 (1973).

5. *Lovisi v. Zabradnick*, 429 U.S. 977 (1976); *Lovisi v. Slayton*, 539 F.2d 349 (1976), 351; *Zablocki v. Redhail*, 434 U.S. 374 (1978), 386; *Hollenbaugh v. Carnegie Free Library*, 439 U.S. 1052 (1978), 1054; *Jarrett v. Jarrett*, 449 U.S. 927 (1980). See also *Bateman*, 429 U.S. 1302 (1976); *Palmore*, 466 U.S. 429 (1984).

6. *Michael M. v. Superior Court of Sonoma County*, 450 U.S. 464 (1981), 470; *Whisenhunt v. Spradlin*, 464 U.S. 965 (1983), 971; *North Muskegon v. Briggs*, 473 U.S. 909 (1985), 910.

7. *Mississippi Gay Alliance v. Goudelock*, 430 U.S. 982 (1977); *Acanfora v. Board of Education*, 419 U.S. 836 (1974); *Gaylord v. Tacoma School District No. 10*, 434 U.S. 879 (1977); *Gish v. Board of Education*, 434 U.S. 879 (1977); *Rowland v. Mad River Local School District*, 470 U.S. 1009 (1985); *Hatheway v. Marsh*, 454 U.S. 864 (1981); *Beller v. Lehman*, 452 U.S. 905 (1981); *Kowalski v. Kowalski*, 475 U.S. 1085 (1986). See also *Mount Diablo Council of the Boy Scouts of America*, 468 U.S. 1205 (1984). On gay and lesbian rights cases after *Roe*, see the works cited in the introduction and chapter five by Cain, Eskridge, Gerstmann, Hunter, Koppelman, Leonard, Murdoch and Price, and Richards, along with Lisa Keen and Suzanne B. Goldberg, *Strangers to the Law: Gay People on Trial* (Ann Arbor: University of Michigan Press, 1998): David A. J. Richards, *Women, Gays, and the Constitution: The Grounds for Feminism and Gay Rights in Culture and Law* (Chicago: University of Chicago Press, 1998); William B. Rubenstein, ed., *Lesbians, Gay Men, and the Law* (New York: New Press, 1993).

8. *Wainwright v. Stone*, 414 U.S. 21 (1973), 22; *Connor v. Arkansas*, 414 U.S. 991 (1973); *Canfield v. Oklahoma*, 414 U.S. 991 (1973); *Enslin v. North Carolina*, 425 U.S. 903 (1976); *Doe v. Commonwealth's Attorney*, 403 F. Supp. 1199 (1975), 1202; 425 U.S. 901 (1976).

9. *Ratchford v. Gay Lib*, 434 U.S. 1080 (1978); *New York v. Onofre*, 451 U.S. 987 (1981); *Gray v. Van Ooteghem*, 451 U.S. 935 (1981), 455 U.S. 909 (1982); *Board of Education of Oklahoma City v. National Gay Task Force*, 470 U.S. 903 (1985); *National Gay Task Force v. Board of Education of Oklahoma City*, 729 F.2d 1270 (1984), 1272. See also *Singer*, 429 U.S. 1034 (1977); *Texas A&M University*, 449 U.S. 1034 (1980), 471 U.S. 1001 (1985).

10. *New York v. Uplinger*, 467 U.S. 246 (1984), 249.

11. *Adams v. Howerton*, 458 U.S. 1111 (1982); 673 F.2d 1036 (1982), 1040–41.

12. *Longstaff v. INS*, 467 U.S. 1219 (1984); *Matter of Longstaff*, 716 F.2d 1439 (1983), 1450. On repeal in 1990, see preface note 11, introduction note 20, chapter two note 8.

13. *J-R Distributors v. Washington*, 418 U.S. 949 (1974), 951–52; *Hamling v. U.S.*, 418 U.S. 87 (1974), 128. *See also Carlson*, 414 U.S. 953 (1973); *Gay Times*, 414 U.S. 994 (1973); *Jenkins*, 418 U.S. 153 (1974); *Erznoznik*, 422 U.S. 205 (1975); *Huffman*, 420 U.S. 592 (1975); *Atheneum Book Store*, 420 U.S. 982 (1975); *Southeastern Promotions*, 420 U.S. 546 (1975); *MTM*, 420 U.S. 799 (1975); *Hicks*, 422 U.S. 332 (1975); *Smith*, 431 U.S. 291 (1977); *Ward*, 431 U.S. 767 (1977).

14. *New York v. Ferber*, 458 U.S. 747 (1982), 764. See also *FCC*, 438 U.S. 726 (1978); *Bethel School District No. 403*, 478 U.S. 675 (1986).

15. *Young v. American Mini Theatres*, 427 U.S. 50 (1976), 63. See also *Doran*, 422 U.S. 922 (1975); *Renton*, 475 U.S. 41 (1986); *Schad*, 452 U.S. 61 (1981).

16. *Brockett v. Spokane Arcades*, 472 U.S. 491 (1985), 494, 498–99. See also *Walter*, 447 U.S. 649 (1980); *Vance*, 445 U.S. 308 (1980); *New York State Liquor Authority*, 452 U.S. 714 (1981); *Michell Brothers' Santa Ana Theater*, 454 U.S. 90 (1981); *Avenue Book Store*, 459 U.S. 997 (1982); *Randall Book Corp.*, 464 U.S. 919 (1983); *Macon*, 472 U.S. 463 (1985); *Young*, 474 U.S. 1070 (1986); *P.J. Video*, 475 U.S. 868 (1986).

17. *Bowers v. Hardwick*, 478 U.S. 186 (1986), 189–92, 195–96. There is an extensive scholarly literature on *Bowers*, *Romer*, and *Lawrence*. See the works cited in note 7, along with Katherine M. Frank, "The Domesticated Liberty of *Lawrence v. Texas*," *Columbia Law Review* 104 (2004): 1399–1426; Suzanne B. Goldberg, "*Lawrence* and the Road from Liberation to Equality," *Texas Law Review* 46 (2004): 309–16; Nan D. Hunter, "Sexual Orientation and the Paradox of Heightened Scrutiny," *Michigan Law Review* 102 (2004): 1528–54.

18. *Bowers*, 199–201, 204–5, 208.

19. Ibid., 209–10, 213.

20. *Michael H. v. Gerald D.*, 491 U.S. 110 (1989), 122–23. See also *Swanner*, 513 U.S. 979 (1994).

21. *Michael H.*, 127, 132. See also *Glucksberg*, 521 U.S. 702 (1997).

22. See *Hartigan*, 484 U.S. 171 (1987); *Webster*, 492 U.S. 490 (1989); *Hodgson*, 497 U.S. 417 (1990); *Akron Center for Reproductive Health*, 497 U.S. 502 (1990); *Rust*, 500 U.S. 173 (1991); *Dalton*, 516 U.S. 474 (1996); *Leavitt*, 518 U.S. 137 (1996); *Lambert*, 520 U.S. 292 (1997); *Mazurek*, 520 U.S. 968 (1997); *Stenberg*, 530 U.S. 914 (2000); *Gonzales*, 550 U.S. 124 (2007).

23. *Planned Parenthood of Southeastern Pennsylvania v. Casey*, 505 U.S. 833 (1992), 851, 857, 984.

24. *Baker v. Wade*, 478 U.S. 1022 (1986); *Sawatzky v. Oklahoma City*, 517 U.S. 1156 (1996).

25. *Carlucci v. Doe*, 488 U.S. 93 (1988); *Webster v. Doe*, 486 U.S. 592 (1988); *Doe v. Woolsey*, 510 U.S. 928 (1993); *Oncale v. Sundowner Offshore Services*, 523 U.S. 75 (1998), 77. See also *Krc*, 510 U.S. 1109 (1994); *Miller*, 516 U.S. 1114 (1996); *Nelson*, 522 U.S. 866 (1997); *Shabar*, 522 U.S. 1049 (1998).

26. *U.S. Army v. Watkins*, 498 U.S. 957 (1990); *Cheney v. Pruitt*, 506 U.S. 1020 (1992). See also *Ben-Shalom*, 494 U.S. 1004 (1990); *Woodward*, 494 U.S. 1003 (1990); *Schowengerdt*, 503 U.S. 951

(1992); *Jackson*, 513 U.S. 868 (1994); *Walmer*, 516 U.S. 974 (1995); *Thomasson*, 519 U.S. 948 (1996); *Selland*, 520 U.S. 1210 (1997); *Richenberg*, 522 U.S. 807 (1997); *Thorne*, 525 U.S. 947 (1998); *Holmes*, 525 U.S. 1067 (1999).

27. *Ward v. Olivieri*, 480 U.S. 917 (1987); *San Francisco Arts and Athletics v. U.S. Olympic Committee*, 483 U.S. 522 (1987); *Hurley v. Irish-American Gay, Lesbian and Bisexual Group of Boston*, 515 U.S. 557 (1995); *Arbeiter v. New York*, 520 U.S. 1213 (1997). See also *Clewis*, 511 U.S. 1030 (1994); *Westboro Baptist Church*, 519 U.S. 1090 (1997).

28. *Boy Scouts of America v. Dale*, 530 U.S. 640 (2000).

29. *Rent Stabilization Association of New York City v. Higgins*, 512 U.S. 1213 (1994); *Knott v. Holtzman*, 516 U.S. 975 (1995); *Hacklander-Ready v. Wisconsin*, 520 U.S. 1212 (1997). See also *Doe*, 522 U.S. 810 (1997); *Lumpkin*, 522 U.S. 995 (1997).

30. See *Pope*, 481 U.S. 497 (1987); *Houston*, 482 U.S. 451 (1987); *American Booksellers Association*, 484 U.S. 383 (1988); *Hazelwood School District*, 484 U.S. 260 (1988); *Fort Wayne Books*, 489 U.S. 46 (1989); *Oakes*, 491 U.S. 576 (1989); *Sable Communications*, 492 U.S. 115 (1989); *FW/PBS*, 493 U.S. 215 (1990); *Osborne*, 495 U.S. 103 (1990); *R. Enterprises*, 498 U.S. 292 (1991); *Jacobson*, 503 U.S. 540 (1992); *Alexander*, 509 U.S. 544 (1993); *X-Citement Video*, 513 U.S. 64 (1994); *Denver Area Educational Telecommunications Consortium*, 518 U.S. 727 (1996); *Reno*, 521 U.S. 844 (1997); *Playboy Entertainment Group*, 529 U.S. 803 (2000); *City News and Novelty*, 531 U.S. 278 (2001); *Alameda Books*, 535 U.S. 425 (2002); *Ashcroft*, 535 U.S. 234 (2002); *Ashcroft*, 535 U.S. 564 (2002); *American Library Association*, 539 U.S. 194 (2003); *Ashcroft*, 542 U.S. 656 (2004); *Mukasey* (2009).

31. *Thornburgh v. Abbott*, 490 U.S. 401 (1989), 413, 415.

32. *National Endowment for the Arts v. Finley*, 524 U.S. 569 (1998), 582, 588. See also *Arcara*, 478 U.S. 697 (1986); *Barnes*, 501 U.S. 560 (1991); *Pap's*, 529 U.S. 277 (2000).

33. *Romer v. Evans*, 517 U.S. 620 (1996), 624, 630–31.

34. Ibid., 632–35.

35. *Equality Foundation of Greater Cincinnati v. City of Cincinnati*, 518 U.S. 1001 (1996), 525 U.S. 943 (1998); *Romer*, 642.

36. *Lawrence v. Texas*, 539 U.S. 558 (2003), 562.

37. Ibid., 564–66.

38. Ibid., 566–67, 571–72, 575.

39. Ibid., 577–79.

40. Lisa Duggan, "The New Homonormativity: The Sexual Politics of Neoliberalism," in *Materializing Democracy: Toward a Revitalized Cultural Politics*, ed. Russ Castronovo and Dana Nelson (Durham, N.C.: Duke University Press, 2002), 175–94.

41. *Lawrence*, 578.

Acknowledgments

This project began many years ago in a graduate seminar on U.S. legal history taught by Mary Frances Berry at the University of Pennsylvania in 1991. I am very grateful for Professor Berry's guidance, Gerald Neuman's suggestions, and Henry Abelove's and Carroll Smith-Rosenberg's mentorship during this stage of my work. For the inspiration of their example and the encouragement they have provided for my work on the history of sexuality, I thank John D'Emilio, Martin Duberman, Jonathan Ned Katz, Elizabeth Kennedy, and Leila Rupp. John and Leila have read and reviewed various components of this book and have responded with consistent generosity and excellent advice. I also extend my heartfelt thanks to my History, Women's Studies, and Sexuality Studies colleagues and students at York University, especially Bettina Bradbury, Stephen Brooke, Marc Egnal, Jerry Ginsburg, Doug Hay, Craig Heron, Molly Ladd-Taylor, Kate McPherson, Jeanette Neeson, Anne Rubenstein, and Miriam Smith.

Librarians and archivists make historical research possible, and in working on this book I have been assisted by the staffs of first-rate research collections, including the Canadian Lesbian and Gay Archives; the Gay and Lesbian Historical Society of Northern California; the Gay, Lesbian, Bisexual, and Transgender Archives of Philadelphia; the Gotlieb Archival Research Center at Boston University; the Human Sexuality Collection at Cornell University; the Labadie Collection at the University of Michigan; the Lesbian Herstory Archives; the Library of Congress; Miller Library at Colby College; the June L. Mazer Collection in Los Angeles; the Seeley G. Mudd Manuscript Library at Princeton University; the National Archives; the Sophia Smith Collection at Smith College; the New York Public Library; the ONE National Gay and Lesbian Archives at the University of Southern California; Robarts Library at the University of Toronto; the Schlesinger Library at the Radcliffe Institute for Advanced Study; Scott Library at York University; the Tarlton Law Library at the University of Texas–Austin; U.S. Citizenship and Immigration Services; the Urban Archives at Temple University; and the Yale University Library's Manuscripts and Archives.

One of the most rewarding aspects of my research on this project has been the opportunity to communicate with some of the book's protagonists and members of their families. For their generosity and their willingness to share their materials, memories, and reflections, I thank Clive Boutilier's niece Patty, members of the Freedman and Rosenberg families (Michael Freedman, the late Paul Laven, the late Jeanette Laven, Michael Meeropol, and Allen Young), Gilbert Cantor's son Anthony Cantor, Alan Levine, Burt Neuborne, and Montague Ullman.

My work has benefitted greatly from the responses of chairs, commentators, co-panelists, and audiences at the annual conventions of the American Historical Association (Ramón Gutiérrez), the American Society for Legal History (Pat Cain and Mary Louise Adams), the American Studies Association (Sharon Ullman), the Canadian Association for American Studies, the Canadian Lesbian and Gay Studies Association, the Committee on Lesbian and Gay History (Vicki Eaklor, Karen Krahulik, and Leisa Meyer), and the Organization of American Historians (Lisa Levenstein and Joanne Meyerowitz), along with the 1950s and 1960s in North America conference at Wesleyan University (Henry Abelove), Connexions: A Working Conference on Race and Sex in North America at New York University, the Queer Matters conference at Kings College (John Howard and Elizabeth Emens), and the Sexual Worlds, Political Cultures conference sponsored by the Social Science Research Council (Margot Canaday, Pippa Holloway, and Leslie Reagan). I was also fortunate to have the opportunity to present my work on this project at the American Bar Foundation (Christopher Tomlins), Case Western Reserve University (Jonathan Sadowsky and Rhonda Williams), Colby College (Pam Thoma), Duke University (Karen Krahulik), Franklin and Marshall College (Abby Schrader), Queen's University, the Radcliffe Institute for Advanced Study (Nancy Cott and Reva Siegel), Rutgers University (Alison Isenberg and Keith Wailoo), Temple University (Bryant Simon and Beth Bailey), the University of California–Santa Barbara (Leila Rupp), the University of Maine–Orono (Liam Riordan), the University of Missouri–Columbia (LeeAnn Whites, Sylvia Lazos, Jean Sternlight, and Mary Jo Neitz), and the University of Pennsylvania (Bob Schoenberg).

For financial support, I am grateful for the three-year research grant I received from the Social Sciences and Humanities Research Council of Canada (SSHRC), a SSHRC conference travel grant, a York University Faculty Association Research Development Fellowship, and the additional support I received form my department, my faculty, and my university. Thanks to the SSHRC grant and other forms of support, I had the excellent research assistance of a large group of students in the Graduate Programs in History and Women's Studies at York: Mark Abraham, Christian Borges, Joyce Clements, Eva Kater, Karen MacFarlane, Ian McPhedran, Harry Nirwal, Joel Regehr, Stephen Schwartz, Susan Smitko, Jon Sufrin, David Tayler, and Joseph Tohill. Tim Retzloff provided expert research assistance in Michigan.

In a perverse way, I am also grateful for the National Endowment for the Humanities grant that I did not receive. As I describe in "Post-Tenure Lavender Blues," published by the History News Network in 2003, my grant proposal for this project received the highest possible evaluation by the NEH's five-person panel of American History and American Studies scholars and was recommended for funding, but NEH chair Bruce Cole, appointed by President George W. Bush, vetoed my grant on grounds that have never been shared with me. In the course of my work on this book, nothing did more to convince me that my project might have historical, intellectual, and political significance.

For publishing my work on the Supreme Court, I thank *Law and History Review* (Christopher Tomlins), the *Organization of American Historians Magazine of History* (Leisa Meyer), *torquere* (Sharon Rosenberg), and the History News Network (Rick Shenkman). "*Boutilier* and the U.S. Supreme Court's Sexual Revolution," published in *Law and History Review* in 2005, was awarded the Audre Lorde Prize for Best Article in Lesbian, Gay, Bisexual, and Transgender History by what was then called the Committee on Lesbian and Gay History, an affiliated society of the American Historical Association. Forthcoming essays drawn from this project will be published in the *Journal of American Ethnic History* (Horacio Roque Ramírez) and *Connexions: Histories of Race and Sex in North America* (Jennifer Brier, Michele Mitchell, and Jennifer Morgan).

At the University of North Carolina Press, my editor Chuck Grench, his assistant Katy O'Brien, assistant managing editor Paul Betz, and copyeditor Jeffrey Canaday guided me with expert care and gentle encouragement through the process of completing this book. I also want to thank David A. J. Richard, Eric L. Muller, and one anonymous scholar who reviewed the manuscript for the press and made a set of suggestions that greatly improved it. I have been very fortunate to receive constructive and caring support from other scholars, colleagues, and friends, including Dana Barron, Angela Blake, Mary Bonauto, Elspeth Brown, Stephen Brown,

Douglas Charles, Elise Chenier, David Cruz, Karen Dubinsky, William Eskridge, Gill Frank, Franca Iacovetta, Laura Kalman, Steven Maynard, Martin Meeker, Joyce Murdoch, Claire Potter, Ian Radforth, David Rayside, Darren Rosenblum, Tuan Samahon, Samuel Silvers, Mark Simonson, Simon Stern, Tom Sugrue, and Bill Woods.

Enduring friendships that began before I became a historian remain a source of great strength, comfort, and joy in my life. For their commitment, loyalty, and love over more than twenty years, I thank Brad Bennett, Linda Carmy, Judy Drager-Davidoff, Barbara Schwartz, and Stacy Sterling. In Maine, where I have lived part-time for more than a decade, Pam Thoma and Andy Dephtereos (now in Washington), Betty Sasaki and Ludger Duplessis, Julie Kay Mueller, and other good friends supported, entertained, and distracted me as I worked on this project. I also thank my cousin Leslie Fishbein, who helped me first imagine that I could be a historian of gender and sexuality. I am deeply grateful for all of the ways that my sister Gayle and my brother Scott have encouraged me. My parents Rhoda and Walter deserve very special acknowledgment for all of the sacrifices they made to help their children succeed and for all of the positive ways they responded when our lives turned out differently from what they may have expected.

By the time this book is published, Jorge Olivares will have lived with me and this project for more than fourteen years. An exceptionally smart reader of texts, a brilliant scholar of Latin American literature, and a Cuban American with keen sensitivity to the traumas and transformations of crossing borders, he has read all of my chapters multiple times, listened to me practice my talks repeatedly, accompanied me on conference and research trips in three countries, and talked endlessly with me about my ideas and my prose. Most of all, I thank Jorge for loving me and letting me love him, which are the greatest joys in my life.

Index

Douglas, William O., 7–13, 232, 239, 254, 281; and obscenity, 10, 35–38, 41–43, 214, 313 (n. 23); and *Griswold*, 13, 28–34, 50, 210–11, 221, 232, 239, 312 (n. 11); and *Loving*, 45–46; and *Eisenstadt*, 47–48, 50, 315 (n. 52); and *Roe*, 53, 316 (n. 63); and *Boutilier*, 78–83, 87–92, 138, 163, 264, 266, 320 (nn. 43, 57), 321 (n. 61)

Doyle, Max, 148

Drugs. *See* Alcohol and drugs

Drum, 146–52; coverage of birth control and abortion, 148, 222–23; coverage of obscenity, 149, 225–26; coverage of bars, 149–50; coverage of *Boutilier*, 152, 248, 260–68

DuBois, W. E. B., 137

Due process, 133, 142; and *Griswold*, 30, 103, 315 (n. 59); and *Loving*, 45, 111, 216, 315 (n. 43); and *Roe*, 53; and *Boutilier*, 60, 81, 83, 88, 144, 154, 168, 171, 180, 251–52; and *Eisenstadt*, 117, 119; and ACLU policy on homosexuality, 159–61; and *Lawrence*, 299–300

East Coast Homophile Organizations, 146

Eastern Mattachine Magazine, 150, 222

Ebony, 217

Eckstein, Ernestine, 143

Eisenhower, Dwight, 8–9

Eisenstadt v. Baird, 13–14, 17, 22, 27–28, 41, 47–56, 58, 76, 93, 315 (nn. 46, 48, 52), 316 (n. 63); litigation strategy in, 20, 97, 114–23, 132–33, 203; post-*Roe* references to, 22, 279, 287, 290, 296, 299, 301; media coverage of, 207–8, 217–19, 223, 228–30; court references to, 230–40; scholarship on, 240–41, 270

Elias, Ralph, 173, 176–77, 201–2

Ellis, Albert, 173, 176, 179, 185, 201

Ellison, Sylvia, 117, 120

Emerson, Thomas, 100–103

Employment discrimination, 27, 140, 143, 152, 154, 157, 159–63, 167, 253, 268–71, 283, 292–93, 295, 332 (n. 74)

Equality Foundation of Greater Cincinnati v. City of Cincinnati, 297–98

Equal protection, 45, 48–49, 81, 102, 111, 114, 117–18, 216, 218, 228, 282, 297–98

Ernst, Morris, 100

Eskridge, William, 59

Europe, x, 46, 54–55, 58–59, 136–38, 144–45, 167, 247, 253, 256. *See also* Great Britain

Evans, Ray, 173, 176, 185

Evans, Robert, 253

Exclusion (immigration), xii, 59–60, 76, 138, 169, 255, 258–59, 285, 319 (n. 40). See also *Boutilier v. the Immigration and Naturalization Service*

Extramarital sex, 8–9, 11, 31–32, 89, 101, 103–4, 113, 119–20, 122, 131, 227, 280, 283. *See also* Adultery

Falsey, Edward, 66–67, 89, 135, 182, 189, 191, 195

Fanny Hill, viii, 10, 13–14, 17, 27–28, 35–44, 47, 50, 56, 295, 312 (nn. 17, 19–20), 313 (nn. 23, 31); litigation strategy in, 20, 97, 104–8, 132–33, 203; and homosexuality, 36–40, 44, 58, 76, 78, 81–82, 93, 106–7, 149, 213, 226, 261; media coverage of, 207–8, 213–17, 226, 231; court references to, 231, 239–40; post-*Roe* references to, 279

Federal Bureau of Investigation, xi, 9, 11–13, 85, 309 (n. 15)

Feminism, 4–5, 55, 98, 116, 120, 123–25, 128–30, 132, 219, 230. *See also* Lesbian feminism

Fetishism, 38–39, 70, 213, 225

Fieldsteel, Ira, 66, 195

First Amendment, 29–30, 35–36, 47–48, 103–6, 128, 147, 284, 293, 295, 312 (n. 11)

Fleming, Robert, 101

Fleuti v. Rosenberg. See *Rosenberg v. Fleuti*

Flores-Rodriguez, 84, 175

Florida, 11, 45, 92, 110, 113, 149, 268, 282

Ford, Clellan, 176

Fornication, 77, 221; laws against, xi, 1, 16, 27, 56, 147, 155, 160, 222, 226–27, 229, 241, 245, 253, 257; and *Griswold*, 14, 17, 32, 104, 211–12, 233–36; and obscenity decisions, 39, 41, 214; and interracial sex and marriage cases, 46, 110, 113, 216, 314 (n. 41); and *Eisenstadt*, 49, 117–23, 218; and immigration, 59; and *Roe*, 131–32, 315 (n. 61); and post-*Roe* developments, 279, 282–83, 295

Forsberg, Joan, 99

52, 128; and *Boutilier*, 58, 76, 93, 167; media coverage of, 207–8, 216–17, 226–28; court references to, 231–32, 234–37, 239–40; legal scholarship on, 245; post-*Roe* references to, 279, 288, 290, 295, 299, 301

Lovisi v. Slayton, 282

Lovisi v. Zahradnick, 282

Lubin, Alex, 109

Lucas, R., 212

Lucas, Roy, 124–25

Luibhéid, Eithne, 59

Macdonald, Dwight, 42–43

Macy, John, 157–58

Manual Enterprises v. Day, 39, 57, 75, 107, 141, 224–25, 260, 312 (n. 19), 313 (n. 20)

Marmor, Judd, 176, 178, 185, 202

Marriage: Supreme Court rulings on, viii, 15, 21; and *Griswold*, viii, 13–14, 17, 20, 27, 29–34, 41, 47–48, 76, 98–104, 114, 209–10, 212, 214, 223, 231–39, 268, 283, 299; and the justices, xiii, 8–9, 11–13; and post-*Roe* cases, 1–2, 282–83, 287–91, 295–96, 299–301; special rights and privileges of, 3, 13, 18, 20, 28, 55, 132, 208, 231, 241; and the sexual revolution, 5, 13; legal regulation of, 6, 27, 45, 216; and sex, 18, 22, 147; and obscenity decisions, 20, 38, 40–41, 43, 105, 107, 236; nonnormative, 27, 45; and *Eisenstadt*, 47–49, 115–23, 218, 227–29, 231–32, 236; and *Roe*, 52–53, 124–32, 219–21, 230, 236; and *Boutilier*, 65, 76–77, 136, 153, 189–90, 274; media treatment of, 208–10, 212, 214, 218–21, 223, 227–30, 250, 268; court references to, 231–41. *See also* Interracial marriage and sex; Polygamy and bigamy; Same-sex marriage

Marshall, Thurgood, 8–10, 28; and obscenity decisions, 35, 40–41, 43, 269; and *Eisenstadt*, 47; in *LaRue*, 53–54, 239; and *Boutilier*, 61, 80, 318 (n. 12), 319 (n. 40); and *Griswold*, 239; and post-*Roe* decisions, 281–82, 287, 290, 339 (n. 64); and *Roe*, 316 (n. 63)

Martin, Clyde, 265

Martin, Del, 141

Marutani, William, 111, 113–14

Massachusetts, viii, 148–49, 233. *See also* Boston; *Eisenstadt v. Baird*; *Fanny Hill*

Masturbation, 8, 38, 89, 199–200, 253, 257

Matlock (U.S. v. Matlock), 281

Matos-Jordan, 60

Mattachine Midwest Newsletter, 266

Mattachine Review, 139, 141, 143, 159, 224

Mattachine Society, 139–41, 143–46, 149–51, 157–59, 176, 197, 225, 227, 261, 265–66, 268. See also *Eastern Mattachine Magazine*

Mattachine Society of New York Newsletter, 145, 225, 227, 261–63, 265–66, 273

Matter of Belle, 256–57, 270–71

McCarthyism, 87, 133–34, 136–37, 166, 200, 203

McCluskey, Henry, 125–27

McConnell v. Anderson, 92, 270

McCorvey, Norma, 20, 54, 125–27. See also *Roe v. Wade*

McLaughlin v. Florida, 45, 110, 113

Mead, Margaret, 176

Media, 1–4, 21–22, 105, 111, 276, 299; gay and lesbian, 139, 141, 222–30, 243, 260–72, 279–80; legal, 240–41, 243, 250–54, 272, 279–80; mainstream, 207–22, 243–50, 272, 279–80

Medicine and medical doctors, 22; and *Boutilier*, xi, 61–92 passim, 151, 171–86 passim, 196, 200, 245, 250–52, 272, 285, 319 (n. 37), 328 (n. 4); and *Griswold*, 22, 29, 98–99; and *Eisenstadt*, 47–48, 117, 122–23; and *Roe*, 51–52, 55, 123–25, 127–28, 219

Meeropol, Michael, 136, 328 (nn. 5, 10)

Mental health and illness, 54, 112–14, 118, 123–24, 275; and immigration, 59, 68–69, 78, 80, 85, 89, 252, 285; gay movement debates about, 151, 156–57; ACLU work on, 164–65, 168–70; *Boutilier* brief comments about, 173, 184, 189, 191, 198, 200, 202, 249, 319 (n. 40). *See also* Psychopathic personality and psychopathology

Merrill, Roy, 125

Mexico, 57, 60, 125, 137

Meyer v. Nebraska, 100, 114, 312 (n. 7), 315 (n. 43)

Michael, Richard, 176

Michael H. v. Gerald D., 289–90

Michael M. v. Superior Court of Sonoma County, 282

and *Boutilier*, 90, 245–46, 248, 273; on
Supreme Court, 208; on *Griswold*, 209–10;
on *Loving*, 216–17; on *Eisenstadt*, 217–18; on
Roe, 220, 316 (n. 63)
Ninth Amendment, 30, 100, 128, 223
Niukkanen v. McAlexander, 138
Nixon, Richard, viii, 8, 10, 40, 215, 218, 228–
29, 269–70
North American Conference of Homophile
Organizations, 269–70
North Carolina, 1–2, 148, 226
North Dakota, 2, 306 (n. 3)
North Muskegon v. Briggs, 282–83
Norton v. Macy, 238
Nudism and nudity, 27, 39, 144, 146, 224, 226,
236, 260
Nukk v. Shaughnessy, 137

Obscenity, x, 9–10, 12, 15–18, 27–28, 207, 241;
post-*Roe* rulings on, 1–2, 22, 207–8, 284–86,
294; rulings after *Fanny Hill*, 40–41, 53–54,
92, 234, 236, 239–40; and children, 40–41,
108, 215, 286, 294; and homophile activism, 57, 140–41, 147–49, 153, 164, 226, 249,
253; and homosexuality, 57–58, 75, 254,
313 (n. 28); and *Griswold*, 103; and *Eisen-
stadt*, 119; media coverage of, 208, 211,
214–16, 218, 222–26, 230, 268–69, 271. See
also *Fanny Hill*; *Ginzburg v. United States*;
Mishkin v. New York; Nudism and Nudity;
Pornography
O'Connor, Sandra Day, 290–91, 295, 298
Off Our Backs, 230
Ohio, 149, 234, 260
Oklahoma, 233, 284, 292
Olinger, Leonard, 176, 185, 200
Olmstead v. United States, 50
Oncale v. Sundowner Offshore Services, 292
One, 139
*One Eleven Wines and Liquors v. Division of
Alcoholic Beverage Control*, 150, 238
ONE Magazine, 139–43, 159, 222, 224–27
ONE v. Olesen, 39, 57–58, 141, 143, 158, 223–24,
249, 253, 260
Oral sex, 2, 27, 44, 63, 143, 211, 223, 228–29,
232–33, 282, 287, 289, 298. *See also* Sodomy

O'Rourke, Eugene, 65–66, 274, 278, 319
(n. 22)
Osborn v. U.S., 239
Oshtry, Norman, 150

Pandering, 37–38, 42, 108, 213–14, 226, 313
(nn. 23, 27)
Paris Adult Theatre I v. Slaton, 40–41, 216,
235, 240
Partisan Review, 220
Pascoe, Peggy, 109–10
Pedophilia, 2, 70. *See also* Children; Minors
Pemberton, John, 100, 114
Pennsylvania, ix, 38, 148–49, 153, 224, 260,
291. *See also* Philadelphia
Perez, 109
Personal Rights in Defense and Education,
152, 263. See also *Pride Newsletter*
Perverts and perversion, 11, 39–40, 68–71, 73,
77, 80, 86, 88, 107, 120, 137, 146, 148, 180,
225, 259, 320 (n. 43)
Philadelphia, ix, 15, 145, 147, 153, 156, 159–60,
243, 269
Philadelphia *Daily News*, 248, 260
Philadelphia Magazine, 248
Physique photography and magazines, 39, 57,
105, 146, 148, 224–25
Pilpel, Harriet: and *Griswold*, 100, 102; and
Eisenstadt, 117–18, 122, 315 (n. 48); and *Roe*,
128, 130; and sex law reform, 160
Planned Parenthood, 9, 19; and *Griswold*, 98,
100–101, 103; and *Eisenstadt*, 114–18, 122, 315
(n. 48); and *Roe*, 124–25, 128, 130–31, 166
Planned Parenthood League of Connecticut,
29, 33, 98
Planned Parenthood League of Massachu-
setts, 115–16, 118–19
Playboy, 5; and obscenity law, 10, 43, 207–8,
213–14; and *Eisenstadt*, 116, 218; and gay
movement, 146; and Supreme Court
media coverage, 208; and *Griswold*, 211–12,
222; and *Loving*, 216–17; and *Boutilier*,
246–48
Playboy Foundation, 116, 212
Poe v. Ullman, 30–32, 98, 104, 129, 160, 233
Polak, Clark: and homophile activism,

Secrecy, 8, 16, 77, 138, 162, 188, 256, 265, 320 (n. 41)

Selwyn, Herbert, 268

Sex discrimination, 117–18, 187, 197, 282, 292, 295–96. *See also* Sexism

Sexism, 33–34, 41–44, 46–47, 50, 54–55, 220, 230. *See also* Sex discrimination

Sexology, 247–48, 265

Sex toys, 2

Sexual assault. *See* Rape and sexual assault

Sexual deviation, deviates, and deviancy: and immigration, xii, 59, 246, 255–56, 271; and homosexuality, 18; and obscenity decisions, 36–37, 39–40, 57, 75, 107, 213, 226, 313 (n. 27); and *Boutilier*, 63–64, 66–70, 79–81, 83–84, 86–87, 174–76, 195, 201–2, 246, 250–53, 320 (n. 57); and ACLU, 159; and post-*Roe* decisions, 284–86, 292

Sexual harassment, 292

Sexually transmitted diseases, viii, 4, 27, 49, 59, 102–3, 112–13, 119, 288. *See also* AIDS; Syphilis

Sexual privacy. *See* Privacy

Sexual revolution, x, 3–6, 9, 13–19, 21–22, 250, 272, 301

Shafer, Drew, 243, 249

Shields v. Sharp, 58

Sickels, Robert, 245

Siminoff v. Esperdy, 137

Skinner v. Oklahoma, 46–47, 114, 129

Smayda v. U.S., 143, 232, 239

Smith, Evander, 143

Smith, Paul G., 66, 70, 176

Sodomy: post-*Roe* cases, ix, xii, 1–2, 279, 281–84, 286–88, 290–91, 295, 297, 299–300; laws against, xi, 1–2; and obscenity decisions, 38–39, 44, 215, 235; cases in 1960s and early 1970s, 58, 92, 121, 125, 148, 223, 229, 233–37, 244–45, 267–69; and immigration law, 59, 257; and *Boutilier*, 63, 77, 135, 194, 261, 265, 277, 318 (n. 18); and *Eisenstadt*, 121, 218, 229; and *Roe*, 125, 229; and sex law reform, 147–49, 155, 164, 212, 222, 241, 243–44, 249, 267; media coverage of, 211–12, 215, 218, 221–23, 227, 229, 243–45, 249, 267–69; and *Griswold*, 212, 222–23, 229,

233–37, 244, 249; legal scholarship on, 253. *See also* Anal sex; Oral Sex

Sohn, Chang Moon, 110

Solicitation, 2, 84, 149, 159, 161–64, 167, 239, 271, 284, 292. *See also* Prostitution

Sontag, Susan, 220

Souter, David, 291, 298

South, 42–43, 110, 112, 142, 165

South Carolina, 231

Stanley v. Georgia, 40–41, 43, 214–15, 257–58, 269, 287

Stearns, Nancy, 128–30, 132

Steele, 255

Sterilization, 4–5, 27, 31, 46–47, 52, 222

Stevens, John Paul, 280, 286–87, 290–91, 298, 300

Stevens, Rosemary, 99

Stewart, Potter, 8–9, 28, 35–36, 38–39, 41, 45, 47, 61, 78–81, 264, 312 (n. 20), 313 (n. 31), 315 (nn. 52, 59), 316 (n. 63)

Stocking, Fred, 107

Stokey, Roger, 118

Stonewall riots, 243

Strict scrutiny, 31, 45, 49, 76, 117, 295

Students, viii–ix, 4–5, 8, 99, 111, 115, 125, 156, 160, 211, 231, 255, 283–84

Sturgis v. Attorney General, 233, 236

Suicide, xi, 9, 245, 273, 276, 291

Supreme Court. *See* U.S. Supreme Court

Syphilis, 8, 194, 333 (n. 44)

Szasz, Thomas, 165, 176, 189, 197, 201–2, 265

Talley v. California, 92

Tavern Guild, 143

Teachers and teaching, 91, 237, 284

Tennessee, 216, 236, 281

Texas, 2, 121, 160, 224, 235, 267, 284, 292, 298–300. See also *Roe v. Wade*

Thomas, Clarence, 291, 298

Time, 146, 211, 219–20, 248, 316 (n. 63)

Tindall, Marie, 99

Toilets, 11, 255

Toobin, Jeffrey, 170

Tovar v. INS, 60–61, 92, 255

Transgender and transsexual, 59, 70, 77, 148, 153, 177–78